A WORLD BANK COUNTRY STUDY

Kazakstan

Transition of the State

The World Bank
Washington, D.C.

World Bank Country Studies are among the many reports originally prepared for internal use as part of the continuing analysis by the Bank of the economic and related conditions of its developing member countries and of its dialogues with the governments. Some of the reports are published in this series with the least possible delay for the use of governments and the academic, business and financial, and development communities. The typescript of this paper therefore has not been prepared in accordance with the procedures appropriate to formal printed texts, and the World Bank accepts no responsibility for errors. Some sources cited in this paper may be informal documents that are not readily available.

ISSN: 0253-2123

Library of Congress Cataloging-in-Publication Data

Kazakstan : transition of the state.
        p.   cm. — (A World Bank country study)
      Includes bibliographical references.
      ISBN 0-8213-3902-8
      1. Kazakstan—Economic policy—1991- 2. Kazakstan—Politics and
government—1991- 3. Structural adjustment (Economic policy)—
Kazakstan. I. World Bank. II. Series.
HC420.5.K294   1997
338.95845—dc21
                                                            97-3838
                                                              CIP

CONTENTS

ABSTRACT

The state sector of Kazakstan has yet to adjust to the sweeping political and economic changes that have accompanied the demise of the former Soviet Union. The country inherited from its Soviet period a level of coverage in public services and infrastructures that it cannot maintain with its own resources. A drastic reassessment of government's role in the economy and social life of the country is increasingly recognized by the authorities. This report seeks to highlight the ways in which reforms in the structures of the state, in the systems of public resource management, and in key programs could facilitate this adjustment. The report identifies five priority directions for the transition of the state: (i) a deliberate shrinking of administrative structures, leading to an (admittedly painful) release of redundant personnel; (ii) a consolidation of the social sector facilities by shifting toward more outpatient and ambulatory treatment in the health sector and increasing student/teacher ratios in education; (iii) the adoption of budget management instruments aimed at selecting priorities among competing needs rather than distributing resources according to exogenously defined uses (as was the case under the command system); (iv) a differentiation of public interventions across the country according to the priorities of local populations, through a gradual devolution of responsibilities to bodies of local self-government; and (v) the creation of personnel management systems which foster motivation, continuity, and professionalism in the civil service.

ACKNOWLEDGEMENTS

This report reflects the findings of a World Bank economic mission which visited the Republic of Kazakstan from August 21 to September 16, 1995. The mission was led by Bernard Funck, and comprised Moncef Belhadjamor (Budget), Guido De Weerd (Administration and Civil Service), Trina Haque (Health and Education), David King (Local Finances), Barbara Ossowicka (Quantitative Analysis) and Laurent Rabate (Budget Execution and Control). Thomas O'Brien prepared a preliminary assessment. Zhanar Abdildina and Natasha Beisenova of the World Bank Resident Mission in Almaty contributed to the mission's work and to this report. Alec McNevin (USAID - Local Finances) also participated in the mission. The mission benefited from the full support of David Nathan (budget adviser to the Ministry of Finance, U.S. Treasury) and S. Ramamurthy (Treasury Adviser to the Ministry of Finance, IMF) and from outstanding contributions from Serik Akhanov and Lyaziza Sabyrova on the evolution of Kazakstan's public finances from the Soviet to the present day.

The mission benefited from the excellent cooperation of the Staff of the Council of Ministers, and particularly from its Center for Economic Reforms and its Department of Finance, Labor and Monetary Circulation, from the Ministries of Finance, Economy, Justice, Transport, Health, Education and Labor, the State Committee for Statistics, the State Committee for Financial Control, the National Bank of the Republic of Kazakstan, the Export-Import Bank of Kazakstan, the authorities of the oblasts of Almaty, South Kazakstan and Kostanai, the authorities of the city of Almaty, as well as the authorities of the rayons of Kapchagai and Talgar (Almaty), Tolebi (South Kazakstan), Federovsky and Mendigara (Kostanai).

CURRENCY EQUIVALENTS
(as of December 30, 1996)

Currency Unit	=	Tenge (T)
T 1	=	US$0.01355
US$1	=	T 73.80

AVERAGE EXCHANGE RATES
Tenge per US$1

1994	1995	1996
36.10	61.37	67.76

ABBREVIATIONS AND ACRONYMS

BESD	World Bank's Economic and Social Database
CPI	Consumer Price Index
CPSU	Communist Party of the Soviet Union
ETF	Economic Transformation Fund
EU	European Union
EXIM Bank	State Export Import Bank of the Republic of Kazakstan
FSU	Former Soviet Union
GDP	Gross Domestic Product
GFS	Government Finance Statistics
GOK	Government of Kazakstan
IFS	International Financial Statistics
IMF	International Monetary Fund
INTOSAI	International Organization of Supreme Audit Institutions
MOF	Ministry of Finance
MOH	Ministry of Health
NAFI	National Agency for Foreign Investment
OECD	Organization for Economic Cooperation and Development
PPP	Purchase Power Parity
PPBS	Planning/Programming/Budgeting System
SCFC	State Committee for Financial Control
SDB	State Development Bank
UNDP	United Nations Development Programme
USAID	United States Agency for International Development

OVERVIEW

A. Need for Reform

1.   After having made great strides toward transforming its economy into a market system, Kazakstan has reached a stage at which the reform of its state apparatus can no longer be delayed. The country inherited from its Soviet period a level of coverage in public services and infrastructures that it cannot maintain with its own resources. On most accounts, the quantity, if not the quality, of public services currently offered by government is on a par with that of higher income OECD countries. But the fiscal resources available to operate and maintain these services have contracted by as much as 75 percent in real terms in the last four years. To date, however, the official reaction has been to spread privations across all activities rather than selecting and focusing on those activities that are deemed most essential. As a result the entire ship of state is rapidly taking in water.

2.   This report will argue that time has come for vigorous action to safeguard key public services. This would involve: (i) consolidating structures and services around key functions, and weeding out others that have a lesser priority or could be performed by the civil society; (ii) differentiating public interventions in response to the preferences expressed by the voters or by the market; and (iii) strengthening selected functions so as to improve their cost-effectiveness.

B. The Size of the State

A Legacy of Highly Developed Public Services

3.   Although it ranks among the lower middle-income countries, Kazakstan inherited from its Soviet past a level of *coverage in public services* equivalent only to levels observed in highly industrialized countries. For instance, with 270 people per physician, and about 100 people per nurse, Kazakstan equals or exceeds even the most generous of the Western European countries. In comparison, Sweden has 400 people per physician. The United Kingdom, which also operates a state health system (the National Health Service), counts 52 people per health personnel, compared to as few as 41 in Kazakstan. In a different area, the paved road density (8.4 km/thousand people) is above the level observed in other similarly vast middle income countries such as Argentina (1.9 km/thousand), Turkey (5.3 km/thousand), Ukraine (3.1 km/thousand), and South Africa (1.4 km/thousand).

4.   Such a high level of provision of public services inevitably translates into *high levels of government employment*. Again, Table 1 shows that, outside of the former socialist economies, Kazakstan compares only with the most heavily industrialized countries of Western Europe in terms of level of public employment. With about 6.4 public employees per hundred population (republican and territorial administrations), it compares with such countries as France, the Netherlands, the United Kingdom, or Italy, whose level of income per capita is more than five times higher than that of Kazakstan (on a purchasing power parity basis). By contrast, the less affluent among the member countries of the European Union (EU), such as Ireland and Greece, have less than 3 percent of their population working for the government.

Table 1: Public Employment in Selected Countries[1]

COUNTRY	GNP PER CAPITA AT PPP[2] ($US)	CENTRAL AUTHORITIES (as % of Population)	LOCAL AUTHORITIES	TOTAL
Kazakstan	2,830	1.5	4.6	6.1
Belgium	20,450	2.7	2.3	5.0
France	19,820	4.6	2.1	6.7
Germany	19,890	1.8	1.7	3.5
Greece	11,400	2.2	0.3	2.5
Ireland	14,550	1.4	0.8	2.1
Italy	18,610	3.8	2.3	6.2
Netherlands	18,080	4.8	1.6	6.4
Portugal	12,400	3.9	1.1	4.9
Spain	14,040	3.1	1.0	4.0
United Kingdom	18,170	1.4	5.1	6.5

[1] Kazakstan (1994); Belgium, Spain (1992); Ireland, United Kingdom (1991);France, Germany, Netherlands (1990); Greece, Portugal (1989).

[2] Purchasing Power Parity; data for 1994.

Sources: Europe Council, World Bank, World Development Report, 1992.

5.   Several factors inherited from its Soviet past help to explain this situation. As was the case across the Soviet Union, an explicit priority was given to public forms of consumption over private forms. In addition, low wage differentials and high education levels facilitated the recruitment of well-trained staff, in education and health for example. The importance given to security considerations, both internal and external, help to explain the continued relative importance of such personnel employed in these sectors (see Table 5). Finally, the fact that after World War II Kazakstan had become a "show piece" of the Soviet Union and was being idealized -- particularly through the Virgin Land ("Tselina")

Chart 1: Evolution of GDP and Fiscal Resources, 1991-1995 (at constant prices, 1991=100)

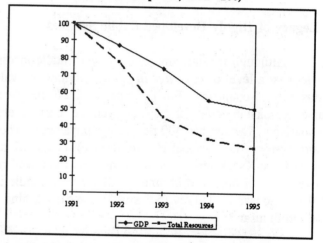

Campaign of the late 1950s -- as the cradle of the new Soviet man, helps explain why the Union devoted a disproportionate amount of resources to its development.[1] The high density of public services in the sparsely populated former *tselina* still bears testimony to this special attention.

---

[1] The fact that a high number of top Soviet leaders (Brezhnev, Ponomarev) grew from the ranks in this process is of course a further contributing factor.

Contraction in Fiscal Resources

6.   Whereas maintaining such a level of service is necessarily costly, the amount of resources available to the fiscal authorities has contracted sharply in recent years: *between 1991 and 1995, the total amount of resources mobilized by the budget declined, in real terms, by a factor of 4* (see Chart 1). Three factors are at play:

(i)   GDP declined by a cumulative 50 percent over the period (see Chart 1), reducing the revenue base for funding public services. This phenomenon has been common to most former Soviet Union (FSU) countries (see Chart 2).

(ii)   Within this reduced revenue base, the state has been unable to maintain its take. Table 2 shows consolidated fiscal revenues collapsing as a percentage of national income: from 36.8 percent of GDP in 1992 to 23.6 percent of GDP in 1995 (excluding grants). Whereas most former socialist countries have had to struggle with the consequences of a rapid erosion of fiscal revenues (see Table 3), rarely has it been so deep and so sudden as in Kazakstan over the last two years, during which consolidated fiscal revenues dropped by as much as 13 percent of GDP.

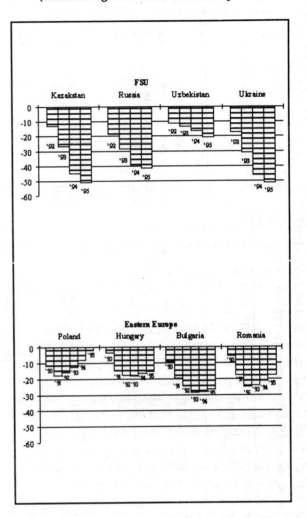

Chart 2: Evolution of GDP in Selected Countries
(cumulative growth rate at constant prices)

(iii)   In mid-1993, Kazakstan lost access to the transfers of resources formerly received, first from the Soviet Union then from Russia. This caused the country a once-and-for-all loss of income of considerable proportion: measured in terms of today's GDP, former transfers of resources ranged between 20 and 25 percent of Kazakstan's GDP. This loss was not offset by the emergence of a net transfer of resources from non-FSU sources. The latter represented only 3.7 percent of GDP in 1994, of which about 2 percent of GDP went to finance the budget (see Table 2).

Table 2: Evolution of the Consolidated Budget, 1992-1995
(in percent of GDP at current prices)

	BUDGET				EXTRABUDGETARY				CONSOLIDATED			
	1992	1993	1994	1995	1992	1993	1994	1995	1992	1993	1994	1995
1. Current Operations												
Current Revenues and Grants	24.5	21.5	17.7	17.5	15.3	15.7	6.1	7.1	38.9	37.2	23.8	23.6
Direct Taxes	7.6	7.8	5.2	5.6	11.5	10.8	4.2	6.3	19.1	18.6	9.4	12.0
Indirect Taxes	13.9	9.3	6.8	4.8	1.5	1.3	0.5	0.0	15.4	10.6	7.3	4.8
Nontax Revenues	0.9	4.4	5.7	6.8	1.4	2.3	1.4	0.0	2.2	6.8	7.1	6.8
Grants	1.7	0.0	0.0	0.0	0.4	1.3	0.0	0.0	2.1	1.3	0.0	0.0
Intragovernmental Transfers	0.4	0.0	0.0	0.2	0.5	0.0	0.0	0.7	..	..	..	..
Current Expenditures	24.7	20.1	14.9	17.7	11.0	11.4	8.5	6.8	34.8	31.6	23.5	23.5
Consumption	17.5	17.5	11.3	13.7	0.6	1.7	0.9	0.8	18.1	19.2	12.2	14.5
Interest Payments	2.2	0.1	1.7	0.2	..	..	2.2	0.0	2.2	0.1	3.9	0.2
Domestic Debt	0.0	0.1	1.6	0.0	..	..	2.2	0.0	0.0	0.1	3.8	0.0
External Debt	2.2	0.0	0.1	0.2	..	..	0.0	0.0	2.2	0.0	0.1	0.2
Transfers to Households	3.0	1.1	0.7	0.8	8.2	7.1	3.9	5.8	11.2	8.3	4.6	6.6
Subsidies	1.5	1.4	1.0	2.3	1.4	2.6	1.4	0.0	2.9	4.0	2.4	2.3
Intragovernmental and Other Transfers	0.5	0.0	0.3	0.7	0.4	0.0	0.0	0.2	..	..	..	..
Current Balance	-0.2	1.4	2.8	-0.2	4.3	4.2	-2.4	0.3	4.1	5.6	0.3	0.1
2. Capital Operations												
Capital Revenues	0.0	2.9	0.3	0.7	0.0	0.0	0.0	0.0	0.0	2.9	0.3	0.7
Capital Expenditures	6.7	5.1	5.6	2.6	4.7	4.1	1.6	-0.5	11.4	9.2	7.2	2.0
Net Lending and Participation	0.0	1.5	2.7	1.6	4.7	4.1	1.6	-0.5	4.7	5.6	4.3	1.1
Investment	6.7	3.6	2.9	1.0	0.0	0.0	0.0	0.0	6.7	3.6	2.9	1.0
3. Overall Balance	-6.8	-0.8	-2.5	-2.1	-0.5	0.1	-4.0	0.8	-7.3	-0.7	-6.5	-1.3
4. Financing									7.3	0.7	6.5	1.3
Domestic									3.1	0.0	4.5	-0.6
Banking System									-2.1	-1.1	3.6	0.9
Other Domestic (residual)									4.4	1.1	0.9	-1.5
External									4.2	0.7	2.1	1.9

Sources: Ministry of Finance, World Bank staff estimates.

Table 3: Evolution of Fiscal Revenues in Selected Countries, 1989-1994

COUNTRY	CHANGE (% of GDP)	LEVEL, 1994 (% of GDP)
Poland	6.5	47.9
Hungary	-6.8	52.3
Bulgaria	-21.9	38.0
Romania	-18.5	32.6
Russia	-4.5	36.3
Kyrgyz Republic	-14.2	24.3
Kazakstan	-21.7	19.0
Uzbekistan	7.8	43.0
Belarus	-1.6	36.6
Ukraine	15.9	42.3

Source: M. de Melo, C. Denizer and A. Gelb, in "Plan to Market: Patterns of Transition," Policy Research Working Paper, World Bank, January 1996.

7.   Further *exacerbating factors* on the expenditure side have strained Kazakstan's fiscal situation. The largest factor was the transfer, starting in 1995, of quasi-fiscal operations from the banking sector to the budget. Whereas this move may ultimately have served to dampen the authorities' appetite for providing backdoor support to enterprises, it remains the case that the costs of the refinancing of inter-enterprise arrears in spring 1994, and of calls on state guarantees on domestic and foreign credits claim a large share of government's shrinking revenue pie.

8.   The brunt of the *fiscal adjustment* therefore fell disproportionately on: (i) transfers to households (-6 percent of GDP in 1992-95) owing largely to the drop in pension payments; (ii) public investment (-6 percent of GDP in 1992-95) which has now virtually stopped; and (iii) operations and maintenance expenditures of public services (-4 percent of GDP) (see Table 2).

Impact on Public Services

9.   Despite this budgetary contraction, the *quantity of public services* supplied to the population has remained largely unchanged, at least on paper. In fact, the number of teachers employed in day schools has actually *increased* during the 1990s, while resources available to the education sector were dropping abruptly[2] (see Table 4). Some efforts have been made in the health sector to reduce the country's in-patient treatment capacity and the number of hospitals beds. Between 1993 and 1994, the number of beds per 10,000 population and the number of doctor's positions (which are associated with the number of beds) fell by about 8 percent and 4 percent, respectively. While these rationalization efforts are commendable, they are not commensurate with the challenge at hand, namely, the decline by almost two-thirds of real resources per capita available to the sector from the beginning of the 1990s. More generally, available evidence indicates that the number of government employees decreased only marginally.

---

[2]   Part of the reason for this increase is the recent efforts to establish schools where instruction is in Kazak rather than in Russian.

Table 4: Number of Schools and Teachers, 1985-1994

	1985	1990	1992	1993	1994
Schools	8,109	8,487	8,654	8,740	8,942
Urban	1,718	1,902	1,977	2,005	..
Rural	6,391	6,585	6,677	6,735	..
Teachers [1]	206.9	248.9	273.7	280.7	270.3

[1] In thousands at the beginning of the school year starting in September of the year.
Source: Goskomstat Statistical Yearbook, 1993 and 1994.

10.   As a result, the amount of *expenditure per public service unit* has declined drastically. Public sector wages have suffered particularly, and by a much larger proportion than those paid in the rest of the economy. Whereas wages in public administrations were on average on a par with those in industry in 1991, by mid-1995, they had decreased to about two-thirds of average industrial wages (see Chart 3). By that date, the purchasing power of public administration wages stood on average at only 40 percent of the 1991 level. Owing to this evolution, the minimum public sector wage corresponds to less than half the subsistence minimum and is insufficient to buy a loaf of bread and a bottle of milk per day. The salary of a secondary school teacher barely corresponds to the subsistence minimum. And even these low wages are paid only sporadically, particularly at the oblast and rayon levels (see Volume 2, Chapter II for a detailed discussion of public sector wages). Many administrations are now sponsoring the development of individual plots or animal husbandry (cattle, pigs, poultry) programs, or of in-kind payments supported by barter transactions with local producers, as an alternative method of providing a living to government employees.

11.   The adjustment between the supply of services and the resources has not affected the quantity of public sector infrastructures or personnel but mainly the *quality of services*. In a number of cases, the situation has reached a point where one can wonder whether any service is rendered at all, or whether existing structures have become little more than empty shells. In the case of primary health care, for example, the demoralization of underpaid personnel, the dearth of basic medical supplies, and the lack of maintenance of care facilities are such that, at some facilities, the resulting deterioration of hygiene

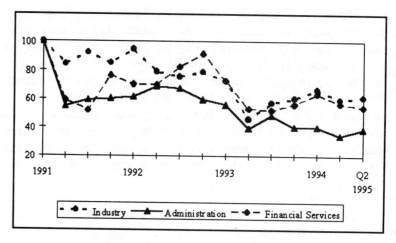

Chart 3: Real Wages in Public Administration, Industry and Financial Services, 1991-1995 (deflated by CPI, 1991=100)

conditions in itself constitutes a major health hazard. This situation of rapid degradation of public services is vividly described in the Human Development Report prepared by the United Nations Development Programme (UNDP), which notes, among other things, that "the collapse of the state-operated health care system, that carried out both preventive and therapeutic activities for the entire population and to a large extent controlled sanitary conditions, has brought about a sharp growth of the incidence of infectious diseases."[3]

The Challenge Ahead

12. The time has come for a different logic to emerge, one that would give priority to ensuring the quality of services -- or at least minimum standards -- and to adjusting the quantity of services "theoretically" supplied to (i) the funding available to meet such standards, and (ii) the preferences expressed by service users. So far, however, the country has been delaying these critical choices while hoping for better times. Unfortunately, there is little reason to believe that, in the foreseeable future, previous levels of resources will again be available to the country so that it can afford the public services it once enjoyed. Even if the anticipated oil rents were to materialize (and if the government were to be successful in capturing them for the budget), such rents would not provide sufficient resources to regain (in real terms) the ground lost since the beginning of the decade.[4]

13. The need to overhaul state structures and practices is increasingly recognized by the authorities. The link between this objective and the reform of public resource management structures and systems (administrative organization, budget management, civil service) is much less well perceived. Crippling rigidities in public resource management, however, hinder the necessary scaling down and redeployment of state services, interventions, administrative structures, and personnel. In most respects, the structures and modus operandi of the state in Kazakstan are the same as they were under the Soviet regime. They hamper resource redeployment in Kazakstan, just as they did during the Soviet days.

14. The next three sections seek to identify where the critical bottlenecks are and to outline an agenda of priority actions to overcome them. Section C deals with the reform of government structures and Section D with the public resource management systems, particularly budget management and the civil service. Section E discusses how these institutional reforms could underpin the necessary redirection of key government programs, particularly in health and education. Finally, Section F puts forward an action program to implement the reforms outlined above.

15. It is important to emphasize from the outset that the transition of the state is not a matter of overnight change. As will become clear in the following paragraphs, it is a matter of determination and persistence. Nor will it take place without hardship for some categories of the service-using public or of the personnel who provide public services. The results, on the other hand, will only become visible over time.

---

[3] *Kazakstan: The Challenge of Transition, Human Development Report 1995,* UNDP. This report should be used as a companion reader for the present report.

[4] Furthermore, the history of the Soviet Union and other countries (e.g., Algeria) illustrates the futility of relying on commodity rents to delay structural reforms. By the 1960s, the Soviet Union had exhausted its scope for extensive growth, and required economic reforms to switch to a more intensive growth pattern. The impetus behind the reform policies advocated by Kossygin and his colleagues waned in the early 1970s, as the commodity boom, from which the Soviet Union benefited vastly, gave well-entrenched structures a new lease on life. Eventually, such procrastination only served to precipitate the final crisis of the 1980s (see S. Fisher and W. Easterly, "The Soviet Economic Decline," *World Bank Economic Review,* September 1995) .

C. The Structures of the State

Overview of Political and Administrative Structures

16.   The country's *political structures* have evolved considerably since the Kazak Soviet Socialist Republic declared its independence and became the Republic of Kazakstan in December 1991. After a first -- failed -- attempt to establish stable political institutions, the country adopted a second Constitution in August 1995 which defines the Republic of Kazakstan as a unitary state[5/] with a presidential form of government and an elected Parliament.[6/]

17.   By contrast, the country's *administrative structures* have remained similar to those in place under the former Kazakh SSR, and, following the tenets of "democratic centralism," are characterized by a high degree of centralization of policymaking combined with as great a segmentation of executive tasks. The President, the Prime Minister, the Deputy Prime Ministers, and their staff assume leadership in the formulation of all government policies and in the control of policy implementation. They are the locus of all policy initiative.

18.   Under them, all state bodies, from the ministries downward, are ordered in vertical hierarchical lines. *Republican administrations* constitute the first tier of administration and comprise the national ministries, state committees -- as well as their field services -- and other national committees and agencies, as well as the administrative establishments and commercial enterprises under their supervision. There are two tiers of *territorial administration* (as defined in footnote 5) which comprise the technical counterparts of republican administrations placed under the administrative authority of the representative of the state in the jurisdiction (*akim*): the oblast level (19 oblasts and 2 national cities, Almaty and Leninsk), and the rayon level (220 rural rayons and 83 towns of oblast importance). Each tier of territorial administration reports to the next upper tier. Together with the republican administration, the two tiers of state territorial administration form part of a "single system of executive bodies of the Republic, and ensure the implementation of the overall nation-wide policies in consideration of the interests and needs of development of their territory" (Art. 87, para. 1, of the Constitution).[7/]

[5/]   This concept of a "unitary" state has fundamental implications for the organization of the state. Legally speaking a *unitary state* is a state in which the authority to make laws resides exclusively with the national authorities. A *federal state* is a state in which the authority to make laws and modify the Constitution (i.e., the national sovereignty) is shared with the territorial components of the country (e.g., states in the United States, regions in Belgium, Länder in Germany). A *confederal state* is an association of states in which the interstate power executes the legal functions delegated to it by the member countries. *Decentralization* can take several forms. It may result from a *transfer or devolution of legislative authority* (under a constitutional act) to *members of a federation* operated under the Constitution. It may also result, in both unitary states and (con) federations, from a *transfer or devolution of executive authority* (by law) to local governments. In the latter context, all local government bodies, elected or not, form part of the executive branch. Finally, governments can provide a measure of autonomy to administrative bodies, local or not, through a *delegation of executive authority* (by executive order). In this case, however the body to which authority is delegated remains in a hierarchical dependence under the terms of the delegation. For the sake of clarity, this report reserves the term *territorial administration* to designate local executive bodies operating under such delegation.

[6/]   The Parliament comprises two Chambers: the Majlis, which is elected directly, and the Senate, which is elected indirectly by a college of maslikhat members. The powers of the legislative branch are restrictively defined by the Constitution.

[7/]   Under this lower tier, there exists also a subadministrative level of state intervention comprising the field services of rural rayons in 2,496 rural localities (aul, selo, settlement), corresponding approximately to the sovkhozes and kolkhozes, and the field services of national cities and oblast towns in 204 urban rayons. They are organized under the authority of a representative of the rayon-level administrator to which they are subordinated.

Main Structural Imbalances

19.　　These government structures and services employ over 1 million people,[8] of whom about 260,000 are at the republican level and about 780,000 are at the territorial level. As indicated in para. 4, such a level of employment has no equivalent among middle-income market economies. A cursory look at the composition of *government employment* provides preliminary indication of where redundancies chiefly reside (see Table 5). The main imbalances lie within the following categories:

- *Autonomous Agencies and Departmental Enterprises*, which are literally teeming at the republican level (and probably also at lower levels, although data are missing that would ascertain this) with close to 100,000 employees (including the vast payroll of the Academy of Science).

- *Oblast and Rayon Administrations,* with over 60,000 employees (excluding the 30,000 working for field services of republican administrations).

- *Health and Education Services*, which together account for about 70 percent of government employment. Health personnel are particularly bloated. They represent about 40 percent of government employment and 2.4 percent of the population.[9]

20.　　In contrast, *Republican Ministries and Ministry Level Administrations* (other than the State Committee for State Security), with less than 10,000 employees, are short-staffed by any standard. The fragmentation of ministerial administrative structures further weakens their effectiveness (see paras. 28-30).

21.　　Previous attempts at *reducing government employment* have shown only very limited success. The decision taken in late 1994, for example, to reduce staff by 25 percent may not have yielded more than a 2 or 3 percent cut in total payroll. Several factors explain this relative lack of success: lack of parallel effort at downsizing administrative structures; absence of necessary information on the structure and composition of the civil service to devise adequate policies (see para. 95); and exemption given to sectors with the largest number of personnel, particularly the social sectors.

22.　　The numbers presented in Table 5, however, clearly show that no critical impact on government employment will be achieved unless structural actions are supported by a reform of health and education policies. These policies are discussed in Section E.

---

[8]　　Excluding staff of the social security system.

[9]　　In comparison, in France, for example, this category of personnel accounts for 14 percent of the civil service and 1.14 percent of the population. Even in the United Kingdom, with its public health care system, health personnel represent only 21 percent of government employment and 1.9 percent of the population.

Table 5: Structure of State Personnel
(estimates for 1994)

REPUBLICAN	
1. Central	
1.1 Ministries	6,800
1.2 State Committees (other than 1.3))	1,100
1.3 State Committee for State Security	6,900
1.4 Other Services	1,600
2. Other Republican Services	
2.1 Republican Field Administrations	30,200
2.2 Embassies	100
2.3 Justice/Order (other than 2.4)	58,300
2.4 State Committee for State Security	6,900
2.5 Armed Forces	63,000
2.6 Academy of Sciences	41,400
2.7 Other Central	42,700
Total	258,900
TERRITORIAL	
1. Oblast Administration	46,100
2. Rayon and Town Administrations	21,500
3. Health	406,000
4. Education	299,100
5. Other Local	0
Total	780,000
Total	1,040,000

Source: World Bank staff estimates based on budget data and authorized positions.

Reforming Republican Administrations

23.   The excessive size of republican structures has resulted from two factors inherited from the Soviet system: (i) weak delineation between the fields of activity of actual administrative services and other types of activities which would not typically belong, in a market economy, to the normal responsibilities of the state; and (ii) fragmentation of ministerial structures arising from former command-and-control principles.

The Realm of the State

24.   The current *demarkation between the "budgetary" sector and the rest of the economy* has resulted from the separation, starting in 1987 under the Soviet Union, of the state's finances from the finances of enterprises. This process, however, affected primarily the "material sphere," leaving within the realm of the state many services that could be provided on a market basis by private or

public corporations or through other institutions of the civil society, such as nonprofit associations or trade unions.

25.   The list of entities funded by the republican budget currently counts 79 groups totaling 2,236 budget units. Of these units, 1,840 are under the supervision of ministry level agencies and another 400 have little to do with public administration, but would best be described as professional associations (e.g., writers' union, or copyright agency); commercial and industrial entities (e.g., road signaling company, hotels, telegraph agency); or administrative establishments (e.g., Academy of Sciences, museums). A careful review of the 1,840 units included in the ministerial groups would bring to light hundreds more entities also corresponding to such descriptions. Indications are that such entities may be as large as public administrations per se and may employ several tens of thousands of persons. Many of these entities could operate on a fee-per-member or tariff-for-service basis.

26.   Pending more detailed design work on the reconfiguration of public administrations, a first major impact in *alleviating administrative structures* could be achieved by:

(i)   Taking an inventory of all administrative structures and of the functions they perform; this inventory does not necessarily need to be sophisticated and could draw upon the information gathered in establishing the new functional and institutional classification of the budget (as discussed in para. 66)

(ii)   Incorporating professional associations, administrative establishments, and industrial and commercial enterprises under separate legal and management regimes

(iii)   Reviewing, one-by-one, their programs, to determine which entities could be privatized on a commercial or nonprofit basis, which others should operate on a tariff basis within the public sector, and which otherwise would require operating subventions from the budget.

27.   The embryo of such a process is actually already under way in many parts of the country. In particular, a number of territorial administrations have introduced a distinction between their "administrative" departments, which continue to be funded through general fiscal resources, and their "productive" departments (e.g., post, telecommunications, aviation, water supply), which are being put "on a self-financing basis." This process remains incomplete, however, partly for lack of appropriate legal forms into which to convert these departments.

Fragmentation of Republican Administrations

28.   With 56 Cabinet-level administrations (22 ministries, 13 state committees, 7 committees and 14 other agencies), *the government of Kazakstan is highly fragmented*. This number of ministry level administrations is two to three times that found in most OECD countries. This fragmentation is further accentuated at the departmental level. There are several hundred first-level administrative units or departments within the republican administrations. In OECD countries, the number of first-level administrative units would typically not exceed 100.

29.   Most OECD countries organize their administrations on the basis of "public services," corresponding to identified "functions" and structured in departments. In these countries, the

departments, not the ministries, are the *basic and stable* modules with which the administration is built. In Kazakstan, in contrast, the functions of the administration are identified at the ministry level and the identification of a new function almost automatically leads to the creation of a new such structure. This accounts for the vastly larger number of first-level units in Kazakstan.

30.   The end result of this process is that ministerial staff, already few in numbers, are very thinly spread across sprawling administrative structures. It is not uncommon for first-level departments to have no more than 20 staff members of all categories -- this indeed is about the average in the Ministries of Economy and Agriculture. The situation at times reaches such an extreme that one wonders whether any functions are performed at all by many departments.

31.   This situation clearly calls for *consolidation*. Indeed, a decision has already been made that, starting in 1996, a main department would need to encompass a minimum of 20 positions, a secondary department a minimum of 10, and a section a minimum of 4. While this measure will reduce to some extent the number of administrative structures and their attendant staffing requirements, it is unlikely to go to the heart of the matter.

32.   A preferable approach would be to consolidate administrations through a process of analysis, selection, and grouping or elimination of their *functions*. Such functional review should precede the finalization of structures and should encompass all administrative establishments operating within the realm of the republican administrations, and not only ministerial administrations. Building upon the administrative inventory proposed in para. 26, such an approach would involve:

> (i)   Conducting a more detailed functional review of the remaining public administrations, and identifying and eliminating redundant functions among the remaining state entities, with automatic closure or privatization of the administrative entities that perform these functions
>
> (ii)   Defining homogeneous organization norms as regards size and organization pattern (e.g., functional or geographic) of administrative structures
>
> (iii)   Aggregating the remaining government functions into large groups of public services and consolidating existing structures into a total of less than 100 first-level departments, taking into account a reasonable span of control
>
> (v)   Grouping departments into a maximum of about 20 ministry level entities, following homogeneous criteria reflecting the policy priorities of the government.

To be comprehensive, and also because of the interlinkages between tiers of administration, territorial administrations should also be encompassed in this process.

Centralization of Policymaking

33.   Another corollary of the current fragmentation of ministerial structures is *a high degree of centralization of policymaking* and control at the top level of the government structure (Prime Minister, Deputy Prime Ministers, and the Staff of the Cabinet of Ministers). This structure is organized as a miniature government and combines the same supra-ministerial roles as those performed under the Soviet regime by (i) the Central Committee and its departments in policy

formulation; and (ii) the Cabinet of Ministers and its departments in controlling the operational activities of the ministries and other state bodies. This centralization weakens the authority and accountability of government ministers and leads to a dilution of political and administrative responsibilities, and a demoralization of ministerial staff.

34. In contrast with the Soviet-era system, the new Constitution defines the Government as a collective body, in which Cabinet members are individually and jointly responsible for government actions. The implementation of this provision will call for a transfer of policy formulation capacities and responsibilities to the ministries, a move which the consolidation of ministerial administrations described above should facilitate.

Reforming Territorial Administrations

35. The creation of local governments, if properly designed, could contribute greatly to the restructuring of public services along more efficient lines. Among other benefits, it would permit public interventions to be tailored specifically to available resource envelopes and to locally perceived priorities. Such flexibility is likely to yield better and more efficient services than do present administrative arrangements, which promote a uniform supply of services nationwide.

Current System

36. In the present system, territorial administrations constitute, in essence, *branches of the state administration*. With a few exceptions (e.g., taxation, law and order), territorial administrations carry out all state functions within their jurisdictions, irrespective of whether the benefits of these functions are purely local or national. Although the state budget is separated into several tiers (rayons, oblasts, republican administrations), these tiers constitute essentially different levels of aggregation of a number of individual budget entities, with little functional or fiscal individuality.[10]

37. In this framework, the *responsibilities of the various tiers of administration* emerge from a process of organizational assignment (i.e., this entity goes to that tier of administration), rather than from one of functional specialization (i.e., this function, for example, primary health care, is performed by that tier of administration). The general rule is that budget entities are assigned to the tier of administration whose jurisdiction corresponds to the catchment area of the service they provide.

38. In practice, territorial administrations, and particularly rayon-level administrations handle most of the public services which are in direct contact with the populations. Territorial budgets finance more than 80 percent of the country's expenditure on education, health, culture and recreation, and transport (see Table 6). About 33 percent of oblast budgets and 60 percent of rayon-level budgets are allocated to education and health (see Table 7). These budgets also handle

---

[10] Two important caveats need to be taken into consideration, which contradict the impression that complete discipline is imposed from the top down. First, the fiscal crisis has produced a growing hiatus between the policy guidelines enacted at the top and the means available to implement them, leaving the republican authorities with no better solution than to let the territorial administrations cope with the resultant difficulties. Second, in the absence of a national civil service (see paras. 95-97), all government departments are staffed with locally recruited personnel -- rather than national civil servants -- whose first loyalty will naturally be to their own jurisdiction.

most welfare programs funded by the state budget,[11] be they in the form of family allowances, assistance to the aged, infirm and handicapped, or consumer subsidies for heating and utilities. Finally, the last major items of expenditures consisted -- until the April 1995 tax reform abolished the special earmarked taxes levied to finance them -- of road maintenance (oblast budget fund) and public transportation (rayon-level passenger transport funds).

Table 6: Allocation of Expenditures between Republican and Territorial Budgets
(1994 actual)

ITEM	REPUBLICAN	TERRITORIAL	STATE	REPUBLICAN	TERRITORIAL	STATE
General Public Services	87.3	12.7	100.0	25.3	4.7	16.2
Defense	99.6	0.4	10.0	7.8	0.0	4.4
Law and Order	79.3	20.7	100.0	9.9	3.2	6.9
Education	17.1	82.9	100.0	4.8	29.4	15.7
Health	13.7	86.3	100.0	2.6	20.5	10.5
Social Security and Welfare	37.4	62.6	100.0	3.5	7.5	5.3
Housing and Utilities	1.3	98.7	100.0	0.1	9.6	4.3
Culture and Leisure	47.2	52.8	100.0	2.0	2.8	2.3
Energy	3.5	96.5	100.0	0.1	3.4	1.5
Agriculture	89.1	10.9	100.0	11.1	1.7	6.9
Industry	97.8	2.2	100.0	0.7	0.0	0.4
Transport and Communication	13.5	86.5	100.0	1.6	12.7	6.5
Other Economic Affairs	81.8	18.2	100.0	14.5	4.1	9.9
Miscellaneous	98.4	1.6	100.0	16.1	0.3	9.2
Total (percent of GDP)	55.8	44.2	100.0	100.0 (10.4)	100.0 (8.2)	100.0 (18.6)

Source: Ministry of Finance; republican expenditures excluding net lending and participation.

39.   Expenditures of territorial administrations are mostly *funded out of general resources*. The new tax code distinguishes, somewhat artificially, between two groups of taxes: five "national taxes" and six "local taxes." The five national taxes are: (i) the income tax on individuals and businesses; (ii) the value added tax (VAT); (iii) excise duties; (iv) the tax on security transactions; and (v) rent payments by mineral resource users. The six "local" taxes include the land tax, the vehicle tax, the tax on property, and three types of fees. In practice, the distinction between national and local taxes is less sharp than their names would suggest. On the one hand, although the republican authorities determine the tax bases and tax rates of the national taxes, 100 percent of the revenues from the individual income tax are earmarked to territorial budgets. The republican budget also shares with territorial budgets the proceeds of the "regulating taxes": the VAT, excise duties, fixed rent payments, and the business income (or profits) tax. On the other hand, while the revenues of the "local" taxes accrue to rayon-level budgets, their bases and rates are centrally set.

---

[11]   Other welfare expenditures are charged to the Social Insurance Fund.

Table 7: Allocation of Expenditures between and within Territorial Tiers
(1994 actual)

ITEM	OBLAST	RAYON	TERRITORIAL	OBLAST	RAYON	TERRITORIAL
General Public Services	32.8	67.2	100.0	3.8	5.2	4.6
Defense	55.6	44.4	100.0	0.1	0.0	0.0
Law and Order	66.5	33.5	100.0	5.2	1.8	3.1
Education	23.7	76.3	100.0	17.3	37.4	29.3
Health	32.9	67.1	100.0	16.8	22.9	20.5
Social Welfare, Housing,	42.6	57.4	100.0	17.9	16.1	16.8
Culture, Leisure, Religion	43.4	56.6	100.0	2.7	2.4	2.5
Agriculture	67.9	32.1	100.0	2.9	0.9	1.7
Miscellaneous	62.5	37.5	100.0	33.2	13.3	21.3
Total	41.1	58.9	100.0	100.0	100.0	100.0
(percent of GDP)				(3.4)	(4.8)	(8.2)

Source: Ministry of Finance.

40. The budget process serves to allocate these general resources among the various strands of the state budget. This process seeks to accomplish two objectives: (i) to ensure a uniform level of services nationwide; and (ii) to induce territorial authorities to cooperate in the collection of national taxes. Expenditure norms seek to achieve the former objective (see para. 62). A complex system of *revenue earmarking* is meant to achieve the latter. In dividing up national resources among budget levels, territorial budgets are first earmarked all or part of the proceeds of the regulating taxes levied within their jurisdiction, up to a maximum defined by their normative expenditure envelopes. The remaining balances are covered by republican "subventions." Neither the sharing rates for the regulating taxes nor the republican subventions affect ex ante the total amount of resources for which each territorial entity is budgeted. Indeed, territorial expenditure budgets are determined independently of the earmarking process, and revenue sharing coefficients vary accordingly. But tax earmarking serves to ensure that for each particular territorial entity the budget resources actually at its disposal *during the execution of the budget* are determined by the revenue efforts of its particular jurisdiction.

41. This mechanism creates only minor rigidities for the ex ante allocation of budget resources (during budget preparation). Considerable rigidities, however, occur at the execution stage as each tenge of resources is parceled out among a myriad of subbudgets according to set coefficients rather than a careful consideration of expenditure priorities. Rigidities would obviously increase dramatically if sharing coefficients were frozen, as is sometimes suggested. Furthermore, given the observed the instability of tax yields over time (see para. 57), such a freeze would make territorial resources much more unpredictable, not less so, thus invalidating the stated rationale for such proposal.

Creating Local Governments

42. In devising a *policy of decentralization*, the authorities would first need to address the following four fundamental questions:

(i)   How many tiers of territorial jurisdiction should the country have?

(ii)   Which form of administrative autonomy should each tier have?

(iii)   At which level of jurisdiction is it preferable to establish local governments?

(iv)   Which responsibilities should local governments be charged with?

Only on this basis can proper fiscal arrangements be defined and established.

43.   **Number of Territorial Tiers.** It is generally desirable to keep the number of tiers of territorial administrations to a minimum. When the number of tiers increases, staffing and other resource requirements also increase, as does the likelihood of overlaps in responsibilities. In view of the immensity of its territory, having two tiers of territorial jurisdiction (see para. 18) seems to be roughly the right balance. It is a common feature among OECD countries, particularly unitary ones. From a demographic point of view as well, the current size of territorial jurisdictions appears broadly appropriate. The average population of the oblast tier (excluding the city of Leninsk) is about 850,000, and that of the rayon tier is just over 75,000. The upper tiers in OECD countries often have average populations as large as the oblasts,[12] but the lower tiers in OECD countries rarely have populations as large as the rayons. To some extent, relatively large local authorities can be advantageous. Many OECD countries have experienced difficulties with local authorities that are too small for some of their functions and yet are so well established that there would be resistance against consolidating them. Despite their demographic size, rayon-level jurisdictions appear to be generally large enough to organize public interventions efficiently while maintaining a direct contact with their populations, particularly given the density of the road network.

44.   **Delegation versus Devolution.** The Constitution of Kazakstan envisages that territorial jurisdictions can be administered in two different ways. On the one hand, territorial jurisdictions may remain part of the national state, but may be administered under a the system of delegation of state authority or "territorial state administration." This is the system currently in place, under which territorial administrations have a certain discretion in implementing national policies in consideration of local circumstances, while still remaining in a subordinate position vis-à-vis republican authorities. But, on the other hand, the new Constitution also opens the door to a devolution of authority to local governments or "local self-administration [...] exercised directly through elections as well as through representative and other bodies of local self-administration [...] established by law" (Art. 89). Under such a system of devolution of authority, vertical hierarchical links would disappear, giving local bodies exclusive authority in the matters transferred to them. Such autonomous local government, however, remains to be established.

45.   **Level of Decentralization.** The next question is to define to which level(s) of jurisdiction this power should be devolved. Article 89 of the Constitution reserves local self-administration for "rural and urban jurisdictions covering territories on which groups of population live compactly" and

---

[12]   Oblasts may, however, have under their supervision a number of lower tier entities which exceed their effective "span of control" (i.e., the number of subordinate units beyond which the efficacy of an organization decreases).

thus would favor the creation of new municipalities.[13] This would appear to be a good place to start, as it is at that level that the most significant impacts of local government should be expected. As noted above, this is the level at which public services are in direct and day-to-day contact with the population (e.g., through utilities, schools, general health care) and at which therefore they are likely to form well-grounded preferences regarding the nature and level of services they receive, and to participate actively in the definition of policies or, for that matter, in the mobilization of resources to support these policies.

46.   For reasons of minimum size of a jurisdiction, it is probably advisable that only localities of national (cities), oblast (towns), or rayon importance (townships) should qualify, at least initially, to be transformed into municipalities. Lower-level localities would remain subadministrative levels, as currently. Such a system would result in a geographical organization of the country, which is not uncommon among countries with vast and sparsely populated territories (e.g., the United States, the Maghreb countries). In such settings local government jurisdictions may often not cover the entire national territory, but may be limited to areas with sufficient population to justify the establishment of specific public services, as well as to generate a sufficient fiscal capacity to operate them. The maintenance of rural roads, for example, may be well within the means of sufficiently populated rural jurisdictions, but may become unaffordable where settlements are few and far between.

47.   **Responsibilities of Local Governments.** The range of functions carried out by Kazakstan's localities (including general health and education, municipal services, public transportation) (see para. 38) is extensive but is fairly conventional by OECD standards. Over time, most of these functions might be transferred to future municipalities.

48.   Three items of expenditures currently funded by the budgets of localities warrant further consideration. First, the range of subsidies given under the heading of social welfare should be examined. If these subsidies are retained, then they should be considered as essentially a form of redistribution. Redistribution is considered to be an activity that should be carried out in a more-or-less uniform way within the nation, and therefore is essentially a matter of central policies. Thus, most of these payments should probably remain a national responsibility. Second, localities do not have responsibility for road building and maintenance in their areas, yet these are very common local functions in OECD countries. Minor roads could well be entrusted to localities. And third, localities and rural rayons provide most of general education and health services. In OECD countries, central governments frequently retain substantial responsibility in these areas.

49.   This transfer of responsibility to municipalities does not need to take place overnight. It may instead be the result of *an evolutionary process*. This devolution process might be tailored so as to proceed in tandem with the development of an autonomous management capacity, as well as democratic practices, at the local level. The authorities may want to begin by devolving a limited set of responsibilities, starting, for instance, with urban infrastructures (e.g., water, district heat, street lighting, sanitation, and public transportation), kindergartens, culture and recreation, and some social services. Such a package would represent about 1.5 percent of GDP. In a second phase, the

---

[13]   The Constitution leaves open the possibility of a devolution of authority in specified matters to oblast (and rural rayons) maslikhats (Art. 86). But such decentralization could only be limited, as these representative bodies would not have their own executives. They might entrust territorial administrations with the execution of tasks under maslikhat authority (Art. 89), but these administrations would remain entirely part of the national executive. The situation of the maslikhats would then be similar to that of the *conseils généraux* in French *départements* before the 1981 decentralization.

responsibility for local roads, and some of the health services, could be transferred to the municipalities. Further along in the process, the authorities would consider the desirability of decentralizing some or all general education.

50.   The responsibilities of local government do not necessarily need to be limited to a specific positive list. The Constitution determines that local governments will be competent "in matters of local significance" for the population. These matters need not be specifically defined. Indeed, many European countries (including Germany, France, Portugal, Spain, and Italy) strive to let their local governments adjust as closely as possible to local priorities by giving them a general responsibility for all local matters. The latter responsibility is understood to include all functions not exercised by a higher authority. Most countries add to this a number of mandatory assignments (matched by commensurate resources), such as hygiene, sanitation, fire protection, local roads or public transportation. In the case of Kazakstan, such mandatory assignments may vary between urban municipalities (e.g., garbage collection) and rural ones (e.g., regulation of agricultural activities).

51.   Furthermore, the emergence of local governments within localities would not necessitate a duplication of *administrative structures*. The head of a jurisdictions's administration could head both of the services which, either during the transition or permanently, would remain part of the state territorial administration within his jurisdiction, as well as local government services. This system of "integrated field services," in addition to being simple to design, facilitates coordination of and cooperation among public activities within the jurisdiction. In such a system, the head of administration would be in charge of executing two separate budgets: the national budget in the jurisdiction and the local government budget as approved by the local council (see para. 74).

52.   However, one concrete aspect of the transformation of localities into municipalities is that the latter would not be subject to the system of norms. Obviously, the national laws would continue to define general rules in certain matters applicable across the country -- or to entrust the government with formulating them -- (school curricula, for example). And obviously local governments would be subject to national laws. But in the discharge of their duties in the fields in which exclusive authority has devolved to them by law, it would be up to the maslikhat, not the state, to define the norms applicable in their jurisdictions.

53.   **Funding Local Governments.** These new municipalities would require their separate sources of funding. It should be underscored from the outset that, in the evolutionary scenario outlined above, the size of local government financing requirements will expand gradually over time, as the process of devolution unfolds and local government responsibilities grow. Therefore, not all the decisions regarding the design of this funding system need to be taken immediately. Indeed, in the course of the devolution process, the country's revenue outlook is bound to undergo substantial change as a result of the ongoing economic transformation, which would cast a different light on different types of fiscal instruments. A fundamental principle, however, should be maintained throughout the process: there should be no devolution of responsibility without a commensurate resource transfer.

54.   In devising a financing system for local government, Kazakstan may want to retain *a high degree of needs equalization* among territorial jurisdictions. Apart from being consistent with the country's tradition, this would also correspond to the notion of equity that people paying equal tax rates in different areas can enjoy similar service levels.

55.   Achieving this objective is complicated by the fact that the *revenues of the country's major taxes are heavily concentrated* in certain areas (see Table 8). For any given tax in any given year, about a quarter of all oblasts raise less per capita than half the national average. This concentration of tax revenues has become more acute over time, as the 50 percent increase in the standard deviation in overall tax yields per capita between the beginning and the end of the period under review (1992-95) indicates. As a result, the gap between the oblasts with the highest and lowest overall yields per capita has widened from a ratio of 5:1 to a ratio of 15:1 between 1992 and 1995. The ranges are even wider if one looks at individual taxes. The degree of variation is even higher when tax yields are compared across rayon-level jurisdictions, instead of across oblasts.

56.   This high concentration results from the fact that *taxes are mostly levied on a production basis rather than on a residence or destination basis*. The personal income tax, which is withheld at the source, is collected chiefly in areas where people work rather than where they live. The profits tax is collected chiefly in the areas of business headquarters. The excise taxes and VAT are collected on an origin basis (i.e., at the point of production or of first import) rather than on a destination basis (i.e., at the point where taxable items are actually consumed). The fixed rents tax arises only in areas with natural resources.

57.   To make matters worse, the geographical distribution of tax revenues is not only uneven. It is also unstable over time. As Table 8 shows, the correlation between revenue performance (as measured by comparing tax yields per capita in each oblast to the national average) from one year to the next is weak. It is even weaker in terms of a longer period of time (four years in the table). Part of this volatility is explained, of course, by the economic turmoil which the country underwent over the period. But such instability is also inherent in the Kazak economy, in view of its heavy regional specialization on various types of commodities (e.g., grain, oil, nonferrous metals) the prices and/or output of which are intrinsically unstable either because the prices of the said commodities on the world market go through wide cycles (as, for instance, in the case of metals), or because production conditions depend heavily on the vagaries of the weather (as in the case of grain).

58.   *Combining tax revenues and grants* could help to reconcile the equalization objective with the above revenue constraint. Volume II, Chapter VII, discusses various taxation options and concludes that the current "local" taxes, together with a portion of the personal income tax, should be considered first candidates for local taxation. Ongoing reforms in the personal income tax, in particular, should make it possible to assign its proceeds on a residence basis. Future municipalities could be allowed to set the rates at which the above taxes would be levied, but only under the form of a surcharge in the case of the personal income tax. To avoid tax escalation, these local taxes and surcharges should be *subject to limits set nationally*.

Table 8: Total Tax Revenues Per Capita
(in percent of mean)

OBLAST	1992	1993	1994	1995
Akmola	134.0	207.8	103.7	114.0
Aktyubinsk	88.3	83.1	122.9	139.6
Almaty	34.3	44.4	40.4	31.2
Atyrau	89.8	94.1	351.1	223.7
East Kazakstan	110.4	100.2	109.5	120.9
Zhambyl	50.6	52.2	41.1	37.9
Zhezkazgan	127.3	88.0	121.9	101.6
West Kazakstan	79.1	72.6	56.9	62.1
Karaganda	179.5	141.6	126.9	121.8
Kzyl-Orda	34.3	35.4	40.6	42.2
Kokshetau	88.1	78.5	63.5	64.3
Kostanai	129.6	103.3	76.8	92.5
Mangystau	161.1	170.9	174.6	246.3
Pavlodar	160.9	158.6	114.8	143.2
North Kazakstan	86.2	85.7	64.6	60.4
Semipalatinsk	56.2	59.3	60.4	57.4
Taldykorgan	54.8	45.4	27.9	19.3
Turgai	155.7	87.7	46.9	38.2
South Kazakstan	56.1	57.9	52.7	52.8
Almaty (city)	152.6	209.1	287.5	283.2
Mean	100.0	100.0	100.0	100.0
Standard Deviation	46.1	52.2	83.6	74.5
Range (Max/Min)	5.2	5.9	12.6	14.6
Correlation				
with previous year	..	81.8	56.3	90.7
with 1992	..	..	..	59.7

Sources: Ministry of Finance and World Bank staff estimates.

59.   These tax revenues could be supplemented by *equalizing grants*. And if Kazakstan wishes to pursue full equalization of differences in resources and needs, an appropriate grant formula can be devised to that effect. The United Kingdom and Sweden, for instance, operate grant programs which ensure that all local governments have the capacity to finance services at standard levels if they levy local taxes at standard rates. Both countries, however, leave it up to local governments to set their own tax rates (within limits) and services at levels of their own choosing rather than at the standard levels. Other options are also discussed in Volume II. With the combination of taxes and grants discussed here, local governments in Kazakstan would not be dissimilar to those in OECD countries, which raise on average some 43 percent of their nonloan revenues from taxes and 39 percent from grants.

D. The Systems of State Management

Budget Management

60.   The need to redeploy administrative structures and public services is recognized increasingly by the Kazakstan authorities. The link between this proposition and the need for budget reform is less widely perceived. International experience, however, demonstrates that effective budget procedures can provide a crucial impetus to, and a key tool for, the reform of public services.

61.   Up to the present, the entire budget process has been dominated at all stages by the *logic of passive distribution* of available resources among existing structures and services, which characterized the Soviet *Gosbudget*. Under this old logic, the allocation of financial resources passively reflected the allocation of real resources. An altogether different logic must emerge: a *logic of selection* among competing services and structures, triggering an adaptation of those structures to policy priorities and resource constraints, even to the elimination of those which rank lowest in the selection process. Under this new logic, finances would direct the real resources, rather than the other way around. This leadership function is exercised most effectively when budget procedures orchestrate, at all levels of government, a process of competition/selection among priorities.

Budget Formulation

62.   **Current Arrangements.** Current budget formulation procedures are not conducive to such selectivity. In the first round of preparation, the expenditure budget is established through the *passive aggregation of norm-based expenditure requests*, which serve to calculate the "input requirement" of a given level of supply of public services. In the planning days, this level reflected the fundamental choices made in the physical planning process. Today, it reflects only the inertia of tradition. Despite the current crisis and the growing gap between normative resource requirements and available resources, the maintenance (at least formally) of the system of norms underwrites a perceived "entitlement" to fiscal resources at all levels of the fiscal chain, which hinders structural reforms.

63.   The fact that a myriad of budget entities participate in the budget process exacerbates the structural rigidities. The basic component of Soviet public finances is the *smeta*, or expenditure allocation document. For each *smeta*, there is a corresponding spending or budget entity. There is a multitude of such entities. The republican tier of administration counts over 2,200 and the territorial tiers may count as many as 40,000. In the first round of budget preparation, each budget entity establishes its own budget submission (based on norms). The latter submissions are simply added up, with little further screening, to form the first draft of the budget. At this level of aggregation, it is virtually impossible for the Ministry of Finance, on its own, to distinguish functional priorities from within the mass of budget submissions. Sectoral ministries hardly participate in the process of screening and prioritizing sectoral budget submissions. They may seek to defend their own *smeta*, but they generally do not assume leadership in the elaboration of other budgets within their sectoral purview. For instance, the Ministry of Education would formulate a budget submission covering the activities of its own administration but would not typically assume responsibility in formulating the *smetas* of the 126 other budget entities under its supervision at the republican level, and even less for the thousands more reporting to territorial levels of administration.

64.   This process also takes place with little consideration for the overall *macroeconomic framework* in which the budget is expected to be executed, and with little apparent conscious effort to program expenditures according to a clear set of policy priorities. It is only in the second round that budget envelopes are cut down in size to fit within the prospective resource envelope. But not even at this stage do programmatic priorities emerge. Instead of making the necessary cuts in expenditure on the basis of functions, the final choices are largely made by nature of expenditure (e.g., wages, operating supplies, transfers). Of course, the *budget classification* used until 1995 did not facilitate such functional choices: at the final stages, proposed budget appropriations were presented only by sectoral "complexes" and by economic nature, rather than by functions and spending departments, considerably obscuring the decisionmaking process.

65.   **Overhauling the Budget Process.** The first step toward transforming the *budget process* into an act of public expenditure programming would be to begin the budget preparation process with the determination of initial *sectoral envelopes*, based on an official forecast of macroeconomic conditions during the forthcoming fiscal year. Once these envelopes had been approved by the Cabinet, they would be conveyed to the sector ministries, with instructions to conduct the preparation of the budget in their sectors within these given parameters. Sectoral ministries would typically be expected to further apportion these envelopes among their subordinate institutions, with similar instructions. The initial envelopes and subenvelopes would be expected to evolve during the budgeting process under the influence of a competitive process and to lead to a sequence of *arbitrations*, and, as a result, also to a *sequence of structural choices* regarding the detail of sectoral policies and the existence, size, and structure of public services: structural choices first within the spending departments, second between the spending departments and the relevant departments of the Ministry of Finance, then through budget conferences between the ministers, and finally, under the leadership of the Prime Minister, to resolve the final disputes. These steps would serve to weaken the pervasive "entitlement mentality" which expenditure norms have created among public services. In this new setting, the point of the budgeting process would no longer be for public services to send resource requisition forms to fiscal authorities, but would be for service managers to convince their peers within subsectors and sectors, and then the rest of the government, that their activities, more than others, warrant the expenditure of scarce budgetary resources.

66.   **Introducing New Budgeting Instruments**. To illuminate better budgetary choices, the Ministry of Finance has developed (with U.S. Treasury and IMF assistance) a more appropriate nomenclature based on a *functional and institutional* classification of fiscal operations. The sketch of this new nomenclature was used for the preparation of the 1996 budget in parallel with the old one. A comprehensive new classification has now been adopted for the republican budget. Beyond the advantages already noted of a functional presentation of government operations, this classification points also toward a rationalization of administrative structures. Indeed, the institutional classification substantially reduces the number of first-rank budget agencies, either as testimony of their recent elimination or by subsuming them into larger expenditure "portfolios." The next steps will be: (i) to make it the sole classification in use for the preparation of the 1997 budget; (ii) to put sectoral ministries effectively in charge of budgeting for these larger portfolios; and (iii) to extend the process to the lower tiers of the budget.

67.   A variety of *budget rationalization methodologies* could be used to facilitate this selection process. If the most radical methodologies, such as zero-base budgeting and the planning/ programming/budgeting system (PPBS) have generally proved unwieldy, some of their insights could

be applied in Kazakstan without too much difficulty. Many countries routinely distinguish among current expenditures between ongoing programs and new measures to highlight some of the trade-offs and policy choices facing the authorities (e.g., which ongoing programs to cut down or terminate, if the government is to afford this or that new initiative). Program budgeting could be implemented successfully in selected sectors, such as education, health, or communications, where the definition of programmatic objectives, efficiency, and performance criteria is more straightforward. More prosaically, most individual categories of expenditure can and should be evaluated according to defined performance objectives, measured by quantitative cost-effectiveness indicators or even simpler measurement of service levels. Section E describes how some of these concepts could be first introduced in the education and health sectors, by moving away from an allocation of budget resources based on the input needs of sectoral facilities to one based on the level of service delivered to beneficiaries.

68.   **The Case of Public Investment.** Adequate procedures are also required to rationalize the management of *public investment*. Although public investment has virtually ceased in Kazakstan, such a situation cannot last. No example exists of a country recovering and sustaining growth without investing in its social overhead capital if only -- as the priority for Kazakstan should be -- to rationalize existing facilities and infrastructures. Furthermore, during recent years public investment activities have been shifted around among many protagonists (including the Ministry of Economy, the Economic Transformation Fund, the State Development Bank, the Ex-Im Bank) in the absence of a conclusive discussion of the role and nature of public investment management. In practice, this function has fallen in abeyance. It now needs to be reinstated.

69.   Public investment management typically involves four specific phases: planning, programming, budgeting, and implementation. The *planning* phase aims to elaborate medium-term economic and social perspectives, as well as development strategies and policies, at both the macroeconomic and the sectoral levels. During this phase, also, emphasis is put on identifying, selecting, and preevaluating investment proposals. In this framework, sectoral ministries would be invited to prepare multiannual investment proposals, identifying and evaluating proposed projects on the basis of common methodological guidelines for the economic and financial evaluation of projects, including the recurrent cost requirements they engender. The *programming* phase seeks to transform the objectives of the plan into operational programs for the state, balancing the respective recourses to policies and investment. The consolidation of investment proposals into a national public investment program (PIP) should follow the same competition/selection logic as that proposed for the budgeting process. The final decisions as to the initiation, phasing, and modulation of investment projects should be made within the *budgeting* framework. The appropriation decision itself would be made taking into consideration, among other things: (i) the macroeconomic conditions under which the budget is expected to be executed; and (ii) the particular aspects of the project proposal, including the economics, the total costs, the nature of the goods and public works to be procured, the financial structure, and the recurrent cost requirements. Finally, whereas the *implementation* of investment projects (e.g., studies and consultations, procurement) takes place under the responsibility of spending agencies, additional precautions need to be taken to ensure avoiding the types of implementation slippage that too easily plague investment projects, particularly cost overruns.

70.   To prepare for the necessary resumption of public investment, Kazakstan should first establish proper institutional frameworks for public investment management and should organize in an efficient way the four functions outlined above: planning, programming, budgeting, and monitoring. Two criteria should guide the authorities in devising any particular arrangement. First, whatever vehicle is

eventually chosen to execute financial transactions related to public investments funded by domestic and external resources (Treasury or Ex-Im Bank), the responsibility for determining development priorities and selecting those projects which meet these priorities best should remain within the government; it cannot be performed by any outside institution. And second, while investment planning and implementation are clear responsibilities of sectoral agencies, the programming functions and the budgeting and monitoring functions need to be closely integrated within the government's fiscal strategy. The role of the Ministry of Finance in this is therefore essential. Whether some of these central functions should be shared with other agencies (e.g., the Ministry of Economy) is an open question. Arguably, decisive progress is more likely to be achieved by concentrating efforts on building up expenditure programming capacities in the one agency which unquestionably requires them, namely, the Ministry of Finance, rather than by dissipating energies across two or more agencies.

Budget Coverage

71.   Budget rationalization would, however, be in vain if the budget did not have complete control over the finances of the state. Considerable progress has already been achieved recently in restoring the unity[14] of the budget through the gradual elimination of most of the *extrabudgetary funds* that existed immediately after independence. Partly as a result of this process, the burden of extrabudgetary funds declined from about 12 percent of GDP in 1993 to about 7 percent in 1995. The Pension Fund, Employment Fund, and Social Insurance Fund[15] have justifiably continued to operate as extrabudgetary funds. The nature of these funds is indeed different from that of regular fiscal operations. They are public insurance funds, managed by parastatal bodies; they are financed not by taxes but by mandatory insurance premiums. As long as the authorities adhere to the *insurance principle* in the field of social protection, it is in their interest to keep the finances of the social security system separate from those of public administrations.

72.   Apart from the above exception, the authorities would be well advised to resist any temptation or pressure to reconstitute or create new extrabudgetary funds. In this context, the reconstitution in early 1996 of the *Road Fund* as an extrabudgetary fund sets an unfortunate precedent. More worrisome is the decision made to finance the *construction of a new capital* in Akmola -- not only outside the framework of the budget, but also to lodge the related transactions in an offshore banking account. There is also no justification for the present state of affairs in which most expenditures financed by foreign borrowing are neither budgeted nor accounted for under the country's normal procedures. Such expenditures should be appropriated, authorized, executed, accounted for, and controlled in the same way as any other budget expenditure.

73.   Another source of the incomplete coverage of the budget is the recent *multiplication of "non-budgetary" resources* mobilized independently by budget entities. Faced with the general dearth of

---

[14]   The principle of budget unity is that all resources and charges of the state should be provided for in a single document. The principle is aimed at giving fiscal authorities (from the Budget Department to Parliament) a comprehensive view of all public finance matters so that they may reach as accurate an understanding as possible of the requirements and implications of public policies, whether in macroeconomic terms (e.g., overall tax burden, share of public spending in aggregate demand) or in microeconomic terms (e.g., cost-effectiveness of expenditure programs).

[15]   Both funded by a social security contribution of 30 percent of payroll.

resources, many budget entities have resorted to raising their own revenues, which they use at their own discretion outside of the framework of budget authorizations. The amount of resources collected in this way is known to be considerable, although no precise figure is available. The rule applicable to these revenues should be simple: the collection of any revenue by any state entity should be explicitly authorized by the budget and accounted for in the budget's books. In those cases where budget entities raises substantial nonbudgetary resources from industrial and commercial activities, the first option should be to incorporate them as commercial enterprises and to consider their privatization where applicable. For those cases where such "commercialization" is not practicable, the authorities should develop a legal and regulatory framework allowing resource-raising entities to deliver fee-based services, while keeping their finances integrated within the state budget, as departmental enterprises (if they remain unincorporated) or as statutory bodies (if they are incorporated).

Unifying the National Budget

74.   Finally, the outcome on the budget side of the devolution policy discussed above (see paras. 42-59) would be to introduce *a clear distinction between two types of budgets: the national budget on the one hand, and the budgets of local governments on the other*. The national budget would cover all of the fiscal activities of the state in matters of general interest, whether administered by central or territorial state administrations, and the local government budgets would encompass the fiscal activities of local governments within their sphere of responsibility. As tax collection becomes more reliable, it would become feasible to restore the unity of the national budget and fund state territorial administrations through normal budget appropriations, rather than through tax earmarking. A measure of autonomy may, however, be retained in favor of territorial administrations, through a system of *delegation of spending authority*, under which system national budget appropriations that are to be executed by state territorial administrations would be regrouped into territorial subbudgets to be executed under the administrative authority of the heads of territorial administrations. Such an arrangement would not represent a dramatic departure from current procedures, but, rather, would put fiscal practices in line with existing administrative arrangements within the state administration. Such an arrangement would allow a much more effective and transparent deployment of fiscal resources according to national priorities.

Budget Execution

75.   There would be little point in strengthening budgeting procedures, however, if the legal and institutional frameworks surrounding the use of public monies were not there to ensure that the budget is executed as planned. Although initial steps have been taken in this regard in the context of the establishment of a new Treasury system, this is unfortunately not yet the case in Kazakstan.

76.   **Conformity between Budget and Execution.** Kazakstan's current budget execution system inadequately ensures the *conformity* of actual expenditures with the approved budget at two levels. At the sectoral level, budget execution should faithfully reflect the allocations among the various public functions entered in the budget as voted, allocations which presumably reflect a careful consideration of public priorities. At the macroeconomic level, budget execution must also permit strict containment of the amount of the budget deficit, thereby ensuring that fiscal policy takes the desired stance.

77.   In fact, the budget seems to be executed in a rather arbitrary fashion. Budget execution data for 1994, for instance, show that appropriations may as well be spent twice over as not at all (see

Table 9). Both underutilization and overutilization of budget appropriations reflect failure to comply with the budget as voted. The discrepancies between authorized and actual expenditures are currently so large as to render meaningless the budget voted by Parliament. These discrepancies have three different sources, each of which calls for a separate remedy.

78.   The first source of discrepancy was, until 1994, a systematic *overoptimism in projecting fiscal revenues*. In 1994, for instance, actual receipts represented only 75 percent of the budget projections. The situation now seems to be improving. For the first time, in 1995, revenue collected for the state budget actually exceeded the budgeted amounts. This should not be a cause for complacency. As the country opens up and develops its natural resource-based activities, the country's macroeconomic performance will become more prone to the fundamental instability of international commodity markets. The authorities may wish to equip themselves to deal with such a volatile fiscal environment by making certain appropriations contingent on the macroeconomic situation (*cyclical funds*).

Table 9: Rate of Execution of the Revised 1994 Budget
(in percent of the revised 1994 budget appropriations)

	REPUBLICAN	TERRITORIAL	STATE
General Public Services	53.6	75.5	55.7
Defence	41.8	n.a.	42.0
Public Order and Safety Affairs	84.1	126.6	90.4
Education	79.1	107.1	101.0
Health	44.0	95.1	82.0
Social Security and Welfare	17.3	30.0	23.5
Housing and Utilities	2.4	1860.6	165.0
Culture, Leisure, Religion	50.6	139.2	76.2
Energy	117.5	n.a.	3320.0
Agriculture	56.9	239.8	62.1
Industry	51.6	n.a.	52.8
Transport and Communications	31.8	n.a.	3320.0
Other Economic Affairs	185.1	2393.8	222.5
Miscellaneous	72.7	143.2	73.2
Total	57.5	97.4	70.2

79.   The second source of discrepancy between budgeted and actual expenditures lies in the *weak legal authority of the budget law*. The state budget of Kazakstan, as defined in the Organic Law of December 17, 1991 or by common practices, appears more like a cash flow forecast rather than a law which *provides and authorizes*. As a result, there is little sanction against obligating expenditures without a proper appropriation. Existing instructions even formally exempt some categories of expenditures (e.g., loans to enterprises, security reserves) from this basic discipline. These exceptions foster more systematic overcommitment.

80.   The new Organic Law of the Budget which the Ministry of Finance is preparing should restate forcefully the binding nature of budget appropriations and should include a provision prescribing that

any person found guilty of committing or abetting any actions that result in the collection of public receipts or the execution of expenditures without authorization by the budget law shall be liable to criminal penalties.

81.   The third, but probably the largest, source of discrepancy is the pervasive use of what is commonly -- if improperly -- known as "*sequestration*"[16] to contain cash outlays within the available cash resources in the Treasury's account. First introduced in 1992 in a bid to bring the budget deficit back under control on a cash basis -- if not a commitment basis -- "sequestration" was codified in 1995 into a thoroughly irrational queuing mechanism. The unacceptable outcome of this procedure is that the state puts itself systematically and deliberately in a situation of defaulting on its payment obligations. Furthermore, the financial choices made under the pressure of circumstances generally lead to the sacrificing of those categories of expenditures which should serve to prepare the future of Kazakstan, such as public investment or the new social programs required for dealing with the hardships of transition. In contrast, the present hand-to-mouth behavior favors wage payments, enterprise subsidies, and, more generally, the maintenance of existing structures.

82.   "Sequestration" must be replaced by orderly budgetary procedures. It is necessary to establish appropriate mechanisms for programming cash flows, and for containing expenditures at the earliest stage (i.e., before obligation), within prospective cash availabilities. A first step has been taken recently in the context of the creation of the new Treasury system. This new system moves away from day-to-day payment decisions on the basis of cash availability to introduce, at the republican level, periodic releases of funds (or *warrants*) by the Treasury Department to spending agencies based on prospective cash flows. This important innovation provides a basis for spending agencies to plan and modulate their expenditure obligations within a set envelope and over a defined period of time, although an admittedly short one. There is still no guarantee that they will actually do so, however. The next step will be to supplement the warrant system with *global obligation control* mechanisms that ensure that spending agencies do not commit funds beyond the warrants available to them. The ongoing computerization of Treasury operations should facilitate this step.

83.   **Security and Efficiency of Fiscal Operations.** Measures are also required to step up *security* against fraud, misappropriation, and the risk of appropriations being squandered. Priorities in this respect involve: (i) establishing internal controls over expenditure obligations within spending agencies; (ii) introducing appropriate procurement regulations; and (iii) strengthening prepayment controls.

84.   For the *global control* by the Treasury over expenditure obligations to be fully effective, it will be essential to supplement the control of the utilization of warrants performed by the Treasury on strictly financial grounds, with *itemized internal controls over expenditure obligations* within each spending agency (Volume II, Chapter V, discusses the options international experience offers in this respect). Such internal controls would go beyond aggregate financial considerations and ensure that

---

[16]   The spread of the term *sequestration* throughout the former Soviet Union has been the source of some confusion as to the nature of the budget control instruments being applied. In practice, it often simply covers *default*. *Sequestration* is a term which designates the cancellation or withholding of appropriations. Sequestered funds are no longer available for obligation. The absence of obligation control in the Soviet tradition makes it difficult to prevent spending agencies from obligating expenditures. In most cases, therefore, the only instrument available to fiscal authorities is their control of the release of funds for the payment of expenditures. It is at that stage, rather than the obligation stage, that the "sequester" is applied. When the expenditure has already been committed, as will commonly be the case for wages, insurance-based social benefits, utilities, and debt service, this practice causes the government to *default* on its payment obligations. No rational budget management system condones such delinquency.

appropriations are used for their intended purposes, and that other regulations pertaining to expenditures (e.g., procurement rules, civil service statutes) are being followed.

85.   Greater efficiency should also be sought in the government's purchases of goods and services, as they amount to almost four times the government's wage bill. Unfortunately, beyond those expenditures funded by international donors, the World Bank particularly, little progress has as yet been made in defining *procurement* rules and procedures. Calls for bids may sometimes be organized for certain expenditures, but such examples are rare. Most purchases are made without systematic recourse to competitive bidding. Even more worrisome, conflicts of interest in government procurement contracts are thought to be rife, opening the door to favoritism and corruption.

86.   Finally, *prepayment controls* need to become more stringent. At present, payment control procedures are hardly defined, and therefore are barely enforced. Furthermore, owing to the poor payment record of the state, suppliers now routinely insist that payment be made prior to delivery. This undermines a chief consideration in controlling outlays, namely, to ensure that the services for which payment is made have actually been rendered. Although retroactive checks can be applied, they will necessarily be unwieldy and will only with the greatest difficulty counter the risk of embezzlement.

87.   Some reforms have been initiated recently. The process of setting up the network of Treasury offices is under way. Treasury offices have begun to implement strengthened prepayment control. Beginning September 1, 1995, all payment orders on the republican budget must be vetted by these offices. The next step would be that the mandatory controls performed by disbursement officers be defined more rigorously, by prescribing for each expenditure category a nomenclature of the required supporting documentation as the basis for verifying that the internal control procedures, mentioned above, have indeed been properly followed, and forbidding disbursement officers to disburse otherwise.

Budget Audit

88.   Properly organized budget audits can play a powerful role in expenditure rationalization. Audit methodologies can range from controls that are internal to government agencies and are geared primarily to the detection of irregularities, to external audits that are intended to assess overall expenditure performance and prepare the way for any necessary reforms. Developing these functions is particularly important in Kazakstan for two reasons. First, under the Soviet institutional system, the controls of all kinds of government agencies were in a very large measure performed by the Party. The sudden disappearance of external controls on the government creates a risk of fraud and misappropriation. Second, the objectives of budget audits go beyond detecting and preventing individual deficiencies. They should also serve to assess the efficiency of government programs, to highlight expenditures or regulations that have become outdated or difficult and expensive to apply, and to correct poorly designed or over-ambitious reforms through the dissemination of successful innovations and experiments.

89.   Current audit systems are poorly suited for these tasks. The existing *internal audits* system has been to a large extent reoriented toward auditing commercial entities. These functions are exercised by the State Committee for Financial Control (SCFC), created in October 1992, by merging the internal inspection units of all government agencies (except for those of a few security Ministries such as Defense, Foreign Affairs, and Interior) with the inspection unit attached to the Ministry of

Finance -- the KRO or control and audit service. The SCFC has the very broad mandate of auditing the financial and commercial activities of ministries, state committees, agencies, territorial executive organs, entities with financial autonomy, and organizations financed by the budget. These very broad terms of reference go even further and cover such matters as assisting the security agencies to combat corruption and crime or auditing foreign exchange and import-export operations. In practice, the SCFC devotes most of its resources, and the time of its 2,975 staff members operating at all levels of government, to auditing commercial firms, particularly for tax compliance.

90.   The emphasis of internal audits should shift to auditing government agencies. This refocusing process will be easier if financial auditing is reintegrated within the Ministry of Finance. This integration will make follow-up actions more effective and will help to strengthen the authority of the Ministry of Finance -- which is important, in the current context of transition, to greater consideration for the demands of budget management. This narrower mandate should also make it possible to reduce staff by abolishing the SCFC units at the rayon level. Finally, it may be advisable to reconsider the reform implemented in October 1992 and once again allow sectoral ministries to develop independent internal inspection systems.

91.   Kazakstan has never had an independent *external audit* function in the budget process. The Constitution adopted in August 1995 provides for the creation of an Accounts Committee, which may take over that function. To date, however, the initial steps taken by the authorities in developing that section of the Constitution[17] point more in the direction of the creation of presidential inspection, duplicating in many respects the functions of the SCFC, rather than toward an external audit capacity. On the one hand, the Committee would have little guarantee of independence. On the other hand, the Committee would wield powers so considerable that they might compromise its review mission by involving it in executive decisions, as well as in private business. If the Accounts Committee is indeed to fill the role of external auditor of the government, a few fundamental principles should be established. First, the tasks of this new institution should be clearly and precisely targeted, and should be limited to public administrations. Second, the new institution should be given the widest possible range of autonomy: free choice of investigation targets, direct access to public opinion through the publication of critical works, and long mandates for its members (the current term of five years would seem to be the minimum recommendable). Finally, the agency should limit its ambitions in an initial stage to the basic, but fundamental, task of verifying the correctness of fiscal accounts. As this capacity is firmly established, the agency could gradually broaden its objectives over time to management audits and, eventually, policy evaluation.

Civil Service Reform

92.   The authorities recognize that the current level of public employment is unsustainable and needs to be cut. The remedy for the present governmental overstaffing will not, however, be in addressing the symptoms rather than the sources of the problem, which lie in the dysfunctional organization of the state sector described above. Any sustainable reduction in government payroll will only come as a by-product of significant revamping of government programs and structures.

93.   At the moment, the fiscal burden of the *wage bill* -- about 15 percent of budget expenditures -- is comparable to the levels observed in middle- and high-income countries. However, under

---

[17]   Presidential Resolution of April 19, 1996.

overall fiscal pressures, its relative size in relation to GDP dropped from 4.8 percent in 1993 to 2.8 percent in 1994. This level is uncharacteristically low by any international standard (see Table 10). Furthermore, this reduced wage bill is spread among an exceedingly large number of employees, as already noted.

94.   As a result, official *individual compensation* is unsustainably low at both ends of the pay scale: wages at the bottom of the scale range well below the subsistence minimum, while wages at the top of the scale represent only a fraction of the wages offered for similar jobs outside the government. As a rule of thumb, the entry-level salary of a general administrator should be at least equal to a country's GDP per capita. Using this yardstick, a specialist's salary should be at least twice as high as it currently is. *Wage differentials*, which range from 1 to 5 among nonpolitical positions, are not unduly compressed, however. The present situation would therefore call for a general, rather than a selective, increase in the wage level. But such an increase should be implemented only in tandem with actual progress in retrenching personnel and strengthening payroll management.

Table 10: General Government Wage Bill in Selected Countries, 1994

COUNTRY	TOTAL EXPENDITURES (% of GDP)	WAGE BILL (% of Expend.)	WAGE BILL (% of GDP)
FSU Countries			
Kazakstan	18.2	15.3	2.8
Russia	46.3	13.5	6.3
Middle-Income Countries			
Czech Republic [1]	51.9	8.3	4.3
Hungary [4]	64.7	11.7	7.6
Romania [2]	44.3	13.6	6.0
Greece [1]	43.1	22.5	9.7
Portugal [4]	48.5	24.7	12.0
High-Income Countries			
Belgium [2]	56.7	17.8	10.1
France [2]	54.4	14.8	8.1
Germany [2]	62.3	18.2	11.4
Ireland [3]	54.2	18.1	9.8
Netherlands [1]	70.9	13.3	9.4
Spain [3]	50.5	19.6	9.9
United Kingdom [2]	56.2	18.6	10.4

Note: Including central and local governments but excluding social security funds.

[1] For 1993.
[2] For 1992.
[3] For 1991.
[4] For 1990.

Sources: IMF: GFS and IFS; World Bank: BESD Data Base.

95.   At present, unfortunately, the *size and composition* of the civil service is not known with any degree of precision. An estimate in excess of a million state employees has been offered in Table 5,

recognizing, however, that this estimate reflects the number of authorized positions rather than the number of persons actually employed. This situation is due to the particular regime under which civil servants are employed. Kazakstan inherited from the Soviet Union a *civil service regime* under which each budget entity recruits and manages its own personnel on a contractual basis to fill centrally authorized positions. In this system, no distinction is made between employment in public administrations and employment in commercial enterprises.

96. A first step toward defining a comprehensive policy in this regard would involve *taking an inventory* of remaining staff after the external boundaries of public administrations have been redefined, as well as of their profiles (e.g., education, seniority). Whereas a degree of decentralization in retrenchment is unavoidable, retrenchment decisions should follow criteria and guidelines established for the entire government. Such an inventory would make it possible to devise *differentiated treatments* applicable to different categories of public employees, including:

(i) The exclusion from the civil service of employees of entities incorporated separately from the state.

(ii) The adoption of specific statutes to govern teachers and medical personnel, the personnel of local governments, and the personnel of the judiciary and legislative branches.

(iii) The early retirement of certain categories of personnel.

(iv) The redeployment, retraining, or dismissal of other categories. Specific severance packages -- beyond the existing two-months' salary payment -- could also be devised once personnel data become available.

97. Retrenchment should be accompanied by measures to strengthen the professional and financial situation of the remaining civil servants. For all its apparent flexibility, the present *civil service system* has many disadvantages. First, it fosters subservience and discipline at the expense of initiative and responsibility. Second, this system creates problems of loyalty, as staff are more likely to dedicate themselves to the interests of their individual employing entity rather than to those of the state at large. Third, the current system subjects the civil service to the vagaries of the political process ("spoils system"). This is particularly damaging in Kazakstan where the turnover in high-level political positions is considerable. Fourth, this type of civil service system is hard to reconcile with one of the basic tenets of democracy: the equal access of all citizens to public office. Finally, when combined with the prevailing "in-line position" wage system under which wage promotion is linked exclusively to hierarchical promotion, such a civil service system creates a built-in incentive for the "mushrooming" of administrative structures.

98. As the authorities elaborate a civil service reform policy, they should consider shifting -- after a genuine staff downsizing -- to a civil service regime more conducive to independence and professionalism. A first critical step in this direction would be for civil servants to be recruited, employed, and managed by the state at large. This is best done on a statutory basis (rather than a contractual one). The fundamental options available in this respect are among position, rank, or mixed systems. Key features, advantages, and disadvantages of each of these systems for Kazakstan are as follows:

- In the *position system* (e.g., in the Netherlands), the salary level is fixed according to the job classification; the grade (and, correspondingly, the salary level) belongs to the job level, whichever individual performs it. The position system is commonly regarded as much superior to the rank system, since it permits wages to be adjusted to the precise features of the job being performed. Capturing these features in job classifications is, however, a highly complex undertaking in practice. And managing human resources under such a system requires monitoring both staff and job profiles. Furthermore, such system may hinder staff mobility, as reassigning a staff member may require finding that person an equivalent position.

- In the *career* or *rank system* (e.g., in France), the salary level or grade belongs to the individual, whichever position the individual occupies. In comparison with the position system, the rank system is relatively easier to implement as it requires only keeping track of personnel profiles. Since grades and wage levels are independent of the position occupied, it becomes easier to reassign staff from one position to the other. Unfortunately, the rank system is much less effective at stimulating staff performance.

- Some countries (e.g., Indonesia) have successfully implemented a *mixed system*, employing, for example, the position system for hierarchical functions; the rank system for other professional and/or clerical functions; and a contractual system for manual workers and temporary employment. This is an option worth considering for Kazakstan.

99.   The introduction of policies should also be accompanied by a substantial improvement in the level and structure of civil servants' wages and by the rationalization of payroll management to remove the opportunities for extralegal compensation and ghost worker schemes which the present system affords.

E. Key Programs

100.   Any critical impact on government employment will also require a review of existing commitments in key expenditure programs -- a review which the instruments proposed above should serve to facilitate. The ongoing fiscal crisis has placed all public expenditures in Kazakstan under enormous pressure. Its impact, however, is being felt differently across and within sectors. Since they are predominantly financed through public sources, education and health services are two areas in which this fiscal shock has had some of the most significant effects. In view of their share in public expenditures (25 percent) and government employment (70 percent), these two sectors remain priority areas for expenditure rationalization. Real resource flows to these sectors are at almost a third of their 1990 levels. In the absence of any major change in service delivery, the sustainability of past health and education achievements is now at issue. As the resource envelopes of the sectors are unlikely to expand again quickly, the current focus of policies should be on promoting a more efficient use of public resources.

Education

101.   The emphasis in *education* expenditures on general education is appropriate (see Table 11). But student to teacher ratios are very low by international standards (see Table 12). These low ratios result from: (i) an excessive specialization in curricula, particularly in vocational and higher education

institutions; and (ii) a funding mechanism designed to keep all classrooms open however marginal they may be.

Table 11: Total Education Expenditures by Facility Levels, 1992-1994
(percentage shares)

	1992	1993	1994
Preschool	4.3	12.1	12.1
Schools	52.3	48.2	46.8
Boarding Schools	5.8	5.1	6.6
Extramural	4.4	3.8	3.7
Vocational-Technical (PTUs, Technikums, etc.)	12.7	13.1	14.3
Higher Education	13.4	13.3	11.9
Other Institutions	4.8	3.4	3.2
Textbooks	0.3	0.3	1.0
State Capital Expenditures	2.0	0.8	0.2
Total	100.0	100.0	100.0

Note: Total expenditures include republican and territorial education budget expenditures.
Sources: World Bank staff estimates based on Local and Republican Budget Execution data, MOF.

Table 12: Student/Staff Ratios in Selected Countries

STUDENT:STAFF RATIOS	KAZAKSTAN (1994)	UNITED KINGDOM (1992)	GERMANY (1992)	TURKEY (1992)	OECD (1992)
Primary/secondary schools					
student:teacher	8.8:1	20.6/15.2	19.6/16.2	29:3/23.4	18.5/14.6
student:all staff	6.1:1				

Sources: 1. Kazakstan - World Bank staff estimates based on Network of Facilities and Personnel data, MOF
2. Other countries -OECD, *Education at a Glance*, Paris, 1995.

102.   Indeed, a major source of the current overstaffing problem in education resides in the methods of resource allocation on the basis of "class-complexes" (i.e., notional class sizes rather than actual student enrollment) applied uniformly per grade level, across the country. Whatever rationale is offered for justifying such calculations, the "class-complex" norms create an incentive for keeping open "marginal" classrooms and courses with low enrollment, whether in schools, vocational institutions, or higher educational establishments.

103.   Two priorities emerge from this situation:

(i)   Revising curricula to focus on more general education courses in schools, and increasing the teaching load, inter alia, by developing multitopic and multigrade methods in general education in low density areas

(ii) Reducing the number of schools and training programs.

104. To stimulate the consolidation of schools, it would be advisable to shift education funding to a *capitation-based funding mechanism* (on a per student basis) or, at the very least, to restrict the application of the class-complex norm to a class size beyond a certain minimum level. Classes or entire schools below such a critical size should be closed or merged with larger establishments.

Health

105. In *health,* the resource allocation patterns show an unfortunate bias toward in-patient and tertiary care, which absorb about three-quarters of available resources (see Table 13). In contrast, polyclinics and ambulatories, which are the main institutions providing outpatient services, have to be satisfied with from 6 to 8 percent of total health spending. The rural network of polyclinic and ambulatory facilities is under particular financial stress, with severe implications for both the equity and cost-effectiveness of health spending.

Table 13: Total Health Expenditures by Facility Levels, 1992-1994
(percentage shares)

FACILITY LEVEL	1992	1993	1994
Hospitals	73.6	71.7	73.1
Polyclinics	6.1	6.8	6.5
Rural Polyclinic and Ambulatory Facilities	1.1	1.0	0.8
Public Health Units	4.1	5.1	4.5
Other Health Activities	14.0	14.9	14.8
State Capital Investment	1.0	0.5	0.2
Total	100.0	100.0	100.0

Source: World Bank staff estimates based on Local and Republican Budget Execution data, MOF.

106. This excessive emphasis on hospitalization is further borne out by a comparison of the basic indicators of in-patient capacity for Kazakstan, OECD countries, and middle- and low-income countries of the region (see Table 14). On all counts (i.e., rate of admission into hospitals, average length of stay in hospitals, and beds/population), the health sector in Kazakstan appears to have placed a comparatively heavier emphasis on in-patient care. Many diseases which are treated on an outpatient basis in other countries are treated through in-patient care in Kazakstan, and, once admitted, patients are often kept for longer periods than is the case outside of the FSU.

107. The permanence of norm-based funding mechanisms underwrites these distortions. At present, sector facilities continue to prepare and submit budgets based on norms or incremental coefficients, while knowing full well that they ultimately will receive considerably less than that. Despite this lack of funding, sector agencies are unlikely to downsize facilities and services for which they seek funding -- the common wisdom being that any effort at rationalization will be self-defeating, as it would only invite further cuts.

Table 14: Availability and Use of Health Care in Selected Countries, 1992 and 1994

	KAZAKSTAN 1994	UZBEKISTAN 1994	RUSSIA 1994	TURKEY 1992	OECD AVERAGE 1992
In-patient admission (% of population)	18.0	19.3	21.0	5.5	16.2
Average length of stay (days)	16.8	14.3	17.0	6.8	14.4
Physicians/000 population	3.7	3.4	3.9	0.9	2.5
In-patient beds/000 population	12.4	8.8	12.2	2.4	8.4

Sources: 1. Kazakstan: Annual Report of the Ministry of Health, 1994. 2. Uzbekistan: *A Survey of Health Reform in Central Asia*, Jeni Klugman and George Schieber, World Bank Technical Paper No. 344, December 1996 3. Russia: Medical Equipment Project, Staff Appraisal Report, World Bank, 1996 4. Turkey and OECD: G.J. Schieber and al. *Health System Performance in OECD Countries*, Health Affairs, 1994

108.   Priority should be given to shifting treatment to cost-effective ambulatory institutions. Recommendations to rationalize resource allocation patterns to cost-effective uses and to encourage the sustainability of effective practices include the following:

(i)   Introducing medical protocols emphasizing ambulatory care where appropriate

(ii)   Strengthening the diagnostic and treatment capacity of polyclinic and ambulatory institutions, and giving them a higher proportion of total health spending

(iii)   Introducing funding mechanisms on the basis of a capitated fund per protocol (i.e., funds to cover protocol treatment for the number of enrolled patients).

109.   The expected impact of these measures would be a decline in the rate of hospital admissions and average lengths of stay, as the demand for costly and lengthy in-patient treatment is reduced. This decline should be accompanied by the closure of entire facilities or wards, rather than by the decommissioning of beds, which may not produce much in terms of actual savings.

F. Reform Objectives, Priorities, and Implementation

110.   Reforming the state is both critical and urgent. International experience identifies two pitfalls in this respect: one of these is a piecemeal approach which seeks to solve problems in a specific field (e.g., excessive government employment) without keeping sight of the existing interlinkages among the different aspects of public management (e.g., public employment and administrative structures or social policies); the other is an overly comprehensive approach, which runs the risk of crumbling under the burden of its own ambitions before it has any critical impact on the ground. The approach suggested in this report is to give the highest priority to reforms that affect the administration as a whole (i.e., reforms that deal with problems common to all state structures and services), and to emphasize reform actions that are likely to foster the sustainability of the overall economic reform program.

111.   Three elements will be key to the success of the undertaking: (i) a clear definition of the objectives to be attained; (ii) a technically and politically feasible sequencing of reform actions; and

(iii) effective institutional support for the design, implementation, and monitoring of this reform agenda.

Overall Objectives

112.   The ultimate goal of the proposed reforms would be to maintain quality public services in areas where public needs, expressed through elections or through the markets, are greatest and where state intervention is warranted under a market economy. Downsizing state structures and services and overhauling public management systems are intermediary objectives toward this ultimate goal.

113.   In revamping government structures, the authorities might seek to achieve the following four objectives over the next two to three years:

(i)   A reduction in the number of first-level departments to less than 100 function-based administrative units operating at the national level

(ii)   A reduction in the number of Cabinet-level agencies to roughly 20 entities, empowered with policymaking, administrative, and budget authority in their area of responsibility

(iii)   The creation of local governments in 287 urban localities as well as perhaps 200-400 rural localities

(iv)   A redefinition of the delegation of authority from republican to territorial administrations.

114.   In the same time frame, the authorities should be able to achieve the following:

(i)   The creation of a national civil service employing, on a statutory basis, in the range of 100,000 professionals at the republican and territorial levels (with separate statutory arrangements for local civil servants as well as teachers and medical personnel)

(ii)   The establishment of budgeting procedures capable of efficiently directing fiscal resources over the short- and medium-terms toward selected public functions.

Priorities

115.   The above goals are undoubtedly ambitious. This report would therefore encourage the authorities to opt for a phased approach, and to sequence the various actions according to their degree of urgency and the requirements for up front political consensus-building and/or for preparatory technical work.

116.   Strengthening budget resource allocation and control mechanisms and downsizing administrative structures deserve the *first order of priority*. This is not only because these are the two areas in which present deficiencies are most crippling, and conversely therefore where some of the largest critical impacts can be expected. Nor is it only because, in the field of budget management at least, concrete proposals are already on the table. Decisive progress in budget management and administrative organization are also prerequisites for putting other desirable steps (for example, the creation of a statutory civil service, the overhaul of social policies, or the development of local

government) on a firm footing. Indeed, budget and administrative reforms would allow the authorities, inter alia, to start addressing one of the two legs of the proposed reform of territorial administration, namely, the establishment of proper mechanisms of administrative and budgetary deconcentration (or delegation) of national authority to existing bodies of territorial administration. Similarly, the education and health sectors could well be selected to pilot budgeting reform initiatives.

117.   While these priority initiatives are unfolding, the authorities would give themselves more time to design *further stages of reforms*. As concerns decentralization, for instance, this "breathing space" could be put to good use: (i) to develop the mechanisms of local accountability and participation -- without which local government is a charade; (ii) to develop a political consensus around the socioeconomic content of decentralization; (iii) to structure jurisdictions and administrations accordingly; and (iv) to devise sustainable systems of local finances. Similarly, this "breathing space" should be used to design, and bring about consensus for, new civil service statutes -- as well as to establish the necessary personnel management systems. Finally, the experience gained through initial efforts at rationalizing social expenditures could then be brought to bear in articulating a more comprehensive, considerate, and carefully targeted reform of social policies and expenditure programs.

Institutional Framework

118.   The successful implementation of the proposed reforms of the state will require both a high degree of political commitment at the top level of the government and appropriate institutional support. Both are needed to ensure that the effort will be sustained despite the entrenched bureaucratic interests it will tackle and the transitional hardship which may be caused for some categories of employees or public service users.

119.   In the areas of *public finances*, the leadership in the reforms would naturally be assumed by the Ministry of Finance. As a matter of fact, a number of proposals along the lines discussed in this report have already been elaborated within the Ministry, with the support of U.S. Treasury, USAID, and IMF advisers, inter alia, in the context of the establishment of the new Treasury system.[18]

120.   In contrast, the leadership and the support function for *administrative and civil service reforms* still need to be organized. Since the reforms concern the entire public administration -- all ministries, all state committees, the units reporting to them, and also the territorial administrations and local governments -- it would be advisable that the leadership role be played directly by the authority with overall responsibility for the entire public administration -- namely, the Prime Minister -- and that the institutional support functions be directly linked to his authority. The support structure would be in charge of the preparation of the program of action, the definition of the strategy elements, and the identification of the stages of the process and of the authority to be responsible for the implementation of each of these stages. The support structure could comprise two specialized divisions, one dealing with public service structures and the other concerned with the civil service. The civil service division could constitute the embryo of a more permanent capacity to ensure the overall management of human resources (including the organization of transparent recruitment procedures).

121.   Finally, the structural adjustments to *education and health* policies proposed above cannot accommodate the current atomization of responsibilities over the sectors: they will require a strong

---

[18]   This reform is also supported by a Treasury Modernization Project from the World Bank.

leadership. To make the sectoral planning of reform and resource needs possible, all education and health facilities not specifically transferred to future municipalities should be brought under the sole jurisdiction of the education and health ministries and their territorial counterparts (within the framework of delegations described in para. 74). Similarly, the Ministries of Health and Education should be put firmly in charge of programming and managing all national expenditures in their respective sectors.

G. Conclusions

122.   The administrative and financial management of the state has yet to adjust to the sweeping political and economic changes that have accompanied the demise of the former Soviet Union. Owing to the ongoing fiscal crisis, however, the resources available to sustain the country's vast network of public administrations and services has shrunk drastically. Rather than leading to a consolidation of public interventions around priority areas, this fiscal contraction has caused a deterioration across the board of the quality of public services.

123.   It is increasingly recognized that such a process of consolidation and redeployment cannot wait much longer. For this transformation, however, there is no blueprint. Most nations have had to confront the challenges facing Kazakstan today. They have responded in accordance with their own national identities and distinguishing characteristics. This international experience is available for Kazakstan to tap.

124.   On the basis of this experience, this report seeks to outline the range of options which the country could consider when charting its own course. It identifies the following five directions for change which should rank highest on Kazakstan's agenda:

(i)   A deliberate shrinking of administrative structures, leading to an (admittedly painful) release of redundant personnel

(ii)   A consolidation of the social sector facilities by shifting toward more outpatient and ambulatory treatment in the health sector and increasing student/teacher ratios in education

(iii)   The adoption of budget management instruments aimed at selecting priorities among competing needs rather than distributing resources according to exogenously defined uses (as was the case under the command system)

(iv)   A differentiation of public interventions across the country according to the priorities of local populations, through a gradual devolution of responsibilities to bodies of local self-government

(v)   The creation of personnel management systems which foster motivation, continuity, and professionalism in the civil service.

CHAPTER I. STRUCTURE OF PUBLIC ADMINISTRATIONS AND SERVICES

A. Introduction

1.1   Volume I showed that the state in Kazakstan is vastly overcommitted in relation to the fiscal resources it is able to mobilize. One symptom of this problem is the uncharacteristically large size of the government payroll. Downsizing this payroll will only be achieved through downsizing government structures. To date, however, the structure of public administrations and services in Kazakstan has changed little from Soviet days. Public administrations and services are still characterized by a large degree of centralization and uniformity as well as an excessively broad definition of the functions and responsibilities of the state.

1.2   The analysis below reveals three main priority areas for reform: (i) consolidating republican government structures; (ii) transforming territorial administrations into local governments, in a gradual and orderly way; and (iii) reforming health and education policies. The present chapter focuses on the first of these priority areas and lays out two major directions for change: (i) eliminating or incorporating separately from the state the many existing entities which no longer perform core administrative functions in a market economy; and (ii) consolidating the presently fragmented administrative structures into larger ministerial agencies, fully in charge of their field of responsibility, on the basis of a review, selection, and regrouping of the *functions* performed by these structures. A similar process should be conducted within territorial administrations.

B. Overview of Government Structures

Current Structure

1.3   The political structures of Kazakstan have evolved considerably in the last five years. In the final days of the former Soviet Union (FSU) in December 1991, the Kazakh Soviet Socialist Republic (Kazakh SSR) declared its independence and became the Republic of Kazakstan. It took a little over a year for the new state to define the fundamental principles of its independent existence. These principles were enshrined in the country's first Constitution, adopted in January 1993. These initial constitutional arrangements proved short-lived and were swept away when the Parliament was declared illegitimate one year after its election in March 1994. The new Constitution, adopted in August 1995, now sets the basic parameters under which the reform of the state will take place. The new Constitution reaffirms (Arts. 2 and 3, para. 4) that the Republic of Kazakstan is a *unitary state*. This concept has fundamental implications for the organization of the state as explained in Box 1.1. The Constitution further determines that the country has a presidential form of government (Art. 2) with an elected Parliament (Art. 49).[1]

1.4   In contrast with these rapid political changes, the country's administrative structures have remained to a large degree unchanged from the days of the Kazakh SSR. Essentially, these administrative structures are still molded according to the tenets of "democratic centralism" (Box 1.2 describes the intellectual and historical roots of these administrative principles). The main features of the current organization and inner workings of the state apparatus (the executive branch) in Kazakstan are outlined in Figure 1.1.

---

[1]   The Parliament comprises two Chambers: the Majlis, which is elected directly, and the Senate, which is elected indirectly by a college of maslikhat members. The powers of the legislative branch are restrictively defined by the Constitution.

1.5   The President and the Cabinet of Ministers, led by the Prime Minister, dominate the executive branch. The Prime Minister, the Deputy Prime Ministers, and the staff (*Apparat*) of the Cabinet of Ministers assume leadership in the formulation of all government policies and in the control of policy implementation. They are the locus of all policy initiative. To carry out their tasks, the Cabinet staff is organized into departments that replicate, on a reduced scale, the ministerial structure. In public finances, for instance, it is the Cabinet department in charge of that sector, not the Ministry of Finance, that lays down the main parameters for the preparation of the budget. In this respect, the Cabinet combines the same supra-ministerial roles as those performed under the Soviet Union by: (i) the Central Committee and its departments in policy formulation; and (ii) the Cabinet of Ministers and its departments in controlling the operational activities of the ministries and other state bodies (1977 Constitution of the Soviet Union, and Soviet Law of July 5, 1978 on the Cabinet of Ministers).

Box 1.1: Some Definitions

A *unitary state* is a state in which the authority to make laws resides exclusively with the national authorities. A *federal state* is a state in which the authority to make laws and modify the Constitution (i.e., the national sovereignty) is shared with the territorial components of the country (e.g., states in the United States, regions in Belgium, Länder in Germany). A *confederal state* is an association of states in which the interstate power executes the legal functions delegated to it by the member countries.

Decentralization can take several forms. It may result from a *transfer or devolution of legislative authority* (under a constitutional act) to *members of a federation* operated under the Constitution. It may also result, in both unitary states and (con) federations, from a *transfer or devolution of executive authority* (by law) to local governments. In the latter context, all local government bodies, elected or not, form part of the executive branch.

Finally, governments can provide a measure of autonomy to administrative bodies, local or not, through a *delegation of executive authority* (by executive order). In this case, however, the body to which authority is delegated remains in a hierarchical dependence under the terms of the delegation. For the sake of clarity, this report reserves the term *territorial administration* to designate local executive bodies operating under such delegation. The term *deconcentration* is sometimes used to characterize this type of administrative arrangement.

1.6   Under the Cabinet of Ministers, all state bodies, from the ministries downward are ordered in vertical hierarchical lines. Republican administrations constitute the first tier, and comprise the national ministries, state committees, and other national committees and agencies, as well as the administrative establishments and commercial enterprises under their supervision. In general, ministries have vertical (or sectoral) responsibilities, whereas state committees have horizontal ones. The role of the republican administrations is to carry out background work for the definition of policy orientation by the Cabinet, to prepare the detailed policy implementation regulations, and to implement policy in their respective spheres or to establish directives for policy implementation by their counterparts in lower tiers of government.

Box 1.2: Historical Roots of Current Government Organization

The politico-administrative system established under the Soviet Union followed a Russian Doll model. Nominally autonomous soviets and identically structured and interlocking administrations replicated themselves almost ad infinitum from the Union to the village level. In this system, each soviet purportedly had legislative authority within its jurisdiction and established within itself a standing executive committee in charge of executive activities. At the same time, all activities in the country were organized so as to create a single Union-wide enterprise, encompassing all aspects of economic and social life. In practice, therefore, each administrative structure was part of a double set of hierarchical lines. It reported to higher sectoral authorities through vertical lines running from the village to the Union level and reported through horizontal lines to the soviet committee to which it belonged. This system of double loyalties inevitably created problems of coordination. Conflicts between these two lines were escalated to the next highest levels.

Given these coordination problems, the real power, however, rested with the Party organization, which operated in parallel in a single hierarchical line. It provided the backbone of the state administration and served to maintain its overall integrity. In keeping with the principles of democratic centralism, the actual lines of authority were pointed upward through the system of soviets, and downward through the administrative apparatus (both controlled by the Party). In this, the Party played three essential functions: (i) policy formulation; (ii) policy coordination and reconciliation of differences among various administrative bodies of government, or between the latter and the rest of the economy; and (iii) control of policy implementation. In this scheme, public administrations, other than Gosplan, were limited to subordinate, atomized executive functions. This lack of policy formulation, coordination, and control within administrative bodies obviously became more acute down the chain of command, and was therefore more severe in Alma-Ata than in Moscow.

This pattern emerged from the dual historical tradition of the Communist Party: utopian and authoritarian. In the utopian days, it had been envisaged that the will of the people -- or that of the proletariat -- would provide a unifying principle to the otherwise "anarchical" system of Soviet power (see V.I. Lenin, *State and Revolution*, 1917). Centrifugal forces, however, set in immediately. The establishment of the Communist Party's monopoly control over political and administrative bodies, as the self-styled repository of the people's will, served to hold these forces in check.

In doing this, the communist leadership drew on a second strand of its tradition: "democratic centralism." To survive the political repression that followed the failure of the first Russian Revolution of 1905, the Social Democratic Party of Russia took the fundamental option to abandon the hope of building a political organization with a broad political appeal, akin to the German Social Democratic Party) and to transform itself into an underground, conspiratorial group of "professional revolutionaries." It adopted organization rules common to all such groups: centralized leadership, strict hierarchies, segmentation of tasks and information flows, compartmentalization of responsibilities, and internal security arrangements through mutual espionage (see V.I. Lenin, *What to do?* 1905). The success of the takeover of October 1917 convinced the communist leadership of the superiority of their organization. This conviction was reinforced by the experience of the Civil War, in which political commissars succeeded in subjugating military units of dubious loyalty to the will of the party. Similar methods were later applied to administrative organizations. Eventually, the autonomy left to soviet organizations came to be understood as that of a field commander, autonomous in conducting his forces toward meeting the overall battle plan, but not in defining it. This framework was codified in the 1927 charter of the Communist Party and the 1936 Constitution of the Soviet Union (which proclaimed the Communist Party to be "the nucleus of all state organizations"). These documents became the blueprint for state organization in all socialist countries, from China to Ethiopia and from Poland to Vietnam.

1.7   Most republican administrations have counterparts at the territorial levels. These counterparts come into two categories as shown in Figure 1.1:

(i)   *Field Services of Republican Administrations*: These services are, in theory at least, under the direct administrative and technical authority of the republican administrations. This situation applies to a relatively minor number of republican administrations, generally to the territorial antennas of state committees (the Tax Inspectorate, under the Ministry of Finance, is also organized in this manner, but this is an exception rather than the norm).

(ii) *Territorial Departments*: This is the more common case. These departments are organized into territorial administrations under a head of territorial administration (*akim* in Kazak language, *glava* in Russian) appointed by the next upper tier of administration; heads of administration serve as representatives of the President and of the Government. Territorial departments are under dual authority: (i) they are under the technical authority of the sectoral administration of the next upper tier (which means that they form part of tall vertical "cylinders" of sectoral administration that reach from the capital down to the village level); and (ii) they are under the administrative authority of the head of territorial administration and thus are also subject to horizontal accountability.

1.8   There are two tiers of territorial administration:

(i)   *Oblasts*: comprising the 19 oblasts and 2 national cities (Almaty and Leninsk) as well as the administrative establishments and commercial enterprises under their supervision. Their akims are appointed by the President of the Republic, on the proposal of the Prime Minister.

(ii) *Rayons*: comprising the 220 rural rayons and 83 urban townships of oblast importance as well as the administrative establishments and commercial enterprises under their supervision. Their akims are appointed by the oblast administration to which they report.

1.9   Under this lower tier, *villages* are subadministrative levels of state intervention comprising the field services of rural rayons in 2,496 rural localities (aul, selo, settlement), corresponding approximately to the sovkhozes and kolkhozes, and the field services of national cities and oblast townships in 204 urban rayons. These services are organized under the authority of a representative of the rayon-level administrator to which they are subordinated.

1.10   Each tier of territorial administration reports to the next upper tier (the Russian Doll model). Together with the republican administration, the two tiers of state territorial administration form part of a "single system of executive bodies of the Republic, and ensure the implementation of the overall nation-wide policies in consideration of the interests and needs of development of their territory" (Art. 87, para. 1 of the Constitution).

1.11   The responsibilities of the various levels of administration emerge *from a process of organizational assignment* (i.e., this entity is subordinated to that administration), *rather than from one of functional specialization* (i.e., this function -- for example, primary health care -- is performed by that level of administration). As was the case in the Soviet Union (for both budget entities and enterprises), budget entities are assigned to one (and only one) level of administration, which is then charged with supervising and funding the budget entity. The general rule is that budget entities are assigned to the administration whose jurisdiction corresponds to the catchment area of the service they provide. There are specific and general exceptions to that rule, however. Specific exceptions are, for example, the fact that a former Union-wide tuberculosis center will be placed under the administration of the oblast of Kustenai, or the fact that teacher training colleges will be under oblast administration in Shymkent, but under republican administration in Almaty. General exceptions are a number of functions considered of national importance (e.g., taxes, state properties, land, justice) that are performed exclusively by republican administrations (and their field services).

Figure 1.1: Current Organization of the Executive Branch

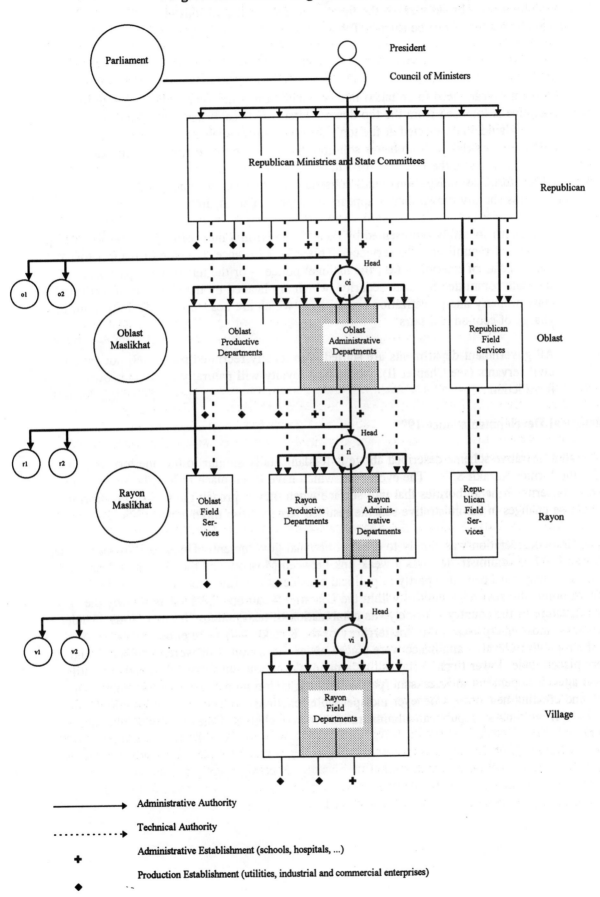

1.12   Since a degree of congruence exists between the notions of "functions" and "organization," it is possible to piece together a broad view of the functional roles of the various levels of administration. Such an attempt can be seen in Table 1.1.

A Few Caveats

1.13   Two important caveats need to be taken into consideration, which contradict the impression that complete discipline is imposed from the top down. First, the fiscal crisis has produced a growing gap between the policy guidelines enacted at the top and the means available to implement them, leaving the republican authorities with no better solution than to leave the territorial administrations to their own devices in coping with the resultant difficulties. Second, the distinction between republican field services and territorial administrations, and, consequently, between technical and administrative authority, is in fact less sharply drawn than it appears on paper. This is, inter alia, because:

(i)   The akims (possibly represented by their deputies) in a number of instances double up as head of republican field services. This is, for instance, the case of the territorial departments of interior -- i.e., the national police -- or the territorial departments of the state committee for state security, which are headed by the akim, or of territorial state property and privatization committees, which are headed by the deputy akim in charge of economic affairs.

(ii)   All government departments are staffed with locally recruited personnel, not national civil servants (see Chapter II), whose first loyalty will naturally be to their own jurisdiction.

Main Structural Developments since 1991

1.14   The administrative scheme described above is fundamentally similar to the one formerly in place under the former Kazakh SSR. The evolutions which have taken place reflect, however, some of the likely concerns of the authorities that will surface when they approach the necessary reform of the state. These changes in administrative scheme resulted largely from three considerations.

1.15   The first consideration was simply to create a national government. Under the Soviet regime, the republican level of administration was a weak link between Moscow and the oblasts, at least in Kazakstan. This may have been due partly to political considerations (the need to keep in check the aspirations of nominally sovereign entities within the Union). It can be explained as well by the productive structure of the country -- namely, its combination of heavy industries and farms. Under the Soviet rules, most enterprises within the territory of the Kazakh SSR were either too large to report to the republican level -- and hence were placed under the Union -- or were too small -- and hence were placed under lower tiers. Establishing a national government involved: (i) incorporating Union-level agencies operating in Kazakstan (particularly the Union ministries) into the republican structures, and creating new ones, whenever indispensable functions were previously exercised only in Moscow; and (ii) building up republican administrations to take charge of the tasks of a sovereign government.

Table 1.1: Allocation of Functions Among Tiers of Administration [1]

SERVICE	RAYON	OBLAST	REPUBLIC
Education	Kindergartens Schools	Some teacher training colleges Vocational colleges	Mos: higher education
Health	General hospitals Polyclinics	More specialist hospitals Specialist dentistry	Research Very specialized treatment
Social Security and Welfare: Goods and Services	Social aid units	Homes for the mentally handicapped Homes for the aged and infirm	
Social Security and Welfare: Transfers		Help to families	Unemployment benefit Sickness benefit State pensions
Social Security and Welfare: Subsidies	Heating subsidies Utility subsidies	Fuel subsidies Transport subsidies	Housing subsidies Long-term loans for housing Subsidies for printing social literature
Defense (and foreign representation)	Some benefits to current and former service personnel		Virtually all
Public Order and Safety		Some police services Fire services	Some police services
Recreation and Culture	Halls of culture Cinema subsidies	Halls of-culture	Subsidies to mass media
Agriculture	Pest control	Veterinary services	Most, especially grain purchases and financial support to agriculture
Transport and Communication	Improvements to public transport	Improvements to public transport	Most, including subsidies to mail services

[1] Functions performed at the village level are included under "Rayon."

1.16   A second consideration was to fill the vacuum created by the disappearance of the Communist Party. This involved: (i) absorbing the policy formulation capabilities of the former central committee departments within the administrative structures (particularly the staff of the Cabinet of Ministers); and (ii) transferring territorial administrations from the authority of the Party (see Box 1.2) to that of government administration strictly speaking. The initial step, under the law of February 15, 1991 on local self-administration, was to dissolve the former soviets and their executive committees and to transfer all the state responsibilities, enterprises, and properties within their jurisdictions to new local government bodies. The country soon began to drift apart, however, with local governments passing conflicting laws, for example, declaring tax-free zones, contracting foreign loans, and embezzling public properties.

1.17   The impending chaos called for the reassertion of national authority. This was the third consideration. Among the first steps, taken in late 1992, were to put all tax administrations under the Republican Tax Inspectorate, and, after calling a halt to all privatization, to transfer all public properties back to the state. The critical moment, however, was the adoption of the country's first Constitution in January 1993, which in practice put an end to local self-government and established the system of territorial administration described above.

C. Structure of State Personnel

1.18   The administrative structures described above, and the public services that they provide, are too large in relation to the country's fiscal capacity. These structures and services employ over 1 million, of whom about 260,000 are at the republican level and about 780,000 of whom are at the territorial level (estimates for 1994).[2]

1.19   A summary overview of the structure of state personnel indicates where the main imbalances lie (see Table 1.2).[3] These imbalances are concentrated in the following areas:

> *Autonomous Agencies and Departmental Enterprises*, which are literally teeming at the republican level (and probably also at lower levels, although data are missing that would ascertain it) and would employ several tens of thousands of staff -- close to 100,000 in fact if the vast payroll of the Academy of Science were included.

> *State Security*, whose payroll exceeds in size the payroll of all central republican administrations taken together.

---

[2]   Not included in these numbers, nor in further discussions, is the administrative personnel of the Pension Fund and Social Insurance Fund. The personnel of these funds may exceed 100,000 employees, though, which is quite considerable. Another source of underestimation is the fact that certain categories of personnel (maintenance personnel, for instance), whose positions do not require central authorization, and are not budgeted for under "wages" but under other categories of operating costs.

[3]   The figures presented in Table 1.2 are rough estimates and reflect authorized positions rather than actual employment. In the absence of any human resource management system, aggregate data on employment simply do not exist at present. Such data were last collected in 1990, after which time the effort was discontinued for financial reasons. Note also that although complete data exist on authorized positions, these are considered highly confidential. The figures presented in Table 1.2 are pieced together from a variety of partial sources and constitute only broad orders of magnitude.

Oblast Administrations, which appear sizable in comparison with republican administrations.

Health and Education Services (reporting generally to territorial administrations), which together account for about 70 percent of government employment. This is excessive by any standards, particularly in the health sector. Health personnel represent about 40 percent of government employment and 2.4 percent of the population. In comparison, in France, for example, this category of personnel accounts for 14 percent of the civil service and 1.14 percent of the population. Even in the United Kingdom, with its public health care system, health personnel represent only 21 percent of government employment and 1.9 percent of the population.

1.20   In contrast, *republican ministries and ministry level administrations* (other than the State Committee for State Security) with less than 10,000 employees seem to be desperately short-staffed by any standards. As will be discussed in Section F, the fragmentation of ministerial administrative structures further weakens their effectiveness.

Table 1.2: Structure of State Personnel
(estimates for 1994)

REPUBLICAN	
1. Central	
1.1 Ministries	6,800
1.2 State Committees (other)	1,100
1.3 State Committee for State Security	6,900
1.4 Other Services	1,600
2. Other Republican Services	
2.1 Republican Field Administrations	30,200
2.2 Embassies	100
2.3 Justice/Order (other)	58,300
2.4 State Committee for State Security	6,900
2.5 Armed Forces	63,000
2.6 Academy of Sciences	41,400
2.7 Other Central	42,700
Total	258,900
LOCAL	
1. Oblast Administration	46,100
2. Rayon and Town Administrations	21,500
3. Health	406,000
4. Education	299,100
5. Other Local	n.a.
Total	780,000
Total	1,040,000

Source: World Bank staff estimates based on budget data and authorized positions.

D. Priorities for Reform

1.21 These observations also delineate the areas of priority for the reform of the state, for which this report will also develop detailed recommendations. These areas include:

Revamping republican structures by drastically pruning parastatal entities and consolidating ministerial ones

Transforming territorial administrations into local governments, in a gradual and orderly way, thereby allowing the local population to reform the service they receive according to their own priorities

Reforming health and education policies with a view to downsizing sectoral facilities and personnel.

E. The New Constitution

1.22 The Constitution adopted on August 30, 1995 introduces a number of fundamental innovations which, when put into practice, would facilitate the design and implementation of these state reforms. Some of the key innovations are as follows:

(i) *Respective Roles of the Legislative and Executive Branches.* This is a critical point in any fundamental law. Similar to the French Constitution, Article 61 of the Constitution clearly delineates a number of areas in which the role of the legislative branch is limited to setting fundamental principles and broad orientations, and in which the executive branch is charged with establishing detailed regulations. Within a broad strategy approved by Parliament, this article gives the executive branch the necessary flexibility to define and update the specific detail, the modalities, and the tactics of implementation of institutional reforms in key areas of state reform such as the following:

- Regime of ownership and other property rights
- Organization and activities of state bodies and bodies of local self-administrations, of the military and the civil service
- Taxation and the establishment of duties and other mandatory payments
- The republican budget
- Education, health, and social security
- Privatization of enterprises and their properties
- Structure of the territorial administration of the Republic.

(ii) *Organization of the Government.* In contrast to the Soviet Constitutions, which gave a supra-ministerial role to the Cabinet and placed the ministries in a hierarchical situation vis-à-vis the Cabinet, the new Constitution (Art. 68) defines the Government as a collective body jointly responsible vis-à-vis the President of the Republic. A revision of the roles of the staff of the Cabinet of Ministers and a consolidation of ministerial administrations are both required for Cabinet ministers meaningfully to discharge these constitutional responsibilities (see paras. 1.44-1.45).

(iii) *Local Self-Administration (Local Government)*. The Constitution opens the door to a devolution of authority to local jurisdictions in matters of local interest (Art. 89).

F. Reforming Republican Administrations

1.23   The excessive size of republican structures has resulted from two factors inherited from the Soviet system: (i) weak delineation between the fields of activity of administrative services (properly speaking) and other types of activity which may or may not belong, in a market economy, to the normal responsibility of the state; and (ii) fragmentation of ministerial structures arising from former command-and-control principles.

Demarcation of Public Administrations

Excessively Broad Delineation

1.24   The list of entities funded by the republican budget counts 79 groups totaling 2,236 budget units. Of these units, 1,840 are under the supervision of ministry level agencies (see Tables 1.3 and 1.4). Another 400 are not really public administrations but rather:

Professional Associations, such as the writers' union, the musicians' union, the playwrights' union, or the Kazak copyright agency

Commercial and Industrial Entities, such as the food company Tagah (five budget units), the road signaling company, hotel complexes, or the Kazak telegraph agency

Administrative Establishments, such as the Academy of Sciences (43 units), the Kazak-Turkish University, the Patent Office, or the Nature Museum.

A careful review of the 1,840 units included in the ministerial groups would bring to light hundreds more entities falling into the above categories.[4/] For instance, among the 187 budget units included in the Ministry of Agriculture group, one would find such professional associations as the Farmers' Union and the Committee of Collective Farms, such commercial and industrial entities as the state joint stock companies (holding) Zhivprom or the production/marketing concern Kazakkrunokarakul, and such administrative establishments as the republican higher school of the agroindustrial complex.

1.25   Such entities require administrative, personnel, and financial management systems that are separate from those of the state. Many of them could operate on a fee-per-member or tariff-for-service basis and could therefore be privatized, transformed into private associations, or organized under a separate legal form.

[4/]   In these lists, each ministerial administration (and each of its field offices, as the case may be) counts as only one budget unit. The balance consists of parastatal entities of one type or another.

Priorities for Action

1.26   The first steps toward alleviating administrative structures should therefore consist of the following:

(i)   Taking an inventory of all administrative structures and of the functions they perform; this inventory does not necessarily need to be sophisticated and could draw upon the information gathered in establishing the new functional and institutional classification of the budget (as discussed in Chapter IV).

(ii)   Clarifying the nature of existing administrative structures on the basis of a unified typology.[5/] The following is an example of such a typology:

   a.   Central Administrative Departments: departments with countrywide competence

   b.   Subnational Administrative Departments: territorial departments executing the assignment of a central department in local jurisdictions

   c.   Specialized Technical Agencies, including laboratories, research stations, educational institutions, etc.

   d.   Public Corporations: entities with separate legal and management regimes, including professional associations, administrative establishments, and industrial and commercial enterprises.

(iii)   Reducing the list of administrative structures, funded directly from the budget, to Categories 1 to 3.

(iv)   If they do not yet exist, creating the appropriate legal forms for incorporating entities under Category 4.

(v)   Reviewing, one by one, the entities in Category 4 to identify those that could:

   a.   Be privatized to commercial or nonprofit organizations

   b.   Operate on a tariff basis within the public sector

   c.   Or would require operating subventions from the budget; the last should be subject to the same functional review as that recommended for administrative departments (see para. 1.38).

[5/]   Pursuant to Article 61, para. 3, a law should establish such a typology as well as the fundamental legal and management principles attached to the various legal forms it creates.

1.27   The last measure would probably constitute the single most effective means of relieving the current administrative congestion and cutting down excessive employment. Indications are that Category 4 entities may be as large as the administrative sector and may employ several tens of thousands of employees. In addition, this process of horizontal devolution would allow the supply of fee/tariff-based services to adjust to the actual demand from the population and the economy through the price mechanism, rather than through necessarily more cumbersome administrative procedures.

Fragmentation of Republican Administrations

Fragmentation at the Ministerial Level

1.28   With 56 separate Cabinet level administrations, the superstructure of the government of Kazakstan is highly fragmented. As of September 1995, it included:

  (i)   *22 ministries*, which generally have sectoral or vertical competencies[6] and are headed by ministers, assisted by vice-ministers and a board of senior staff members[7] (see Table 1.3)

  (ii)   *13 state committees*, which generally have horizontal competencies (i.e., responsibilities that cut across the sectors handled by ministries); they are headed by chairmen, assisted by vice-chairmen and a board of senior staff members (see Table 1.4)

  (iii)   *7 committees and 14 other agencies* under the Cabinet of Ministers (see Table 1.5).

1.29   Most state committees, as well as the Ministries of Finance (Tax Inspectorate) and Justice have field services operating at the oblast level (called "territorial committees" when they report to state committees) and sometimes also at the rayon level (see Table 1.6). The domestic security apparatus and the judiciary branch are also organized at the national level (see Table 1. 7).

---

[6]   The Ministry of Economy, formerly called the State Committee for Planning (Gosplan), is an exception to that rule.

[7]   The "board" of a ministry is another legacy of the Soviet administrative system, dating back to 1967 (General Rules for Ministries, adopted by Decree of the Cabinet of Ministers of the Soviet Union of July 10, 1967). These "boards" originate from the fact that ministries and state committees were considered production enterprises. They were the head office of a vertical enterprise group, reporting to their parent holding, the Cabinet of Ministers. Members of the "board" are appointed by decree and their position is explicitly registered within the ministry's establishment. The "board" sits regularly and establishes the ministry's work program and also, at least in theory, makes decisions on staff recruitment. The minister is chairman of the "board." Disagreements between the "board" and its chairman can be brought to the attention of the Cabinet of Ministers.

Table 1.3: Structure of Ministries

MINISTRIES	NUMBER OF UNITS[1]	STAFFING
Ministry of Geology	32	59
Ministry of Agriculture	187	260
Ministry of Construction and Housing	1	131
Ministry of Culture	49	52
Ministry of Defense	148	849
Ministry of Ecology and Biological Resources	83	161
Ministry of Economy	9	451
Ministry of Education	127	137
Ministry of Power and Coal	n.a.	61
Ministry of Finance	479	1,064
Ministry of Foreign Affairs	6	301
Ministry of Health	59	128
Ministry of Industry and Trade	1	258
Ministry of Information and Mass Media	45	68
Ministry of Interior	44	1,536
Ministry of Justice	68	162
Ministry of Labor	22	121
Ministry of Oil and Gas	n.a.	71
Ministry of Social Protection	8	91
Ministry of Science and Technology	76	69
Ministry of Tourism and Sport	18	73
Ministry of Transport and Communications	172	249
Total Ministries	**1,634**	**6,352**

[1] Number of units indicates the number of budget entities, including field services, reporting to a particular administration.
Sources: Various decrees, staff of the Cabinet of Ministers, World Bank staff estimates.

Table 1.4: Structure of State Committees

STATE COMMITTEES	NUMBER OF UNITS[1]	STAFFING
State Price and Antimonopoly Committee	22	106
State Committee for Emergencies	1	n.a.
State Committee for Statistics and Analysis	21	n.a.
State Committee for Finance Control	22	206
State Committee for State Security	25	6,874
State Committee for Nationalities	1	41
State Committee for Material Resources	13	51
State Committee on Utilization of Foreign Capital	n.a.	39
State Committee on Water Resources	31	50
State Committee for Management of State Property	22	51
State Committee on Land Relations and Land Use	n.a.	51
State Customs Committee	26	343
State Committee for Privatization	23	96
Total State Committees	**207**	**7,909**
Total without State Committee for State Security		1,034

[1] Number of units indicates the number of budget entities, including field services, reporting to a particular administration.
Sources: Various decrees, staff of the Cabinet of Ministers, World Bank staff estimates.

Table 1.5: Structure of Other Republican Bodies

OTHER REPUBLICAN BODIES	NUMBER OF UNITS[1/]	STAFFING
National Aerospace Agency	2	50
National Union of Composers	1	n.a.
National Committee for Securities	n.a.	96
Patent Office	1	24
Presidential Office	1	n.a.
Principal Department of Border Guards	19	437
Prosecutor's Office	22	453
Production Unit of the Presidential Cabinet	n.a.	68
Republican Guard	1	n.a.
Republican Society of Veterans Council	1	n.a.
Sanatoria and Hospitals	8	n..a.
Security Service of the President	1	n.a.
Presidential Staff	16	n.a.
Society of Foreign Cultural Relations	1	11
Standards Bureau	21	40
State Control on Trade	n.a.	7
State Technical Commission on Information Security	n.a.	49
Supreme Court	1	218
Committee for Staff Certification	1	39
Technical Control Committee	9	41
National Archives	8	20
Total Other Central Administrations	114	1,553

[1/] Number of units indicates the number of budget entities, including field services, reporting to a particular administration.
Sources: Various decrees, staff of the Cabinet of Ministers, World Bank staff estimates.

Table 1.6: Structure of Republican Field Services[1/]

REPUBLICAN FIELD SERVICES	STAFFING
Tax Inspectorate	20,368
Customs Department	4,519
Territorial Committee for Statistics and Analysis	649
Inspectorate for Free Mass Media	34
Territorial Committee for Management of State Property	510
Territorial Committee for Privatization	181
Territorial Committee for Land Relations and Land Use	474
Territorial Antimonopoly and Price Policy Committee	505
Territorial Committee Standards for Mining	377
Center for Standards and Meteorology	220
Territorial Fishery Committee	7
Territorial Justice Department	754
Territorial Department of Ecology and Biological Resources	1,265
State Inspectorate for Labor Security	316
Territorial Committee for Financial Control	n.a.
Total Republican Field Services	30,179

[1/] The number of budget entities reporting to these administrations is included in the total number posted for their parent structures at the republican level.
Sources: Various decrees, staff of the Cabinet of Ministers, World Bank staff estimates.

Table 1.7: Territorial Structure of
Domestic Security Apparatus and Judiciary Branch[1/]

JUSTICE AND SECURITY UNITS	STAFFING
Oblast Departments of the State Committee for State Security	6,874
Oblast Department of the Ministry of Interior	38,624
Department of the Penitentiary System, Ministry of Republican Affairs	7,229
Oblast Prosecutor's Office	6,772
Oblast Arbitration Court	440
Oblast Court	1,110
Ordinary Courts	4,111
Total Justice and Security Units	65,160

[1/] The number of budget entities reporting to these administrations is included in the total number posted for their parent structures at the republican level.
Sources: Various decrees, staff of the Cabinet of Ministers, World Bank staff estimates.

1.30   The number of ministry level administrations is two to three times that found in most OECD countries. The United Kingdom has some 20 ministries, Sweden has 14, Italy has 19, and the United States has 14 Cabinet level departments (and 9 major executive agencies).

1.31   The source of this discrepancy is as follows. Most OECD countries organize their administrations on the basis of "public services." These public services correspond to "functions" and are structured in departments. The departments, not the ministries, are the *basic and stable* modules with which the administration is built. In this scheme, ministries are created by grouping departments; the form of this grouping varies over time according to the changing emphasis of government policies. In this system, modifications in the government structure affect the administrative structures only indirectly. The basic modules remain stable. In Kazakstan, in contrast, the functions of the administration are identified at the ministry level; there are as many ministries as there are basic functions. It is only in a second stage that these ministries are divided into departments. In this system, ministries are created by a decree that describes in very general and vague terms the sector of which the ministry is in charge and lists the main departments. On this basis, it is up to the ministry to organize its own structure within the limits of its authorized positions.

1.32   This system of organization has many drawbacks, which result in the following:

(i)   Dilution of the concept of public service and of the principles applying to it (e.g., continuity of service, permanence of activity)

(ii)   Overlapping responsibilities (the same function is exercised by several entities, as is currently the case with "foreign relations," which has a department in virtually every administration, often headed by a vice-minister or deputy akim) or lack of coverage of other responsibilities (a function is not performed because all units deny that it is their attribution, as is currently the case with the liquidation of bankrupt state enterprises)

(iii)   Difficulties in coordination and blurred lines of authority (it is questionable how much authority ministries have over their own staff, compared to the Staff of the Cabinet of Ministers)

(iv)   Multiplication of ministry level structures (the identification of a new function almost automatically leads to the creation of a new such structure)

(v)   Politicization of any administrative decision, since the creation or elimination of a particular function for administrative reasons necessarily affects the composition of the government.

Internal Fragmentation of Ministerial Administrations

1.33   This fragmentation is further accentuated at the departmental level. There are several hundred first-level administrative units or departments within the republican administrations. In OECD countries the number of first-level administrative units would typically not exceed 100.

1.34   As has been noted above, the list of first-level units which compose a ministry (called "department" or "sector") is established by the decree that creates the ministry. On this basis, the detailed structure of a ministry is defined by ministerial decision: departments are subdivided into divisions, divisions into sections, and so on. This is the theory. In practice, however, ministry organization charts may vary considerably from this blueprint:[8] sections may be juxtaposed to divisions; a number of sectors may not be structured into departments but may report directly to a vice-minister; and departments may not have divisions under them. Ministerial structures also appear to be created without reference to any organizing principle, such as function (e.g., production, personnel, finances), type of output, or geographical area.

1.35   Whereas this fragmentation can essentially be traced back to the divide-and-control mentality which characterized "democratic centralism," a second factor also comes into play: the civil service system. As will be seen in Chapter II, the latter is structured according to an "in-line position system," wherein civil servants' grades are linked to this hierarchical position. In such a system there is considerable pressure to create administrative structures to satisfy career ambitions or to allow for re-deployment through lateral moves of redundant personnel (who would otherwise be downgraded).

1.36   The end result of this process is that ministerial staff, already few in numbers by any international standard, are very thinly spread across sprawling administrative structures. The situation at times reaches such an extreme that one can wonder whether any function is performed at all by many departments, particularly in view of the prevailing widespread absenteeism. Nor is it always clear whether the function purportedly performed is worth performing at all or whether it constitutes merely a vestige of central planning. Whole departments may often employ no more than a dozen staff members at all levels (professional and support). For example, although the functions of the ministry itself have become hard to discern, the Ministry of Economy has 18 departments for a total of 360 job positions. Similarly, the Ministry of Agriculture has 14 departments, employing an average of less than 20 people. And the situation is the same in just about any ministry level administration.

Priorities for Action

1.37   The situation described above clearly calls for the consolidation and strengthening of republican administrations. Indeed, a decision has already been made that, starting in 1996, a main department will need to encompass a minimum of 20 positions, a secondary department a minimum of 10, and a section a minimum of 4. While this will reduce to some extent the number of

---

[8]   Actual organization charts are confidential.

administrative structures and their attendant staffing requirements, it is unlikely to go to the heart of the matter which is to consolidate administrations through a process of analysis, selection, and grouping or elimination of their *functions*. The review of these functions should precede the normalization of structures. It should also encompass all administrative establishments operating within the realm of the republican administrations, and not only ministerial administrations.

1.38   Building on the administrative inventory proposed in para. 1.26, such an approach would involve the following steps:

(i)   Conducting a more detailed functional review of the remaining public administrations, identifying and eliminating redundant functions performed by entities under Categories 1, 2, 3 and 4c, with the automatic closure or privatization of the administrative entities that perform functions made redundant

(ii)   Defining homogeneous organization norms as regards size, organization pattern (e.g., functional, geographic), taking into account a reasonable span of control

(iii)   Aggregating the remaining functions into large groups of public services

(iv)   Consolidating existing structures into public service based departments created by Presidential decree[9]

(v)   Grouping departments into ministry level entities through a Presidential decree on the reallocation of departments and other public entities among ministries.

1.39   Whereas common management principles provide sufficient guidance for the first four steps described above, there are few general rules for the grouping of departments into ministries. It is advisable, however, to take the following into consideration:

(i)   Each ministry should have authority over its entire field of responsibility (e.g., the Ministry of Finance should have authority over all public finance matters)

(ii)   Each ministry should cover only those functions that fall within its field

(iii)   No ministry should be in charge of conflicting functions (e.g., mining and environment)

(iv)   Each function should be attributed to one -- and no more than one -- ministry (to avoid positive and negative conflicts of attribution)

(v)   The total number of ministries should be small enough to enable the Council of Ministers to meet efficiently, as a collective policymaking body (a successful coordination meeting is more or less impossible when the number of participants exceeds two dozen).

1.40   Box 1.3 provides an example of how such a process could be successfully conducted.

---

[9]   Pursuant to Article 44.3 of the Constitution, which determines that the President "upon proposal of the Prime Minister determines the structure of the government of the Republic... as well as forms, [and] abolishes other executive bodies of the Republic not entering the Government."

Box 1.3: Successful Administrative Downsizing: The Case of Guinea

In many countries, weak performances of public administrations constitute a major obstacle to sustained development. For this reason, a number of public administrations, among industrialized as well as developing countries, have undertaken administrative reforms over the last 20 years. The case of Guinea (Conakry) offers an example of how such reforms can be successfully carried out. It is also a particularly relevant case because until the death of President Sekou Touré in 1984, the Republic of Guinea was organized along Marxist-Leninist principles and characterized by the domination of the Party-State, central planning, absence of separation of powers between branches and political institutions (party, legislative, executive, judiciary branches), and a closed economy.

Within months of the foundation of the second Republic in 1984, the new regime adopted a recovery program, supported by the IMF, the World Bank, and other donors. The burden of public administrations quickly emerged as a major obstacle to such endeavors. Public administrations were indeed plethoric in terms of personnel and in terms of structures. They counted about 15,000 departments and 125,000 employees for a population of about 6.3 million. A diagnostic study commissioned by the authorities highlighted the following issues: administrative centralization, fragmentation of public administration, duplication of responsibilities among services, unclear assignments, confusion between the legal regime applicable to public administrations and commercial state enterprises, weak civil service management, and erratic wage payment. This situation engendered a high degree of corruption. Furthermore, the new authorities were frustrated by the fact that existing procedures for budget management and execution did not allow them to direct budget resources toward their new policy orientations.

In the beginning of 1985, the government decided to launch a vast program of administrative reforms and established an institutional framework for implementing it in a coordinated and integrated fashion. This included a steering committee composed of senior administrative officers, and a technical unit in charge of preparing and carrying out government decisions. The latter unit was also the locus of donor financial and technical support for the reforms.

Administrative reforms proceeded in three phases.

During the first phase, administrative reforms focused mainly on supporting other structural measures. In parallel with the removal of domestic barriers to trade and the elimination of compulsory sales of agricultural products to state trading companies, the latter companies were closed down together with state livestock trading companies, state livestock farms, and the six state banks. An initial group of other state bodies which no longer belonged to the realm of the state was also eliminated or transferred. During this phase, the authorities conducted an inventory of existing public administrations and of the functions they performed. They also elaborated modern methodologies for administrative organization.

The second phase focused on actually designing the new administrative structures and initiating their introduction on a pilot basis. Emphasis was placed on alleviating concomitantly the burden of administrative procedures and reducing the field of intervention of the state. In parallel, new delegation techniques were elaborated to decongest the senior decision-making level of the government, foster a sense of responsibility within the civil service, and prevent downsizing from resulting in higher centralization. During this phase, also, the operations of supra-ministerial structures were also rationalized.

Finally, the third and last phase consisted in the general implementation of administrative normalization measures.

Civil service reforms proceeded in parallel. The first steps were taken in 1995 with the transfer of the army and security forces to a specific regime, and the removal from the civil service of employees of state commercial and industrial entities, as well as of state banks. A first civil service census was then taken. Beyond revealing many existing anomalies (e.g., 'ghost workers,' misrepresentation of family status, employees past retirement age), this census laid the basis for defining specific policies for personnel reduction (e.g., early retirement, voluntary departures, layoffs with severance payments, aptitude tests).

Although the reform process had its ups and downs, it succeeded within three years in establishing a more "performing" and motivated administration. By the end of 1988, the civil service had shrunk to 50,000 employees, and a new career and wage system had been introduced, which involved a 118 percent increase in the average level of civil service wages.

Problems of Coordination

1.41   At the moment, unfortunately, the result of the current fragmentation of ministerial structures is a high degree of centralization of policymaking and control at the supra-ministerial level -- the Cabinet of Ministers and the Presidential staff. Both are currently organized as miniature governments. The implementation of the new Constitution, particularly the sections concerning the President and the Government, calls for an adjustment of these structures to their new functional roles, as discussed in the following paragraphs.

1.42   The current role of the Cabinet of Ministers, its Deputy Prime Ministers, and staff extends considerably beyond the usual coordination and logistics functions of that level of government, and indeed beyond the requirements of the new Constitution. As a legacy of the Soviet form of government (see para. 1.22) -- reaffirmed in a resolution of April 20, 1995 determining its organization -- the staff of the Cabinet of Ministers, among other functions, manages the activities of the Cabinet; keeps the seal of the Republic; formulates the main direction of government policies and monitors their implementation; reviews draft legislation; organizes the registration, codification, publication and execution of laws and regulations; and interprets the decisions of the Cabinet of Ministers.

1.43   The Cabinet staff's structure duplicates that of the government (see Table 1.8). The Cabinet is headed by a Chief of Staff, appointed by the President, with ministerial rank. Its department heads are appointed by the Cabinet; they attend Cabinet meetings. In addition to departments in charge of functions belonging to the Prime Minister (e.g., chancellery, relations with the President, relations with the Parliament, press service), the Cabinet staff includes sectoral departments in charge of directing the activities of all the ministries. For the Prime Minister, however, the drawback of this arrangement is that it involves his authority in sectoral decisions which in practice are hard for him to assess and monitor, unnecessarily putting at stake both his administrative responsibility (as head of the Cabinet administration) and his political responsibility (vis-à-vis the President and the Parliament), and therefore the stability of the entire government. For the members of the government, this arrangement serves to weaken the authority extended to them by the Constitution and their accountability in their fields, which leads to a dilution of political and administrative responsibilities and a demoralization of ministerial staff.

1.44   Section V of the new Constitution regarding the government and the responsibilities of the Prime Minister gives the latter the leadership and coordination role within the government defined as a collective body. To carry out his duties, the Prime Minister would require support departments for horizontal, supra-ministerial, and intersectoral functions (i.e., functions that concern all ministries and state committees, rather than vertical or sectoral functions). Examples of such horizontal functions are as follows:

    (i)   *Managing the government's work*[10] (e.g., managing the government's agenda, inter-ministerial coordination, and coordination with consultative bodies; monitoring the execution of Cabinet decisions; maintaining the Cabinet Secretariat; registering/publishing government acts)

---

[10]   These are the functions of the "secretariat general of the government" in francophone countries; the Cabinet Office in the United Kingdom; and the *Bundeskanzleramt* or Chancellery in Germany.

(ii)   *Supporting the Prime Minister in his capacity as head of the government* (e.g., protocol, relations with Parliament, cipher code, technical advisers)

(iii)   *Supporting the Prime Minister in his capacity as head of the state administration*, on behalf of the President (e.g., administrative organization, civil service).

Table 1.8: Structure of the Staff of the Cabinet of Ministers

1 - Administrative Office of the Prime Minister

2 - Administrative Staff of the Advisory Group to the Prime Minister

3 - Chancellery of the Prime Minister

4 - Press Service

5 - Office for Relations of the Cabinet of Ministers with the President

6 - Department of Territorial Development

7 - Department of Industry and Commerce

8 - Department of Construction, Transport and Communication

9 - Department of Agricultural Industry and Environmental Protection

10 - Department of Technical and Scientific Progress

11 - Department of Economic Policy

12 - Department of Finance, Employment and Monetary Circulation

13 - Department of Defense

16 - Department of International Relations

17 - Department of Economy and Finance

18 - Department of Personnel Organization

19 - Secretarial Commission for Special Merit Pensions

20 - Department of the Interior

   a. Administrative Staff of the Committee for Emergencies

   b. Supreme Consultative Council for Science and Technology

   c. Center for Economic Reform under the Cabinet of Ministers

   d. Association of Industries and Enterprises under the Council of Ministers

   e. Liaison Office with Religious and Public Associations

Source: Government of Kazakstan, List of Budget Entities.

1.45   The implementation of the Constitution may require a review of the organization of these supra-ministerial structures to determine which ones would help the Prime Minister deliver his mandate and which ones might be best left to the other ministries. Box 1.4 provides examples of how these functions are organized in the United Kingdom, Germany, France, and Senegal. The latter two countries are probably the most relevant examples for Kazakstan, as they are unitary countries with rather similar presidential regimes.

1.46   A similar functional review might also determine how best to organize the Presidential staff to assist the President in carrying out his responsibilities under Article 44 of the Constitution without compromising his authority in sectoral matters. The present structure of the Presidential staff is presented in Table 1.9. Box 1.5 indicates how the presidential staff is organized in Senegal, where presidential powers are comparable to those exercised by the President of the Republic of Kazakstan.

Table 1.9: Structure of the Presidential Staff

1. First Deputy
2. Deputy
3. Special Representative to the President under the Parliament
4. Administrative Office of the President
5. Legal Council
6. General Inspectorate
7. Department of Information and Analysis
8. Presidential Spokesman
9. Department of Science and Technology
10. Department of Political Analysis
11. Department of Foreign Affairs
12. Office of Presidential Protocol
13. Department of Defense
14. Department of Finance
15. Department of Economic Policy

Other Units Under the Presidential Staff

1. Kindergarten Number 212
2. Kindergarten Number 239
3. Kindergarten Number 1
4. Pioneer Camp
5. Department of Almaty Affairs
6. Department of Interior
7. Department of Natural Supplies
8. Azman Hotel Complex
9. Djalin Hotel Complex
10. GOH Unit
11. Workshop
12. Cinematographic Unit
13. Department of Civil Aviation
14. Museum of Nature
15. Presidential Guard
16. Department of Forestry

Source: Government of Kazakstan, List of Budget Entities.

Box 1.4: Supra-Ministerial Organization in Selected Countries

Counties usually have supra-ministerial administrative structures, under the authority of the Prime Minister. These structures do not duplicate ministerial functions but rather execute some of the functions which are common to all ministries, and support the Prime Minister in his dual capacity as head of the government and head of state administration. This box presents the situation in France, the United Kingdom, Germany, and Senegal.

France

1. General Secretariat of the Government (including departments for information and documentation, legislation and verification, and the official gazette)
2. General Services (including civil and military advisers)
3. Directorate for Administrative and Financial Management of the Prime Minister's Departments
4. Department for Administrative Organization and Relations with Public Service Users
5. Secretariat of the Inter-Ministerial Committee for European Economic Cooperation
6. Secretariat of the National Council for Crime Prevention
7. General Secretariat of Defense Services (government communication center, service for security of information systems, institute for high defense studies)
8. Delegation for Air Space
9. Inter-Ministerial Committee for Nuclear Security
10. State Secretariat in charge of Relations with Parliament
11. State Secretariat for Administration and Civil Service
12. State Secretariat for Administrative Reforms
13. State Secretariat for Human Rights

United Kingdom

Prime Minister's Office
1. Private Office
2. Secretariat for Appointments
3. Press Office
4. Political Office (including relations with political parties)
5. Policy Unit (evaluation of public policies)
6. Foreign Affairs Adviser
7. Efficiency Unit

Cabinet and Civil Service Office

1. Secretariat of the Cabinet, including for groups of advisers (foreign affairs and defense - - economic affairs - European affairs - interior, social affairs and relations with Parliament -- science)
2. Central Statistical Bureau
3. Civil Service Management Bureau

Germany

1. Legal and Administrative Department (administrative and financial management of the chancellery - statistics - administrative law - planning of government agenda - relations with Länder - relations with Parliament, government information system)
2. Foreign Relations Department
3. Department of Interior, Social Affairs and Environment
4. Department for Economy and Finance
5. Department for Social and Political Analysis (including relations with social and religious groups, and with the press)
6. Intelligence Department

Senegal

1. General Secretariat of the Government
2. Private Office of the Prime Minister (including technical advisers)
3. Financial and Administrative Department (management of the Prime Minister's departments)
4. National Archives
5. National Palaces
6. Department of National Parks
9. National Printing Press

Box 1.5: Organization of Presidential Staff in Senegal

In presidential regime, supra-governmental administrative structures would typically have a double structure: one part would be in charge of supporting the President in the discharge of his technical attributions, as head of the executive or as commander of the armed forces, and the other part would be in charge of the relations of the President with other parts of society. Here is the case of Senegal.

Private Office

1. Private Secretariat
2. Protocol Department
3. Press Department
4. Documentation Department
5. Architecture Bureau
6. Presidential Palace

Secretary General Office of the President

1. Administrative and Financial Management Department
2. Cipher Office
3. Security Department
4. High Chancellery of National Orders
5. Secretariat of the High Judiciary Council
6. Secretariat of the High Council for National Defense
7. General State Inspection
8. Office of the Financial Adviser
9. Office for Organization and Methods, and Administrative Reforms
10. General Inspection the Armed Forces
11. Military Staff of the President
12. Office of the Legal Adviser
13. Office of Technical Advisers

G. Reforming the Territorial Administrations

1.47   The restructuring of the territorial administrations could proceed along the same lines as those applicable to the republican administrations, namely, through: (i) devolution of state activities to fee-based or tariff-based entities, public or private; and (ii) selection and consolidation of the remaining state functions. Such a process is already under way in many parts of the country. In particular, a number of territorial administrations have introduced a distinction between their "administrative" departments (i.e., those belonging to the "nonmaterial sphere"), which continue to be funded through general fiscal resources, and their "productive" departments (i.e., those belonging to the "material sphere"), which are being put "on a self-financing basis" (see Figure 1.1). This process remains incomplete, however, partly for lack of appropriate legal forms into which to convert these departments. The "productive" departments remain for the most part within the territorial administrations and continue to be subject to the same management rules as the "administrative" departments. This, to a large extent, defeats the purpose of autonomy. In particular, the staffing of the productive departments (about 1,800 positions) continues to be determined by budget norms. The creation of the appropriate legal forms for these departments (see para. 1.25) should help the process unfold.

1.48   Far greater strides toward rationalizing public services at the territorial level should be expected from two other reforms:

(i)   The *devolution of responsibility to future local governments* would make possible the differentiation of state interventions across the country and would permit an adjustment of the supply of local services to the preferences of the populations concerned and to their willingness to pay (see Chapter VII).

(ii)   A *reform of education and health policies* should make it possible to downsize sectoral facilities by streamlining curricula and moving toward capitation-based funding mechanism in education and shifting medical treatment from its present focus on in-patient care to more cost-effective outpatient treatment and ambulatory institutions. These policies are discussed in greater detail in Chapter VIII.

H. Reform Agenda and Framework

1.49   Reforming the state is both critical and urgent. The international experience, however, should help guard against two opposite pitfalls: on the one hand, a piecemeal approach which seeks to solve problems in a specific field (e.g., excessive government employment) without keeping sight of the existing interlinkages among the different aspects of public management (e.g., public employment and administrative structures or social policies); and on the other hand, an overly comprehensive approach, that runs the risk of crumbling under the burden of its own ambitions, before it has any critical impact on the ground. The approach suggested in this report is to give priority to reforms that affect the administration as a whole, to act on the problems common to all state structures and services, and to emphasize reform actions that are likely to foster the sustainability of the overall economic reform program.

1.50   Two elements will be key to the success of the undertaking: (i) a clear definition of the objectives to be attained; and (ii) an effective institutional support for the design, implementation, and monitoring of a feasible agenda of reform actions.

Overall Objectives

1.51   The ultimate goal of the reform would be to maintain quality public services in areas where public needs, expressed through elections or through the markets, are greatest and where state intervention is warranted under a market economy. Downsizing of state structures and services should serve to foster this ultimate goal.

1.52   In revamping government structures, the authorities might set themselves two objectives for the next two to three years:

(i)   Reducing the number of first-level departments to fewer than 100 function-based administrative units operating at the national level.

(ii)   Cutting down the number of Cabinet-level agencies to roughly 20, and empowering them with nationwide policymaking, administrative and budget authority in their area of responsibility. This would be accompanied by a parallel downsizing of administrative structures at the territorial level.

Institutional Framework

1.53   The successful implementation of the proposed reforms of the state will require both a high degree of political commitment at the top level of government and appropriate institutional support. Both are required to ensure that the effort will be sustained despite the entrenched bureaucratic interests it will tackle and the transitional hardships it may cause to some categories of employees or public service users.

1.54   The leadership and support function for administrative reform (and civil service reform, as Chapter II will make clear) would need to be organized. Since the reforms concern the entire public administration, all ministries, all state committees, the units reporting to them, and also the territorial administrations, it would be advisable that the leadership role be played directly by the authority with overall responsibility for the entire public administration (i.e., the Prime Minister) and that the institutional support functions be directly linked to his authority. This support structure could comprise two specialized divisions, one dealing with public service structures and the other concerned with civil service, each of them having a regulation subunit and a management subunit.[11]

Next Steps

1.55   This structure would be in charge of formulating a strategy for administrative reform, preparing an action program, and identifying the various steps in the process and the administrative authorities responsible for their implementation.

1.56   In the light of the priorities identified in this chapter, such an action program would include the following steps:

(i)   Taking an inventory of existing structures and their main functions (in conjunction with the formulation of a new budget nomenclature)

(ii)   Classifying existing structures according to an agreed typology

(iii)   Redefining the concept of public service on the basis of functions

(iv)   Reviewing staffing norms

(v)   Reducing the size of the administration by defining more sharply the new external boundaries of public administrations and reducing the number of structural units.

---

[11]   As will be discussed in the next chapter, the civil service division could constitute the embryo of a more permanent capacity to ensure the overall management of human resources (including the organization of transparent recruitment procedures).

CHAPTER II. THE CIVIL SERVICE

A. Introduction

2.1   With a payroll in excess of 1 million, Kazakstan's civil service is clearly oversized. As a result, public wages have been depressed to unsustainably low levels. Previous attempts at reducing public employment have shown only mixed success. The decision taken in late 1994, for instance, to reduce staff by 25 percent may not have yielded more than a 2 or 3 percent cut in total payroll. Several factors explain this relative lack of success: (i) lack of parallel efforts at downsizing administrative structures; exemptions given to sectors with the largest staffs (social sectors); and (ii) the absence of information on the structure and composition of the civil service. A deeper impact should be expected from the policies proposed in Chapter I (i.e., redefining the boundaries of public administrations; consolidating administrations along functional lines and redeploying the remaining personnel accordingly; and bringing public service decisions closer to the ultimate beneficiaries through decentralization). This last policy will be further discussed in Chapter VII.

2.2   Retrenchment should be accompanied by measures to strengthen the professional and financial situation of the remaining civil servants. Many of the present difficulties arise from the type of civil service regime that Kazakstan inherited from the Soviet Union, under which civil servants are recruited on a contractual basis by each individual agency, rather than on a statutory basis by the state at large, and offered unattractive career structures. The authorities would be well advised to shift, after a genuine staff downsizing, to a statutory regime conducive to independence and professionalism, and to bring about a substantial improvement in the level and structure of public wages. These policies should be accompanied by a rationalization of payroll management.

2.3   A critical element for the success of the civil service reforms discussed above will be the creation of a central capacity, first to conduct the reforms, and, more permanently, to ensure the overall management of human resources.

2.4   This chapter examines these various points in turn. Section B relates the existing uncertainties regarding the size of the government payroll to the prevailing civil service regime. Section C reviews recent achievements in cutting down government employment and suggests other approaches. Section D discusses the options Kazakstan has for strengthening its civil service regime, and Section E discusses the implications of these options for wage policy. Finally, Section F puts forward suggestions for strengthening the institutional framework for civil service management.

B. Size of the Civil Service

2.5   The size and composition of the civil service is not known with any degree of precision. Chapter I offered an estimate in excess of 1,000,000 state employees (see Table 1.2) but acknowledged that this estimation reflected the number of authorized positions rather than the number of people actually employed. This situation is due to the particular regime under which civil servants are employed (see Section D, below). As a result, there is no central agency charged with civil service management nor is there any centralization of the personnel data needed for elaborating human resource strategies at the government level. As has been noted, the last effort at collecting such information dates from 1990.

C. Policies for Civil Service Reduction

2.6   The authorities recognize that the current level of public employment is unsustainable and needs to be cut. Previous attempts at reducing public employment have shown only mixed success. In late 1994, for instance, the authorities issued instructions to reduce personnel by 25 percent. As it transpired, no more than 2 or 3 percent of the total payroll was actually cut. In the case of ministerial administrations, Cabinet of Ministers Resolution 874 of November 1994 indeed eliminated about 20 percent of the authorized positions at that level (from 7,370 positions to 5,948). But the resolution also authorized the creation of 927 new positions, as some positions eliminated in one area were recreated in another. For example, the downsizing of the staff of the Ministry of Economy was achieved in part by eliminating the National Agency for Foreign Investment (NAFI) under the Ministry; this Agency, however, was reincarnated as a committee under the Cabinet of Ministers. This disappointing result was achieved at the cost of maximum turmoil within public agencies, as staff were first dismissed *en masse*, in agency after agency, before being subsequently rehired on a selective basis.

2.7   Two main factors explain this relative lack of success. First, the staff reduction policy was carried out as a numerical exercise, focusing exclusively on cutting down authorized positions, rather being part of a deliberate effort at pruning administrative structures, based on a clear sense of functional priorities. Second, the effort was unbalanced: it focused exclusively on cutting the payroll of republican and territorial administrations, but left the largest sources of public employment partly or totally untouched (parastatals and social sectors, respectively). This imbalance also reflects a lingering perception that administrations, compared with other functions, have essentially non-productive activities.

2.8   The present government overstaffing will not be remedied by addressing the symptoms rather than the sources of the problem, which lie in the dysfunctional organization of the state sector described in Chapter I. It is also crucial that any downsizing policy be perceived by state employees as being part and parcel of a *positive* approach aimed at a desirable objective, rather than as a vexing or punitive activity. Such an objective could be defined as:

Strengthening public administration capacities to make the entire public service more efficient and better able to serve its beneficiaries.

2.9   Achieving this objective would involve: (i) redefining the boundaries of public administrations; (ii) consolidating administrations and services along functional lines, and redeploying the remaining personnel accordingly; and (iii) bringing public service decisions closer to the beneficiaries by creating autonomous local governments at the municipal level. These policies are outlined in Chapters I and VII. No sector of the government should be a priori exempt from downsizing measures. Specifically, the social sectors, as the largest public employers, will need to be included in the effort.

2.10   Whereas a degree of decentralization in retrenchment is unavoidable, retrenchment decisions should follow criteria and guidelines established for the entire government if the overall objective mentioned above is to prevail over favoritism and cronyism. The design of such guidelines would require a good knowledge of the profiles of existing staff. A first step toward defining a comprehensive policy in this regard would involve *taking an inventory* of the remaining staff after the external boundaries of public administrations have been redefined, as well as of their main features (e.g., education, seniority). Taking such an inventory alone might lead to substantial retrenchment, as it should weed out cases of double employment as well as some of the current "ghost workers." It should also establish the foundation of a personnel data base, which would become a key instrument for civil service management. To make this possible, it is essential that the type of information collected through the personnel inventory, as well as the structure of the resulting personnel data base, be tailored to the requirements of the civil service regime in favor of which the government would have opted. The first such requirement would be to give each civil servant an identification number to be used uniformly in all civil service management activities, starting with the management of the payroll (see Section F, below).

2.11   Collecting such information would make it possible to devise differentiated treatments applicable to different categories of public employees, including the exclusion from the civil service of employees of entities incorporated separately from the state; the early retirement of certain categories of personnel; and the redeployment, retraining, or dismissal of others. Specific incentives for voluntary departures may also be offered beyond the existing two months' salary payment. It is critical, however, that such incentives be carefully targeted. When offered universally, such incentives would often cause a weakening, rather than a strengthening, of administrative capacities -- as the best employees are the first to leave -- and might fail to achieve any genuine retrenchment, when the positions occupied by departing employees need to be refilled.

2.12   Retrenchment should be accompanied by measures to strengthen the professional and financial situation of the remaining civil servants through the introduction of a statutory regime conducive to independence and professionalism, and a substantial improvement in the level and structure of public wages. These two measures will be discussed in the next two sections.

D. Civil Service Regime

Fundamental Options

2.13   When reforming its civil service, the first fundamental choice Kazakstan will need to make is to opt for a particular type of civil service regime. Civil service regimes typically fall within one of the following categories:

> *Open system*: Civil servants are employed by individual units under contractual arrangements similar to those applicable in the rest of the economy. Rules may be provided to regulate the activities, but not the specific employment situation, of civil servants, which is governed by regular labor legislation. This was the civil service system of the USSR; it is still in place in a number of former socialist countries, including Kazakstan.

> *Statutory system*: In this concept, the state is considered a specific nonprofit organization of general public interest, which requires distinct rules from those applicable to commercial entities. Civil servants are employed by the state under uniform staff rules set unilaterally by the state, defining the reciprocal rights, duties, and guarantees of the state and its employees, the fundamental rules of recruitment, career development, and remuneration, and management principles; such rules normally seek to guarantee the equal access of citizens to the civil service based on their talents, and promotion based on merit, and also seek to ensure the continuity of public services. Most Western countries and international organizations (such as

the UN, World Bank, EU, OECD) have adopted this system. Within a statutory system, the system known as the "position system" is different from the "rank system" or "career system."[1]

-   In the *position system* (e.g., in the Netherlands), the salary level is fixed according to the job classification; the grade (and, correspondingly, the salary level) belongs to the job level, whichever individual performs it.

-   In the *career system* (e.g., in France), the salary level or grade belongs to the individual whichever position he/she occupies.

Opting for one or the other has fundamental implications for the future of the entire public sector financial and administrative management system.

Current System

2.14   Kazakstan inherited from the FSU an *"open system."*[2] Spending units recruit, employ, and dismiss their staffs at will subject to the country's labor laws and the government's system of wage grids (see next section). The wage grids borrow some of the features of a position system (see Table 2.1). They consider three levels of civil servants: (i) at the top are the country's political authorities, elected representatives, and other politico/administrative authorities; (ii) at the bottom are support staff, including secretaries, accountants, and typists; and (iii) in the middle are professional staff, called "specialists" (including administrative officers, as well as teachers, engineers, economists, researchers, and doctors and other health personnel) and lower level managers. These grids structure all jobs and the corresponding wages along hierarchical lines, line positions being predominant and in a higher salary bracket than other positions.

2.15   Beyond its apparent flexibility, the open civil service system has many disadvantages. They stem from its fostering subservience and discipline at the expense of initiative and responsibility. First, an open system creates problems of loyalty, as staff are more likely to dedicate themselves to the interests of their individual employing entity rather to those of the state at large. The dubious loyalty of the territorial tax inspections to central tax authorities is one such example. Another manifestation of this problem is the constant "turf battles" waged by government agencies. This stems from the fact that each employee's career perspectives are more intimately linked to the success of his/her own agency in preserving and possibly expanding its turf than to the employee's dedication to the service of the state as a whole.

---

[1]   Some countries are using a mixed classification system (e.g., the Philippines) or a combination of rank and position systems (e.g., Indonesia).

[2]   In Soviet times, however, appointments to management positions were governed by the *nomenclature* system. The *nomenclature* was a comprehensive list of appointments that were controlled by the Party. Although only roughly 10 percent of the Soviet population belonged to the CPSU, practically all the Deputies to the Supreme Soviet, Ministers, heads of important enterprises and farms, Army personnel, trade union officials, research institute elites, etc. -- both at the all-Union and republican levels -- were members of the Party and their appointments were approved by the relevant Party committees.

Table 2.1: Wage Scale for Professional Staff of the Republican Administration

CATEGORY OF FUNCTIONS	NET MONTHLY SALARY	PERCENT INCREASE
Minister, State Committee Chairman	4,600	8.70
Vice-Minister, Deputy Minister	4,200	4.76
Department Chief	4,000	5.00
Ambassador	3,800	1.32
Main Department, Chief	3,750	9.33
Main Department, DeputyChief	3,400	4.41
Autonomous Sector, Chief	3,250	7.69
Autonomous Sector, Deputy Chief	3,000	3.33
Autonomous Sector, Manager	2,900	5.17
Sector, Manager	2,750	(9.09)
Political Adviser, Foreign Affairs	3,000	3.33
Manager, Foreign Affairs	2,900	5.17
Economic Adviser, Foreign Affairs	2,750	3.64
Assistant to Minister	2,650	0.00
General Sector, Manager	2,650	9.43
Principal Specialist, 3rd Secretary, Foreign Affairs	2,400	20.83
Specialist Category 1, Foreign Affairs	1,900	7.89
Specialist Category 2, Foreign Affairs	1,750	8.57
Specialist, Foreign Affairs	1,600	n.a.

Source: Cabinet of Ministers Resolution 974, April 14, 1995.

2.16   Second, the open system subjects the civil service to the vagaries of the political process ("spoils system"). This is particularly damaging in Kazakstan where the turnover in high-level political positions is considerable. Each new appointment brings with it deep changes in the management of the agencies concerned -- changes which may or may not be inspired by the long-term interest of the state. A recent decree-law of December 25, 1995 on the Public Service makes matters even worse. It stipulates, for instance (Art. 29), that should a minister resign (individually or with the rest of the government), his deputies, assistant, and advisers follow suit as well as all the heads of departments, agencies, committees, divisions, and autonomous bodies under his/her authority. Similarly, should the head of an oblast or national city resign (individually or with the termination of the President's mandate), all heads of territorial administration subordinate to him/her also tender their resignation. The fate of the entire superstructure of the state is thereby made dependent on the ups and downs of the country's political life.

2.17   By contrast, a common feature of the development of modern states has been the attempt to foster the professionalism, loyalty, and independence of their personnel, as well as the continuity of the state, by isolating their careers from political interference. Even countries (such as the United States) that have maintained some elements of a "spoils system" have also endeavored to strictly regulate its effects.

2.18   Third, an open system is hard to reconcile with one of the basic tenets of democracy: the equal access of all citizens to public offices.

Option for Reforms

2.19   A first critical step toward strengthening the civil service would be for civil servants to be recruited, employed, and managed by the state as large. This can be done on a contractual or on a statutory basis.[3/] One can indeed envisage that uniform contractual rules for civil servants could be established through a system of collective bargaining with labor representatives. Few countries have adopted such an option, which is reckoned to be unwieldy and is sometimes also considered as undermining the authority of the state.[4/] As noted above, statutory regimes come in two forms: the *position system* or the *rank or career system*.

2.20   The pros and cons of each of the systems for Kazakstan are as follows. The *position system* is commonly regarded as much superior to the rank system, since it permits wages to be adjusted to the precise features of the job being performed. Capturing these features in job classifications is, however, a highly complex undertaking in practice. And managing human resources under such a system requires monitoring both staff and job profiles. Furthermore, such a system may hinder staff mobility, as reassigning a staff member may require finding the staff member an equivalent position.

2.21   By comparison, the *rank system* is relatively easier to implement, as it requires only keeping track of personnel profiles. Given that grades and wage levels are independent of the position occupied, it is also easier to reassign staff from one position to another. Unfortunately, the rank system is much less effective at stimulating staff performance.

2.22   The two systems, however, are not so different fundamentally that it would be impossible to combine them or to shift from one to the other. In both position and rank systems, level and grade ought to be closely related to formal education and training. In any sound civil service system the main rank or position categories are based on educational background. Both systems require monitoring of human resources -- their particular skills, experience, and positions within the public services. A central management and information updating system is a prerequisite for both systems. As both systems require job descriptions and approved organizational staffing charts or "staffing laws" and also personnel management tools, it remains possible to shift from one system to another or to mix them.

2.23   Indeed, some countries (e.g., Indonesia) have successfully implemented a *mixed* system. For example, the position system is used for hierarchical functions; the rank system is employed for other professional and/or clerical functions; and the open system is followed for manual workers and temporary employment. This is an option worth considering for Kazakstan.

2.24   A new statutory regime should be introduced only following substantial administrative reform and should be reserved for the perhaps 100,000 permanent white collar employees remaining with nonincorporated state entities. Temporary and manual workers would remain under an open regime.

[3/]   Under the Constitution of Kazakstan, the authority to regulate the civil service is divided between the legislative branch and the executive branch. Art. 61, para. 3(3) of the Constitution determines that the legislative branch establishes the fundamental principles, organizational norms, and activities of state bodies and bodies of self-administration, as well as civil and military service. Within these parameters, the President upon proposal of the Prime Minister determines the structure of the government, establishes, abolishes, and reorganizes executive bodies (Art. 44, para. 3), and establishes a unified civil service system for all entities funded from the state budget (Art. 44, para. 9). A similar division of labor also exists in other countries, such as France, the United Kingdom, and Belgium. Pursuant to this constitutional principle, the civil service law should avoid going into to much detail and should rather leave to the executive sufficient flexibility to ensure an efficient management of the civil service.

[4/]   New Zealand is a recent exception. It chose in 1988 to shift from a statutory regime to a system of collective bargaining under the labor law.

Political personnel (members of the government, elected representatives) are not part of the state's permanent personnel and do not belong in a statutory civil service (they are presently covered by the civil service regulations). Their financial and legal situation needs to be defined in a different framework. Similarly, in keeping with the principle of separation of powers, the administrative personnel of the legislative and judiciary branches cannot be submitted to the authority of the executive branch and therefore require their separate regimes.

E. Wage Level and Structure

2.25 Reducing the civil service would create room for improving compensation for the civil servants who would be subsumed under the new statutory system. At the moment, the overall size of the wage bill appears to be manageable, but it is spread among too many employees. As a result, official individual compensation is unsustainably low at both ends of the pay scale: wages at the bottom of the scale range well below the subsistence minimum, while at the top of the scale wages represent only a fraction of the wages offered for similar jobs outside the government. Owing to the particularities of payroll management (see paras. 2.53-2.56), actual wages may in fact vary arbitrarily. Nonwage compensation, varying with grades, may also constitute a decisive element of the employment package.

2.26 A general increase in the wage level would be in order. But it should be implemented only in tandem with actual progress in retrenching personnel and strengthening payroll management.

Macroeconomic Aspects

2.27 Under fiscal pressures, the overall size of the wage bill has actually dropped to very low levels. From 4.8 percent of GDP in 1993, government wage expenditures fell to 2.8 percent of GDP in 1994, as is seen in Table 2.2 (actual budget outcome).[5] This level is extremely low by any international standard (see Table 2.3) and should be considered incompressible. It certainly pales in comparison with the 8 percent of GDP which the country devoted in 1994 to other purchases of goods and services. Aggregate budget savings should be sought within this latter category of expenditures rather than in the global wage bill.

Table 2.2: Size of General Government Wage Bill
(actual budget outcome)

BUDGET	WAGES		REVENUE (%)		EXPENDITURE (%)		CURRENT EXPENDITURE (%)		GDP (%)	
	1993	1994	1993	1994	1993	1994	1993	1994	1993	1994
Total 1/	1,298	13,198	17.7	15.75	18.26	13.80	21.00	19.01	4.84	2.84
Republican	417	5,152	8.37	10.22	9.35	8.32	14.97	13.56	1.56	1.11
Territorial	881	8,046	34.16	24.12	28.76	21.01	34.23	22.35	3.29	1.73

1/ Excluding Social Security.
Source: Economic and Functional Classification of the Budget, Ministry of Finance, Center for Economic Reforms.

---

[5] Note that these numbers do not include the wage bill of the social security system. The latter represented another 1 percent of GDP in 1994-95.

Table 2.3: General Government Wage Bill in Selected Countries, 1994

COUNTRY	TOTAL EXPENDITURES (% GDP)	WAGE BILL (% EXPENDITURE)	WAGE BILL (% GDP)
FSU Countries			
Kazakstan	18.2	15.3	2.8
Russia	46.3	13.5	6.3
Middle-Income Countries			
Czech Republic 1/	51.9	8.3	4.3
Hungary 4/	64.7	11.7	7.6
Romania 2/	44.3	13.6	6.0
Greece 1/	43.1	22.5	9.7
Portugal 4/	48.5	24.7	12.0
High-Income Countries			
Belgium 2/	56.7	17.8	10.1
France 2/	54.4	14.8	8.1
Germany 2/	62.3	18.2	11.4
Ireland 3/	54.2	18.1	9.8
Netherlands 1/	70.9	13.3	9.4
Spain 3/	50.5	19.6	9.9
United Kingdom 2/	56.2	18.6	10.4

Note: Including central and local governments but excluding social security funds.
1/ For 1993.
2/ For 1992.
3/ For 1991.
4/ For 1990.
Sources: IMF: GFS and IFS; World Bank: BESD Data Base.

2.28   With government employment largely unchanged, average government wages have fallen considerably behind those in the rest of the economy. By mid-1995, wage differentials between industry and finance on the one hand and public administrations on the other had widened by 50 percent compared to their levels at the time of independence. The differential has grown even larger in comparison with the private sector. This is the result of the infrequent adjustment of the minimum wage which serves as a numerator to calculate government salary (see Figure 2.1 and next section). The same policy also explains how pension payments were cut from 7 percent of GDP in 1992 to about 4 percent of GDP in 1994-1995.

2.29   It is commonly agreed as a benchmark that the entry-level salary of a general administrator should be at least equal to a country's GDP per capita. Using this yardstick, a "specialist's" salary should be at least twice as high as it currently is.

2.30   The present fiscal crisis is too acute, however, for the government to envisage wage improvements of such magnitude without drastic cuts in payroll.

Basic Wage Structure

2.31   As was noted above, the structure of the civil service wage system follows some of the precepts of a "position system." This system is made up of 14 wage scales that associate wage levels to categories of government positions. Table 2.1 shows the first of these tables which cover the professional staff of republican administrations. Other tables cover, for instance: the professional staff of autonomous republican agencies (table 2); the professional staff of oblast administrations (table 3); the professional staff of the city of Leninsk (table 4); the professional staff of other city administrations (table 5); the professional staff of autonomous agencies of the city of Leninsk (table 8); the professional staff of autonomous agencies of other cities (table 9); the professional staff of rayon administrations (table 10); the staff of notary offices (table 11); the support staff of all state agencies (table 12); the staff of village administrations (table 14). The pay scales for cities, rayons, villages, and notary offices are further differentiated by type and/or size of location. Wage tables are updated periodically at the same time as the Cabinet of Ministers adjusts the minimum wage, which they follow (see Figure 2.1).

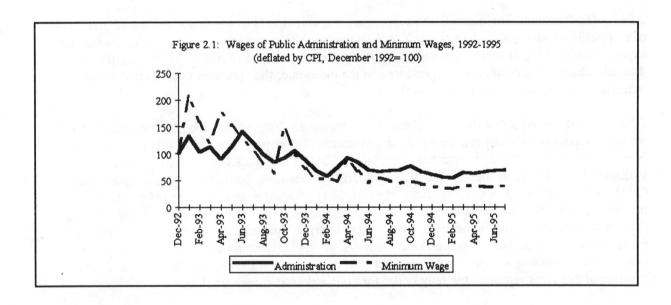

Figure 2.1: Wages of Public Administration and Minimum Wages, 1992-1995
(deflated by CPI, December 1992= 100)

2.32   All pay levels are calculated on the basis of a reference wage or numerator (the "minimum wage") and a system of coefficients measuring the "weight" of each job. For example:

Specialist position in a given agency . . . . Coefficient 4.2
Minimum wage . . . . Tenge 261.7
Net basic monthly wage . . . . 4.2 X 261.7 = 1,100

or

Section chief position in a given agency . . . . Coefficient 8.53
Minimum wage . . . . Tenge 261.7
Net basic monthly wage . . . . 8.53 X 261.7 = 2,200

A seniority bonus is added to this basic wage, which increases with the number of years of service (3-5 years: 10 percent; 5-10 years: 15 percent; 10-15 years: 20 percent; 15-20 years: 25 percent; more than 20 years: 30 percent).

2.33   In the aggregate, the wage differentials involved in these grids are reasonable: they range from 1 to 5 among nonpolitical positions. It would be unwise to compress them any further, as this would certainly lead to a further demoralization of the civil service.

2.34   The "positions coefficients," however, may not correspond to the actual work load and level of responsibility attached to the position. It is commonly agreed among human resource management experts that job weights should updated every five to seven years. Unfortunately, despite the dramatic changes the country has experienced in the meantime, the "position coefficients" have remained unchanged since Soviet Union times.

2.35   As was noted above these wage scales are structured along an "in-line position system" in which hierarchical positions are, under all circumstances, better paid than "specialist positions." [6] Furthermore, similar positions earn better salaries the higher one goes in the country's territorial structure: for instance, the basic wage of a "specialist" varies from 1,000 tenge at the rayon level (table 10) to 1,600 tenge at the republican level (table 1). Career perspectives therefore revolve primarily around moving to managerial positions (even among engineers or surgeons) and climbing the hierarchical and territorial ladders. This system deprives specialist professions and lower administrative tiers of the best professional elements. It also constitutes a built-in incentive for the observed mushrooming of administrative structures, particularly at the republican level, in which managerial positions represent the only outlet for civil servants' career ambitions.

2.36   Translating the categorization of personnel put forward in the public service decree-law of December 1995 into actual pay scales would only make matters worse. The latter legislation collapses all existing classifications of administrative staff into a single "in-line" scale along hierarchical lines. This scale comprises 16 job classes -- i.e., 8 categories x 2 steps per category (see Figure 2.2). Three of the basic defects of this structure are: (i) it includes political positions (e.g., President, ministers) and the administrative staff of the legislative branch; (ii) it does not establish any link between job classification and level of education; and (iii) the career prospects it offers are

---

[6]   This system also used to ensure higher salaries for jobs monopolized by the Communist Party.

extremely limited. With only two steps per category, the only real career perspective is to climb up the hierarchical ladder. To achieve this, a government employee of Kazakstan needs a job vacancy of a higher level in the line position. This can be obtained in one of two ways: the retirement or compulsory departure of a government employee "owner" of the "position" or job of a higher level; or the creation of supplementary jobs of a higher level (e.g., more divisions and thus more management positions). This constitutes a source of conflict within the administration and a built-in incentive for the "mushrooming" of administrative structures. Furthermore, an employee has lesser career perspectives in a small department than in a department with several directorates and branches and a high number of jobs. The "line position" system also pushes the high-level technicians (e.g., doctors, veterinarians, engineers, teachers, computer specialists) toward managerial jobs -- the only jobs belonging to the high-level salary scales. To the weaknesses already prevailing in the existing pay scale, such a system would add a lack of recognition of the diversity of professional situations of state employees -- a diversity which requires differentiated career paths.

2.37   Instead of proceeding in that direction, Kazakstan should first opt for one type or the other of civil service regime and then develop a wage structure accordingly. If the choice is in favor of a position system, a typical procedure for elaborating a revised wage structure would be as follows. Jobs or positions are grouped together, according to job content, in order to form homogenous job classes or families requiring the same *kind* of qualifications or technical, managerial, or scientific skills. Each of these classes is in turn divided into grades according to the *level* of difficulty, complexity, or responsibility and skills required. There are mainly two methodologies for evaluating job levels: job ranking and job rating. In the job ranking method, positions within a class are compared to a fully evaluated reference position. In the point rating method, the various characteristics of the position being evaluated are tallied on the basis of a predetermined point scale for each element, the total score determining the job level. *Such exercise should only be undertaken for the remaining government white collar positions after the administrative restructuring described in the above paragraphs and in Chapter I has taken place.*

2.38   If the authorities prefer to opt for a rank system, the procedure would first involve establishing a personnel classification by: (i) defining different "hierarchies" corresponding to the existing levels of education in the country's education system; (ii) dividing "hierarchies" into classes or grades that define a career structure; and (iii) further dividing grades into "steps" or "echelons" along which progress is linked to seniority and performance evaluation. A second step would be to convert each existing salary level into an equivalent hierarchy, grade, and step level, and attribute the said level to the employee occupying the related position. *Again, such an exercise should only be undertaken for the white collar workers who are to remain with the state service after administrative reorganization.*

2.39   The actual design of new wage scales under either of these two systems (or under a mixed system) should be based on macroeconomic assessment of their immediate implications (through the conversion of wage scales) as well as their medium-term implications (through the career prospects they offer). This, however, would require a much better knowledge of the characteristics of the existing staff (e.g., education, seniority) than is currently available, a knowledge which would be acquired via the above recommended staff inventory.

Figure 2.2: New Job Classification for Administrative Staff

Category	Class (rank or grade)															
top	1	2														
1			3	4												
2					5	6										
3							7	8								
4									9	10						
5											11	12				
6													13	14		
7															15	16

Notes: 1) Top category - positions: the Prime Minister; the State Secretary; the Head of the Administration of the President; Deputy Prime Ministers.

2) First category - positions: the Head of the Apparat of the Government; the Head of the state body directly subordinated and accountable to the President of the Republic; ministers; chairpersons of state committees; akims of the oblasts, towns of republican importance and the capital of the Republic; the Chairperson of the Central Electoral Commission; Deputy Heads of Administration of the President and Apparat of the Government; assistants and advisers of the President of the Republic; the Representatives of the President; the heads of the Apparat of the Chambers of the Parliament; the heads of the structural offices of the Administration of the President; the heads of the central executive bodies, not members of the government.

3) Second category - positions: deputy heads of state bodies, directly subordinated and accountable to the President of the Republic; deputy ministers; deputy chairpersons of state committees; deputy akims of the oblasts, towns of republican importance and the capital of the Republic; deputy heads of the Apparat of the Chambers of the Parliament; deputy Chairperson, secretary and members of the Central Electoral Commission; deputy heads of the structural offices, state inspectors of the Administration of the President; deputy heads of Administration of the President and Apparat of the Government; Representatives of the Government; the heads of the structural offices of the Apparats of the Government and the Chambers of the Parliament; the assistants and advisers of the Chairpersons of the Senate and the Chairperson of the Majlis of the Parliament, Prime Minister and deputies; heads of sectors of the Administration of the President; deputies of the heads of other central executive organs, non-members of the Government, akims of districts and towns of oblast subordination.

4) Third category - positions: heads of departments, agencies, committees: heads of divisions of independent divisions; assistants and advisers of first heads of state bodies, directly subordinated and accountable to the President of the Republic; ministers, chairpersons of state committees, as well as first heads of other central executive organs, non-members of the Government; heads of sectors of the apparats of the Government and the Chambers of the Parliament, chief and senior experts, consultants, experts, senior reviewers, reviewers of the Administration of the President, the Apparats of the Government and the Chambers of the Parliament.

5) Fourth category - positions: deputy heads of departments, agencies, committees, divisions, independent divisions and heads of divisions of state bodies, directly subordinated and accountable to the President of the Republic; ministers, state committees, as well as other central executive organs, non-members of the Government; heads of departments, division offices of local executive organs of oblasts, towns of republican importance and the capital.

6) Fifth category - positions: deputy akims of districts and towns of oblast importance; chief leading specialists of state organs; directly subordinated and accountable directly to the President of the Republic; ministers, state committees, as well as other central executive organs, non-members of the Government, deputy heads of departments, divisions, offices of local executive organs of oblasts, towns of republican importance and the capital of the Republic; chief and leading specialists for the Apparats of maslikhats, local executive organs of oblasts, towns of republican importance and the capital of the Republic.

7) Sixth category - positions: heads of departments divisions, offices of district and oblast importance, district and towns of local executive organs; heads of structural offices of the Apparats of maslikhats of districts, towns of oblast importance, specialists of departments, divisions, offices of oblast, towns of republican importance and the capital; of local executive organs, rural townships, towns of district subordination, local executive bodies, the Apparat of maslikhats of oblasts, towns of republican importance and the capital.

8) Seventh category - positions: specialist of districts, towns of oblast subordination, districts in towns of local executive bodies, rural, settlements, towns of district subornation of local executive organs, their divisions, the Apparats of maslikhats of districts, towns of oblast importance.

Other Compensation

2.40   The current compensation package also includes a number of bonuses and indemnities, some of which are in-kind payments.[7/] The compensation package can also be augmented by extralegal devices which the current payroll procedures afford, such as ghost worker schemes. There would be little point in seeking to rationalize the pay structure without closing the existing loopholes that have allowed these schemes to flourish.

2.41   *Indemnities*. There are mainly two types of indemnities. On the one hand, wage supplements, ranging from 15 to 25 percent of basic wages, are paid to civil servants working in hardship or environmentally damaged zones (these percentages are doubled in rayons surrounding the Aral Sea). On the other hand, in a bid to develop the countryside, the government has created specific supplements paid to social workers in villages and auls, equivalent to 25 percent of basic wages.

2.42   *Bonuses*. The wage budget of all budget entities also includes an incentive fund equivalent to four months of total staff salaries. This amount is used at the discretion of the head of the entity. It can be used in regular installments or for lump-sum annual payments. In practice, however, this fund can be used as a slush fund to finance special pay deals with privileged employees, outside the framework of the official wage policy. It would be preferable to place such bonuses within a formal and transparent incentive system as part of the wage reform described above.

2.43   *In-Kind Benefits*. Dachas, cars, access to certain sanatoria or to scarce goods, as well as other in-kind payments, traditionally formed a substantial part of the compensation package for Soviet civil servants: often they determined their ranks more surely than did formal wages. Whereas many of these benefits are now disappearing, access to government housing remains a crucial form of non-wage payment.

2.44   *Extralegal Schemes*. The current decentralization of payroll management (see Section F, below) affords many opportunities for extralegal payments. Budget entities may not fill their authorized positions, or may fill them only with 'ghost workers' and improve their average wages by pooling their authorized wage bill among fewer employees than are authorized. Or they may claim higher positions than they actually require and use the extra resources in the same manner. In addition, there is little safeguard against government employees belonging to more than one payroll.

2.45   These possibilities, combined with the use of the incentive fund, may lead to situations in which actual compensations are set arbitrarily, or more exactly, are a function of each employee's bargaining power.[8/] Rationalizing payroll management is therefore a necessary complement to rationalizing public wages.

[7/]   Civil servants are also entitled to one month of paid leave at the minimum wage.

[8/]   Note that the public service decree-law further debases government wage policy by allowing employees recruited from the private sector to retain their previous salary levels.

F. Civil Service Management

2.46   A critical element for the success of the civil service reforms discussed above will be the creation of a central capacity, first to conduct the reforms and more permanently to ensure the overall management of human resources. At present the only human resource function exercised at the government level is the establishment of authorized positions. Almost all other personnel functions are carried out by individual budget units. Civil service management is thus in effect spread among tens of thousands of administrative structures. This prevents the emergence of deliberate human resource strategies responsive to the government's development program and managed within the context of public expenditure programming.

Personnel Norms

2.47   At present, personnel management revolves around the concept of norms (*normy*). These norms relate the volume of goods or services provided as determined in the plan's objectives (*zadanie*) or indicators (*pokozatel*) to the maximum quantity of resources made available to achieve the objectives. Government resolutions annually determine personnel norms (i.e., the maximum number of authorized positions and the wage bill for all government bodies).[9] These norms are established and monitored by three different departments of the Ministry of Finance: the State Apparatus Department, the Social Sphere Department (education, health, and other social services), and the Sovereignty Sphere Department (interior, defense, national security). Their only concern is a financial one.

2.48   Once norms have been established, these departments seek to monitor only the "fill ratio" of the norms, on the basis of quarterly reports sent to them by all budget entities around the country. These reports, however, are not consolidated nor do they contain any profile information on the personnel actually occupying authorized positions.[10]

Recruitment

2.49   Currently, there are no standardized recruitment procedures. Each administrative entity, as well as autonomous agencies, recruits it own staff autonomously. In principle, the recruitment process is supervised by the entity's administrative committee or board; in practice, the process may be much more informal. Although the recruiting entities may occasionally advertise vacancies, there is no systematic and public procedure for calling for applications, or evaluating them. In some cases candidates are recruited directly from specialized schools. This is the case, for instance, for judiciary functions, economists, and some functions within the Ministries of Finances, Interior, Education, and Health.

---

[9]   For instance, Cabinet of Ministers Resolutions 1,179 of October 21, 1994 and 1,189 of August 25, 1995 (respectively, on staffing and wage bills of ministries, state committee, and other republican structures, including field services, the judiciary system, and the security apparatus) or Cabinet of Ministers Resolution 1,371 of December 5, 1994 (on staffing of territorial administrations). These resolutions, together with budget data, constitute the main sources for elaborating Table 1.2.

[10]   In the absence of such information, the Ministry of Finance is left to apply notional average wages to authorized positions, to calculate the wage budget.

2.50   The "board" of an agency (see Chapter I, footnote 7) is charged with examining applications, possibly interviewing candidates, and finally recruiting the selected candidate. The board also determines the level of employment and the corresponding salary of the candidates. The only available guidelines are contained in a "qualification guide" dating from the Soviet Union era which indicates the requirements for candidates for different positions. Whatever its value, the said guide no longer seems to be widely used.

2.51   As Kazakstan moves to strengthen its civil service, it would be well advised to adopt two of the basic principles of modern civil services, and indeed of democratic government: (i) equal access of all citizens to public offices; and (ii) recruitment on the basis of talent. These principles imply that all eligible candidates for government jobs should be given equal opportunity to be recruited (access rules), and that recruitment decisions should be based on transparent and nondiscriminatory rules (selection rules). Access rules apply to the government; they regulate eligibility criteria, job definitions, and publicity requirements, whereas selection criteria apply to the candidates (e.g., nationality, qualification, physical aptitude, age, education).

2.52   Equal access to government jobs is best guaranteed by a system of competitive entry examinations. To permit the largest possible degree of uniformity in selection decisions, a single central entity should be charged with organizing such examinations, in consultation with the relevant technical departments as far as the content of the examination is concerned. This would be one of the main functions of the proposed central civil service agency.

Payroll

2.53   At present, the security of wage payments is not sufficiently guaranteed. The process is almost entirely in the hands of spending units. Wages are paid in cash by the units' paymaster (generally the accountant or deputy accountant). The paymaster calculates wages monthly and consolidates them into a payroll statement which is submitted to the Finance Department of the level of administration to which the unit belongs. With the Finance Department's approval, the paymaster withdraws the net amount from the spending unit's account at the local branch of the National Bank, after transferring mandatory and voluntary wage levies (income tax, pension, social insurance, trade union fee) to the relevant accounts.

2.54   The weaknesses of this system are as follows. In the absence of a consolidated personnel data base or of personnel identification numbers, it is impossible to validate the calculations made by the spending units' accounts (e.g., validity of the calculation parameters, status or even presence of employees). This opens the door to the paymaster's colluding with his colleagues in producing misleading personnel information. There is also some a posteriori control in that the wages covered by the payroll statement have indeed been paid.[1] The fact that the Finance Departments do not have any administrative authority over the spending units' accountants further aggravates the risk of fraud.

2.55   A first step toward strengthening payroll management would be to establish a complete personnel roll where all state employees are identified by an identification number and where the main features of their employment situation are centralized (e.g., grade, position, age, seniority, residence,

---

[1]   For instance, in the absence of an employee, the paymaster would not typically return the unpaid wage to the bank, but would keep it and possibly loan it to other colleagues.

family situation). Over the medium-term, this data base could also serve as a basis for introducing a procedure of wage payment by bank transfer rather than in cash.

2.56   More immediately, in view of the lingering reluctance of private individuals to maintain bank accounts, priority should be given to tightening cash payment procedures. Substantial improvement could be achieved by separating the functions of calculating the payroll from the actual payment of wages. The first function would continue to be exercised by the spending units' authorizing officer (*rasporiaditel*), but actual payment would be made by under the authority of the Finance Departments (*finorgan*) or by the Treasury (depending on how the division of labor emerges between these two departments). The authorizing officer would establish, on a monthly basis, an itemized payroll statement providing detailed calculation parameters for each employee, and consolidated by budget item. This payroll statement would then be transferred to the Finance Departments, which would verify its validity (against the personnel data bases), and would approve its payment. Actual cash payment would executed by paymasters appointed by the Finance Departments (rather than by the spending units) and, preferably, chosen from within their staff.

Creation of a Civil Service Agency

2.57   The success of the measures in this chapter and in Chapter I for achieving a substantial strengthening of Kazakstan's public administration and civil service will depend largely on the existence of a consistent leadership. It is therefore essential that institutional support be provided for managing this endeavor. Since the reforms concern the entire public administration, all ministries, all state committees, the units reporting to them, and also the territorial administrations and local governments, this institutional support can be efficacious only if it is directly linked to the authority with the overall constitutional responsibility for the entire public administration (i.e., the Prime Minister). This reform commission could be progressively converted into a specialized public agency with ministerial rank (Civil Service Commission or Ministry) in charge of managing the civil service and updating statutory rules.

G. Conclusions

2.58   Reforming the civil service system is an essential part of the broader effort to downsize government. On the one hand, as this chapter and the previous chapter have made clear, no sustainable result can be achieved in cutting down government employment without first downsizing structures and services. Conversely, if the objective of such downsizing is to strengthen, not to weaken, the effectiveness and responsiveness of government interventions in selected core functions, parallel efforts are required to establish the civil service as a permanent body of professionals, motivated to dedicate themselves to the longer-term interest of the state. For this twofold aim, this chapter has identified priority actions in four areas: (i) staffing; (ii) employment rules; (iii) remuneration; and (iv) personnel management.

2.59   As concerns staffing, the objective of the proposed reforms would be to strengthen public administration capacities and to make public services as a whole more efficient and less costly. Priority actions would involve:

- Taking a (computerized) inventory of authorized staffing levels
- Taking an inventory of the actual staffing of all budget entities and establishing a permanent updating system
- Reviewing the staffing of the health and education sectors in relation to reassessment of sectoral policies
- Formulating severance incentives
- Adjusting staffing levels to the requirements of restructured administrations.

2.60   As concerns employment conditions, the proposed move, after an initial downsizing of the government payroll, from an open regime to a statutory one would aim at establishing a body of public administration professionals entrusted, under the authority of the government, with ensuring the quality and continuity of state public services. Priority actions would be as follows:

- Opting for a particular type of civil service regime (rank, position, mixed) for the professional staff of the state
- Defining the principles governing the personnel of other government entities (local government personnel, teacher and medical personnel, personnel of parastatal entities and of the legislative and judiciary branches)
- Adopting civil service statutes defining the terms and conditions of civil servants' employment, remuneration, and careers.

2.61   Within this new statutory system, the authorities should introduce a more motivating remuneration system, in terms of both salary level and career structure, taking into consideration overall budgetary constraints and human resource management capabilities. This would involve:

- Designing a new remuneration system in accordance with the new civil service statutes
- Preparing new incentive systems in conjunction with the introduction of a performance evaluation system
- Centralizing payroll management under the dual control of the Treasury and the future civil service agency.

2.62   Finally, to operate this new personnel system, the government will need to establish a human resource development capacity in charge of managing regulations and personnel, and to provide the required management tools to the employing agencies. The first steps in this process would be the following:

- Establishing a central agency responsible for managing and coordinating civil service rules and remuneration policy, as well as for the recruitment, careers, payment, and termination of employment of civil servants
- Defining the personnel management functions of employing departments
- Establishing proper linkages between personnel management and fiscal management systems.

CHAPTER III. FISCAL CHOICES AND ADMINISTRATIVE STRUCTURES

A. Introduction

3.1   The need to redeploy administrative structures and public services is recognized increasingly by the Kazakstan authorities. The authorities also recognize that such redeployment is likely to cause hardships for both personnel and users, as the level of employment and the volume of services provided (at least in theory) will need to decline. The link between this proposition and the need for budget reform is less widely perceived. International experience, however, demonstrates that the activation of effective budget procedures can provide a crucial impetus to, and a key tool for, the reform of public services.

3.2   Before the particular techniques involved in budget reform -- from the planning to the execution and evaluation stages -- are reviewed (as will be done in the next three chapters), it is important to highlight the fundamental changes required in the budgetary logic itself. Up to the present, the entire budget process has been dominated at all stages by the *logic of passive distribution* of available resources among existing structures and services, which characterized the Soviet *Gosbudget*, as this chapter will make clear (see also the background paper prepared in conjunction with this report on "The Soviet Legacy in the Public Finances of Kazakstan"). Under this old logic, the finances followed the real resources. An altogether different logic must emerge: a *logic of selection* among competing services and structures, triggering an adaptation of those structures to policy priorities and resource constraints, even to the elimination of those that rank lowest in the selection process. Under this new logic, it is up to the finances to direct the real resources.

3.3   The following three factors contribute to the present distribution logic:

(i)   The surviving system of budgetary norms engenders a supply-driven mentality and sanctions the primacy of physical allocation decisions over financial ones

(ii)   The atomization of budget units obscures budgetary decisions

(iii)   The architecture of the public finance system prevents a differentiation of public interventions.

3.4   These points will be discussed in turn in Sections B, C, and D, respectively.

B. Passiveness of Public Finances

3.5   Affecting the entire budget process is a system of technical norms inherited from the planning system. Like production norms, these norms relate a given supply of public services (for example, number of hospital beds) to resource requirements, first in physical terms (for example, number of beds x meal per bed), then in financial terms (number of meals x cost of a hospital meal) -- the level of supply itself being determined exogenously. In the planning days, this level reflected the fundamental choices made in the physical planning process (see Box 3.1). Today, it reflects only the inertia of tradition.

3.6   The current use of these norms will be further detailed in the next chapters. At this stage, suffice it to underline that, despite the current crisis and the growing hiatus between normative resource requirements and available resources, the subsistence (at least formally) of the system of norms underwrites a perceived "entitlement" to fiscal resources at all levels of the fiscal chain. It justifies the general attitude of denial of the fiscal crisis and the resulting resistance to structural changes.

3.7   One example will illustrate the situation. Having aggregated the budget request of its subordinate bodies calculated on the basis of national norms, Oblast X submits to the Ministry of Finance an "incompressible" expenditure budget for 1995 of 11 billion tenge. In view of the overall fiscal constraints, the Ministry authorizes only 5.7 billion. The oblast protests that this amount will enable it only to pay wages and will not cover such expenditures as students' stipends, kindergarten lunches, and school heating, not to mention the acquisition of operating supplies or the completion of school construction initiated five years previously. Having failed to mollify the Ministry of Finance, the oblast administration decides not to cut services but rather to call on the population and local enterprises for financial contributions and to seek a loan from Almaty (of no less than 4.5 billion tenge), in view of the fact that "the resource requirements of the public services in the oblast are covered for only 40 percent." Not surprisingly, seven months into the fiscal year expenditure commitments were running at close to 90 percent of the authorized budget and payment arrears equivalent to 25 percent of committed expenditures had accumulated. Similar situations are common at all levels of administration, republican or territorial.

3.8   Whatever the legitimate needs of that particular oblast are, what is striking in this example is (i) the refusal, at all points in the process, to conceive that existing public services

---

Box 3.1: Financial Planning in the Soviet Era

Soviet financial planning had a subordinate role in the overall planning process. The financial plans were the derivatives of the plans for output, allocation of resources, capital investments, and labor. They served to ensure that economic units would have the rubles required to acquire the material resources they needed, based on technical norms, to meet the output targets established through the physical planning process. Thus, planning of the usage of financial resources neither preceded nor controlled the formulation of other types of plans. It performed, however, a "control by the ruble" function for checking the validity of physical planning. Balancing the financial plans validated the overall balance of the physical plans.

There were several types of financial plans: the Consolidated Financial Plan; the State Budget; the financial plans (balances of incomes and expenditures) of enterprises, associations, and soviet farms; the financial plans of budget-financed institutions; the financial plans of collective farms; the financial plans of enterprises and organizations of consumer cooperative units; the State Social Insurance Budget; the Cash and Credit Plans of the Gosbank and the Stroibank.

Because of the direct involvement of the state in economic life, the State Budget had a relatively significant importance. On average, about 50 percent of the net material product or about 40 percent of the GDP were concentrated in the State Budget.

In brief, the purpose of the budget process was for the budget entities to requisition from the public finance system the monetary resources needed to achieve agreed planning targets in much the same way as they requisitioned material supplies through Gosnab.

---

may not be a God-given right, and (ii) the incapacity to rank priorities and to choose, among competing budget claims, which services will be funded and which will be reduced or discontinued. So overpowering is the system of norms that the received wisdom is that existing public services have to be funded to capacity under any circumstances.

C. Atomization of Public Finances

3.9   The atomization of the public finance system exacerbates the structural rigidities. The basic component of Soviet public finances is the *smeta*, or expenditure allocation document. For each *smeta*, there is a corresponding spending or budget entity (which possibly groups together several administrative units). This spending or budget entity is an administrative body that is autonomous in the preparation of its budget (which is based on nationally mandated expenditure norms) and in the execution of that budget. Each budget entity is headed by an authorizing officer (*rasporiaditel)*, supported by at least one accounting officer. At the budget preparation stage, the *smeta* of a budget entity constitutes its budget request. After budget approval, the *smeta* returns to the budget entity as an executory document, detailing its appropriations by nature of expenditure: for example, personnel, social security contributions, stipends, maintenance.

3.10   There is a multitude of such entities, and they are extremely heterogeneous. As was noted in Chapter I, the republican tier of administration counts over 2,200 of these entities. Some entities are overly aggregated: for example, each sectoral ministry constitutes one single *smeta*, a situation that prevents a detailed allotment of the budget by large functions located at the department or sub-department level. In contrast, other entities may be minuscule. This atomization becomes exponential at the territorial level. If one were to extrapolate on the basis of the example in Box 3.2, there might be as many 40,000 budget entities operating at the territorial level with their own *smeta*.

Box 3.2: The Russian Doll Model in Practice: The Case of the Kostanai Oblast

The Kostanai oblast encompasses 14 rayons and 8 towns of oblast subordination. Each of these entities constitutes a first level of centralization of *smeta*.

Take the example of the Mendigara rayon. Until 1994, the rayon budget was subdivided into 14 separate budgets: that of the rayon administration itself plus those of 13 villages. Each of these villages received a share of revenues and also executed, under the supervision of the higher echelon (the rayon), part of the expenditure budget.

Since 1994, however, this lower level of territorial administration has been eliminated and its activities have been subsumed under the control of rayon-level administrations. Village-level budgets have therefore been consolidated with the rayon level. The village level has remained a basic level of centralization and aggregation of *smeta*. A village centralizes about 12 *smeta*: 2 kindergartens, 3 schools, 1 club, 1 library, 3 primary health care centers, 1 ambulatory polyclinic, plus the village administration, now an outpost of the rayon administration. In total, in Mendigara, about 150 *smeta* (i.e., 13 villages x 12 budget entities) are centralized at the village level and are consolidated into 12 rayon-level *smeta*.

The rayon administration budget itself centralizes 15 *smeta* corresponding to infrastructures of services with rayon-wide catchment areas: 1 rayon administration,1 culture department, 1 sports department, 2 veterinary stations, 1 vocational training center, 1 rayon administration, 1 maslikhat, 1 pension fund (*raisobes*), 1 children's home, 1 republican police operation, 1 traffic police operation, 1 police children's home, 1 for the 5 hospitals, and 1 for social assistance units located in villages. Village level *smeta* (12) and the rayon administration's own (15) are therefore centralized into 27 documents at the rayon level.

The same process takes place at the oblast level, which centralizes rayon *smeta* and combines those of budget entities with oblast-level catchment areas into about 200 oblast-level *smeta*.

D. The Russian Doll Model

3.11   In this system, the budget is constructed, in the first instance, by successive aggregation of individual *smeta* from the bottom up (as is seen in para. 3.9 and Box 3.2), all molded by the same national norms. The process is essentially passive and involves adding up resource requests rather than selecting among them.

3.12   This atomization combined with the norm system creates extraordinary rigidities in the resource allocation process, as thousands of institutions converge on fiscal authorities with claims to resources, which not only remained unscreened as they proceed through the administrative chain, but also are solidly entrenched by expenditure norms. Such an architecture may have been consistent with a planning system under which policy choices as to the location and level of services were made exogenously. Without this, such a structure considerably obscures policy choices and rigidifies expenditure patterns.

3.13   The rules that determine the assignment of budget entities to this or that budget further hinder a differentiation of public services across the country. The principle is that each entity is assigned to the administration in the jurisdiction in which it operates. As these entities are all state administrations, this assignment can occur irrespective of whether the said entity performs functions which are of local or of higher interest. The state budget may well be separated into several tiers (rayons, oblasts, republican administrations), but these tiers constitute essentially different levels of aggregation of a number of individual *smeta*, with little functional or fiscal individuality. Furthermore, since fiscal resources are essentially pooled at the national level, no one has an interest in requesting less than the norm or is allowed to request more than the norm.

3.14   This version of the concept of budget unity is deeply rooted in the Soviet tradition. It reflected the unity of the state, and beyond, a certain conception of the unity of the people and of the equality of Soviet citizens (see Box 3.3).

3.15   The concept of budget unity is fundamental and, indeed, it needs to be reasserted. It is, however, not incompatible

Box 3.3: Fiscal Centralism in the Soviet Era

Although the USSR was a federal state, the budget was constructed on a centralized basis. The principle of *democratic centralism* revealed itself in the ways in which a budget of a lower-level organization was included in the budget of a higher-level organization, or a lower-level budgetary authority was forbidden to reduce its planned revenues or expenditures.

This concept dates from the first days of the Soviet regime, when the entire country was drifting apart. This situation led Lenin to declare in 1918: "The centralization of finances and the concentration of our forces is essential; unless these principles are applied in practice, we shall be unable to carry out our economic reforms that will provide every citizen with enough to eat and the possibility of satisfying his cultural needs (...). An urge towards decentralization is to be observed (...) and it is quite natural because the centralism of the tsar and the bourgeoisie engendered hatred of and disgust for all centralized authority among the masses. I regard centralism as the means of providing a subsistence minimum to the working people. I am in favor of the broadest autonomy for local Soviet organizations but at the same time I believe that if our work of consciously transforming the country is to be fruitful, there must be a single, strictly defined financial policy, and that instructions must be carried out from top to bottom. From you we expect a decree on the centralization of the country's finances" (Report to the All-Russia Congress of Representatives of Financial Departments, May 1918).

with a devolution of authority at the local level within the context of a unitary state. This report will even argue that a properly designed devolution process would permit the unity of the budget to be restored where it has been unnecessarily compromised (see Chapter VII).

3.16   The present drift of fiscal practices, not decentralization, constitutes the real challenge to the integrity of the budget. In the absence of a selection process among services and programs through competition for budgetary resources, underfunded services have come to compete in the marketplace for non5fiscal resources. These resources take many forms but mostly originate in commercial activities: for example, a vocational training school may venture into building construction, or a health facility may rent commercial space. Although no aggregate number is available to gauge the importance of these nonbudgetary resources, the consensus is that they are large. The problem with these "nonbudgetary" resources is not that public services would charge for the services they render -- within proper regulation, this might even be desirable. The problem is that agencies are undertaking other activities than the ones they are budgeted for in order to keep in existence public services which may not actually be delivered -- or even needed, for that matter. Increasingly, therefore, the level at which public services are being *actually* funded and delivered is decided outside the budget.

E. Conclusions

3.17   The administrative reforms described in Chapter I are critical. International experience, however, shows that such initiatives are unlikely to be effective, and may even remain a paper exercise, unless they are supported in the day-to-day business of running government affairs by a commonly perceived budget constraint (i.e., by procedures which institutionalize the competition between services and programs for scarce resources).

3.18   With the abolition of central planning, the role of the budget in resource allocation needs to change fundamentally. Under the planning system, the budget was in the ancillary position of allocating financial resources according to the physical resource pattern established by the plan. Without central planning, the budget exercises a leadership role in the allocation process, by mobilizing and deploying fiscal resources to steer real resources in the direction set by overall government policies. This leadership function is exercised most effectively when budget procedures orchestrate, at all levels of government, a process of competition and selection among priorities. A number of initial steps have been taken in that direction, as will become clear in the next chapters. Considerably more remains to be accomplished, however, for such logic to permeate all phases of the budget cycle, from its preparation (see Chapter IV) to its execution (see Chapter V) and its audit (see Chapter VI).

CHAPTER IV. EXPENDITURE BUDGETING

A. Introduction

4.1   As was noted in Chapter III, the budget of Kazakstan has not yet made the transition that would give it the leadership role in the allocation of public resources. It remains characterized by its passiveness in the indiscriminate aggregation of expenditure requests, and passiveness also in the final apportioning of austerity across all spending entities.

4.2   Concrete suggestions will be given in Section C, below, for shifting from the microeconomic and supply-driven approach to budgeting to a macroeconomic and functional approach that enables fiscal resources to be deployed according to defined policy priorities. Budget rationalization techniques and an improved nomenclature would serve better to enlighten policy and structural choices. Rationalizing budgetary choices would, however, be pointless if the "optimal allocation" arrived at could be circumvented during the budget execution; hence it is necessary to reinforce the binding nature of budget appropriations (which is highlighted in Section D). Ex ante rationalization would also be in vain if the budget did not have complete mastery over the finances of the state. This chapter will begin by considering this basic issue (Section B).

B. The Scope of the Budget

4.3   Proper budget management starts with proper budget coverage. The first order of business in Kazakstan is to recalibrate the scope of the budget so that it covers *all and nothing but* the activities which rightfully belong to the realm of the state in a market economy.

Coverage

4.4   The *nothing but* referred to above was described in Chapter I. It would consist of introducing a *sharper demarcation between public administrations and other service activities*, based on a functional review of their roles in the new market environment. A similar process was initiated under the Soviet Union in 1987, with the separation of the state finances from those of enterprises. This process, however, affected primarily the "material sphere," leaving within the realm of the state many services that could very well be provided on a market basis by private or public corporations or through other institutions of the civil society, such as nonprofit associations or trade unions. Chapter I gave some indication of the broad scope there is in this field for pruning budgetary commitments.

4.5   At the same time that the span of the budget is being reduced in this manner, its coverage should expand to restore the budget's complete mastery over the state's own financial operations. Three principles are commonly considered essential in this respect:

> *Unity*: <u>All resources and charges of the state are provided for in a single document</u>. This principle of comprehensiveness affects the presentation of the budget. The principle is aimed at giving fiscal authorities (from the Budget Department to Parliament) a comprehensive view of all public finance matters so that they may reach as accurate an understanding as possible of the requirements and implications of public policies, whether in macroeconomic terms

(e.g., overall tax burden, share of public spending in aggregate demand) or in microeconomic terms (e.g., cost-effectiveness of expenditure programs).

Universality (or gross budget rule): <u>All revenues are accounted for their gross amount,</u> without any offsetting operation against spending items. This principle of transparency affects the nature of budget authorizations. Its corollary is an interdiction forbidding all spending agencies to increase their resources beyond their budget appropriation, in any way that is not provided for by the budget law itself.

Nonearmarking: <u>All revenues serve to fund all expenditures.</u> This principle seeks to avoid the fragmentation of the budget and thereby to leave complete room for maneuvering to fiscal authorities in allocation decisions. It serves to underpin the necessary fiscal solidarity among government agencies.

Countries adapt these principles to their own circumstances and often tolerate certain relaxations of some of their more stringent aspects. But, as is explained immediately below, budget practices in Kazakstan infringe these three rules in more serious ways.

Unity

4.6   Despite recent progress, the budget of Kazakstan still presents an incomplete picture of the state's financial operations, mainly as regards quasi-fiscal operations and expenditures funded by foreign borrowing. Considerable progress has already been achieved, however, in restoring the unity of the budget through the gradual elimination of most *extrabudgetary funds* that existed immediately after independence. This progress came about in two steps. First, in 1994 most of the previous extrabudgetary funds were reintegrated in the budget. This reform concerned the following six funds: (i) the Economic Transformation Fund; (ii) the Passenger Transport Funds; (iii) the Employment Fund; (iv) the Road Fund; (v) the Environment Protection Fund; and (vi) the Mineral Resource Protection Fund. Table 1.1 showed that this reform caused the burden of extrabudgetary funds to decline from about 12 percent of GDP in 1993 to about 5 percent in 1995. Even within the budget, however, these funds initially retained their specific funding sources, in the form of payroll contributions for funds (i), (ii), and (iii), and of various user charges for funds (iv), (v), and (vi). The second step was taken when all these levies (with the exception of the social funds, discussed immediately below) were eliminated with the tax reform of April 1995. As a result, the special funds themselves fell into abeyance.

4.7   The *social funds* are an exception, and a justified one. The Pension Fund and the Social Insurance Fund[1] have continued to operate as extrabudgetary funds, while the Employment Fund[2] has become one again. In addition, a Compulsory Medical Insurance Fund started to operate in early 1996. The nature of these funds, however, is different from that of regular fiscal operations. The social funds are public insurance funds, managed by parastatal bodies; they are financed, not by taxes, but by mandatory insurance premiums. As long as the authorities adhere to the *insurance*

---

[1]   Both funded by a social security contribution of 30 percent of payroll.

[2]   Funded by an employer contribution of 2 percent of payroll.

principle in the field of social protection, it is in their interest to keep the finances of the social protection system separate from those of public administrations.

4.8   Apart from the above exception, the authorities would be well advised to resist any temptation or pressure to reconstitute or create new extrabudgetary funds. In this context, the reconstitution of the *Road Fund* in early 1996 creates an unfortunate precedent. Roads are crucial to the economy of Kazakstan, and sufficient funding must be provided for their maintenance.[3/] But other sectors could make a similar claim. And if it is true that other countries (e.g., Japan, New Zealand) have successfully operated similar funds, few of these countries have undergone fiscal strains of the same magnitude as Kazakstan. When the resources available to maintain all public infrastructures are painfully few, the little room for maneuvering that fiscal authorities have should not be artificially hampered by exempting any particular sector from sharing in the austerity.

4.9   More worrisome is the decision made to finance the *construction of a new capital* in Akmola, not only outside of the framework of the budget, but also to lodge the related transactions in an offshore banking account. First, there is no reason why this particular expenditure item should not compete for public funding with other expenditure priorities, such as maintaining basic health or paying decent pensions. Second, assuming that this proposal would indeed receive higher priority, the international record of cost overrun and misappropriation in this type of project pleads unequivocally for putting its implementation firmly under the control of the Treasury.

4.10   There is also no justification for the present state of affairs in which most expenditures financed by foreign borrowing are neither budgeted nor accounted for under the country's normal procedures. These expenditures should not be treated specially. On the contrary, foreign borrowing should be regarded by all interested parties -- fiscal authorities, spending agencies, legislative bodies, and the general public -- as just another way of financing the country's expenditure programs, and should be treated as such within the budgetary framework. Foreign-funded expenditures should be appropriated, authorized, executed, accounted for, and controlled in the same way as any other budget expenditure. Not only would this ensure full transparency to the use of borrowed funds, but it would help to reassure all interested parties that foreign borrowing is directed toward the country's priorities.

Universality

4.11   There is a second reason why at the moment the budget presentation and accounting of fiscal transactions is incomplete: namely, the recent *multiplication of "nonbudgetary" resources* levied independently by budget entities. Faced with the general penury of resources, many budget entities have resorted to raising all manner of revenues, which they use at their own discretion outside of the framework of budget authorizations. In many cases the distinction between a "nonbudgetary resource" and a simple bribe may be tenuous. It should be emphasized that this situation is entirely legal, even if it is in clear contradiction of a fundamental principle of budget management. The amount of resources so collected is known to be considerable, although no precise figure is available. In theory, such a figure could be obtained as, pursuant to old regulations, all nonbudgetary proceeds should be deposited in specific accounts at the National Bank and all nonbudgetary transactions should

---

[3/]   See "Kazakstan: Transport Sector Review," World Bank, Draft Sector Report, February 1996.

take place in its books. But in practice these regulations are little observed and no attempt is made to consolidate those records that exist.

4.12 Whereas the need to provide economic incentives to both suppliers and users of public services, particularly in times of fiscal crisis, is legitimate, it cannot be done outside the framework of the budget. The rule should be simple: the perception of any revenue by any state entity should be explicitly authorized by the state budget and accounted for in the state budget's books. The simplest way to achieve this is to pool all miscellaneous payments received by state agencies with all general resources of the state budget and require these agencies to seek normal budget authorization for all their expenditures, including those expenditures that they formerly funded with nonbudgetary resources. However, where nonbudgetary resources arise from industrial and commercial activities, the first option should be to incorporate these entities separately from the state and to consider their privatization where applicable (as discussed in Chapter I).

4.13 Not all situations lend themselves to such clear-cut treatment. More flexible techniques can also be envisaged, including the following:

Annex Budgets: This framework can be applicable for departmental enterprises (i.e., agencies undertaking commercial or industrial activities which, for one reason or the other, the state has decided not to incorporate). Such agencies would typically have their own resources and expenditures, including some nonfiscal resources and expenditures resulting from their normal commercial or industrial activities. All these financial activities could be traced in specific budgets, annexed to the state budget but submitting to the same regulations. To allow performance monitoring, such agencies should also be required to maintain financial accounts and statements similar to those of normal commercial enterprises.

Statutory Bodies: Administrative entities which deliver fee-based services (e.g., education, health services) might be incorporated under a specific legal form, allowing them to be managed autonomously. Such statutory bodies could operate a specific budget covering their own receipts as well as a government subvention, if necessary, on the resource side, and their operating expenses on the other, while keeping these budgets integrated within the state budget.

In both cases, however, only the budget law would be empowered to create and abolish both annex budgets and statutory bodies, as well as to authorize their revenues and expenditures.

Nonearmarking

4.14 Other than in the situation described above, the major instance of earmarking concerns the funding of territorial budgets. As will be described in Chapter VII, these subdivisions of the state budget are funded mainly through a procedure of earmarking shares of general resources. This mechanism, justified by the need to enlist the cooperation of territorial administrations in the collection of national taxes, creates only minor rigidities for the ex ante allocation of budget resources (during budget preparation). Indeed, territorial expenditure budgets are determined independently of the earmarking process, and revenue sharing coefficients vary accordingly. Rigidities would obviously increase dramatically if these coefficients were frozen, as is sometimes suggested. Considerable rigidities, however, occur at the execution stage as each tenge of resources is parceled

Box 4.1: The Budget Preparation Process

The preparation of the state budget follows the schedule outlined below:

Phase 1: Preparation of the budget outline. The staff of the Cabinet of Ministers (Department of Finance, Labor and Monetary Circulation) takes the lead in formulating the Budget Directive. The Department formulates a first outline of the budget based on: (i) a review of the state of execution of the ongoing budget, changes in taxation and administrative structures, evolution of the external debt; and (ii) a number of policy assumptions regarding the evolution of the minimum wage and of some key prices. This first outline is used to determine the base parameters of the budget, particularly the target level of the deficit. These parameters are submitted for the approval of the Prime Minister and the Cabinet. They issue the Budget Directive to the Ministries and territorial administrations.

Phase 2: Formulation of the draft budget. Following this overall directive, the Ministry of Finance issues detailed instructions to all budget entities regarding the calculation of their budget request, particularly as to the use of expenditure norms and incremental factors, and the estimation of fiscal revenues. The formulation of the draft budget starts. Each budget entity calculates its own *smeta* and centralizes it with the finance department of its level of subordination. The latter checks that the *smeta* have been established according to the set methodology. In parallel, the Ministry prepares its own estimate of expenditure requirements administration by administration, and of prospective fiscal resources. After various rounds of centralization, budget requests are verified and consolidated by the Department of the Budget of the Ministry of Finance. If a gap arises, as has been the case in recent years, the latter Department cuts back the requests and brings them back within the expected resource envelope, according to an order of priorities among types of expenditure (four categories are untouchable, including wages). This process also enables the revenue shares earmarked to the various levels of administration to be defined (see Chapter VII). The draft state budget is submitted by the Ministry of Finance to the final arbitration of the Deputy Prime Minister in charge, who submits the final draft of the state budget to the Prime Minister and the Cabinet, which finalizes it.

Phase 3: Approval of the budget. With the endorsement of the President, the republican part of the budget is sent to Parliament. Under the new Constitution, the two chambers discuss the proposed republican budget in separate sittings (Art 54.2), and approve it in a joint sitting (Art 52.2). The authority of Parliament is, however, attenuated by Art 61.6 of the Constitution under which "laws reducing state revenues or increasing state expenditures can only be submitted to Parliament if accompanied by a positive resolution of the government." The republican budget determines the sharing rates of the various national taxes with territorial budgets.

Phase 4: Detailed allotments. On this basis, the Ministry of Finance initiates the final budget allotment process. As concerns republican administrations, detailed allotment is carried out by the Ministry of Finance. As concerns territorial budgets, the Ministry of Finance informs the financial departments of the various oblasts of their revenues and invites them to establish their final budgets on this basis -- as well as on the basis of guidelines regarding expenditure priorities by nature of expenditure. The final oblast budget is, nominally at least, approved by the oblast maslikhat: the latter budget contains revenue sharing rates with subordinate administrations. The finance department of the oblast proceeds to the detailed allotment of the part of the oblast budget relevant for oblast-level administrations and invites the rayon-level finance departments to finalize the budgets of their jurisdictions. A similar process ensues at the rayon level.

The process of establishing territorial budgets is described in further detail in Box 7.3.

out among a myriad of subbudgets in function of set coefficients rather than according to the priorities of the moment.

4.15   This report will argue (see Chapter VII) that this situation might best be remedied by the development of meaningful local government and by the accompanying separation of state and local budgets, each with its own source of funding. It will also argue that once tax collection has become sufficiently reliable, the authorities may be well advised to do away with the earmarking of revenue shares to the territorial strands of the state budget and to fund their activities through normal appropriations from the national budget. In addition to its benefits for budget management, the latter would have the advantage of putting fiscal practices in line with budget realities.

C. Formulation of the Budget

4.16   The procedures which lead to the budget formulation are not conducive to selectivity. The essential features of this process have been highlighted in Chapter III. In the first round of preparation, the expenditure budget is established through passive centralization of norm-based expenditure requests, which serve to calculate the "input requirement" of a given supply of public services. This process takes place with little consideration for the overall macroeconomic framework in which the budget is expected to be executed, and with little apparent conscious effort to program expenditures according to a clear set of policy priorities. It is only in a second round that budget envelopes are cut down to size to fit within the prospective resource envelope. But not even at that stage do programmatic priorities emerge. Instead of modulating the necessary cuts by expenditure functions, the final choices are largely made by nature of expenditure (e.g., wages, operating supplies, transfers). Of course, the current budget classification does not facilitate such functional choices: at the final stages, proposed budget appropriations are presented only by sectoral "complexes" and by economic nature, but not by functions, which considerably obscures the decision-making process. The various administrative steps involved in preparing the budget process are summarized in Box 4.1.

4.17   A fundamental transformation of the budgeting approach is now in order -- a transformation under which the budget would become the main instrument of government economic policy in terms of overall macroeconomic management and in terms of microeconomic resource allocation. In such a setting, the *physical* resource allocation which still operates on its own inertia must be subjugated to the *financial* direction of the budget. The following paragraphs describe how this should be done. In a nutshell, a revamped process would involve bringing the competing financial requirements of public services and programs within expenditure envelopes defined (eventually within a multiyear framework) on the basis of government macroeconomic and policy priorities. New budgeting techniques, starting with an improved budget nomenclature, should make it possible to orchestrate this selection on the basis of functional priorities and efficiency considerations.

Macroeconomic Framework

4.18   The need to integrate the government's budget program within a larger macroeconomic framework is increasingly well understood, but only small progress has been made in the direction of this integration. The Department of Finance, Labor and Monetary Circulation incorporates such considerations in the preparation of the initial budget directive, based on discussions with the Ministry of Finance and the Ministry of Economy. The scope of this exercise, however, remains quite limited and focuses almost exclusively on determining an overall deficit and the conditions under which it can be financed domestically (with foreign borrowing taking place by and large outside the budget). The government currently lacks the active capacity to place budget developments within a broader context, such as relating revenue outlook to the evolution of the various tax bases (and the latter to other aspects of government policy in the field of price or distribution policies) and relating expenditure programs to external balances. In addition, no framework is in place to include government financial policies within a medium-term plan. This is the framework within which many fiscal decisions (e.g., investment, indebtedness) unfold. In 1993-94 the Ministry of Economy launched the preparation of a medium-term indicative plan, which would have achieved this, but the effort fizzled out with the many staff changes at the Ministry. Efforts are also under way, with USAID technical assistance, to build up a revenue projection capacity within the Ministry of Finance. At the moment, however, fiscal authorities must stumble along, with the IMF programs as the only benchmarks for their decisions.

4.19   It would be helpful to resume the effort started two years ago to prepare a medium-term indicative program, based on a comprehensive macroeconomic framework, and to insert the annual budget programs within that framework. An administrative capacity needs to be established to that effect, with adequate staffing and equipment. Locating this capacity within the Ministry of Finance may possibly offer the best guarantee that such a macroeconomic programming exercise will be closely integrated with the determination of the country's financial priorities.

4.20   A multiannual macroeconomic program (covering three years, at least) could also form the basis for formulating *medium-term expenditure programs*. Even if the budget is established on an annual basis, the activities of the state are of a more permanent nature and the implications of its fiscal policies commonly extend beyond the ongoing year. A number of expenditure items, for instance, have their own dynamics: (i) the wage bill is influenced by the organization of career structures and the patterns of administrative organizations; (ii) investment expenditures are typically executed over several years, with annual installments of variable orders of magnitude; (iii) these expenditures in turn generate more permanent operation and maintenance requirements; (iv) the public debt service has its own profile, determined by the volume and terms of public borrowing; and (v) similarly, on the revenue side, some important categories of revenues may be transitory (e.g., privatization proceeds) while others may have downward trends (e.g., central bank profits) or upward trends (e.g., royalties from new exploitation of natural resources). A medium-term budget framework would enable the fiscal authorities to prepare the required strategies, associate sector ministries to these financial concerns, and apprise the business community and the general public of the government's stance, allowing them to plan their activities accordingly. Several OECD countries, such as Australia, Denmark, Germany, Sweden, and the United Kingdom actually base their annual budgets on published medium-term expenditure plans.

Expenditure Programs

4.21   At the moment, expenditure priorities emerge, a posteriori as it were, through the bottom-up consolidation of *smeta* (see Box 4.1), transforming a key policymaking process into a mere accounting exercise. At no point does one witness the active pursuit of sectoral and subsectoral priorities. Taking the preparation of the 1996 budget as an example, the circular sent by the Ministry of Finance in August 1995, inviting spending agencies to engage in preparatory activities, limits itself to reminding them what the 1995 allocations were but is mute as to policy guidelines for the next year; nor were these priorities defined in any specific term in the initial budget directive from the Cabinet. Further evidence of this is the fact that sectoral ministries hardly participate in the process. They might seek to defend their own *smeta*, but they generally would not assume leadership in the elaboration of other budgets within their sectoral purview.[4/] The entire preparation process therefore comes across as a number-shuffling exercise rather than as a debate on the objectives to be attained, the programs to be executed, the activities to be carried out, and the means available to do so. Even at the final stage, when the draft budget is approved, what budget debate there is appears to be

---

[4/]   Some ministries may be more enterprising than others in this respect. For instance, the Ministry of Health has issued directives to the territorial health departments for the preparation of the 1996 budget.

limited to arguments about broad expenditure aggregates (e.g., wages, office supplies) rather than about programmatic priorities. An alternative budgeting cycle is proposed in Box 4.2.

Box 4.2: An Alternative Budgeting Cycle

An effective budget formulation procedure should seek to ensure that all the parties concerned are aware of the policy framework and financial conditions under which the budget is prepared, and that they understand which priorities have been established, which activities have been selected and the performance that is expected in carrying them out. The process should therefore involve all the administrations concerned by the budget -- both on the revenue and on the expenditure side, central and local departments, decision-makers as well as administrators in an active consultation process. Procedures established by the Ministry of Finance should define precisely the various steps of budget formulation, the responsibilities of the parties concerned, the work to be undertaken, the output expected, and the timetables which need to be met.

The budgeting process may be divided into *4 phases*, divided into *14 steps*, for a total duration of *32 weeks*.

Phase 1 - *Budget Forecasting*: This phase would involve analyzing short- and medium-term economic and financial trends, elaborating the macroeconomic framework of the budget, and defining overall budget aggregates (revenue and expenditures), based on revenue projections and expenditure profiles. This phase would aim at delineating fiscal priorities and options in order for the budget to ensure the normal operation of the state, while contributing to growth (among other things, through judiciously selected investment programs) and to financial and monetary stability.

This phase would last for *8 weeks* and involve *4 steps*: elaborating economic and fiscal projections, defining options, setting budget envelopes, and formulating the budget circular from the Ministry of Finance to spending and revenue departments.

The process would be conducted by the Ministry of Finance and would lead to the presentation by that Ministry of a first draft budget for the approval of the Cabinet. On this basis, the Minister of Finance would issue the budget circular.

Phase 2 - *Elaboration*: This phase would involve the preparation by spending departments of budget proposals, based on the budget circular and under the leadership of the relevant sectoral ministries, the formulation of proposed sectoral budgets by the sectoral ministries, and submission of the latter to the Ministry of Finance; and arbitration between conflicting claims on budget resources, first between sectoral departments and the Budget Department (budget conferences), second between the Minister of Finance and sectoral colleagues, and finally, if necessary under the authority of the Prime Minister.

At the end of this phase, which would last *10 weeks* and involve *three steps* (preparation, budget conferences, political arbitrations), the draft budget is technically finalized.

Phase 3 - *Budget Law*: This phase would involve the preparation of the draft budget law by the Ministry of Finance, its approval by the Cabinet, and its adoption, after debate and amendment, by Parliament.

This phase may take *10 weeks* and cover *4 steps*: draft budget law, approval of the draft by the Cabinet, discussion and adoption of the budget law by Parliament, and promulgation of the budget law by the President.

Phase 4 - *Budget Effectiveness*: During this phase, the Ministry of Finance actually puts budget appropriations at the disposal of spending agencies.

This last phase would necessitate *4 weeks* to perform *3 steps*: detailed allotment of budget appropriations, establishment of budget fascicles by spending agency, and, as the case might be, transitory funding of spending agencies based on already approved allotments if the budget has not been approved on time by Parliament.

4.22   The first step toward transforming the budget into an act of public expenditure programming would be to open the budget preparation process with the determination of initial *sectoral envelopes*, based on official anticipations of macroeconomic conditions during the forthcoming fiscal year. These initial envelopes would reflect government policies as to: (i) the relative share of fiscal operations in the economy; (ii) within the resources devoted to the state activities, the sectors that the authorities will want to emphasize in view of their economic role or social impact (e.g., health, education, the environment); and (iii) within these sectors, the types of activities that the government will seek to promote during the forthcoming exercise (e.g., preventive health care, pest control). The purpose of the budget process would then be to identify and select the most appropriate implementation techniques to achieve the objectives set within given envelopes. The role of initial envelopes would not be to cast the budget into a final pattern from the beginning but rather to establish benchmarks for the ensuing selection process. Once they have been approved by the Cabinet, these envelopes would be conveyed to the sector ministries with instruction to conduct the preparation of the budget in their sectors within these given parameters. Sectoral ministries would typically be expected to further apportion these envelopes among their subordinate institutions with similar instructions.

4.23 The above procedure would reverse current practices in two ways. First, sectoral ministries would be closely associated with the financial and economic concerns of the government and with the implementation of the fiscal strategies to deal with these concerns. Second, and perhaps more important, this step would serve to weaken the pervasive "entitlement mentality" which expenditure norms have created among public services. In this new setting, the point of the budgeting process would no longer be for public services to send resource requisition forms to fiscal authorities. Instead, it would be for public services to first convince their peers within subsectors and sectors, then the rest of the government, that their activities deserve a higher claim on scarce resources than others. In other words, the burden of proof would be reversed, forcing spending units to justify their existence in relation to policy objectives and their performance in pursuing these objectives.

4.24 The initial envelopes and subenvelopes would be expected to evolve during the budgeting process under the influence of the competitive process and to lead to a sequence of *arbitrations*, and, as a result also, to a *sequence of structural choices* regarding the detail of sectoral policies and the existence, size, and structure of public services: structural choices first within the spending departments, second between the spending departments and the relevant departments of the Ministry of Finance, then through budget conferences between the Ministers, and finally under the leadership of the Prime Minister to resolve the final disputes.

4.25 In many sectors such new practices may require that sectoral ministries gain full authority over their field of responsibility. Their introduction will therefore need to proceed in parallel with the reform of territorial budgets described in para. 4.15 and in Chapter VII, Section D.

Norms

4.26 With the competitive procedures just described, expenditure norms, at least as currently designed, should naturally fall into disuse. At the moment, spending agencies are to use norms or guidelines for most, if not all, of their items of expenditure. These norms were established under central planning, and at times date back to the 1950s. Extremely detailed fill-in tables serve to calculate these norms. Owing to the recent high inflation and volatility of relative prices, however, some norms have become impossible to calculate using established methodologies, and the Ministry of Finance has accepted that spending agencies use another, simpler approach and prepare their *smeta* by adjusting "last year's" spending by some approved incremental factors.

4.27 The recourse to norms -- which reflect the requirements of the services more than those of their users -- bears testimony to the persistence of the central planning mindset. For example, for hospital expenditures, the norms consider such factors as the number of beds and the number of bed-days, the number of visits to polyclinics attached to hospitals, and the expenditure on bottled milk given to mothers. It is easy to see that if Oblast A has in the past been given more funds than Oblast B, then it might have more beds and so also might be able to have more bed-days, and it might also be able to spend more on bottled milk; but it might not have more visits to the polyclinic. In the same way, for ambulance services, the relevant factors include the number of stations, the number of staff, and the number of people given first aid at home. Again, Oblast A might have been given more funds than Oblast B in the past and so might have more stations and more staff, but it would not necessarily treat more people at home.[5]

4.28   Under any circumstances, measuring actual needs through norms is likely to remain an evasive objective. First, calculating accurate norms would require the use of detailed cost-accounting techniques for the estimation of unit costs reflecting the variety of actual situations on the ground. Second, also because of this variety, the use of uniform norms, rather than fostering equity may achieve the reverse.[6] Third, when used systematically, expenditure norms tend to rigidify cost structures, as they remove any incentive to improve performance through technological or organizational changes.

Budget Rationalization Methods

4.29   Efficient budgeting would require that each expenditure be justified *on its own merit*, not according to any ready-made formula. This, however, does not preclude the use of objective criteria in budget formulation. A number of methodologies are commonly used in this respect to rationalize budgetary choices. Some radical methodologies have been tested in different countries, including zero-base budgeting and the planning/programming/budgeting system (PPBS). These radical approaches have more often than not yielded mixed results, owing, in large part, to the sheer

---

[5]   Other examples of factors affecting norm expenditures include the following:

(a)   For wages for staff in hospitals for mentally handicapped people, there is a set number of approved staff per 100 beds and there are set wages for staff.

(b)   For wages for schoolteachers, rayons use approved student-staff ratios to determine staff needs and they use approved wage rates to determine wage costs.

(c)   For heating costs in hospitals, there is a formula which allows for the age of the building, its volume in cubic meters, and the coldness of the area in which it is situated.

(d)   For blankets in hospitals, a total number of approved blankets is set depending on the number of beds, and then the expenditure norm is the cost of replacing a standard allowable annual percentage for write-offs.

(e)   For subsidies to public transport companies for discounted fares, estimates are made of average ticket prices, average numbers of journeys per person, and number of people eligible for discounts.

(f)   For subsidies on cinema losses, an estimate is made of the estimated income from spectators at standard ticket prices and of the estimated expenditure of screening in the oblast.

(g)   For subsidies on heating, the budget allowance is the difference between the estimated cost of supplying heat -- these estimates allow for items such as the total number of square meters of housing, the number of days on which heating will be required, and also average temperatures -- and the revenue that would arise if units of heating were sold at the standard tariff.

[6]   See Alex MacNevin and George Ianev, *Intergovernmental Fiscal Relations in Kazakstan*, USAID, July 1995. This report provides a number of illuminating examples of the vicissitudes of the expenditure norms. The norm "class complex" is one of them. "The logic of using class complexes stems from the size of the country and the disparities in population density. In densely populated areas like Almaty, for example, there are 35-40 students in a class, whereas in a small village out in the rural areas, there are only 5-7 students in a class. Hence per student (operating costs should) differ significantly. To smooth out this difference, the oblast finance departments take an average class size and calculate all expenditures associated with it. The result is a "class complex" (which is applied uniformly per grade level). This methodology has managed to accumulate a number of supporters at the local level and is sympathetically looked upon by the Ministry of Finance. In our opinion it introduces great inefficiencies (as) it seems to favor financially the rural areas with small classes and punishes the cities -- undesired redistribution."

complexity of implementing them. But some of their insights could be applied in Kazakstan without excessive difficulty and would bring in critical improvements in budget management. Box 4.3 illustrates this point with the recent experience of Australia.

Box 4.3: The Impact of Budget Reforms in Australia

The Labor Government which took office in Australia in 1983 was more successful than most in cutting back public expenditures, which had been one of its main political objective. Central government expenditures were brought back from about 28 percent of GDP in 1983-84 to 24 percent in 1989-90. The government's political will was obviously key to this success. It does not account for it entirely, however. After all, other governments came to office during the 1980s with a proclaimed desire to "roll back the state" and achieved much less than that. It took, for instance, almost a decade for the British Conservative Government which came to power in 1979 just to reduce government expenditures below the level that existed when it took office (and even that achievement was short-lived as expenditure began escalating almost immediately thereafter).

The decisive factor in Australia's experience was that political will was supported by effective reforms in budgeting, among which the following stand out:

(i) *Expenditure Control Framework*: "At the outset, the Government established the Expenditure Review Committee (ERC), which consists in a permanent group of senior ministers, which examine the budget implications of all policy proposals. The creation of the ERC has been accompanied by a greater emphasis on the sound justification of such proposals. [...] It has been aided by an expenditure control framework based on a system of three-year *forward estimates* which describe the cost of continuing all existing policies and programs."[1] This has had two positive consequences. The first one is to concentrate the attention of decision-makers on strategic questions regarding substantive changes in expenditure programs, and away from the minutia of the calculation of baseline estimates. Second, spending agencies have been forced to think systematically about the medium-term consequences of their proposals. "The close consideration of the outyear consequences of all decisions has also reduced the magnitude of the government's budget task, with the forward estimates for the budget showing a real decline as the government commenced preparation of its 1987, 1988 and 1989 budgets. This contrasts with the previous approach where, between one budget and the next, the typical experience was for the estimates to blow out, with major savings required just to restore (the previous year's levels)."[1]

A further factor has been, starting in 1987, the consolidation of the expenditure portfolio from 28 to 16 and the introduction of *portfolio targets*. "The requirement (by the ERC) that each minister who proposes spending measures should put forward proposals to fully offset their cost by a complementary set of savings proposals in the same portfolio is a powerful device for giving spending and savings proposals a similar prominence in budget formulation."[2]

These measures were combined with efforts to devolve responsibilities to spending departments, in particular "the consolidation of all salary and administrative expenses into a single *running cost* appropriation whereas previously there had been 20 or more items [...]. The estimates of running costs are part of the forward estimate system and are maintained in real terms less an efficiency dividend of 1.25 percent [...] This formulation of running costs estimates has replaced the previous interventionist and incremental approach so that Finance no longer needs delve into the details of an agency's operation seeking minor savings."[1]

(ii) *Financial Management Improvement Program* (FMIP): These reforms were complemented by initiatives under the FMIP launched in 1984 to shift the emphasis of budgeting from dollar inputs to program outcomes. Two salient features of this program are the obligation made to evaluate all spending programs at least once every five year, and the rule that every new spending proposal needs to be accompanied by a description of arrangements made for its evaluation, as well as of the evaluation criteria against which the performance of the proposed programs will be assessed.

[1] "*Australia's Budgetary and Financial Management Reforms*," Michael Keating and Malcolm Holmes, Governance: An International Journal of Policy and Administration, Vol. 3, No. 2, April 1990; [2] "*Managing Budgetary Outlays 1983-84 to 1992-93*," Geoff Dixon, in Federalism and the Economy, Brian Galligan, Editor, Federalism Research Center, Australian National University, 1993.

From Zero-Base Budgeting to Distinguishing Ongoing and New Programs

4.30   Zero-base budgeting was designed in reaction to the "entitlement" mentality. It consists in budgeting every year from a "clean slate" by requiring all spending agencies to justify fully and rank all their expenditure programs. It has often proved overly ambitious administratively to carry out such an exercise every year. Such a comprehensive review may best be undertaken at regular intervals and may be quite in order after the momentous changes Kazakstan has undergone. A scheduled approach -- one sector after the other -- has proved less administratively demanding and therefore more likely to be carried out in a meaningful manner. This is the approach which the United Kingdom has been following over the last few years. A more modest but potentially highly effective version adopted by many countries (e.g., France, Australia) consists of routinely distinguishing among current expenditures between ongoing programs and new measures, and only requiring full justification for the latter. "Ongoing programs" correspond to the minimum appropriation required to maintain public services at the level of the previous year (equivalent to a service's previous year's appropriation less non-renewable appropriations plus adjustment to needs). New measures are the expenditure programs proposed to be introduced with the new budget. This methodology has often been misconstrued as a license automatically to roll over ongoing programs, but properly used it can highlight some of the trade-offs and policy choices facing the authorities (e.g., which ongoing programs should be to cut down or terminated, if the government is to afford this or that new initiative).

From PPBS to Performance Criteria

4.31   PPBS seeks to shift the emphasis of budget decisions from the input requirement to the actual results of budget programs, measured in quantifiable units. It consists of organizing all government programs around a certain number of quantitative program objectives (eradication of tuberculosis, for example), in order to determine which combination of institutional measures and budget resource allocations across agencies would maximize the attainment of these objective. Although the PPBS idea possesses some obvious attractions, the difficulties involved in structuring budgets along programmatic lines when spending agencies are organized, in the best of circumstances, along functional lines have often been insurmountable. A slightly more modest approach, involving program budgets limited to a few key sectors, has been more successful. Some sectors, such as education, health, or communications, where the definition of programmatic objectives, efficiency, and performance criteria is more straightforward, lend themselves more readily to program budgets.

4.32   More prosaically, most individual categories of expenditure can and should be evaluated according to defined performance objectives, measured by quantitative indicators. Such an indicator can simply seek to curb the evolution of a service's operating budget at constant prices. More refined instruments can be elaborated to measure cost-effectiveness. Even expenditure norms have been effectively used in some countries, such as France. But, unlike Kazakstan, such norms were then used in an attempt to curb some categories of costs (e.g., hospital costs) and not to set a minimum standard of services.

4.33   Whichever methodologies Kazakstan chooses to adopt to rationalize budgetary choices, no methodology should involve automatic budget allocation. Rationalization methodologies serve to *support* the evaluation of budgetary choices, not to substitute for them. Budget evaluation methodologies should be determined for each exercise by the Ministry of Finance and conveyed in the budget circular from the Ministry to the spending agencies.

D. Public Investment Management

4.34   The impact of improved procedures will only be felt over time as public investment gradually recovers from the present trough. Public investment has virtually ceased in Kazakstan. It collapsed from over 6 percent of GDP in 1992 to close to nil in 1995. In view of the depth of the fiscal crisis, it is understandable that the country prefers to use its meager resources for today's consumption rather than setting resources aside to look after tomorrow's consumption. And yet, such a situation cannot last. No example exists of a country recovering and sustaining growth without investing in its social overhead capital.

4.35   Adequate procedures are also required to rationalize public investment budgeting. Investment programming is not distinct from budget programming in general, but is only a particular aspect of it. Investment programming uses similar approaches and needs to be closely integrated within the budgeting function.

4.36   During recent years public investment activities have been shifted around among many protagonists (see Box 4.4), in the absence of a conclusive discussion of the role and nature of public investment management. In practice, this function has fallen in abeyance. This function now needs to be rehabilitated, and the government's leadership role in setting policy objectives and priorities, making strategic choices, and selecting particular projects needs to be reinstated and organized. The remainder of this section reviews the functions that need to be performed, and this being clarified, the institutional framework in which such functions might be carried out.

Public Investment Process

4.37   Public investment management typically involves four specific phases: planning, programming, budgeting, and implementation. The *planning* phase aims at elaborating medium-term economic and social perspectives as well as development strategies and policies, at both the macroeconomic and sectoral levels. Such an exercise would, in the first place, identify global sectoral priorities and the resource envelope at the disposal of the country to fulfill them -- or that it could reasonably expect to mobilize. In a number of industrialized countries (e.g., Japan, France) and in most developing ones, this phase results in the preparation of a *development plan* which is discussed and approved by the government.

4.38   The *programming* phase seeks to transform the objectives of the plan into operational programs for the state, balancing the respective recourses to policies and investment. As is true for all aspects of government action, a piecemeal approach to public investment decisions is unlikely to foster an efficient achievement of national priorities and sectoral strategies -- hence the importance of a *public investment program*. During the programming phase, emphasis is put on identifying, selecting and preevaluating investment proposals. In this framework, sectoral ministries would be invited to prepare multiannual investment programs, identifying and evaluating proposed projects on the basis of common methodological guidelines for the economic and financial evaluation of projects, including the recurrent cost requirements they engender. The consolidation of investment proposals into a national public investment program (PIP) should follow the same competition/selection logic as proposed for the budgeting process. At the consolidation stage, programs and projects proposed by the sectors are screened on the basis their prospective efficiency in reaching development objectives, their consistency with sectoral strategies, their scores on economic and financial evaluation criteria, the status of preparation of feasibility technical studies, the proposed financing schemes, and also the

Box 4.4: The Tribulations of the Economic Transformation Fund

The Economic Transformation Fund (ETF) was established in 1992 to finance investments for: (i) integrating national infrastructure (such as power grids and pipelines); (ii) vertically integrating production at the national (instead of FSU) level; (iii) converting the military complex to civilian activities; and (iv) completing ongoing capacity expansion projects. The Fund's resources were also used to extend financial support to politically or socially sensitive areas, such as city-factories or coal mines. The Fund benefited from a special levy on enterprises' operating expenses and lent its resources for 2 to 10 year maturities and at a 6 to 12 percent interest rate. The resources of the ETF amounted to more than 2 percent of GDP in 1993. But they rapidly declined thereafter owing mainly to sequestration measures by the Ministry of Finance. The special levy was eventually abolished with the April 1995 tax reform.

The Fund was initially put under the authority of the Ministry of Economy, which started developing four priority National Programs (nonferrous metals, food and consumer goods industries, transport and telecommunications, and energy) and a number of other smaller programs. Actual lending operations were handled by the Department of Capital Accumulation of the National Bank. In practice, rational allocation procedures were never firmly established and the Fund was largely used at the discretion of the Cabinet of Ministers. Not surprisingly, the ETF's loan portfolio quickly became delinquent and suspicions arose as to the proper utilization of these resources.

In September 1994, the government established the State Development Bank (SDB), which inherited the portfolio of the ETF, together with the staff of the Department of Capital Accumulation of the National Bank. The SDB became operational in March 1995. Under the SDB, the procedures for managing the ETF remained essentially unchanged.

(i)   ETF was funded through budget appropriations. The 1995 budget appropriated 9 billion tenge. However, by September 1995, only 1.2 billion tenge had been released.

(ii)   The SDB had no independent capacity to evaluate and monitor investment lending. As concerns its public investment activities, the SDB operated on instructions of the Cabinet of Ministers, specifying project by project the borrowing entity and the selected suppliers. The role of the SDB was limited to executing disbursement transactions, without as much as checking on the actual delivery of the goods or works.

(iii)   As regards private sector financing, the SDB's discretion was greater; little such financing actually took place, however.

It quickly appeared that some SDB functions, particularly as regards the on-lending of foreign credits, duplicated those of the State Export-Import Bank (EXIM). In August 1995, a decision was made to merge the SDB, together with the ETF portfolio, into EXIM. Finally, in April 1996, the government agreed to assume financial responsibility for the inherited ETF portfolio by putting it on a managed fund basis and taking it off the balance sheet of EXIM. EXIM is planning an internal review of ongoing projects and outstanding portfolios. In view of what is known about the quality of the latter, it would seem that a thorough external audit would be more in order.

status of execution of other investment projects in the sector. Final arbitration and approval are given by the Cabinet of Ministers.

4.39   Public investment programming should not be a one-off affair driven by the formal requirement of producing a programmatic document every so many years, but should be a continuous process of project identification and evaluation, leading to a "pipeline" of projects, constantly refined and updated, which will feed into the state budget or which can be submitted for the consideration of foreign financiers.

4.40   The final decisions as to the initiation, phasing, and modulation of investment projects should be made within the *budgeting* framework. The selection of a particular project within the PIP would authorize a particular budget appropriation, but would not mandate it or substitute for it. The appropriation decision itself would be made, taking into consideration, among other things: (i) the macroeconomic conditions under which the budget is expected to be executed; and (ii) the particular aspects of the project proposal, including the economics, the total costs, the nature of the goods and public works to be procured, the financial structure, and the recurrent cost requirements. To permit its phasing and monitoring, each project should be identified by a specific budget line.

4.41   The responsibility of financial authorities does not stop there. Whereas *implementation* of investment projects (e.g., studies and consultations, procurement) takes place under the responsibility of spending agencies, additional precautions need to be taken to avoid the types of implementation slippage that all too easily plague investment projects, particularly cost overruns. In addition to the normal budget execution procedures, executing agencies would therefore also be required to establish project accounts to monitor with a greater degree of precision the financial *and physical* execution of each of the projects under their supervision. The ministry in charge of the investment budget monitors the utilization of investment appropriations in relations with progress in implementation and prepares, on a regular basis (annually) and based on the reports of executing agencies, a report to the Cabinet of Ministers on the execution of the PIP, laying out the results obtained, the observed slippage, and the corrective measures proposed.

Institutional Framework

4.42   To prepare for the necessary resumption of public investment, Kazakstan should first establish proper institutional frameworks for public investment programming and execution. At the moment, such frameworks do not exist. Box 4.5 presents some of the available options for organizing this administrative function. Two criteria should guide the authorities in espousing any particular arrangement. First, whatever vehicle is eventually chosen to execute financial transactions related to public investments funded by domestic and external resources (Treasury or EXIM), the responsibility for determining development priorities and selecting those projects which fit them best will remain the government's own; at the same time, the government will also remain accountable to Parliament for the efficient execution of projects. Second, investment programming needs to be closely integrated within the budget function. The Ministry of Finance therefore plays a central role from the planning (definition of macroeconomic and fiscal strategies) to the implementation stages (outlays monitoring).

4.43   Whether some of the public investment management functions should be shared with other agencies, such as the Ministry of Economy, is an open question. Two further considerations should be noted in this respect. First, it would be hard to justify -- in the light of what was said in Chapter I about the need to reduce the number of Cabinet-level agencies -- maintaining a Cabinet-level agency if investment programming were its sole substantive function. Second, a critical mass is more likely to be achieved quickly if expenditure programming capacities are built in the one agency, which undoubtedly requires them (i.e., the Ministry of Finance), rather than in two separate ones.

Budget Nomenclature

4.44   Rather than illuminating the terms of the budgetary choices (as a good nomenclature should do), the nomenclature that Kazakstan inherited from the Soviet system and used until 1996 has tended to obscure these terms. This nomenclature of expenditures is structured in four levels:[2] (level 1)

---

[2]   By comparison, the expenditure nomenclature of the Soviet Union budgets distinguished: Groups (*Gruppy*), Divisions (*Razdely*), Chapters (*Glavy*), Sections (*Paragrafy*), and Articles (*Stat'i*). The Groups reflected "complexes," the institutional arrangements for expenditure allocation: national economy; sociocultural measures; defense; state authorities bodies; etc. Chapters within the Groups showed expenses by ministries and departments (for example, Chapter 82 in Group 1 was the Ministry of Agriculture). Sections referred to expenditures on certain kinds of enterprises and organizations (section 8 "Zone agrochemical laboratories" in Chapter 82). Articles indicated various (earmarked) types of expenditures used for financing enterprises and organizations (Article 24 "State planned capital investments of khozraschet enterprises," or Article 31 "Operational expenses").

Box 4.5: Institutional Framework for Public Investment Management

Organizing the institutional framework for public investment management consists in dividing up in an optimal way the four following functions: planning, programming, budgeting, and monitoring. Existing models come broadly into four categories.

Planning-Programming-Budgeting-Monitoring: The Republic of Korea offers the best example of a country which successfully integrated all four functions under the authority of an Economic Planning Board (EPB). The latter was established in 1961, incorporating the Budget Bureau (transferred form the Ministry of Finance) and the Statistics Bureau. EPB was later made responsible for price policy, fair trade, project appraisal, and the monitoring and evaluation of project performances.

A lesser and considerably less effective version of this model has consisted in a number of developing countries (including, for instance, many African countries) separating their budget into an investment budget, with a planning agency in charge, and a current budget under the responsibility of the Ministry of Finance. The typical pitfalls of this approach to public investment management are that planning agencies (i) are often more preoccupied with the allocation of resources than with the availability of these resources, causing macroeconomic imbalances, and (ii) have commonly tended to concentrate on new projects rather than on completing half-finished ones or ensuring funding for the maintenance of existing ones (as the latter is charged to a different budget).

Planning-Programming/Budgeting-Monitoring: A more effective arrangement is in place in Thailand where the National Economic and Social Development Board prepares indicative plans and investment programs but leaves the actual budgeting decisions to the Budget Bureau (in the Prime Minister's Office), which also monitors (together with the Ministry of Finance) investment implementation and evaluates their performance. A country like Tunisia, which for many years had operated a separate investment budget under its Planning Ministry, decided in 1995 to adopt a similar framework and reunified its budget.

(Planning)/Programming-Budgeting-Monitoring: OECD countries do not generally distinguish between the management of public investment and that of other categories of public expenditures. A number of these countries, including Japan, France, and the Netherlands, however, have found it useful to establish alongside the public finance management system a development planning capacity. The role of these agencies, however, is essentially one of research, consensus building, and recommendation.

---

complex or economic sectors (e.g., energy, agriculture and agroindustries, machine tool industry); (level 2) ministries and departments; (level 3) certain categories of enterprises; and (level 4) expenditures from earmarked revenues. At the final approval stage, the presentation of the budget presents only the first level of aggregation. In parallel, expenditures are classified in 20 categories of an economic nature.

4.45   Such categorization is a hindrance to the satisfactory understanding and analysis of the content of budget submissions. In particular, the concept of "complexes" was tailored to the requirements of the central planning structure but has no particular relevance to the present context. What is far more important, by its emphasis on the sectoral and economic characteristics of expenditures, this classification obscures the key element on which budgetary decisions should be based: namely, *their functions*. In many cases even the most detailed disaggregation fails to capture that notion. This is the case, for example, with most ministries which present only one *smeta* (classified by nature of expenditure) covering all of their operations. The *smeta* is therefore the ultimate irreducible level of budget information.

4.46   To redress this weakness, the Ministry of Finance has developed (with U.S. Treasury and IMF assistance) a more appropriate nomenclature based on a *functional and institutional* classification of fiscal operations. An economic classification will continue to operate in parallel. To facilitate the financial management of the budget, this new nomenclature was also made consistent with the chart of Treasury accounts. The sketch of this new nomenclature was used for the preparation of the 1996 budget in parallel with the old one. This first sketch still required further refinement, however, as it had been established by equating *smetas* with functions. Whereas the method is a useful approximation for "small" *smetas*, it proved too crude when *smetas* covered entire ministries. Also, the institutional nomenclature still stopped at the first hierarchical level of spending agencies, without detailing fiscal operations to the second and the third hierarchical levels.

4.47   A comprehensive new classification has now been adopted (Decree of the Ministry of Finance of May 26, 1996) which is applicable to the republican budget starting June 1, 1996. Beyond the advantages already noted of a functional presentation of government operations, this classification also points toward a rationalization of administrative structures. Indeed, the institutional classification substantially reduces the number of first-rank budget agencies, either as testimony of their recent elimination or by subsuming them into larger expenditure "portfolios." The next steps will be to: (i) make it the sole classification in use for the preparation of the 1997 budget, and to discard the previous one, in order to force all participants in the budget process to think in the new mode rather than in the old one; (ii) to put sectoral ministries effectively in charge of budgeting for these larger portfolios; and (iii) to extend the process to the lower tiers of the budget.

E. Approval of the Budget

4.48   Programming expenditure, rationally, would be in vain if the legal and institutional frameworks surrounding the use of public monies were not there to ensure that the budget is executed as planned. This touches on a fundamental aspect of the budget as an instrument of economic management. The budget is not merely a declaration of intent; it is a law which *provides and authorizes*. By contrast, the state budget of Kazakstan, as defined in the Organic Law of December 17, 1991 or by common practices, appears more like a cash flow forecast (see Chapter V).

4.49   This notion of authorization is essential, however. The budget authorization creates both rights and obligations for spending as well as revenue departments. It allows spending departments to use public monies, but only for specific purposes and within clear limits. It authorizes revenue departments on an annual basis to levy all (and nothing but) the taxes and other mandatory payments provided for by the budget law, following the provisions of the specific legislation establishing these revenues.[8] The notion of authorization would also be the source of the legal accountability (sanctioned by criminal penalties) which accompanies the use of public monies (for example, the obligation of tax collectors to collect all assessed revenues, or the interdiction made to obligate expenditures without a proper appropriation).

4.50   These basic and commonly accepted notions were well recognized under the Soviet Union, but they seem in many case to have fallen into disuse with the breakdown of the financial discipline that accompanied the demise of central planning. These notions are not trivial in the context of Kazakstan today. As is documented in Chapter V, it is not uncommon for spending agencies to spend beyond their appropriations or even without an appropriation, or, conversely, for appropriations to remain unexecuted without being formally rescinded.

---

[8]   In Anglo-Saxon countries, however, revenue legislation provides sufficient legal authority for government to raise revenues. The budget law, in these cases, "provides and authorizes" only expenditures, the revenue side of the budget constituting only "approved estimates." Note also, that the United States budget legislation separates the expenditure approval process in two different steps: the "authorizations," which give agencies the authority to carry out a certain number of well-defined activities, and the "appropriations," which provide funding to agencies for the purposes defined in the agencies' authorizations.

4.51   The new Organic Law of the Budget which the Ministry of Finance plans to prepare should restate forcefully the binding nature of budget appropriations. Although detailed regulations and denominations may vary from one country to another, the rule in most countries is for *regular appropriations* to be restrictive: they set the *maximum amount* that spending agencies can obligate and pay for the *purpose intended* by the budget law within *one fiscal year*.[9/] Some categories of expenditures may require more specific appropriations. There might, for example, be *indicative appropriations* for funding mandatory expenditures (e.g., public debt service, pensions) which cannot be evaluated with full precision at the beginning of the fiscal year.[10/] These cases should, however, be restrictively defined in the budget law. Countries with strictly annual budget cycles may have specific appropriations for multi-year public investments, distinguishing for each project between *obligation appropriations* (the authority given to obligate the full amount of a project) and *outlay appropriations* (the authority to pay that part of the investment project executed that falls due during the fiscal year).

4.52   Different types of appropriations may therefore coexist. But the point is that appropriations define and restrict the conditions under which public monies can be used. Such rigor is the only basis on which to ensure that the execution of the expenditure budget correspond to plans, hence to reassure the authorities that the efforts at rationalizing expenditure programming suggested above would not readily be circumvented during the implementation phase of the budget -- the phase discussed in Chapter V.

F. Conclusions

4.53   Considerable progress still needs to be made for budgeting to transform itself into a process of selection among competing claims for resources within a finite resource envelope. The formulation of a new Organic Law on the Budget, currently at the draft stage, provides an excellent opportunity to establish such new principles. The main priorities identified above are the following:

(i)   Establish firmly the *authority of the budget and its control* over the finance of the state by:

-       Refraining from creating new extrabudgetary funds and including within the budget framework all the resources of budget entities, including the current "nonbudgetary resources" and the proceeds of foreign borrowing

-       Reasserting the legal authority of the budget law, supported by appropriate criminal sanctions.

[9/]   In the United States, where the Constitution does not specify that appropriations should be annual, only the authority *to obligate* under regular appropriations from the federal budget lapses with the fiscal year, not the authority to make payment for expenditures that are already obligated. The federal budget also has *multiyear appropriations* which authorize obligations beyond the current fiscal year. Many other countries and, most U.S. states and local governments, however, have outlay-based appropriations, under which the authority both to obligate and also to pay lapses with the fiscal year.

[10/]   In the United States, these are usually covered by *permanent appropriations* which Congress does not need to vote every year (again, owing to the absence of an annual limit on obligations).

(ii)   Shift from the current microeconomic and supply driven approach to a *macroeconomic and functional approach* by:

- Inserting the budget within a short- and medium-term macroeconomic program and establishing to that effect a macroeconomic forecasting capacity within the Ministry of Finance

- Formulating the budget on the basis of expenditures envelopes reflecting macroeconomic projections and policy priorities, and budget rationalization techniques and performance criteria, rather than expenditure norms

- Putting sectoral ministries in charge of elaborating budget submissions covering all budget entities within their area of responsibility and formalizing arbitration mechanisms at all stages of preparation, culminating with budget conferences at the political levels for the final decisions

- Fully implementing the new functional and institutional classification of fiscal operations as the sole budget nomenclature for the republican budget starting in 1997 and extending it to territorial budgets.

(iii)   Reinstate within the government, and preferably within the Ministry of Finance, a capacity to program and manage public investment.

CHAPTER V. BUDGET EXECUTION

A. Introduction[1]

5.1   Budget execution systems should help achieve three objectives. First, it is necessary to ensure *conformity* of expenditures with the approved budget at two levels: (i) at the sectoral level, budget execution must faithfully reflect the presumably optimal allocations among the various public functions financed by the budget, allocations that are entered in the budget as voted; and (ii) at the macroeconomic level, budget execution must also permit a strict containment of the amount of the budget deficit. The second objective is that the execution system must have a built-in measure of *flexibility* to allow the authorities to tailor expenditure volume to macroeconomic possibilities and, where necessary, redeploy expenditures during the course of the year to take account of economic developments and changes in receipts inflow. Finally, the execution system must ensure maximum *security* against fraud, misappropriation, and the risk of squandering part of the appropriations.

5.2   Kazakstan's expenditure execution system does not meet these requirements. First, the practice of "sequestering" expenditures creates such discrepancies between authorized and actual expenditures as to render meaningless the budget voted by Parliament. Furthermore, the financial choices made under the pressure of circumstances generally lead to the sacrificing of those categories of expenditures which should serve to prepare the future of Kazakstan, such as public investment or the new social programs required for dealing with the hardships of transition. In contrast, the present hand-to-mouth behavior favors wage payments, enterprise subsidies, and, more generally, the maintenance of existing structures (Section B). Second, the control of the deficit is more apparent than real, owing to the accumulation of payment debts (*zadolzennost*), at the republican level as well as the territorial levels (Section C). Third, the absence of procurement regulations opens the door to favoritism and corruption. And finally, the government's poor payment record has led an increasingly large number of suppliers to require advance payment, with the attendant risk of embezzlement through payments without counterpart (Section D).

5.3   A number of reforms are currently being implemented to improve this situation. The establishment of a Treasury Department within the Ministry of Finance is beginning to allow control over the use of budget appropriations and will soon permit a global control over the flow of expenditure obligations. The next order of priorities should involve, among other matters:
(i) subjecting the abuses of budget authority (particularly obligating expenditure without corresponding appropriation) to criminal penalties; (ii) moving from a global to an itemized control of expenditure obligations (*rasrechenie*); and (iii) introducing competitive procurement rules and outlawing (and systematically driving out) conflicts of interest in government contracts.

---

[1]   This chapter deals exclusively with the execution of expenditure budgets. Paragraphs 5.36 and 5.42 and Box 5.4 are taken from *Fiscal Management in Russia*, A World Bank Country Study, March 1996 .

B. Conformity between Authorized and Actual Expenditures

5.4   The budget preparation process is deemed to have identified the expenditure priorities as the basis for allocating the available resources to the most efficient economic or social uses. The objective of conformity between the actual budget and the approved budget is therefore to ensure that this optimal allocation is achieved. This is far from the case presently in Kazakstan.

Arbitrary Execution of the Authorized Budgets

5.5   A comparison of the projected and actual budgetary expenditure figures shows that actual expenditure matches the budget estimates only in random cases. There is a wide discrepancy between budgeted expenditures and actual expenditures. On the one hand, some expenditures exceed the amounts originally authorized (see Table 5.1 which compares the actual budget outcome in 1994 with the revised budget approved in July of that year). For example, budget execution data for the oblast of Kostanai for the first seven months of the year show that the appropriations for the entire year had already been drawn on by 137 percent for the operations of state agencies, 112 percent for those of security agencies, 118 percent for the culture and information sector, and as much as 168 percent for resources channeled to "various enterprises," a chapter for which the resources originally authorized were admittedly very low.

Table 5.1: Execution of the Revised 1994 Budget
(in millions of tenge)

	REPUBLICAN			TERRITORIAL			STATE		
	Rev. Budget	Actual	%Realiz.	Rev. Budget	Actual	%Realiz.	Rev. Budget	Actual	%Realiz.
General Public Services	22,747	12,197	53.6	2,356	1,778	75.5	25,103	13,975	55.7
Defense	8,987	3,761	41.8	0	15	n.a.	8,987	3,776	42.0
Public Security	5,657	4,759	84.1	980	1,241	126.6	6,637	60,006	90.4
Education	2,920	2,310	79.1	10,495	11,235	107.1	13,415	13,545	101.0
Health	2,837	1,247	44.0	8,248	7,840	95.1	11,085	9,087	82.0
Social Security and Welfare	9,866	1,705	17.3	9,500	2,851	30.0	19,366	4,556	23.5
Housing and Utilities	2,065	50	2.4	198	3,684	1,860.6	2,263	3,734	165.0
Culture, Leisure, Religion	1,893	958	50.6	770	1,072	139.2	2,663	20,302	76.2
Energy	40	47	117.5	0	1,281	n.a.	40	1,328	3,320.0
Agriculture	9,389	5,344	56.9	274	657	239.8	9,663	6,001	62.1
Industry	697	360	51.6	0	8	n.a.	697	368	52.8
Transport and Communications	2,390	761	31.8	6,254	1,281	n.a.	40	1,328	3,320.0
Other Economic Affairs	3,776	6,991	185.1	65	1,556	2,393.8	3,841	8,547.8	222.5
Miscellaneous	10,717	7,788	72.7	88	126	143.2	10,805	79,145	73.2
Total	83,981	48,278	57.5	39,228	38,206	97.4	123,209	86,484	70.2

Source: Ministry of Finances

5.6   On the other hand, other expenditures may be made during the year that were not initially provided for or authorized. An example in 1994 is "resources transferred to territorial budgets in application of reciprocal accounts" (i.e., loans converted into grants). Another example, in the first quarter of 1995, is "loans made to enterprises," representing expenditure of over 1 billion tenge during the quarter, although there is no such appropriation.

5.7   Under most headings, expenditure items are being implemented only in part or not at all. Examples from the 1994 republican budget include expenditures related to the consequences of the Semipalatinsk nuclear explosions, the Chernobyl disaster and the ecological disaster in the Aral area, with zero actual expenditure, against appropriations totaling 6.5 billion tenge (i.e., 6 percent of the total expenditure estimates of the 1994 budget as amended in July). In the case of investments, actual expenditure was under 1 percent of the total estimates of over 2 billion tenge.

5.8   The average rate of execution of the 1994 state budget (70 percent for the overall state budget, 57 percent for the republican budget) masks such wide disparities that there is evidently no real relationship between the approved and the actual budgets. This is not an acceptable situation, since *it renders the entire budget process pointless* and makes it impossible to reap the fruits of applying budget constraints to government agencies and forcing them to prioritize expenditures as part of the budget preparation.

Defective Control of the Deficit

5.9   Compliance with an overall deficit level compatible with the country's macroeconomic objectives is as important in budget execution as compliance with sectoral choices. This objective is achieved only apparently, at present. As we have seen, the practice of sequestration applied at the republican budget level causes outlays to be aligned on receipts volume, increased by the accepted deficit (financed by various means shown on the resources side of the budget under the heading "means of covering the deficit"). In this way the deficit on a cash basis is indeed contained, but often artificially. Frequently, only the monetary consequences of expenditure operations (i.e., outlays), not the expenditure itself, are being deferred or prevented. This leads to an accumulation of payment arrears.

5.10   In the case of territorial budgets, no cash deficit is in principle permissible. But in practice large deficits are run during the course of the year. These deficits inevitably have to be absorbed by the republican budget, at least in part.

5.11   Significant as these cash deficits are, they reflect only part of the situation, since only expenditures actually paid are recorded. In addition, large payment arrears are also contracted by the budgets, chiefly for wages and salaries. According to Ministry of Finance data based on systematic surveys of the oblasts, total debt as of August 15, 1995 came to 6.6 billion tenge -- about half of it accounted for by wage and salary arrears. A similar survey of the agencies financed by the republican budget found a lower debt volume, of the order of 325 million tenge. Aggregate debt as of August 15, 1995 for all budgets taken together thus came to 7 billion tenge (equivalent to about 2 percent of GDP over the period).

Sources of Discrepancy

5.12   Both underutilization and overutilization of budget appropriations reflect a failure to comply with the budget as voted. Three different types of causes have been at play: (i) overestimation of the revenue budget; (ii) the nonbinding nature of budget appropriations; and (iii) the practice of sequestration (see Box 5.1). These three sources of discrepancy are different in nature and call for separate remedies.

Discrepancy between Budgeted and Actual Revenues

5.13   Up until 1995, the budget clearly overprojected revenue estimates. In 1994, for instance, actual receipts represented only 75 percent of the budget projections. This situation, which was not limited to Kazakstan but affected most of the former Soviet transition countries, is explained primarily by underlying macroeconomic instability, and particularly by the unexpected growth of payment arrears across the economy. With regard particularly to budget receipts, many very large enterprises awaiting privatization or restructuring built up large tax debts. Many individuals whose salaries are no longer paid, or are paid only in kind (barter), have also built up debts of various kinds to the state. Another factor was no doubt the desire not to enter overly pessimistic data in the initial budgets with regard to the continued contraction of national product, and the resulting tendency to exaggerate the expected receipts.

5.14   The situation now seems to be improving. For the first time in 1995, a more cautious approach to revenue budgeting was adopted. In the event, revenue collected for the state budget actually exceeded budgeted amounts (197 billion tenge in actual revenues as compared to 192 billion in the original budget and 187 billion in the revised budget).

5.15   But economic uncertainty will not go away. As the country opens up and develops its natural resource-based activities, it will become more prone to the fundamental instability of international commodity markets. *Cyclical funds* are a device often used to permit the adjustment of the budget to an uncertain macroeconomic environment. This device involves providing that certain appropriations are not available automatically but only if the macroeconomic situation conforms to the favorable scenario. Otherwise, the appropriations are not made available to the agencies.

Expenditures without Budget Appropriations

5.16   Government instructions confer certain rights to spend without prior authorization. Two main expenditure categories show substantial utilization of resource allocations without any corresponding appropriation:

Box 5.1: Sequestration vs. Default

The spread of the term *sequestration* throughout the former Soviet Union has been the source of some confusion as to the nature of the budget control instruments being applied. In practice, it often simply covers *default*.

Sequestration is a term which designates the cancellation or withholding of appropriations. Sequestered funds are no longer available for obligation. The absence of obligation control in the Soviet tradition makes it difficult to prevent spending agencies from obligating expenditures. In most cases, therefore, the only instrument available to fiscal authorities is their control of the release of funds for the payment of expenditures. It is at that stage, rather than the obligation stage, that the "sequester" is applied. When the expenditure has already been committed, as will commonly be the case for wages, insurance-based social benefits, utilities, and debt service, this practice causes the government to *default* on its payment obligations. No rational budget management system condones such delinquency.

(i) *Loans to enterprises*. As was indicated earlier, expenditure under this heading was relatively high as of the end of first quarter 1995. The argument put forward in defense of such practices is to protect the confidentiality of such loans, and therefore limit the demand for such interventions. This is unlikely to be effective. On the contrary, the risk of proliferating demand and of pressure to expend is more likely to stem from the lack of selectivity in loan approval conditions which confidentiality affords. In any case, whenever a precedent arises, the information is likely to be quickly disseminated through informal channels to other potential beneficiaries.

(ii) *Setting up of reserves* (expenditures of the Committee for Material Resources). Expenditures under this heading also seem very high. The setting up of reserves, provided for by a directive of August 20, 1992, takes place even if no appropriation has been made. While it is possible that urgency can justify, in very narrowly defined circumstances, a flexible expenditure procedure with retroactive appropriations, nothing can justify the total lack of expenditure appropriations.

5.17   These exceptions foster more systematic overutilization. As we have seen, beyond these two exceptional examples of large unauthorized expenditures, much more frequent cases of expenditure in excess of appropriations are to be found in republican budgets and, above all, in territorial budgets. It can of course be difficult to predict the required amount of an appropriation even in the case of compulsory expenditures. This traditionally applies to court judgments, for example. But, as was discussed in Chapter IV, except for certain specifically designated cases where exceptions are justified by the nature of the expenditure, the ceiling on the appropriation budgeted for a given expenditure category should constitutes a legal authorization which cannot be exceeded unless the authorization itself is amended.

5.18   The desire to strictly enforce this basic principle of budgetary law has led some countries (e.g., France and the United States) to impose severe criminal penalties for noncompliance, severe enough to deter any violation in practice. In Kazakstan, where the law on the principles of the budgetary law is currently under discussion, it would be advisable to include a provision prescribing that any person found guilty of committing or abetting any actions that result in the collection of public receipts or the execution of expenditures without authorization by the budget law shall be liable to criminal penalties. This provision could be repeated each year in the budget law itself.

The "Sequestration" Practice

5.19   In a bid to bring the budget deficit back under control on a cash basis, if not a commitment basis, the authorities introduced in 1992 a mechanism to contain cash outlays within the available cash resources in the Treasury's account. This mechanism is commonly, if improperly, known as "sequestration" (see Box 5.1). An instruction of February 20, 1995 clarified the various administrative practices which had developed in this respect since 1992 and sought to define a formal basis for dealing with payment requests coming from spending agencies.

5.20   The rules established involve funding priorities that give short shrift to the priorities identified in the voted budget. Furthermore, these rules are both unclear and contradictory. They establish two types of priority orders, which are difficult to reconcile among themselves and are even more difficult to reconcile with the official budget, for example:

(i)   First, a number of broad categories are designated as priority items, involving, in decreasing order of priority, wages, social security contributions, stipends, pensions, the celebration of the 150th anniversary of the poet Abai, ...

(ii)   Second, the instructions define a separate method of prioritizing outlays by apportioning percentages of receipts by periods of five days. For example, "during the second and fifth period of five days, wage and social security contributions are paid up to 90 percent of available receipts. Stipend outlays are made in equal parts during the second and third periods of five days, up to a maximum of 10 percent of available receipts."

5.21   The key point is that any rationality which the budgeting process may have had is brushed aside in favor of a summary apportioning among broad natures of expenditures, and apparently random distributions among the various institutions financed by the republican budget. The proliferation of unclear or inapplicable rules results in a sort of ad hoc execution of budgetary expenditures, reflected in the deferral of all expenditures not absolutely essential in the short-term -- such as investments and new social programs -- that have not yet turned into well-entrenched entitlements.

5.22   This situation deprives the republican budget of all capacity to prepare, on the economic side, for the necessary infrastructure investments and, on the social side, for redeployment of the essential subsidies to provide better cushioning of the impact of the transition on employment. By attending to the most pressing demands, it sanctions long-established customs -- for example, by assigning essential priority to wages and salaries without due attention being paid to selecting those units which are to continue to be financed by the budget and those which are not. In the same way as the build-up of payment arrears for the public enterprises, the practice of sequestration makes it possible -- but only in appearance -- to defer indispensable structural choices. This takes place at the cost of underinvestment and neglect of maintenance, which rapidly becomes both dangerous and costly.

5.23   "Sequestration" is a budgetary practice that must be replaced by orderly budgetary procedures. Such procedures may involve measures which would make original appropriations unavailable to spending agencies (through impoundments and ultimately rescission of appropriations) following shortfalls in revenue collection or other macroeconomic considerations. But these procedures need to be carefully regulated to protect the integrity of the budget process, as will be discussed in Section C.

5.24   At a more basic level, however, it is not acceptable for the state to put itself systematically and deliberately in a situation of payment suspension. Therefore, it is necessary to establish appropriate mechanisms for programming cash flows, and for containing expenditures at the earliest stage (i.e., before obligation), within prospective cash availabilities. This is the role of the obligation control procedures described below (see paras. 5.25-5.31).

Controlling Expenditure Obligations

Rationale

5.25   To prevent such difficulties, countries have developed systems to monitor and regulate expenditure obligations (see Box 5.2). Under such systems, expenditures are controlled to the maximum possible extent upstream of payment, enabling the necessary appropriations to be blocked out in the accounts, so that the amounts that remain available for new expenditures are known at any given time. The concept of obligation unfortunately does not form part of the Soviet public finances tradition and has not yet been defined in Kazakstan. There is no mandatory procedure subjecting decisions with a financial impact to prior financial control, even in the form of simply posting and assessing the amounts involved.

5.26   This situation leads precisely to the lack of coherence and arrears build-up referred to earlier. Because of the current lack of prior controls, enterprises apparently very often refuse to deliver goods or services ordered before receiving payment from the agency. The agency, however, then runs the risk of improper payment if a service paid for in advance is not actually performed. These two situations -- late payment and premature payment by government -- both exist in Kazakstan and are equally unsatisfactory.

5.27   Bringing expenditure obligations under control therefore appears to be the top priority for improving budget execution. Such control of expenditure obligations can be performed in a variety of ways. It can be carried out in a very detailed manner and for each expenditure

---

Box 5.2: The Notion of Expenditure Obligation

An obligation represents the legal commitment of an expenditure by an agency of the government to another party. While the concept of payment or outlay is an obvious one, since it corresponds to a disbursement, whatever its origin, the concept of obligation is much more difficult to pin down and in fact depends on the various expenditure categories that can be identified.

In principle, it is necessary to define, for each expenditure category and each ministry or government agency with budget and accounting autonomy, a key factor, prior to the taking of the decision, that creates an expenditure obligation.

-    In the case of goods and services purchases, the obligation occurs before the contract is concluded, which implies that all contracts are transmitted to the financial agency responsible for posting the obligations to the accounts, before being notified to the other contracting party. In the case of non-contract purchases, an order voucher, supported by a quantities/cost estimate, must be transmitted.

-    Similarly, in the case of personnel expenditures, several types of decisions help create obligations (i.e., rights of wage-earners). Generally speaking, individual recruitment or regrading decisions trigger obligations and therefore verification of availabilities in terms of appropriations or jobs; collective decisions are subjected to more comprehensive monitoring.

(*itemized control*). It can also be performed much more globally, based on aggregated data, where it is not considered important to monitor the financial impact of each individual expenditure decision but rather to group the expenditure authorizations for each ministry or agency together under specific time periods (*global control*). In principle, however, only itemized obligation control can effectively guarantee that expenditures will not overrun the limits set. It is too late to do this at the time of payment, since failure to pay can only generate debts and perhaps even legal proceedings or major difficulties for the suppliers that are not paid.

Introducing Obligation Control

5.28   A first step away from "sequestration" practices and toward establishing a global obligation control mechanism has been taken recently in the context of the creation of the new Treasury system. This new system moves away from day-to-day payment decisions on the basis of cash availability to introduce, at the republican level, periodic releases of funds (or *warrants*) by the Treasury Department to spending agencies, based on prospective cash flows. These warrants represent the maximum outlays that spending agencies can present for payment on a specific line item appropriation during a certain period of time. These warrants are currently extended on a bimonthly basis. As the fiscal situation stabilizes, the Treasury intends to bring the duration of these warrants to a month. The intention is also to extend the warrant system to territorial budgets before the end of 1996. This important innovation provides a basis for spending agencies to plan and modulate their expenditure obligations within a set envelope and over a defined period of time, although an admittedly short one. There is still no guarantee that they will actually do so, however.

5.29   The next step will be to supplement the warrant system with global obligation control mechanisms that ensure that spending agencies do not commit funds beyond the warrants available to them. The ongoing computerization of Treasury operations should facilitate this evolution. The purpose would still be essentially a financial one. It would aim at containing the aggregate flow of obligations within approved appropriations, rather than checking the validity or efficiency of individual expenditure decisions.

5.30   For this global control by the Treasury to be fully effective, however, it will need to be based on more refined, detailed upstream controls of each individual item of expenditure (or each group, in the case of small routine expenditures). It will therefore be essential to augment the control performed under the warrant system, on strictly financial grounds, with internal controls with more diversified objectives, within each spending agency. Such control will seek to ascertain first, in financial terms, that the expenditures authorized are compatible with the available appropriations, and second, that the operations financed conform with other expenditure regulations (e.g., on civil service or on procurement).

5.31   Actual procedures followed vary appreciably from country to country, depending on national traditions and the desired degree of constraint. International experience ranges between two poles (see Box 5.3). At one end, this prior control function can be placed entirely under the authority of each individual minister. This is the system in place in the United States. At the other end, prior control can also be exercised directly by the Ministry of Finance -- through specialized financial officers located in each ministry (or group of small ministries). This system is used France and in most francophone countries. The British system (also used in many Commonwealth countries) lies in-between these two poles, financial comptrollers being under the administrative authority of spending agencies but under the technical authority of the Treasury. A comparison of the two ends of the spectrum of intraministry financial controls (United States and France) shows the following advantages and disadvantages:

(i) The *United States system* gives spending agencies the responsibility and incentives to enforce the control and to look for savings opportunities or to put forward only regular expenditures. Given the fact that the same institution executes and controls expenditures, this system provides fewer guarantees of financial probity than one with checks and balances. Therefore, it needs to be accompanied, as is the case in the United States, by highly developed a posteriori audit capacities.[2]

(ii) The checks and balances of the *French system* offer the advantage of more rigorous control, since in practice the financial control necessarily extends from checking the availability of appropriations and correctly calculating the expenditures to assessing the timeliness and validity of the expenditures themselves. However, a diminution of

---

[2]   Even so, a report issued by the U.S. General Accounting Office in November 1989 concluded that "the Federal Government still lacks internal control and accounting systems necessary to effectively operate many of its programs and safeguard its assets. Moreover many of the weaknesses are long-standing and have resulted in billions of dollars of waste." (Manual on the Federal Budget Process, Congressional Research Service, Library of Congress, Washington, D.C., December 24, 1991.)

Box 5.3: Financial Control in France, the United Kingdom, and the United States

The financial control system set up in *France* in 1922 is based on a simple principle: to be valid, every financial decision taken by a minister must be approved by a financial comptroller, who is himself under the authority of the Minister of Finance. The latter thus exercises a kind of tutelage or supervisory jurisdiction over his colleagues. The comptroller is responsible for exercising a priori control, prior to the obligation. The comptroller approves the use of appropriations and can slow them down if he feels the appropriations are being drawn down too rapidly. He performs primarily a strictly financial check, verifying that the necessary appropriations are available. In practice, however, the comptroller's action extends to assessing the validity of the operation, in particular sanctioning cases presented for regularization where the expenditure has already been made (for instance, he will deny approval of a contract awarded without competitive bidding when such a procedure is required). Where the comptroller refuses to give his approval, the disbursement officer must refuse to pay.

The system in place in the *United Kingdom* is broadly similar to the one used in France. The only significant difference is that financial comptrollers belong administratively to the spending agencies. They are nonetheless appointed by the Treasury and remain under its technical authority. They are charged with implementing control regulations established by the Treasury, not by the spending agencies.

Within the federal government of *the United States*, spending agencies have much greater spending autonomy and can obligate funds within the warrants issued by the Treasury (the latter also operates all disbursement functions). The financial operations of an agency take place under the authority of a chief financial officer, who reports directly to the head of the agency. "The basic principle of internal control is that each agency should have primary responsibility for ensuring that its resources are used properly and efficiently. The Federal Managers' Integrity Act requires each agency to establish internal control systems, in accordance with standards prescribed by the Comptroller General, which provide 'reasonable assurance' that (1) obligations and costs are in compliance, with applicable law; (2) funds, property, and other assets are safeguarded against waste, loss, or abuse; (3) revenues and expenditures are properly recorded." (Manual on the Federal Budget Process, Congressional Research Service, Library of Congress, Washington, D.C., December 24, 1991.) Internal management systems are audited annually by the General Accounting Office.

---

competence can set in among spending agencies, which may feel only partly responsible for the financial outcomes of the decisions they make.

5.32 In brief, existing systems mix empowerment and rigor in various doses. In view of the serious nature of the current lapses in financial discipline within spending agencies, and of the underdevelopment of the audit expenditure function (see Chapter VI), Kazakstan should prefer to err on the side of rigor. A control system akin to the British model may offer just the appropriate dosage.

C. Need for Flexibility during the Year

5.33 To control the deficit effectively, the authorities must be able to adjust the original authorizations in the light of macroeconomic developments during the fiscal year, particularly the actual inflow of receipts. At a more detailed level, limited reallocation among the various ministries or expenditure sectors may also be required in light of actual appropriation drawdowns during the year.

5.34 The margins of flexibility must, however, be strictly defined. Unless the budgetary process is to become meaningless and cease to play an effective role in expenditure selection, the scope for amendment of the budget must be strictly limited. This can be achieved by subjecting such revisions to procedural formalities tailored to the impact of the amendments, in the following ways. Amendments to the detailed allotment should be acceptable at the initiative of spending agencies, but only within a single budget line item. Amendments with wider implications or deriving from new decisions should require the approval of the Ministry of Finance, or, if merited, approval on a government-wide basis. Finally, major decisions (those affecting the magnitudes of original appropriations) should be submitted to Parliament for advance approval, or to regularize necessary amendments decided on by the executive in cases of urgency. However, the procedures *actually* followed in Kazakstan suffer from a marked lack of clarity at all of the stages described above.

Role of the Legislative Branch

5.35   In principle, budget amendments have to be approved by Parliament. In practice, cases of budget adjustments approved by Parliament are rare. In addition to the two 1994 budget laws submitted to and approved by Parliament, six other vintages of the 1994 budget were adopted by the executive. This practice appears to confirm the existence de facto of a sort of right of administrative amendment of the budget not provided for by the Organic Law on the Budget. There is a clear need, borne out by international experience, to grant the administration some authority to reallocate appropriations. This autonomous power should, however, be strictly circumscribed in legal terms if authorization by Parliament is to remain meaningful. The executive branch might, for example, be authorize to freeze existing appropriations when circumstances justify it, but its authority to fund activities beyond original appropriations should be limited to emergency situations and subject to regularization by the legislative branch.

Role of the Government

5.36   Measures are gradually being taken to strengthen the role of the Ministry of Finance within the government: The draft law on the principles of budgetary law provides that new decisions with financial repercussions shall be submitted to and appraised by the Ministry of Finance before being approved by the government. In fact, current practice apparently assigns a key role in this appraisal process to the Office of the Prime Minister. There is a need, however, for a clearer separation of functions: financial and technical appraisal should be the sole responsibility of the Ministry of Finance, with the Prime Minister's Office responsible rather for arbitrating conflicting priorities and taking account of political constraints.

5.37   It is necessary to reassert the Finance Ministry's role in the preparation of governmental decisions with financial repercussions. Decisions made by the government during the year must not worsen the deficit or increase payment arrears. Internal procedures should be adopted to improve the consistency of ministerial and presidential decisions with overall fiscal policy. To ensure at least a minimum of fiscal discipline, the Ministry of Finance must be systematically informed of policy proposals by other government agencies that are likely to have fiscal consequences. Before any decision is made, these fiscal consequences should be systematically quantified by the proposing unit and the Ministry of Finance. If the cost of the proposal is greater than the available reserves included in the budget, compensating cuts in other programs or increases in tax revenues should be required. It is not uncommon in many countries for the Ministry of Finance to have considerable powers in such matters.

Internal Adjustments within Spending Agencies

5.38   The scope for spending agencies to reallocate funds within appropriation expenditure categories varies depending on the budget or period concerned. In the case of the republican budget, a radical change was introduced in December 1993. Until then, spending agencies enjoyed substantial autonomy and could reallocate appropriations within their agencies. Now, appropriations are broken down under narrowly defined specific items or "articles," and the practice of sequestration has intensified the partitioning of appropriations: agencies are financed by means of circumscribed funding allocations, each corresponding to a specific object, and reallocation to other items, even more urgent ones, is out of the question. Moreover, the refusal by the Ministry of Finance to accede to the wish of the expending ministries to maintain contingency appropriations available to meet urgent needs, makes the distribution of appropriations among the various agencies and the various items even more inflexible. The only course of action available to meet an urgent request by an agency is to "recall" appropriations already assigned to some other agency -- apparently a very delicate operation in practice. Territorial budgets, on the other hand, are characterized by greater flexibility in the reallocation of appropriations, at least in theory. In practice, with regard to the inadequacy of the appropriations, this flexibility is less significant as most of the funding is concentrated on a very small number of items, primarily those relating to personnel remuneration.

5.39   The budget crisis at the republican level as well as the territorial level clearly complicates the choices between two conflicting objectives: the need to allow room for maneuvering to appropriations managers, who are best placed to perform priority ranking, and the desire to concentrate the available resources on essential needs (managers can be tempted to favor less essential needs in the belief that payment of salaries will take place later in any event, in response to staff pressure).

5.40   A reasonable compromise may be to maintain a rigid distinction between the lines for personnel, investment, and maintenance, and those for operations (e.g., utilities, office supplies), and to monitor the latter only at the aggregate level. In this case, monitoring of appropriation drawdowns would continue to distinguish expenditure items following the existing nomenclature, but internal redeployments would be authorized at the spending agencies' discretion.

D. Need for Efficiency and Security of Budget Outlays

5.41   A third requirement with respect to budget execution procedures is to ensure the maximum possible security for payments (i.e., protection against fraud and misappropriation) and to ensure the efficiency of expenditure. In all countries the special risks that characterize not only large organizations but also public agencies, particularly the lack of a precise and readily available synthetic indicator such as profit, have justified the enactment of specific protective rules: strict separation of functions, allowing reciprocal control between officials; multiplication of internal pre-expenditure controls; specific capping procedures for large unit expenditures; and, in particular, the systematic requirement of competitive public bidding. Essentially, such procedures and precautions are not yet in place in Kazakstan or, indeed, in most of the FSU countries.

Need for Procurement Rules

5.42   Procurement rules -- designed to enhance expenditure efficiency -- are in the embryonic stage in Kazakstan. Little progress has been made in defining rules of procedure, notably recourse to competitive bidding, designed to boost expenditure efficiency (i.e., obtaining the best value for money). Calls for bids may sometimes be organized for certain expenditures, but such examples are rare and most purchases are made without systematic recourse to competitive bidding. Competitive or not, there are no standardized procurement procedures. Government agencies typically lack quarterly and monthly purchasing plans, competitive bidding requirements for contracts above certain levels, standardized specifications for procurement, and conflict of interest regulations.

5.43   A fortiori, no institution is charged with harmonizing procurement practices between different republican agencies and between the republican and territorial levels of government or coordinating and advising on public procurement issues across the board. Commissions could be established to provide guidance and advice to contracting agencies in order to improve procurement methods, to assist in the awarding of different types of contracts, or to study the impact of public procurement on various sectors. Coordination and harmonization could bring consistency, help prevent conflicts, and alleviate delays -- gains that are particularly obvious in cases of infrastructure cofinancing by different levels of government, where conflicting regulations may arise. The United States federal procurement system provides an example of decentralization with some coordination (see Box 5.4).

Box 5.4: U.S. Federal Government Procurement

Public procurement by the U.S. federal government can be undertaken by several agencies. Procurement of certain items, mostly large-volume purchases, is carried out by the General Services Administration (GSA), principally for domestic purchases. The Federal Supply Service (FSS) buys, stores, and distributes a variety of goods for GSA. Other agencies, such as the U.S. Agency for International Development (USAID) and the Department of Defense, also have contracting authority. GSA publishes a Government Supply Catalog that lists complete item descriptions, prices, the name of the winning bidder and the period of bid validity. Any item in the catalog can be purchased directly from the listed supplier at the listed price since GSA has already conducted a formal competition. Many purchases up to a value of $25,000 are made through the catalog.

Construction, goods, and commodities. According to Federal Acquisition Regulations (FAR), all U.S. federal government contracts costing more than $25,000 must be awarded competitively under the terms of the Competition in Contracting Act (CICA) of 1984. CICA requires "full and open" competition by sealed bids. All advertisements are published in the *Commerce Business Daily* (CBD), a publication of the U.S. Department of Commerce. Exceptions to the application of CICA must be justified in writing. There is a long list of exceptions under the classification "Other than Full and Open Competition." This list includes sole-source procurement. Prebid conferences at which general procurement information is made available to potential bidders are an important part of the process.

Consultants. Procurement by negotiation is allowed for required technical services. A request for proposals (RFP) is summarized in the CBD. The evaluation process for such services includes weighing and rating proposals, establishing a competitive range, and negotiating with firms scoring within the competitive range.

Cofinancing between the federal government and local governments. Source of financing determines which standards and regulations should apply. For instance, for construction of a highway crossing different states, federal funds and funds from these particular states will be used. The construction is subject to the Federal Highways Act. Federal standards of construction and federal regulations will apply.

Source: *Fiscal Management in Russia*, A World Bank Country Study, March 1996.

Strengthening Expenditure Controls at the Payments Stage

Existing Controls

5.44   In Kazakstan, as in all the former Soviet republics, control over final outlays was performed at two levels: (i) at the aggregate level, by the Ministry of Finance at the republican level and the territorial departments of finances at the territorial level (*finorgan*) when approving the regular releases of funds to the spending agencies' accounts at the National Bank; and (ii) on an item-by-item basis by the National Bank, which executes the payments. The bank's role is limited to physical execution of the payments, after checking that the necessary appropriation funds are available and undertaking various other checks (for example, correct description of the debtor).[3]

5.45   Unfortunately, payment control procedures are hardly defined, and therefore are barely enforced. Disbursement orders drawn up by spending agencies are transmitted without supporting documentation. This rules out detailed analysis and verification of the reality of the proposed expenditure. Moreover, neither the compulsory prepayment controls at the National Bank nor the disbursement officer's personal liability are spelled out precisely anywhere. No directive pertaining to the nature of prepayment controls is currently applied. Such a directive apparently existed under the Soviet Union but it was not reinstated in the legislation of Kazakstan nor has it been replaced (see Box 5.5).

Box 5.5: Data on Republican Budget Execution

Kazakstan's budget execution problem is a problem not of availability of data but rather of utilization of the data to monitor and improve the budget choices process. The 220 computer centers of the National Bank centralize the operations effected throughout the territory on a very regular basis and thereby enable the National Bank to draw up a detailed situation statement by major accounts, aggregated every five days. Consequently, all the budget execution data published by the Ministry of Finance derive from National Bank data, with more or less detailed reprocessing. The National Bank's information system furnishes information that is not only rich and reliable but also available relatively quickly, as follows:

-       Every five days, an overall statement of is sent to the Ministry of Finance consolidating all accounts with a common code in order to obtain figures for receipts inflow, operating expenditures, and investment expenditures.

-       Every month, based on more complete data, the Finance Ministry's Budget Bureau (General Directorate of the Budget) prepares a monthly monitoring table, amplified by data on the execution of territorial budgets transmitted by the Bank and verified within the Ministry by the Treasury Directorate.

-       Every quarter a detailed breakdown of the data available to the National Bank is published in a "Report on Execution of the State and Republican Budgets for the Quarter." The territorial budget execution data are also centralized, and the Bank's data on republican expenditures are compared with those of the spending ministries. The quarterly report is not available until a month and a half after the end of the quarter.

There is, however, little utilization of this information and no utilization of the most complete document -- the quarterly budget execution report.

---

[3]   This means, incidentally, that the restrictions in terms of item-specificity of the appropriations can be interpreted more or less strictly, depending on the instructions given to the various financial agencies at the oblast level.

5.46 Furthermore, a number of factors greatly complicate any attempt at establishing such control procedures. First, owing to the poor payment record of the state, suppliers now routinely insist that payment be made prior to delivery. This cuts the ground from under the chief consideration in controlling outlays (i.e., that the services for which payment is made have actually been rendered). Although retroactive checks can be applied, they will necessarily be unwieldy and will only with the greatest difficulty counter the risk of embezzlement.

5.47 The second critical risk to the security of payments arises from the complete decentralization of personnel management. As described in Chapter II, every one of the 40,000 or so budget entities recruits and manages its personnel independently, within its authorized positions. Similarly, it calculates and pays the wages of personnel on its own. Payment is made in cash on the basis of nominative lists. This absence of any centralization of personnel management is an invitation to fraud under many forms: misgrading of personnel, miscalculation of wages, 'ghost worker' schemes, enrollment of the same personnel on different payrolls, etc.

Reform Priorities

5.48 Some reforms have been initiated recently. The process of setting up the network of Treasury offices is under way. The Treasury offices have begun to implement strengthened prepayment control. Beginning September 1, 1995, all payment orders on the republican budget were to be vetted by these offices. While it is still too early to draw all the potential lessons from this control, it is already apparent that the defects mentioned earlier concerning the control performed at the National Bank centers persist: the control procedures are not defined sufficiently systematically and precisely. Moreover, in the transition phase, in which the Treasury offices continue to be separate from the payment agencies, the control circuit, already complex, becomes even more so.

5.49 It is therefore proposed that the mandatory controls performed by disbursement officers be defined more rigorously, by prescribing a nomenclature for each expenditure category of the required supporting documentation (see Box 5.6), as the basis for verifying that the internal procedures have been properly followed.

5.50 While these controls may seem very stringent, their purpose is to ensure consistency between the basic expenditure and its assigned budget utilization. Ensuring this conformity is a difficult task: it involves examining cost and quantities estimates, invoices, and so on, and comparing them with the specific categories covered by the appropriations. No single check can suffice to achieve this. The successive checks performed at the obligation and payments stages therefore have to comprise a coherent system, rounded out later by the a posteriori audits. These are discussed in Chapter VI.

Box 5.6: Prepayment Controls in France

In France, the controls performed by the disbursement officer under his responsibility comprise checks on:

- The quality of the work of the expenditure control officer or his delegate
- The existence of an adequate appropriation balance
- The validity of the obligation
- The external validity of the expenditure (i.e., complete justification by means of the necessary documentation)
- The accuracy of the settlement calculation
- The proper application of the lapsation rules by the financial control officer
- The absence of garnishment or distraint and other obstacles to

E. Conclusions

5.51   Whereas some initial steps have been taken, major progress is still required before budget execution mechanisms come to meet the three basic performance criteria laid out in this chapter: conformity between budget and actual outcomes, flexibility during the fiscal year, and the efficiency/security of budget outlays. The ongoing transformation of the Treasury system, with the assistance of the IMF, the U.S. Treasury, and the World Bank, have put many of the recommendations presented in this chapter on the authorities' agenda. The order of the day is now to proceed vigorously with their implementation. Key actions toward meeting the above criteria would be as follows.

5.52   As concerns conformity between budgeted and actual expenditures:

- Discontinue "sequestration" practices
- Extend the warrant system to territorial budgets
- Supplement this system with control mechanisms over expenditure obligations, first at a global level, then on an item-by-item basis
- Subject abuses of budget authority (e.g., incurring obligations without proper appropriations) to criminal penalties
- Include selected categories of expenditures within "cyclical funds," to be released only if certain macroeconomic assumptions materialize.

5.53   As concerns the flexibility during the execution of the budget:

- Restore contingency appropriations
- Clarify the respective authorities of spending agencies, the Ministry of Finance, the Council of Ministers, and Parliament in modifying the budget during its execution
- Formalize the authority of the Ministry of Finance in all government decisions which have financial implications
- Extend line-item autonomy for current operating supplies to spending agencies.

5.54   As concerns the efficiency of expenditures and their security against fraud and misappropriation:

- Adopt and enforce competitive procurement regulations
- Prohibit, and systematically root out, conflicts of interest in government contracts
- Centralize payroll management under the dual control of the Treasury and the proposed civil service agency (see Chapter II)
- Prescribe for each expenditure category a nomenclature of supporting documentation to be controlled before payment and forbid disbursement officers to disburse otherwise.

VI. BUDGET AUDIT AND EVALUATION

A. Introduction[1]

6.1   Budget audit and evaluation are particularly important in transition countries, for two reasons:

-    Reforms need feedback. Budget audits go beyond detecting and preventing individual deficiencies. They can also contribute to reforms in a positive way. First, they serve to assess the efficiency of existing programs and to highlight regulations that have become outdated and difficult and expensive to apply. Second, they can also help to identify and correct poorly designed or overambitious reforms. And third, they can further the dissemination of successful innovations and experiments.

-    Some of the previous control mechanisms have disappeared. Under the Soviet institutional system, controls of government agencies were in very large measure performed by the party -- without any legal basis. The sudden disappearance of external controls of government has created a real risk of fraud and misappropriation.

6.2   Audits can take different forms, ranging from *internal controls* to government agencies and geared primarily to the detection of irregularities, to *external audits*, designed to provide (to the legislative branch, the general public, and the executive branch itself) an independent assessment of probity of the executive's fiscal management, and to *budget evaluation,* intended rather to assess policy performances and possibly pave the way for any necessary reforms.

6.3   The current audit arrangements are poorly suited for these tasks. If internal controls exist under the State Committee for Financial Control (SCFC, or *Gosfincontrol*), the apparent proliferation of fraud and irregularities -- sometimes denounced or even penalized by SCFC -- reflects the weakness, rather than the strength, of existing controls, which are not sufficiently deterrent. Furthermore, the internal audits system has been reoriented to inspecting commercial enterprises rather than government departments.

6.4   As to external audit, the new Constitution provides for the creation of an Accounts Committee in charge of evaluating budget execution, which could serve as the locus of such a function. Unfortunately, as initially set up, the institution would lack the minimum autonomy which meaningful external audit requires. Finally, the budget evaluation function stills needs to be developed and organized.

B. Updating the Internal Control System

The State Committee for Financial Control (SCFC)

6.5   The SCFC is the main institution in charge of internal financial control within the government. It was created by bringing together all technical and financial inspection capacities previously spread across government agencies (see Box 6.1). It is organized at the national level and

---

[1]   Paras. 6.15, 6.19, 6.23-6.29 are borrowed from *Fiscal Management in Russia*, A World Bank Country Study, March 1996.

has offices at all levels of administration. Out of a total staff of 2,975, only 170 are assigned to head office, however. Most of the staff are assigned to the lower tier of administration (rayon level).

Box 6.1: Formation of *GosFinControl*

The pre-1992 situation: a multitude of internal controls in the various ministries. In Kazakstan, as in the former Soviet Union, internal control of government agencies was performed, until 1992, by internal inspection units within each agency. The units performed both a technical and a financial function and covered the agency's administrative services, as well as entities and enterprises subordinated to it.

The inspection unit attached to the Ministry of Finance -- KRO, or control and audit service -- had a more extensive role, its competence extending to all government departments and to the agencies and enterprises under their authority. The KRO already had a very dense network and a very large staff.

The 1992 reform. In October 1992 it was decided to elevate the KRO from a Ministry of Finance agency to a State Committee rank. This gave it the rank of ministry (and its chief the rank and prerogatives of a minister). On the one hand, this elevation of the financial inspection service to autonomous status served the objective of promoting control of government, necessary at a time when party control was disappearing. On the other, it is in line with the ongoing "centrifugal" process of proliferation of autonomous agencies in the Kazak administration, described earlier.

At the same time, it was decided to bring together within this new institution the functions performed until then by the various ministerial inspection units, except for those of a few security ministries such as defense, foreign affairs and interior, which retained their inspection units. In the latter cases, the financial inspection responsibilities are exercised jointly by the State Committee for Financial Control (SCFC) and the retained ministerial inspection units.

Excessively Broad Definition of the Functions of the SCFC

6.6   The SCFC's responsibilities are excessively broad and diverse, as is clearly evident from the resolution organizing it (October 7, 1994). This resolution (Article 1) defines the SCFC as "the central organ of the state apparatus responsible for the financial inspection of the financial and commercial activities of the ministries, state committees, agencies, territorial executive organs, entities with financial autonomy and organizations financed by the budget." This general mission covers both the conventional tasks of a financial inspection unit and other, more extensive, tasks of financial inspection of private enterprises in order to furnish assistance requested by the judicial authorities or to exercise control over certain operations.

6.7   *Conventional responsibilities.* Some of the many "functions" or responsibilities specifically identified in this resolution relate particularly to public agencies or entities that have received public funds. Thus, the resolution provides that the Committee "shall control and verify the effectiveness of off-budget and social expenditures against government funds within the limit of the receipts collected against government funds"; "periodically control the execution of the government budget in accordance with the instructions of the organs of state authority," and, finally, "draw up proposals designed to ensure economical, appropriate (in terms of budget allocation) and efficient use of state funds and of resources, including those in foreign exchange." In addition to these internal control functions, the resolution expressly provides that the Committee shall be "responsible for training the...other agencies in financial control techniques and for defining the necessary bookkeeping methodology to prevent the incorrect utilization of funds and their misappropriation."

6.8   *Other responsibilities*. These very broad terms of reference go even further, and some of the tasks listed extend well beyond the public sphere. The resolution states, for example, that the Committee's functions include "assisting the security agencies in combatting corruption and criminal behavior within the sphere of the economy" (point 5). Among the "functions" described under point 6, intended to facilitate achievement of these objectives, the Committee "shall, with the participation of other organs and exchange control authorities, control the records and accounting pertaining to foreign exchange and import-export operations and other operations connected with external economic relations, in order to verify their completeness and objectivity, and shall also control residents' foreign exchange operations."

6.9   The resolution similarly prescribes that the Committee, "within the limits of its competence and pursuant to law, shall control the proper use of government subsidies and financing, resources and assets, received pursuant to agreements, deriving from state-owned enterprises and organizations, and also, in connection with letters, statements and complaints by citizens, in private enterprises, agricultural concerns and other commercial organizations, including mixed-capital enterprises with foreign shareholders."

6.10   *Risk of dilution of the Committee's control activities*. This multitude of tasks creates first of all a risk that the Committee's activities, being spread too thinly, would be executed in a superficial or haphazard way. Given such a wide spectrum of tasks, it would seem impossible for the Committee to formulate a coherent work program geared to both deterrence and identification of needed remedies. The reports submitted by the Committee to the President of the Republic for 1994 and the first half of 1995 confirm this risk. They report a diverse collection of cases of misappropriation, abuse of authority, or simply poor management -- ranging from the theft of livestock in the former sovkhozes to the awarding of contracts which damage the financial interest of the state. These statements are supported by figures, precise only in appearance, without any ranking of the violations and other problems encountered or any analysis of their deep-seated causes and ways of remedying them.

6.11   *Risk that internal control will focus unduly on enterprises*. The heterogeneous nature of the agencies controlled by the Committee also creates a risk of skewed selection of the financial inspection targets (i.e., of the Committee tending to neglect the government agencies and public services -- which are more difficult to control for reasons of accounting technique and administrative sociology -- in favor of controlling enterprises, which are easier and in every respect more rewarding targets for the financial inspectors). The SCFC's organization structure indeed suggests that enterprises, rather than administrative departments, account for the bulk of the financial inspections performed (a reproach, in fact, voiced by the Ministry of Finance). Of the Committee's eleven departments, three perform general tasks (methodology, human and financial resources, miscellaneous matters) and only two are responsible for controlling the agencies financed out of budget funds (the budgetary agencies' inspection department, and the security and defense agencies' inspection department). In contrast, no less than six separate departments are devoted to inspecting the various enterprise sectors.

6.12   This implicit priority may have been understandable when the state owned most of the productive sector, or even more recently when large volumes of assistance were provided to enterprises in the form of foreign loan guarantees, import-export privileges, and directed loans. Certainly, the violations detected put into question the exact nature of the latter policies. For example, the report on the Committee's activities for the first half of 1995 (quoted in the press on this point) noted that a large part of the directed credits had not been applied to their intended purposes. But such priority has lost its justification now that budget assistance to enterprises is waning.

6.13   An unfortunate side effect of this quasi-exclusive attention has been to contribute to a proliferation of overlapping controls over enterprises. For example, the SCFC is authorized to reassess tax returns in parallel with the tax authorities, or to control foreign exchange operations alongside the central bank. This type of duplication of efforts is unlikely to be efficient. A division of roles is required which clearly defines those specialized controls that are left to specialized agencies and those of a more general nature that are left to the SCFC. Beyond efficiency considerations, such a division of roles would also foster a better protection of the rights of the persons or enterprises inspected.

Priorities for Strengthening Internal Control

6.14   Priorities for strengthening internal control would therefore appear to be as follows:

(i)   Shifting the focus of activities to controlling government agencies.

(ii)   Limiting more strictly the controls applied to enterprises.

In the case of state enterprises, the authorities should in the first place avoid the repetition of systematic and often routine inspections and retain only a smaller number of more widely spaced inspections.

Concerning private enterprises, these should be inspected by the SCFC only to the extent that they receive public assistance. Furthermore, the scope of these inspections should be restricted by specifying, at the time the assistance is given, the nature of the obligations entered into and defining, at the time of the decision to provide the assistance, the information requirements the enterprises have to meet. Private enterprises that receive earmarked subsidies would normally only have to demonstrate that these requirements have been fully met. This verification can normally be performed without requiring enterprises to disclose all of their books to the SCFC. Submitting a "utilization account" showing the uses made of the entirety of the expenditures financed by the subsidy should be a sufficient basis for control. Only if an enterprise fails to produce such a utilization account, or if there are reasonable grounds to suspect untruthful statements, should an inspection of the enterprise's complete accounts be allowed.

(iii)   Bringing the financial inspection within the Ministry of Finance. The above re-redirection of activities will be easier if financial inspection is reintegrated within the Ministry of Finance. This integration will make the follow-up action to the inspection more effective and help to strengthen the authority of the Ministry of Finance, an important objective in the current context of transition to greater consideration for the demands of budget management.

(iv)   Reducing staffs by abolishing the inspection units at the rayon level. As is seen above, a large proportion of the SCFC's staff work in the rayons. These units are small and their staffs have a narrow range of action. As a result, the controls they perform tend to become routine or overdetailed. Distancing the inspection units further from the local echelon would allow them to diversify the control themes and contexts and thereby enrich the inspectors' experience, and would also give them a role in the dissemination of successful practices. By retaining the financial inspection units only at the oblast level, it should be possible to control all the government agencies, public enterprises and subsidized private enterprises sufficiently closely, especially if the principle of periodic but in-depth controls is applied.

(v)   Developing separate technical inspection systems in each ministry. The possibility should be reopened for each ministry to set up a specific inspection unit with both technical and financial control tasks. This would enable the recommendations and requests from the financial inspection to be communicated more efficiently, and would ensure more genuine deterrence. It would hence be advisable to reconsider the reform implemented in October 1992 (see Box 6.1) and opt to set up a few high-caliber inspection capacities within key spending agencies.

(vi) Reaffirming the pedagogical role of internal audit. The reform recently implemented in Argentina and described in Box 6.2 demonstrates the importance of the advisory assistance role in setting up internal controls within each ministry, provided with management tools tailored to each specific situation.

Box 6.2: The New Internal Audit Organization in Argentina

Argentina's 1992 innovative Law on Financial Management and Control Systems of the Public Sector created the new internal control and audit agency, the National Syndic Office. This new office has jurisdictional and financial autonomy and answers directly to the Office of the President. The office is jointly managed by a head syndic, appointed by the President, and three adjunct syndics, nominated by the head syndic and appointed by the President. The National Syndic Office has the power to contract with institutions outside the public sector to carry out audits and evaluations of budget programs.

The National Syndic Office is charged with establishing norms and procedures for all internal audits and coordinating the internal audit offices operating within each spending unit. The National Syndic Office is organized under the paradigm of centralized norms and procedures and decentralized operations and implementation. The audit procedures developed by the Syndic Office are universal and integrated, covering all operation aspects of the spending unit including budget, financial, and economic assets. Audits consist of an ex post examination of all financial and administrative activities of the spending unit, based on the principles of efficiency in the use of resources and effectiveness in the attainment of the unit's objectives.

The head of each spending unit is responsible for conducting internal audits according to the norms prescribed by the National Syndic Office, using specialized personnel inside the spending unit who are exclusively assigned this responsibility. Internal auditors cannot participate in any way in activities they are supposed to audit.

The National Syndic Office is also charged with supervising compliance with accounting principles, which are established in cooperation with the external audit agency, the National Audit Office.

The National Syndic Office must report immediately to the Office of the President all infractions with negative consequences to the public sector. General reporting obligations are to the President, the National Audit Office, and the general public on a periodic basis.

Source: *Fiscal Management in Russia*, A World Bank Country Study, March 1996.

C. Creating an Independent External Audit Agency

The Accounts Committee

6.15   An effective system of budgetary audit needs more than internal inspection and control mechanisms. It needs an audit institution that is fully independent of the executive or that reports exclusively to the legislative branch of government, since the executive branch of government cannot be expected to be strict and objective about its own operations. This external audit institution is typically charged with final oversight and ex post auditing of all budget expenditures, to prevent and uncover inappropriate or fraudulent use of funds.[2]

6.16   Kazakstan has never had an independent ex post audit function in the budget process. Such an institution did not exist in the FSU. The Constitution adopted in August 1995 provides for the creation of an Accounts Committee, which may take over that function. To date, however, the initial steps taken by the authorities in developing that section of the Constitution[3] point more in the direction of the creation of presidential inspection, duplicating in many respects the functions of SCFC, rather than toward that of developing an external audit capacity.

6.17   On the one hand, the Committee would have little guarantee of independence. It is directly subordinated to the President, who can dismiss its members before their -- already quite short -- term of office of five years. Moreover, the Committee does not seem to have full control over its work program. On the contrary, the founding resolution envisages that it would carry out tasks set by the President. In addition, nothing is said of the publicity of the Committee's findings, either directly vis-à-vis the general public or indirectly through elected representatives.[4] And finally, the level and structure of the salaries of its members are determined by the President, and the latter's office also provides for the Committee's operating supplies.

6.18   On the other hand, the Committee wields powers so considerable that its members may compromise its review mission by involving it in executive decisions. The Committee's field of investigation includes state as well as private bodies, in which it even has the right to interfere through injunctions. Members of the Committee also have the right to attend sessions of Parliament, as well as meetings of the Cabinet of Ministers, the Board of the National Bank, and the boards of other government agencies. The Committee can even refer its decisions to police authorities to determine whether any crime is involved in the matters investigated.

Lessons from International Experience

6.19   There is a wide diversity of organizational structures and of objectives assigned to supreme audit institutions around the world. Despite this diversity, however, a few general features apply to most supreme audit institutions worldwide:

---

[2]   Detecting breaches of financial and accounting norms and exposing irregular practices represent the most common forms of control of the supreme audit institution, according to members of the International Organization of Supreme Audit Institutions (INTOSAI), which is a United Nations organization with headquarters in Vienna, Austria.

[3]   Presidential Resolution of April 19, 1996.

[4]   The only case where the founding resolution envisages the Committee's communicating to Parliament is as part of the Government's report on the execution of the budget, which it concludes.

(i) The external audit institution's independence from the executive branch of government is indispensable to the effective discharge of its mandate. It normally rests on several principles:

- Plans for audit and control are selected independently of the administration.
- Extensive powers of investigation are granted to the external audit institution.
- Special protection of tenure is extended to its members.
- Reports and audits are to be publicized either directly or through the intermediation of the legislature. Publicity is especially important if the administration refuses to change certain practices.

(ii) Supreme audit institutions are not granted directly enforceable decision power unless they are constituted as *judicial* authorities, and as such are independent of the executive and the legislature.[5]

(iii) Supreme audit institutions concentrate almost exclusively on external ex post audits of government accounts. In addition to verifying the formal accuracy of the accounts and the lawfulness of operations, supreme audit institutions are beginning to evaluate the efficiency of budget programs and policies.[6]

6.20 These features and principles distil the experience gained by many countries in trying to run an effective external audit function. They suggest the following considerations relevant to Kazakstan:

(i) It is important, first of all, that the tasks of external audit be clearly and precisely targeted and in particular that they be restricted to government agencies.

(ii) It is important that the new institution be given the widest possible range of autonomy: free choice of investigation programs, direct access to public opinion through the publication of critical works, and longer official life (the current term of five years would seem to be the minimum recommendable).

(iii) While the purpose of the audit needs to be narrowly specified, it is, on the other hand, important that the institution's auditing methods, and hence its responsibilities, be broadened and diversified. In an initial stage, the agency should limit its ambitions to the basic but fundamental task of verifying the correctness of fiscal accounts. As this capacity is firmly established, the agency could gradually broaden its objectives and include management audits responsibilities. Eventually, it will be desirable for the external audit further to expand to policy evaluation (see next Section).

6.21 External audit institutions around the world have a history of trial and error in defining their power and influence as they adapt generally accepted principles to their national institutional context. A similar process of adaptation is to be expected in Kazakstan.

---

[5] Findings and recommendations of audits performed by the General Accounting Office, which reports to the U.S. Congress, or the Federal Audit Office in Germany, which is independent but not constituted as a judicial authority, are not directly enforceable. Findings from audits performed by the Court of Accounts in France or Italy are directly enforceable because the supreme audit authority in these two countries is constituted as an independent institution with judicial authority.

[6] In some instances supreme audit institutions are charged with the task of controlling expenditure obligations. This is the practice in Italy and Belgium, although ever-broader exceptions to this practice have been established.

Box 6.3: Budget Evaluation Techniques: Measurement of Efficiency and Performance

The evaluation of a budget program relies heavily on the measurement of its efficiency and performance. The general objective of these techniques is to establish on a scientific basis the relationships between the resources used in a program, the actual outcomes, and the initial objectives of the program. Evidence on efficiency and performance is also used to:

- Provide consistent and credible information to decisionmakers
- Improve planning of activities and setting goals
- Ensure a better allocation of time, manpower and materials
- Simulate the effects of reductions in funding.

Measuring efficiency: Two types of efficiency are generally identified. Technical efficiency refers to the correct use of available technologies. It is achieved when the maximum level of output is obtained from the inputs actually used. Allocative or economic efficiency refers to the production of a level of services or output with the least possible cost. The achievement of allocative efficiency presumes that technical efficiency is being attained, and in addition that the input combination or technology used is the one that minimizes the costs of production.

Techniques for measuring efficiency range from simple analysis of input ratios, regression techniques relating unit costs to level of output, and frontier analysis. This last uses statistical data to recognize the difference between the most efficient units of production (those on the frontier) and other less efficient units. The practical application of the concept of efficiency to the public sector is made more difficult by the multidimensional nature of the public function and the complexity of quantifying actual outputs.

Measuring performance: Efficiency is part of the measurement of performance. However, the strict measurement of efficiency is not always possible owing to the lack of data. In addition, performance involves the concepts of quality of goods or standards of service provision, and the overall quality of the contribution by a particular organization. Performance also implies a degree of accountability for the results achieved and consequently a potential reaction by decisionmakers or by the public at large.

The measurement of performance generally relies on the use of performance indicators. These indicators should help relate the objectives of the program, the resources allocated to the program, and the actual outcomes. Common indicators include volume or number of cases handled, average productivity and costs, time frame for task completion, demand for the service versus availability of the service, and general fulfillment of the overall goals of the organization. To be useful for management control and policymaking, performance indicators have to be compared to anchors or benchmark indicators. The latter can be represented by particular norms or standards, time series of past experiences, actual performance in similar activities, or performance in control groups. Data on benchmark indicators have become more available following the increasing adoption of management information systems in the public sector.

Evaluation: By itself, evaluation has the objective of improving program and agency effectiveness and is viewed as an aid to decisionmaking and management. Management-oriented evaluation seeks to stimulate awareness in three areas:

- Policy and program formulation; that is, to what extent are objectives still relevant, what new objectives are desirable, and what are the clients' needs?
- Program implementation; that is, the suitability and effectiveness of organizations, their methods, procedures, and time tables.
- The impact of completed programs; that is, the distribution of benefits, other unintended effects, and possible waste of resources.

Once programs are selected for evaluation, an initial determination needs to be made about the kind of information required and the sources of that information. It is also necessary to determine over what period of time the questions will have to be answered. Determining the design of the evaluation involves a choice between a sample survey, a case study approach, a field experiment, or the use of data already available. The process of evaluation begins with data collection and analysis and concludes with reporting to the relevant authority. Accountability is incomplete if the findings of an evaluation are not made available to the general public. Timeliness of the reports and actual clients on the policymaking side are crucial for relevance. These aspects underscore the importance of systematic and sustained evaluation practice.

This box borrows heavily from T. Carlyle and A. Premchand, Public Expenditure Management, Chapter 9, International Monetary Fund, Washington, D.C., 1993.

D. Developing a Budget Evaluation Capacity

6.22   Probity and accuracy are two key concerns which justify the existence of ex post budget reviews. They are not the only concerns, however. Countries around the world are paying increasing attention to efficiency considerations (have public expenditures produced value for money?) and are stepping up their *budget evaluation* capacities to assess expenditure performance. The growing awareness is due to the quandary in which many governments have found themselves, caught between mounting pressures to rein in aggregate spending and the intrinsic difficulty of identifying lower priority activities in the absence of competition for many government services. The challenge of tackling expenditure inertia is even more pressing in the case of Kazakstan, as has been noted throughout this report. At this stage, however, the function of budget evaluation is simply not organized in any systematic fashion, nor is the concept as yet fully at home within the Government of Kazakstan. This section therefore attempts to summarize the relevant highlights of the recent international experience with budget evaluation procedures and institutions.

6.23   *How is budget evaluation performed?* Evaluations are carried out periodically during implementation or after completion. Not all government activities need to be evaluated regularly. In some cases the costs of evaluation may be higher than the benefits produced. At minimum, evaluations should analyze the financial and physical performance of programs, explain any deviations in results from stated objectives, and recommend change.

6.24   Evaluations rely heavily on methodologies used in the social sciences (see Box. 6.3). The use of these methodologies has introduced higher and more objective standards and has facilitated the identification of perverse or undesirable effects and of discrepancies between stated objectives and those actually pursued by the program. What ultimately determines the effectiveness of evaluations, however, is how explicitly performance indicators have been defined. In the older tradition in countries where budget evaluation has been performed for many years (such as the United States or the United Kingdom), evaluation has been on bureaucratically defined standards with less explicit performance indicators. Recently, countries with innovative approaches to public finance management, such as New Zealand and Australia, have put more emphasis on defining and quantifying performance indicators for individual spending units. This should significantly facilitate and improve the evaluation of each agency's performance.

6.25   *What institution is in charge of evaluation?* A notable feature of the international experience is that most countries rely on a wide range of institutional resources, rather than a single one, to carry out the evaluation function: institutions in charge of external audits, institutions carrying out internal audits, budget planning offices, and, sometimes, private institutions under contract, including universities and research institutions.

6.26   Following a period of experimentation, many countries have assigned responsibility for budget evaluation to their supreme audit institution, expanding their traditional roles in control and audit. Many countries have formalized this enlargement of duties in specific legislation.[2] Just about every member country of the International Organization of Supreme Audit Institutions (INTOSAI) has seen the need to expand the classic audit and control functions of supreme audit institutions to include budget evaluations.

---

[2]   Recently, this has been the case in Switzerland, Belgium, Japan, and Chile.

6.27   Other countries have entrusted the evaluation function to the budget office. Argentina's law on financial management and control systems of the public sector of 1992 assigns responsibility for determining the norms and procedures for the evaluation of all budget expenditure programs, and for conducting these evaluations, to the National Budget Office. In Canada, the Treasury Board has a review policy requiring reviews/studies, evaluations, and internal audits of key activities to be undertaken by departments. As part of this policy, the Treasury Board requires that departments and agencies, as part of their annual business plans, to provide public notification of plans for future review of key activities.

6.28   Some countries follow more complex arrangements. In the United States, several agencies handle the evaluation function, following a similar methodology, although most program evaluations are carried out by a specialized department in the General Accounting Office, the supreme audit institution in the country. Often, the General Accounting Office contracts out these evaluations to academic and research institutions. In Germany evaluations are carried out by individual ministries, the independent Federal Audit Office, and other institutions. Parliamentary commissions also conduct evaluations for legislated programs and new policies and social experiments. In France, budget evaluation programs are coordinated by the Supreme Council for Evaluation. The council performs few evaluations itself, contracting most of them out through a competitive bidding system. Qualifying institutions bid for particular evaluation projects, presenting a detailed description of the methodology they would follow in the evaluation.

6.29   In France and other countries, the enabling legislation for some programs or the text of the budgetary appropriations contains a requirement for periodic evaluations of certain programs. France plans to use this approach more systematically. Each legislative proposal would be accompanied by an evaluation study quantifying as precisely possible the potential impact of new policies.

E. Conclusions

6.30   Both internal and external audits have an important role to play, not only in detecting misappropriation and fraud, but also in assisting in the structural reform of government programs by helping to identify redundancies and to spread innovations and best practices. This chapter has formulated a number of recommendations which would put audit mechanisms in a stronger position to meet these tasks. These recommendations are summarized below.

6.31   As concerns internal audits, the recommendations are to:

-       Shift the emphasis of internal audits from commercial enterprises to government
        agencies
-       Reintegrate financial inspection within the Ministry of Finance
-       Reduce the financial inspection staff by abolishing existing units at the rayon level
-       Allow sectoral ministries to develop separate technical inspection systems.

6.32   As concerns external audits, the recommendations are to:

-       Redirect the mandate and institutional arrangement of the Accounts Committee from
        internal inspection to external audit

- Give this institution a clear and precisely targeted mandate, preferably limited to public administrations, as well as the widest possible range of autonomy
- Establish firmly the institution's accounting audit capability, then gradually extend its mandate so as to include, over time, policy evaluation.

6.33 And as to budget evaluation, the recommendations are to:

- Create a first evaluation capacity within the Budget Department, and diversify institutional sources over time, including through a gradual expansion of the role of the Accounts Committee
- Mandate that any new expenditure proposal be accompanied by evaluation criteria, a timetable, and the appropriate institutional arrangements.

CHAPTER VII. THE REFORM OF TERRITORIAL ADMINISTRATION

A. Introduction

7.1   A reform of territorial administration, if properly designed, could contribute greatly to the restructuring of public services. It would promote a moving away from a uniform supply of services nationwide and would permit the differentiation of public interventions in response to locally perceived priorities. The main aim of this chapter is to consider how territorial administration at the local level in Kazakstan might develop into a more genuine system of democratically controlled local government. It also reviews the options that the international experience offers in this respect.

7.2   Two related key points should be borne in mind in this report. First, Kazakstan is a young republic which is newly introducing market reforms and hence is undergoing a period of substantial change; given the uncertainties that characterize any such period, it is likely that any reform will be taken on a gradual basis. Second, because the process of reform is likely to be evolutionary, it is important also to understand the present system before considering options for reform.

7.3   In the present system, as presented in Section B, territorial administrations constitute essentially branches of the state administration. With a few exceptions, territorial administrations carry out all state functions within their jurisdiction, whether of local or of national significance. These activities are mostly funded out of general resources, as Section C determines, with a view to achieving a uniform level of services across the country. A complex system of tax earmarking and grants serves to combine this objective with that of inducing territorial authorities to cooperate in the collection of national taxes. Section D argues that the present system of delegation of state authority to territorial administrations could evolve over time into a devolution of responsibilities to local governments. Kazakstan's new Constitution envisages that such a devolution would favor the creation of new municipalities. This would appear to be a good place to start. These new municipalities would require their separate source of funding. Property and income taxes would be first candidates. These tax revenues could be supplemented by equalizing grants. These fiscal issues are discussed in Section E. This policy would allow for a clearer distinction between a unified national budget on the one hand, and local government budgets on the other.

B. Structure of Territorial Administrations

Structure of Territorial Jurisdictions[1/]

7.4   The current territorial organization of Kazakstan is governed by a decree-law of December 9, 1993, which distinguishes between two categories of jurisdictions, namely, regions and localities.

(i)   *Regions*: A region is a part of the territory of the Republic covering a number of localities, created and administered in the interest of the Republic. Regions come in two tiers, oblasts and rayons, which can be defined as follows:

[1/]   Since Kazakstan is a unitary country (see Chapter I), the structure of its territorial jurisdictions is a matter of administrative organization. Art 2., para. 3 of the Constitution stipulates that "the territorial jurisdictions of the Republic, the location and status of its capital are determined by law."

a.   *Oblasts:* Territorial divisions of the Republic, comparable to provinces
b.   *Rayons:* Rural subdivisions of an oblast.

(ii)   *Localities:* Localities are sections of the territory, in which groups of more than 50 people live compactly and which can be administered by local representative and executive bodies. Localities come in two groups: urban localities and rural localities.

Urban localities include the following:

a.   *National cities:* Of republican subordination (Almaty and Leninsk)
b.   *Towns:* Of oblast subordination, with a population of at least 50,000
c.   *Townships:* Of rayon subordination, with a population of at least 10,000, two-thirds of which are workers and their families, state housing, industrial enterprises...
d.   *Villages:* Or settlements, with a population of at least at least 3,000, established near industrial enterprises, railway stations, health facilities....

Urban localities can be subdivided into urban rayons.

(iii)   *Rural localities* include the following:

a.   *Aul (selo):* Of a least 50 people, 50 percent of which are farmers and their families, corresponding generally to the limits of sovkhozes and kolkhozes
b.   *Other localities:* Included in the nearest locality.

7.5   This structure may seem complex. In practice, however, these units are administered by two tiers of territorial administration, as is seen in Chapter I, and are financed by two similar tiers of the state budget. Oblasts and national cities belong to the first tier of administration, which reports directly to the republican government. Rural rayons and towns of oblast subordination belong to the second tier, which reports to oblast authorities. There was formerly a third tier -- at the village or aul level -- but this was incorporated in the rayon level in 1994. These entities now constitute "sub-administrative" levels of public intervention, as is found in many other countries.[2]

7.6   The importance of the notion of "localities" in the present report is that it is the level at which the Constitution and the law envisage that local governments could be created.

7.7   The terms "rayon" and "oblast" are used generically in this report to encompass all entities participating in that tier of administration. More precise denominations (such as "rural rayon" or "national city") are used when it is necessary to be more specific.

---

[2]   "Parishes" in Scandinavian countries and in Great Britain; "wards" in some cities in the United States; "*Ortshafte*" in North-Rhine Westphalia (Germany); "*barrios*" in the Philippines; "*mahalles*" in Turkey.

Size of Territorial Jurisdictions

7.8   It is generally desirable to keep the number of tiers of territorial administrations to a minimum. When the number of tiers increases, staffing and other resource requirements also increase, as does the likelihood of conflicting responsibilities. In view of the immensity of its territory, a two-tier territorial administration system seems the right balance for Kazakstan. It is a common feature among OECD countries, particularly unitary ones.

7.9   From a demographic point of view, the size of territorial jurisdictions appears broadly appropriate. The average population of the oblast tier (excluding the city of Leninsk) is about 850,000. Oblasts range from 313,000 to 1,300,000. The average population of the rayon tier is just over 75,000 (see Table 7.1). In the oblast of Almaty, the populations of the rayons range from 16,500 to 145,200. The upper tiers in OECD countries often have average populations as large as the oblasts,[3] but the lower tiers in OECD countries rarely have populations as large as the rayons. To some extent, relatively large local authorities can be seen as advantageous. Many OECD countries have experienced difficulties with local authorities that are too small for some of their functions and yet are so well-established that there would be resistance to reform.

7.10   Despite their demographic size, rayons appear to be generally large enough to organize public interventions efficiently while maintaining a direct contact with their populations, particularly given the density of the road network. It is usually considered that when roads allow people to move at a speed of 50 km/h, the lower jurisdiction can be as large as 8,000 km^2 (compared with 1,200 km^2 if normal speed is limited to 20 km/h). Table 7.1 indicates that the average area of rayons corresponds more or less to that level, except in oblasts with very low population density. Such a criterion matters less at the oblast level, which requires less direct contact with the populations.

---

[3]   Oblasts may, however, have under their supervision a number of lower tier entities which exceed their effective "span of control" (i.e., the number of subordinate units beyond which the efficacy of an organization decreases).

Table 7.1: Size and Structure of Territorial Jurisdictions

OBLAST	1,000 km²	Pop.1994 x 1,000	Pop. km²	Rayons	Towns total	Other urban local.	Other rural local.	Rayons av.km²	Rayons av.pop.
Total Kazakstan	2,724.9	16,942.4	6.2	220	83	204	2,496	12.4	77.0
1. Akmola	92.0	869.6	9.5	12	6	14	151	7.7	72.5
2. Aktyubinsk	300.6	760.2	2.5	16	7	3	150	18.8	47.5
3. Almaty	72.7	962.9	13.2	11	4	9	133	6.6	87.5
4. Atyrau	118.6	457.7	3.9	8	1	15	57	14.8	57.2
5. East Kazakstan	97.5	961.0	9.9	12	6	19	102	8.1	80.1
6. Zhambyl	144.3	1,052.0	7.3	10	4	13	142	14.4	105.2
7. Zhezkazgan	312.6	493.4	1.6	7	4	22	65	44.7	70.5
8. West Kazakstan	151.3	674.3	4.5	16	2	4	164	9.5	42.1
9. Karaganda	115.4	1,305.5	11.3	9	6	17	106	12.8	145.1
10. Kzyl-Orda	220.0	606.3	2.8	8	3	11	97	27.5	75.8
11. Kokshetau	78.2	674.9	8.6	16	4	9	194	4.9	42.2
12. Kostanai	113.9	1,082.5	9.5	14	4	13	205	8.1	77.3
13. Mangystau	165.6	338.5	2.0	4	3	10	19	41.4	84.6
14. Pavlodar	124.8	965.9	7.7	12	3	8	164	10.4	80.5
15. North Kazakstan	45.0	620.6	13.8	12	4	1	149	3.8	51.7
16. Semipalatinsk	185.8	839.2	4.5	15	3	13	149	12.4	55.9
17. Taldykorgan	118.5	737.9	6.2	12	6	9	136	9.9	61.5
18. Turgai	111.8	313.2	2.8	10	3		144	11.2	31.3
19. South Kazakstan	117.3	1,969.2	16.8	16	8	11	168	7.3	123.1
Almaty (city)	33.0	1,185.4	35.9	8	1	2			
Leninsk (city)	6.0	71.6	11.9		1	1	1		

Source: Statistical Yearbook of Kazakstan, 1993.

Institutional Framework[4/]

7.11   Formally, state territorial administration is exercised by two state bodies: a deliberative one -- the maslikhat, or local council -- and an executive one, the head of administration (*akim* in Kazak, *glava* in Russian).

Maslikhat

7.12   In practice the role of the maslikhat is marginal at best. Whereas prevailing laws give them a fairly wide range of responsibilities,[5/] they have not been given a field of authority separate from that of the state. The responsibilities they have are to be exercised within the bounds set by republican authorities. In this context, the role of the local council is to help adapt national decisions to the circumstances of its jurisdiction. The budget of the jurisdiction is one example. This budget is to be approved by the maslikhat, but at the same time it remains part of the state budget and as such is almost completely determined by regulations, norms, and resource allocation decisions made centrally. In this context, the role of the maslikhat appears to be of little consequence, and its approval authority to be purely formal (see Box 7.2). In brief, the existence of the local council appears at this stage more like a remnant of the former local soviets rather than an active ingredient of popular participation in decisions of local interest.

7.13   The maslikhat could find a new functional role in the context of the creation of local governments, as is described in Section D, below.

Box 7.1: Local Soviet Administration

In Soviet times, each territorial level had a soviet or council of people's delegates. The local soviet was part of the legislative branch. This situation is the source of a lingering confusion between decentralization and federalism (see Box 1.1). A hierarchical line linked the soviet upward to the Union level Supreme Soviet.

The soviet designated among its members a number of standing committees (10 to 15), in charge, inter alia, of monitoring on a continuous basis the activities, resources, social services, production, etc., of the entities assigned to their particular soviet (Art. 147 of the Soviet Constitution). The soviet also established within itself a an executive committee in charge of implementing the decisions of both higher levels of authority and its own. Executive committees included a number of departments, established by regulations. Although they emanated from a legislative body, executive committees were integrated in the executive branch. They were in charge of supervising the work of the other standing committees as well as of all state entities under their subordination. In practice, however, the executive committee itself was under the tutelage of the first secretary of the party in that jurisdiction.

The authority of the executive committee was limited not only because it reported in actual practice to the local party organization, but also because all local actions, plans, budgets, organization, etc., remained integrated within those of the next upper soviet, and onward up to the national level. Through this Russian Doll model, the state maintained its formal unity.

[4/]   The authority of bodies of territorial administration is a matter of some legal confusion. It is determined by two sets of legislation: the law of December 15, 1991 on local self-administration (amended in January 1992 and April 1993), and the decree-law of December 10, 1993 on local representative and executive bodies, which partly supersedes the former, without, however, formally abrogating it. Furthermore, some of the provisions of both legislations conflict with the new Constitution. This is particularly the case with Art. 60 of the decree-law of December 10, 1993 which gives Parliament the authority to cancel decisions of local maslikhat. This may have been consistent with the Soviet system, where local soviets were part of the legislative branch (see Box 7.1), but not with a unitary regime where they form part of the executive branch and are therefore submitted to executive, not legislative, authorities.

[5/]   The formal responsibilities of the maslikhats are defined in two different documents. The Constitution gives them the following prerogatives: (i) approval of the jurisdiction's development plans, socioeconomic programs, budget and execution reports; (ii) decisions of territorial jurisdictions within their competencies; (iii) hearing of reports from the head of the administration; (iv) decisions on their own internal structure; and (v) responsibility for defending the legitimate interests of their citizens in the implementation of national policies. These prerogatives are further elaborated in the decree-law of December 10, 1993. Arts. 40 and 41 of that law set a number of limited responsibilities in the fields of: urban planning, social order, public security, hygiene regulations, fire protection, among other things. Elected members of the maslikhats are also part of the electoral college for the appointment of the members of the Senate.

Structure of Territorial Administrations

7.14   Territorial administrations are headed by a representative of the President and the government: the head of administration. The latter is the repository of state authority within the jurisdiction (see Box 7.2). He is supported by deputy heads of administrations, a "board" of senior staff (as is the case within republican administrations). He supervises the jurisdiction's "own" departments (as different from "constitutional" departments (see next paragraph).

7.15   As is explained in Chapter I, there are two types of state administration at the territorial level, each with its own rules:

(i)   *Territorial departments* (a.k.a. *own departments*), under the *administrative authority* of the head of territorial administration and the *technical authority* of the relevant sectoral

---

Box 7.2: Authority of Heads of Territorial Administrations

The head of a local administration represents the state in its jurisdiction. Under the Constitution and the decree-law of December 10, 1993, his responsibilities include: preparing the jurisdiction's development plans and budget, formulating the detailed organization chart and staffing plans of its administrations based on the list of departments and staffing norms set by the Cabinet of Ministers, appointing heads of departments, coordinating the allocation of agricultural lands, monitoring economic activities within the jurisdiction, managing goods and passenger services belonging to the state, regulating and registering the use of labor, enforcing environmental, hygiene, and safety standards, supervising education and health services.

The head of administration is a political appointee. Like a minister, his term expires with that of the President. Heads of administrations are appointed by the next upper level of the executive branch, heads of oblasts by the President, heads of rayons by the oblast head, and so on.

---

administration of the next upper tier; they are funded out of the jurisdiction's own tier of budget and their heads of departments are appointed by the head of territorial administration, in consultation with the relevant sectoral administration of the next upper tier.

(ii)   *Field services of higher tiers of administration* (a.k.a. *constitutional departments*), under the *administrative and technical authority* of the higher tier; they are funded out of the budget of that upper tier and their heads of departments are appointed by the next upper level of administration to which they report, in consultation with the head of territorial administration of the jurisdiction in which they operate.[6]

For example, at the oblast level are the oblasts' own departments (road fund, for example) as well as constitutional departments (territorial privatization committee, for example). Similarly, at the rayon level are the rayons' own departments (such as education) as well as constitutional departments, reporting either to the republican level (for example, the rayon branch of the tax inspectorate) or to the oblast level (for example, road maintenance brigades).

7.16   The distinction between own and constitutional departments is blurred when the head of administration or (one of his deputies) is appointed, in his capacity of representative of the state, as head of a constitutional department, as is the case for a number of departments. The head of

---

[6]   Territorial finance departments are an exception to that rule. They are under the administrative authority of the head of territorial administration but have all the other characteristics of constitutional departments.

administration doubles up, for instance, as head of the republican police or head of the territorial department of state security, while one of the deputies is also head of the territorial committees for managing state properties and for privatization.

7.17. The structure of an oblast's "own" administration mirrors, by and large, that of republican ministries. It comprises the following:

(i) The *oblast apparat* (akin to the Staff of the Cabinet of Ministers) subdivided into three sectors: (a) general administration and control; (b) social sphere and territorial development; and (c) organization and control of lower tiers.

(ii) *Sectoral departments*, which are counterparts of republican ministries. Oblasts increasingly distinguish the "productive" departments (e.g., industry, telecommunications, agriculture) from the others, and put the former on a "self-financing" basis. Self-financed departments, however, remain subject to national staffing norms (see Table 7.2).

Table 7.2: Structure of Oblast Administrative Personnel
(based on authorized positions)

	Maslikhat Total	Remun.	Akim and Deputies	Deputies	Deputy Heads	Of which Notarial Offices	Other Sectors	Autonomously Financed Sectors	Total Remun.
Total Kazakstan	1,555	156	1,635	18,931	100	823	20,292	1,784	42,898
Akmola	92	8	75	914	5	41	1,283	27	2,312
Aktyubinsk	117	8	85	1,065	5	28	1,095	59	2,317
Almaty	77	8	85	1,048	5	29	959	42	2,147
Atirau	47	7	60	551	4	26	647	29	1,298
East Kazakstan	92	8	80	997	5	45	1,518	48	2,656
Zhambyl	72	7	85	1,204	5	37	1,209	20	2,530
Zhezkazgan	57	7	70	702	5	41	834		1,618
West Kazakstan	92	8	80	1,006	5	34	1,216	23	2,338
Karaganda	77	7	85	1,173	5	68	1,499	76	2,845
Kzyl-Orda	57	7	70	662	5	18	812	23	1,579
Kokshetau	102	8	80	1,187	5	42	851	135	2,266
Kostanai	92	8	85	1,443	5	48	1,204	568	3,313
Mangystau	37	7	50	412	4	16	504	10	987
Pavlodar	77	7	85	1,268	5	47	1,230	24	2,619
North Kazakstan	82	8	70	782	5	26	825	25	1,715
Semipalatinsk	92	8	80	998	5	41	1,061	34	2,186
Taldykorgan	92	8	75	987	5	34	680	123	1,878
Turgai	67	7	70	653	4	17	462	319	1,515
South Kazakstan	122	8	85	1,507	5	60	1,453	49	3,107
Almaty (city)	7	7	150	330	6	122	872	100	1,465
Leninsk (city)	5	5	30	42	2	3	78	50	207

Source: Resolution 1,371 of the Cabinet of Ministers, December 5, 1994 (health and education not included).

7.18   The "own" administrations of lower tiers have a similar structure, except that the number of "own" departments may be much smaller. Sectors under "own" departments at the oblast level may be under "constitutional" departments one tier down, their activities being performed by field services of the oblasts' own departments rather than by rayon-level departments.

C. Finances of Territorial Administrations

Territorial Structure of the Budget

7.19   As has been seen in Chapter I, public services are assigned to the various levels of administration not on a functional basis (i.e., according to the type of activity being funded) but on an organizational basis: specific "budget organizations" are assigned to specific levels of budget on the basis of the "catchment area" that they serve.[2/] Chapter III described how this organization rule was reflected in the architecture of the budget -- through the assignment of *smeta* to different levels of the state budget.

7.20   The territorial structure of the state budget reflects that of the state itself. The state budget is presented in two strands: republican and territorial. The former centralizes the *smeta* of entities assigned to the republican level, whereas the latter centralizes by oblast the *smeta* of entities assigned to territorial administrations.

7.21   All public services are supposed to be funded uniformly, and mainly from general resources, based on a common measure of needs at the national level: the expenditure norms. The main purpose of the budget process is to ascertain the level of these normative requirements and to dispatch available resources to equalize the level of fulfillment of needs nationwide. The remainder of this section: (i) discusses in more detail the expenditures actually carried out by territorial administrations; (ii) examines how these expenditures are funded; and (iii) assesses how this mechanism succeeds in its intended purpose of equalizing the provision of public services (it probably does rather well).

Key Expenditure Assignments of Territorial Administrations

7.22   The organizational structure of expenditure assignment can be regrouped for statistical purposes into a functional presentation, as was provided in Chapter I, Table 1.1, which shows the main expenditure functions funded by oblast and rayon budgets. Key expenditure assignments of the territorial administrations are also shown -- in quantitative terms this time -- in Table 7.3 (based on budget execution figures for 1994). The figures for territorial budgets cover all oblast and rayon spending. The total level of this spending was about 8.2 percent of GDP in 1994. This is less than half the share of GDP accounted for, on average, by subcentral governments in OECD countries. But OECD countries have found that government spending typically rises as a percentage of GDP as GDP rises, so it could be expected that the figure in Kazakstan would be lower than the OECD average.

2/   Under the central planning system, all legal entities (enterprises and administrations) were similarly assigned to their level of "subordination" and their finances incorporated in the budget of that particular level. The present configuration of services was obtained by weeding productive enterprises out of the state budget, starting in 1987.

7.23   Territorial budgets finance more than 80 percent of the country's expenditure on education, health, culture and recreation, energy, and transport. Conversely, about 60 percent of total spending from territorial budgets is accounted for by education, health, and social security and welfare.[8/] Some indication of how expenditures are divided between oblasts and rayons is given in Tables 7.4 and 7.5. Table 7.4 shows the actual allocation for the whole country in 1994 and Table 7.5 the 1995 allocation in one oblast, that of Almaty.[9/] Rayons typically handle about 60 percent of all local spending: rayons accounted for 58.9 percent of the total local spending shown in Table 7.4, and the rayons in the oblast of Almaty accounted for 57.9 percent of the local spending shown in Table 7.5. The following paragraphs therefore concentrate mainly on the three principal items of spending: education, health, and welfare.

Table 7.3: Allocation of Expenditures between Republican and Territorial Budgets
(1994 actual)

	REPUBLICAN	TERRITORIAL	STATE	REPUBLICAN	TERRITORIAL	STATE
General Public Services	87.3	12.7	100.0	25.3	4.7	16.2
Defense	99.6	0.4	10.0	7.8	0.0	4.4
Public Order and Safety	79.3	20.7	100.0	9.9	3.2	6.9
Education	17.1	82.9	100.0	4.8	29.4	15.7
Health	13.7	86.3	100.0	2.6	20.5	10.5
Social Security and Welfare	37.4	62.6	100.0	3.5	7.5	5.3
Housing and Utilities	1.3	98.7	100.0	0.1	9.6	4.3
Culture and Leisure	47.2	52.8	100.0	2.0	2.8	2.3
Energy	3.5	96.5	100.0	0.1	3.4	1.5
Agriculture	89.1	10.9	100.0	11.1	1.7	6.9
Industry	97.8	2.2	100.0	0.7	0.0	0.4
Transport and Communication	13.5	86.5	100.0	1.6	12.7	6.5
Other Economic Affairs	81.8	18.2	100.0	14.5	4.1	9.9
Miscellaneous	98.4	1.6	100.0	16.1	0.3	9.2
Total (percent of GDP)	55.8	44.2	100.0	100.0 (10.4)	100.0 (8.2)	100.0 (18.6)

Source: Ministry of Finance; republican expenditures exclude net lending and participation.

[8/]   There is some spending on transport and communication: this is a combination of payments from road fund receipts to oblast road funds and the use of special funds from transport development receipts for subsidizing and improving public transport. From July 1, 1995, both these items disappeared from local budgets.

[9/]   The oblast of Almaty surrounds the City of Almaty and has its administrative headquarters in that city; but local public services in the City of Almaty are the responsibility of the city, not the surrounding oblast.

**Table 7.4: Allocation of Expenditures between and within Territorial Tiers
(1994 actual)**

	OBLAST	RAYON	TERRITORIAL	OBLAST	RAYON	TERRITORIAL
General Public Services	32.8	67.2	100.0	3.8	5.2	4.6
Defense	55.6	44.4	100.0	0.1	0.0	0.0
Public Order and Safety	66.5	33.5	100.0	5.2	1.8	3.1
Education	23.7	76.3	100.0	17.3	37.4	29.3
Health	32.9	67.1	100.0	16.8	22.9	20.5
Social Welfare, Housing and Utilities	42.6	57.4	100.0	17.9	16.1	16.8
Culture and Leisure	43.4	56.6	100.0	2.7	2.4	2.5
Agriculture	67.9	32.1	100.0	2.9	0.9	1.7
Miscellaneous	62.5	37.5	100.0	33.2	13.3	21.3
Total (percent of GDP)	41.1	58.9	100.0	100.0	100.0	100.0
				(3.4)	(4.8)	(8.2)

Source: Ministry of Finance, 1994 actual outcome.

**Table 7.5: Allocation of Expenditures between Territorial Tiers in the Oblast of Almaty
(1995 revised budget)**

	OBLAST	RAYON	TERRITORIAL	OBLAST	RAYON	TERRITORIAL
General Public Services	45.2	54.8	100.0	3.8	3.4	3.6
Defense	0.0	100.0	100.0	0.0	2.2	1.3
Public Order and Safety Affairs	94.9	5.1	100.0	4.0	0.2	1.8
Education	23.9	76.1	100.0	17.3	40.1	30.5
Health	27.6	72.4	100.0	15.7	29.8	23.9
Social Security and Welfare	66.9	33.1	100.0	46.5	16.7	29.2
Housing and Utilities	0.0	100.0	100.0	0.0	0.1	0.0
Culture, Leisure, Religion	67.6	32.4	100.0	3.9	1.4	2.4
Agriculture	31.3	68.7	100.0	0.4	0.6	0.5
Transport and Communications	52.2	47.8	100.0	7.3	4.9	5.9
Miscellaneous	50.6	49.4	100.0	1.0	0.7	0.8
Total	42.1	57.9	100.0	100.0	100.0	100.0

Source: Ministry of Finance (using IMF definitions).

Education

7.24   Rayons provide almost all kindergartens and schools; there are exceptions in the principal towns of some oblasts, where the oblasts provide the schools. While rayons supply most schools, oblasts assume responsibilities for overall logistics and policy coordination. Thus, in the oblast of South Kazakstan, the oblast's responsibilities include supplying books, providing inservice teacher training, inspectin0g schools, controlling school standards, and making the most effective use of experienced teachers. Oblasts generally provide vocational colleges and sometimes (for example in the oblast of South Kazakstan but not in the oblast of Almaty) they provide teacher training colleges. Aside from oblast teacher training colleges, higher education is chiefly a republican responsibility.

Health

7.25   Rayons supply polyclinics, which chiefly offer general practitioner services and dentists, and they also supply general hospitals. Oblasts supply hospitals that offer specialist treatment, such as children's hospitals, tuberculosis hospitals, and hospitals for the chronically ill. Oblasts also supply specialized dental services.

Social Security and Welfare

7.26   Spending under this heading can be divided into spending on goods and services, spending on transfers, and spending on subsidies.

(i)   *Spending on goods and services*: This is divided between oblasts and rayons. Oblasts provide homes for the aged and infirm, though apparently Almaty also has one such home that is financed from the republican budget. Oblasts also supply homes for the mentally handicapped. Rayons provide "social aid units" which assist people who, despite being disabled or old, live at home. The units help these people with activities such as shopping and cleaning.

(ii)   *Spending on transfers*: This consists mainly of family allowances, which are administered by oblast-level services. Family allowances are limited to low-income families (i.e., the lowest 20 percent income category). The main categories of allowances include: (a) single parent families; (b) families with many children; (c) families of servicemen; and (d) families with handicapped children living at home. In addition to these payments, there are payments to selected groups such as people affected by the Chernobyl disaster. Finally, rayons make some transfers in kind by giving food to poor and retired people; these transfers are financed half by charities.

(iii)   *Spending on subsidies*: This is handled by both oblasts and rayons. It is likely that budgetary cuts will lead to pressure to reduce these subsidies. There are several components, which include: (a) heating subsidies;[10] (b) utility subsidies; (c) electricity, gas, and liquid and solid fuel subsidies;[11] and (d) transport subsidies. Rayons are chiefly responsible for the first two items while oblasts are chiefly responsible for the last two. The main groups eligible for discounts following the revised 1995 budget are shown in Table 7.6. Some discounts take the form of subsidized prices but many, especially those for utility services, are in the form of lump sums, such as the cost of heating an apartment of a standard size or the cost of renting a telephone line.

---

[10]   Heating subsidies are paid to providers of heating. These providers supply heat to most apartments and also to some houses. They are subsidized to compensate them for supplying heat at subsidized prices. Subsidized prices are offered to most homes but not to apartments that are owned by enterprises, as is explained below in the discussion of housing and amenity services. The subsidized prices for heating are determined centrally, so the subsidy that is paid to each enterprise is equal to the difference between its costs and its revenues at the subsidized prices.

[11]   Utility subsidies are paid to enterprises that supply certain utilities -- chiefly heating, water, and telephones -- to compensate them for offering discounts to selected groups. Likewise, electricity, gas, liquid and solid fuel subsidies, and transport subsidies, are paid to the enterprises producing these items to compensate them for offering discounts to selected groups. The relevant groups vary from item to item and also a little over time, according to central government regulations.

Table 7.6: Main Groups Eligible for Discounted Prices

GROUP	UTILITIES	ELECTRICITY	GAS, LIQUID AND SOLID FUEL	TRANSPORT
WWII veterans	✓	✓	✓	✓
Widows of men killed in WWII	✓	✓	✓	X
Holders of orders and medals	✓	✓	✓ (gas only)	X
Invalids[1]	✓	✓	✓	✓
Poor citizens	✓	X	✓ (gas only)	X
Chernobyl victims	X	✓	✓ (liquid only)	X
Mothers with large families	X	✓	✓ (not coal)	✓
Cowboys	X	✓	✓ (not gas)	X

[1] Some invalids are eligible for only some discounts.
Source: Amended State Budget, July 11, 1995.

Other Functions

7.27 Oblast and rayon level administrations also handle a range of other programs, including programs in the following fields:

(i) *Defense*: Rayons provide subsidies to enterprises producing heating, water, and telephones for supplying these services at discounts to current and former service personnel and their families.[12]

(ii) *Public order and safety*: Oblasts supply fire services and also supply police services in conjunction with the republic.

(iii) *Housing and amenity services*: Rayon accounts include subsidies to "nonprivatized apartments." These subsidies are in fact just another form of heating subsidy.[13]

(iv) *Recreation and culture*: Both rayons and oblasts provide "halls of culture" which contain facilities such as libraries, concert halls, theaters, lecture rooms, and club rooms. In addition, rayons give subsidies to cinema enterprises to offset the losses they incur in rural districts.

(v) *Agriculture, forestry, and fishing*: Oblasts handle pest control while rayons supply veterinary services.

---

[12] The figures in Table 7.4 suggest that in 1994 this minor function was shared between oblasts and rayons.

[13] Before the market reforms, many enterprises built apartments for their employees. The enterprises paid the full price for the heating supplied to the apartments but sold it on to the occupants at a discount. Some occupants still work for the enterprises that own their homes, and they still receive subsidized heat at the enterprises' expense. Other occupants now work for other employers. This item of expenditure covers payments to the enterprises owning these apartments for continuing to offer heat at a discount to former employees. When these apartments are eventually privatized, their occupants will automatically qualify for heating subsidies. So this item of spending will be transferred to the social security and welfare heading.

(vi) *Transport and communication*: Until July 1995, roads were maintained by a Road Fund. This fund received contributions from road users, chiefly in the form of a 1 percent tax on enterprise turnovers. From January 1, 1994 to mid-1995, 30 percent of the receipts from these contributions were paid to the republican level road fund while 70 percent were paid to the oblast level road funds. The republican road fund maintained roads of national importance and oblast level road funds maintained roads of local importance. These user charges were, however, abolished with the April 1995 tax reform, and from July 1, 1995, the date of effectiveness of the tax code, road funds temporarily ceased to exist. The Road Fund was however recreated in early 1996 and is now funded by a new gasoline tax. Until July 1995, oblasts, and to a greater extent rayons, received some funds from a transport development levy whose proceeds were earmarked to subsidize public transport, chiefly for purchasing new vehicles and subsidizing operating costs. These funds were also de facto abolished with the tax reform. The result has been significant increases in public transport fares.

Funding Arrangements

Overview

7.28   Expenditures undertaken by territorial administrations are funded mainly *through general resources*. These resources are allocated through revenue earmarking or subventions. The revised 1995 budget revenues for territorial administrations are shown in Table 7.7, where it can be seen that 15.8 percent of their resources arise from "subventions" or grants, while the rest arises from taxes and nontax revenues. Some so-called local taxes do exist, but in practice their yields count for little. But the main taxes are all national. Allocation of these resources is made through the budget process. This process seeks to accomplish two things: (i) to ensure a uniform level of services nationwide; and (ii) to ensure the collection of national taxes. Expenditure norms seek to achieve the former. A complex system of revenue earmarking is meant to achieve the latter. In dividing up national resources among levels of budget, territorial budgets are first *earmarked* for all or part of the proceeds of the taxes of the originating territory, up to a maximum defined by their expenditure envelope defined by (i). The remaining balances are covered by republican "subventions."

7.29   Neither the sharing rates nor the republican subventions affect ex ante the total amount of resources for which each territorial entity is budgeted. But tax earmarking serves to ensure that for each particular territorial entity the budget resources actually at its disposal *during the execution of the budget* are determined by the revenue efforts of its particular jurisdiction. The role of revenue sharing arrangements is chiefly to entice territorial tax administrations, which may have stronger local than national loyalties, to collect national taxes on their own territory before calling on other resources. Tax assignment rules are also tailored to this necessity. They are mostly levied on a production basis (i.e., the stage at which territorial administrations are more likely to exercise influence) rather than on a residence or destination basis. The resulting pattern of revenue yield is, not surprisingly, extremely uneven across the country, and so are the discretionary equilibrating subventions from the republican budget. For this reason, also, the report will argue that most national taxes, with the possible exception of the personal income tax, would be unfit to fund the local governments to be created.

Table 7.7: Combined Oblast and Rayon Revenues
(revised 1995 budget)

	REVENUE (%)
Tax on individual incomes[1]	21.98
Tax on corporate incomes[1,2]	20.52
Value added tax[1,2]	9.30
Excise taxes[1,2,3]	12.18
Fixed rent payments[1,2]	0.68
Land tax[4]	5.79
Taxes on motor vehicles	0.96
Property tax/state duties	1.74
Nontax revenue	6.05
Other levies	0.13
Road fund	4.38
Nature protection fund	0.52
Subventions	15.76
Total	**99.99**

[1] These taxes are shared by the oblasts with the rayons. Oblasts decide what shares of their revenue entitlement from each tax may be kept by each rayon.

[2] These taxes are shared by the Republic with the oblasts. The Republic decides on the revenue entitlement of each tax for each oblast (see Table 7.10).

[3] The figure includes the revenue from taxes on gasoline and diesel fuel.

[4] Until mid-1995, 10 percent of land tax revenues were paid to the republican budget.

Source: Ministry of Finance (using IMF definitions).

7.30   These points will be discussed in more detail in the rest of this section, starting with a review of the major sources of tax revenues for territorial budgets, and then examining the procedures under which they are allocated.

Revenue Sources

7.31   Under the April 1995 tax code, taxes fall into two groups: five "nationwide taxes" and six "local taxes" (for a description of the main taxes, see Annex 1). Their relative importance is shown in Table 7.7.

The five nationwide taxes and the relevant parts of the code are as follows:

(i)   The income tax on individuals and businesses (legal entities) - Part II
(ii)   The value added tax (VAT) - Part III
(iii)   Excise duties - Part IV
(iv)   The tax on security transactions - Part V
(v)   Taxes and payments by mineral resource users (or "fixed rent payments") - Part VI.

The six "local" taxes and the relevant parts of the decree are as follows:

(i)   The land tax - Part VII[14]/
(ii)   The vehicle tax (or auto-inspectorate tax) - Part VIII
(iii)   The tax on property - Part IX
(iv)   Business registration fees
(v)   Fees to perform specific activities
(vi)   Auction fees.

The last three items are not conventional taxes and are regarded here as nontax revenues. The six local taxes are in fact all rayon taxes. Three of these taxes are covered in detail by the decree while three are merely noted in it as their details have yet to be determined.

7.32   In practice, the distinction between nationwide and local taxes is less sharp than their names would suggest. On the one hand, although the tax bases and tax rates of the nationwide taxes are determined at the central level, and although the revenues from these taxes are at the disposal of the central government, 100 percent of the revenues from the individual income tax are earmarked to local authorities. Furthermore, central authorities share with territorial budgets the proceeds of the *regulating taxes*: the VAT, excise duties, fixed rent payments, and the business income (or profit) tax. On the other hand, while the revenues of the local taxes accrue to rayon budgets, their bases and rates are centrally set.

The Problem of Heavily Concentrated Tax Revenues

7.33   The revenues of the individual income tax and the four regulating taxes are heavily concentrated in some areas. This is the case, for obvious reasons, for fixed rents payments which occur only in the six oil producing oblasts. But the per capita yields of the other taxes are also extremely uneven, as is shown clearly in Table 7.8. For any given tax in any given year, about a quarter of all oblasts raise less per capita than half the national average. This concentration of tax revenues has become more acute over time, as the 50 percent increase in the standard deviation in overall tax yields per capita between the beginning and the end of the period under review (1992-95) indicates. As a result, the gap between the oblasts with the highest and lowest overall yields per capita widened from a ratio of 5:1 to a ratio of 15:1 between 1992 and 1995. The ranges are even wider if one looks at individual taxes. In 1995, for example, the oblasts of Taldykorgan generated 10 times less in personal income tax per capita and 23 times less in profit tax per capita than Mangystau. Similarly, it generated 18 times less in VAT per head of population and as much as 74 times less in excises than the City of Almaty.

7.34   The distribution of tax revenues within oblasts is just as uneven. Within the oblast of Almaty, for instance, the ranges are sometimes even larger. Thus, Table 7.9 shows that the ratio is 12:1 for the individual income tax, 24:1 for the profit tax, 28:1 for VAT, and is unmeasurable for excise duties where some rayons receive no revenues at all.

7.35   This high concentration results to a large extent from the way in which tax revenues are allocated to different areas, specifically, for the following taxes:

14/   Prior to the implementation of the 1995 tax decree, 10 percent of land tax revenues were paid to the republican budget.

(i)   *The personal income tax*, being withheld at the source, is collected chiefly in areas of work rather than on a residence basis. To ensure a precise allocation of revenues to areas of residence, it would be necessary for employers to keep records of where each of their employees lives and then pay the taxes they deduct to the relevant areas. Likewise, enterprises paying interest and dividends should also pay the deducted tax to the areas where the recipients live.

(ii)   *The profit tax* is collected chiefly in the areas of business headquarters.

(iii)   *The excise taxes*[15] *and VAT*[16] are collected on an origin basis (i.e., at the point of production or of first import) rather than on a destination basis (i.e., at the point where taxable items are actually consumed).

(iv)   *The fixed rents tax* arises only in areas with natural resources.

---

[15]   Producers typically pay to the areas where they produce, so these revenues accrue on an origin basis. But enterprises with branches or plants in different areas may make a single payment to one area, thus causing a departure from the origin approach. It should be noted that in countries where taxes of this sort are allocated to subcentral governments, there is a tendency to favor the destination principle. This essentially requires the tax to be collected from retailers rather than from producers. There are important consequences stemming from the replacement on 1 July 1995 of the former taxes on gasoline and diesel by excise taxes on fuel. The former taxes were paid by fuel depots. In the oblast of Almaty, the revenues accrued to the rayons where the depots were located, except for one depot (the largest) which was an oblast enterprise and paid its tax to the oblast. The upshot was that the oblast received a large sum and that six of its subordinate rayons also received some revenue while six others received none. The total revenue from this tax amounted to about 2.3 percent of the combined expenditure of the oblast and its subordinate rayons. But the new excise duties on road fuel are collected from fuel producers. There are no such producers in the oblast of Almaty, so there are now no revenues at all from this excise tax for the oblast or its rayons. In short, the distribution of tax revenues has become more concentrated as a result of this change.

[16]   To see the problem, suppose first that Kazakstan was a closed economy -- that is, one with no exports and imports -- and suppose that each production plant paid its VAT to its local tax office. In this case, VAT would accrue on an origin basis. But if enterprises have plants or branches in different areas and yet maintain central accounts and pay to a single office, then the allocation of proceeds will follow the origin basis less closely. This is the situation in Kazakstan because the 1995 tax code envisages that enterprises with branches or plants in different areas may choose whether to pay to one tax office or to several different ones.

        Another problem arises with imports which are usually taxable. Suppose a car importer in oblast A imports a car. The importer charges VAT at 20 percent of its selling price when selling the car to a retailer in oblast B. Thus, oblast A receives far more than 20 percent of the value of production in A. This problem would be solved if imports were exempt so that the importer would charge VAT only on the difference between its selling price and its importing price.

        A more serious problem arises with exports which are generally exempt. Suppose a carpet maker in oblast C sells a carpet to an exporter in oblast D. The carpet maker charges VAT at 20 percent of the selling price and sends this amount to its own oblast. When the exporter sells the carpet to a foreign firm, it does not charge VAT; but it does demand a refund of the VAT which it paid on its purchase. Thus, oblast D actually loses tax revenue on the sale. This problem would be solved if exports were taxable, because then oblast D would acquire the VAT on the sale of the carpet to the foreign firm.

Table 7.8: Tax Yields per Head for Oblasts and City of Almaty (as a percent of mean)

OBLAST	VAT				PERSONAL INCOME				INCOME TAX (Ind. Ent.)				PROFIT TAX				EXCISES				TOTAL TAX REVENUES			
	1992	1993	1994	1995	1992	1993	1994	1995	1992	1993	1994	1995	1992	1993	1994	1995	1992	1993	1994	1995	1992	1993	1994	1995
Akmola	179.5	217.8	164.7	172.0	125.6	121.2	113.8	80.0	456.1	124.5	63.8	122.5	88.0	252.0	58.7	94.7	97.2	164.4	67.4	48.9	134.0	207.8	103.7	114.0
Aktyubinsk	84.6	76.3	78.2	96.8	89.2	80.2	111.9	133.0	29.8	56.4	56.7	78.7	92.6	87.4	162.1	199.6	87.1	112.5	126.0	83.5	88.3	83.1	122.9	139.6
Almaty	26.0	35.8	39.0	27.3	50.3	64.9	54.8	42.6	13.3	34.1	28.1	62.6	39.0	42.3	35.9	28.4	13.5	30.2	24.8	21.6	34.3	44.4	40.4	31.2
Atyrau	78.1	73.1	498.3	202.0	94.2	104.4	209.7	209.9	16.7	30.3	29.0	104.6	107.7	110.1	369.0	247.9	44.2	69.1	49.7	268.0	89.8	94.1	351.1	223.7
East Kazakstan	81.0	90.0	86.1	142.5	100.8	71.4	93.2	120.5	18.9	113.3	255.1	155.6	143.3	119.4	121.5	97.1	161.8	148.3	199.2	130.5	110.4	100.2	109.5	120.9
Zhambyl	15.3	47.3	28.6	35.9	56.9	53.3	44.4	45.9	19.7	59.3	51.9	56.6	69.4	41.2	39.6	29.3	204.3	179.4	100.4	59.3	50.6	52.2	41.1	37.9
Zhezkazgan	157.9	83.9	45.8	73.4	133.9	143.7	172.2	187.9	76.0	60.4	51.0	122.6	104.4	70.4	163.5	82.9	3.8	7.1	35.1	16.7	127.3	88.0	121.9	101.6
West Kazakstan	84.7	79.7	53.1	57.1	77.1	79.8	70.4	71.2	53.7	88.4	83.8	89.3	58.1	51.4	48.7	59.8	199.2	166.8	78.7	63.6	79.1	72.6	56.9	62.1
Karaganda	165.9	164.4	147.0	138.1	167.1	149.0	154.8	146.9	129.6	143.3	130.3	123.3	210.6	124.0	102.8	104.1	110.2	85.2	84.3	39.2	179.5	141.6	126.9	121.8
Kzyl-Orda	38.7	37.6	36.1	37.8	28.0	28.1	49.4	48.2	13.8	27.9	18.3	24.7	28.1	33.7	40.3	46.7	68.3	68.2	33.6	21.4	34.3	35.4	40.6	42.2
Kokshetau	104.8	77.1	64.8	65.3	118.4	104.0	80.1	73.0	210.7	141.6	96.4	79.3	46.5	57.5	43.3	52.7	141.2	147.2	127.5	83.6	88.1	78.5	63.5	64.3
Kostanai	171.9	113.8	71.0	67.5	145.9	132.7	99.7	114.1	207.4	289.2	189.1	186.0	87.5	86.2	75.1	111.4	6.8	25.3	25.3	38.9	129.6	103.3	76.8	92.5
Mangystau	116.9	188.0	160.1	195.6	176.0	161.1	192.8	290.0	34.8	112.5	424.6	139.7	227.0	181.0	193.1	314.4	0.3	1.5	42.4	10.5	161.1	170.9	174.6	246.3
Pavlodar	165.5	142.7	78.2	55.5	162.0	176.3	152.2	158.9	31.3	45.8	26.0	35.6	159.2	168.3	133.6	195.8	133.3	115.7	35.0	261.3	160.9	158.6	114.8	143.2
North Kazakstan	80.9	86.0	62.2	63.0	130.9	118.2	76.6	72.6	125.1	183.2	234.5	180.1	52.3	46.1	46.8	42.3	227.9	268.2	141.8	85.1	86.2	85.7	64.6	60.4
Semipalatinsk	54.9	70.5	76.7	84.7	52.9	47.8	49.7	48.4	25.3	41.6	36.9	59.1	58.2	54.7	53.9	41.2	65.6	70.2	64.2	36.2	56.2	59.3	60.4	57.4
Taldykorgan	60.1	49.6	23.0	19.5	56.6	56.1	38.8	30.0	42.0	51.4	46.8	65.2	53.8	40.0	27.8	13.7	7.6	9.6	10.5	4.7	54.8	45.4	27.9	19.3
Turgai	252.6	78.3	35.4	40.1	124.3	129.9	67.1	56.5	66.6	162.7	95.5	113.8	76.4	80.2	48.1	25.1	9.1	20.5	17.1	22.2	155.7	87.7	46.9	38.2
South Kazakstan	43.0	44.4	45.0	48.1	37.5	41.7	41.9	36.9	83.0	54.2	37.8	46.8	80.0	81.3	66.2	51.3	57.9	56.4	41.2	139.7	56.1	57.9	52.7	52.8
Almaty (city)	141.8	218.0	306.8	357.6	140.2	192.3	217.4	194.9	190.2	156.0	195.3	196.6	162.7	211.1	281.6	262.3	217.9	267.4	498.0	347.1	152.6	209.1	287.5	283.2
Mean	100.0	100.0	100.0	100.0	100.0	100.0	100.0	100.0	100.0	100.0	100.0	100.0	100.0	100.0	100.0	100.0	100.0	100.0	100.0	100.0	100.0	100.0	100.0	100.0
Standard Deviation	62.1	57.2	114.1	82.3	45.6	47.7	58.7	71.1	107.8	66.8	104.0	50.9	56.0	62.2	90.7	89.5	78.2	76.0	107.8	96.2	46.1	52.2	83.6	74.5
Range (Max/Min)	16.5	6.1	21.7	18.3	6.3	6.8	5.6	9.7	34.3	10.4	23.2	8.0	8.1	7.5	13.3	22.9	701.7	173.9	47.5	74.4	5.2	5.9	12.6	14.6
Correlation																								
with previous year	...	60.5	42.7	78.4	...	93.5	79.7	93.6	...	54.9	56.3	71.4	...	68.8	48.5	85.0	...	55.0	62.2	62.6	...	81.8	56.3	90.7
with 1992	...	...	...	25.2	...	...	...	70.2	...	...	...	42.0	...	...	...	74.0	...	...	...	44.2	...	...	...	59.7

Source: Ministry of Finance.

Table 7.9: Tax Yields per Head for Rayons in the Oblast of Almaty
(as a percent of mean, revised 1995 budget)

RAYON[1]	POPULATION	INDIVIDUAL INCOME TAX	PROFIT TAX[2]	EXCISE DUTIES[3]	VAT[4]
Balkhash	28,200	47.2	12.6	0.0	53.0
Zhambul	91,800	48.8	51.6	0.0	42.1
Iliy	120,100	140.7	231.5	56.4	172.1
Kaskelen	145,200	149.3	100.0	320.5	124.5
Kegen	16,500	96.5	72.3	0.0	62.5
Kurtin	30,200	62.2	27.7	0.0	30.0
Raimbek	53,900	21.4	22.2	0.0	14.5
Talgar	138,100	113.3	99.0	71.8	108.5
Uygur	62,500	34.0	22.9	56.4	24.8
Chilik	89,300	44.7	47.7	25.6	49.1
Enbekshikazakh	111,900	100.6	84.5	205.1	65.9
Kapchagai[1]	45,400	246.6	304.3	17.9	398.4
Total/Mean	933,100	100	100	100	100

[1] Strictly speaking, Kapchagai is a city, not a rayon, but it has the status of a rayon.
[2] The figures exclude a small amount of tax (39 million tenge) paid directly to the oblast.
[3] The figures exclude the revenues from petrol and diesel fuel, as they were not part of excise taxes in 1995.
[4] The figures exclude a small amount of tax (13 million tenge) paid directly to the oblast.

Source: The Oblast of Almaty Finance Office.

7.36   This excessive concentration of tax revenues is bound to create problems. Some areas may feel they are "subsidizing" the rest of the country while others are heavily dependent on subventions. However, this is not really correct. Although the incidence of taxes is notoriously hard to assess, there is no doubt that with taxes such as excise duties much of the incidence falls on the consumer, not on the producer. There is, therefore, no real way in which the few areas with numerous producers can be said to be raising their large tax sums wholly from their own residents. But the belief held by some areas that they are subsidizing others might cause problems. In the worst scenario, it could lead to pressures to secede. Less seriously, unequal per capita tax yields have resulted in different areas receiving different shares of the shared taxes. This may not be very popular in the areas with low shares. These areas may not complain very much as long as territorial administrations are little more than local branches of the national government. But if local autonomy were to increase, they might well start to complain that they were being harshly treated.

Instability of Tax Revenues over Time

7.37   To make matters worse, the geographical distribution of tax revenues is not only uneven. It is also unstable over time. As Table 7.8 shows, the correlation between revenue performance (as measured by comparing tax yields per capita in each oblast to the national average) from one year to the next is weak. It is even weaker when one looks at a longer period of time (four years in the table). Part of this volatility is explained, of course, by the economic turmoil that the country underwent over the period. The resulting volatility of relative prices and profitability necessarily affected related tax bases, particularly those of indirect and profit taxes. By contrast, in the absence of a competitive labor market, the relative inertia of employment and wages helps to explain the much greater stability of the personal income tax yields. But such instability is also inherent in the Kazak economy in view of its heavy regional specialization on various types of commodities (e.g., grain, oil, nonferrous metals) the prices and/or output of which is intrinsically unstable, either (as, for instance, in the case of metals) because the prices of the said commodities on the world market go through wide cycles, or because (as in the case of grain) because production conditions depend heavily on the vagaries of the weather.

Revenue Sharing and Subventions

7.38   Revenue sharing and subvention serve to offset the impact of this high geographical concentration and volatility over time of tax revenues. In the budget process described below, the Ministry of Finance ultimately approves a figure for the level of consolidated spending in each oblast. This consolidated spending figure contains not only the oblast's own spending but also the spending of its subordinate rayons. The Ministry also approves forecasts for the tax and nontax revenues of the lower tiers. At this point, there is a large gap between the approved spending and the forecast revenues of the oblasts.

Revenue Sharing and Subventions for the Oblasts

7.39   To bridge this gap, the government first earmarks to the oblasts all the revenue from the individual income tax that is raised in their areas. Next, it earmarks to the oblasts specified shares of four shared taxes (the so-called regulating taxes), namely, excise taxes, VAT, fixed rents, and profit taxes. These shares vary from oblast to oblast and are also liable to change when the budget is revised during the course of a year. The shares agreed in the revised 1995 budget are shown in

Table 7.10 (note that there are no shared tax revenues in Leninsk which is supported chiefly by the Russian Federation). Finally, for those oblasts in which even the receipts from the individual income tax and the approved shares of the regulating taxes are inadequate, the Ministry pays subventions, that is general grants. Table 7.10 shows the oblasts receiving subventions.

Table 7.10: Tax Shares and Subventions for Oblasts
(revised 1995 budget)

OBLAST	EXCISE TAX SHARE (%)	VAT SHARE (%)	FIXED RENTS TAX SHARE (%)	PROFITS TAX SHARE (%)	SUBVENTIONS? YES/NO
Akmola	100	50	-	90.0	No
Aktyubinsk	100	50	100	51.3	No
Almaty	100	100	-	100.0	Yes
Atyrau	10	10	10	39.5	No
East Kazakstan	100	100	-	100.0	Yes
Zhambyl	100	100	-	100.0	Yes
Zhezkazgan	100	100	-	42.7	No
West Kazakstan	100	100	100	100.0	Yes
Karaganda	100	50	-	54.0	No
Kzyl-Orda	100	100	100	100.0	Yes
Kokshetau	100	100	-	100.0	Yes
Kostanai	100	50	-	29.4	No
Mangystau	10	10	10	19.7	No
Pavlodar	20	20	20	26.2	No
North Kazakstan	100	100	-	100.0	Yes
Semipalatinsk	100	100	-	100.0	Yes
Taldykorgan	100	100	-	100.0	Yes
Turgai	100	100	-	100.0	Yes
South Kazakstan	100	100	-	100.0	Yes
Almaty	20	20	-	8.9	No
Leninsk	0	0	-	0.0	Yes

Source: Ministry of Finance.

7.40   Using both variable tax-sharing rates and subventions may seem complex, but the procedure is simple. Consider first the 14 oblasts with no fixed rents tax shares. Nine of these are allowed to keep 100 percent of the revenues from the other three regulating taxes and, as these 100 percent shares are inadequate, they are also given subventions. Where 100 percent shares of the three other regulating taxes would prove more than adequate, the oblasts are given less. In one case, only the profit tax share is reduced. In three cases, the VAT share is reduced to 50 percent and the profit tax share is set below 100 percent. In the final case, the city of Almaty, both the VAT and excise tax shares are cut to 20 percent and the profit tax share is set below 100 percent. Turning to the six oblasts which do enjoy shares from the fixed rents tax, there are two cases in which even 100 percent from the remaining three regulating taxes proves inadequate, so that subventions are paid. But again, where 100 percent shares of the regulating taxes would prove more than adequate, the oblasts are given smaller shares and no subventions.

7.41   Table 7.11 shows for each oblast its total revenue and its percentage revenue from each of these three sources for the revised 1995 budget. It can be seen that while nine oblasts (including City of Almaty) require no subventions, 11 do require subventions. And in some cases the level of subventions is very high, rising in five cases to over 50 percent of total revenue and in two cases to nearly 70 percent.

Table 7.11: Local Revenues, Shared Tax Revenues, and Subventions
(revised 1995 budget)

OBLAST	LOCAL REVENUES (%)	SHARED TAX REVENUES (%)	SUBVENTIONS (%)
Akmola	36.17	63.83	0.00
Aktyubinsk	52.25	47.75	0.00
Almaty	31.27	15.87	52.85
Atyrau	74.77	25.23	0.00
East Kazakstan	45.56	43.11	11.33
Zhambyl	27.94	27.64	44.42
Zhezkazgan	69.14	30.86	0.00
West Kazakstan	35.71	38.76	25.54
Karaganda	63.12	36.88	0.00
Kzyl-Orda	13.84	16.19	69.97
Kokshetau	29.73	36.67	33.59
Kostanai	67.85	32.15	0.00
Mangystau	88.32	11.68	0.00
Pavlodar	77.83	22.17	0.00
North Kazakstan	35.03	32.54	32.43
Semipalatinsk	23.36	26.60	50.04
Taldykorgan	20.69	10.45	68.86
Turgai	26.49	19.16	54.35
South Kazakstan	23.91	47.24	28.85
Almaty	74.52	25.48	0.00
Total[1]	45.03	32.13	22.84

[1] The totals include figures for Leninsk.
Source: Ministry of Finance.

Revenue Sharing and Subventions for the Rayons

7.42   The sole objective of the Ministry of Finance is to ensure that the oblasts have reasonable funds. It is then up to the oblasts to divide these funds among themselves and their subordinate rayons. In fact, the oblasts use very similar procedures to those of the Ministry. They earmark to each rayon a share of the individual income tax and the four regulating taxes, and where necessary they also top up this income with subventions.

7.43   A useful insight into this process is provided by the oblast of Almaty. Table 7.12 shows the tax shares for the main taxes (except the then separate tax on gasoline and diesel) for 1995. The oblast set the shares for some rayons at less than 100 percent as it seemed that these rayons would still have adequate revenues and would need no subventions. However, when revised budgets were prepared later in 1995, it turned out that all the rayons would need subventions. Some of these could have been avoided by raising the rayons' tax shares, but instead the tax shares were left alone and subventions were allowed for all rayons. Thus, some rayons are "losing" some of their tax revenues to the oblast and are also receiving subventions from the oblast.

Table 7.12: Tax Shares within the Oblast of Almaty, 1995[1]

RAYON[2]	PERSONAL INCOME TAX SHARE (%)	CORPORATE INCOME TAX SHARE (%)	VAT SHARE (%)	EXCISE DUTIES[3] SHARE (%)	SUBVENTIONS? YES/NO
Balkhash	100	100	100.0	100	Yes
Zhambul	100	100	100.0	100	Yes
Iliy	100	25	47.0	100	No[4]
Kaskelen	80	40	29.4	100	No[4]
Kegen	100	100	100.0	100	Yes
Kurtin	100	100	100.0	100	Yes
Raimbek	100	100	100.0	100	Yes
Talgar	100	100	100.0	100	Yes
Uygur	100	100	100.0	100	Yes
Chilik	100	100	100.0	100	Yes
Enbekshikazakh	100	30	100.0	100	Yes
Kapchagai [2]	80	100	75.3	100	No[4]

[1] The table covers the main taxes. The rayons all keep 100 percent of the land tax, the tax on motor vehicles, and the property tax, although until July 1, 1995 they had to pay 10 percent of the land tax to the Republic. They also keep 85 percent of the Nature Protection Fund receipts (the remaining 15 percent going to the Republic).

[2] Strictly, Kapchagai is a city, not a rayon, but it has the status of a rayon.

[3] These rayon revenues exclude the receipts from the gasoline and diesel tax which accrue largely to the oblast; this is because the tax shares were set before fuel taxes were regarded as excise taxes.

[4] At the start of 1995, when the tax shares were fixed, it was expected that these areas would not require subventions; in fact, when the revised 1995 budgets were prepared and it was too late to alter the tax shares, it was found that they would all need subventions.

Source: The Oblast of Almaty Finance Office.

7.44   As the tax shares for the rayons are so often 100 percent, it might seem that the oblast would receive few tax revenues for itself. However, because tax shares are applied on an origin basis, most tax revenues arise in relatively few areas. Consequently, the oblast can raise significant sums if it shares in the revenues in these few areas and acquires no tax revenues from other areas. Table 7.13 shows the division of tax and other revenues between the oblast of Almaty and the rayons. Admittedly, the oblast receives relatively little of the tax on individual incomes. But it receives almost half the revenue from the profit tax, and it receives about a third of the revenue from VAT, even though in each case it takes a share in only 3 areas out of 12. It also receives about two-thirds of the total excise tax receipts shown in Table 7.13, as these are taken to include the taxes on gasoline and diesel which are excluded from the shares shown in Table 7.12.

Table 7.13: Division of Revenues in the Oblast of Almaty
(revised 1995 budget)

REVENUE SOURCE	OBLAST (%)	RAYON (%)	TOTAL (%)
Tax on personal income	2.02	19.29	12.03
Tax on profits	9.02	7.29	8.02
Value added tax	5.42	8.11	6.98
Excise taxes[1]	4.56	1.80	2.96
Fixed rent payments	0.00	0.00	0.00
Land tax	0.00	1.99	1.15
Tax on motor vehicles	0.00	1.98	1.15
Property tax	0.00	2.36	1.37
State duties	0.44	3.46	2.19
Nontax revenue	3.39	4.72	4.16
Other levies	0.37	3.77	2.34
Road Fund	9.05	1.81	4.85
Nature Protection Fund	0.00	1.05	0.61
Subventions	65.73	42.37	52.20
Total	100.00	100.00	100.00

[1] Includes levy on motor fuel which was a separate tax in the first part of 1995.
Source: The Oblast of Almaty Finance Office.

The Budget Process

7.45   The determination of the above revenue-sharing arrangements and subventions is one of the two outcomes of the budget -- the other being the expenditure envelopes of budget organizations. In brief, this process is conducted in a uniform fashion across the country, based on norms and incremental factors determined at the republican level (see Box 7.3 for a more detailed description). First, under a bottom-up process, the rayons and oblasts prepare draft budgets showing forecasts of revenue for the following year and also forecasts of spending. Each oblast then consolidates its own budget with those of its subordinate rayons and submits the consolidated result to the Ministry of Finance. It seems that the main use, in practice, of the oblasts' consolidated budgets is to suggest some amendments to the Ministry's own estimates.

7.46   The decisive process, indeed, goes from top to bottom. The Ministry of Finance prepares its own drafts at the same time as the oblasts and rayons are preparing their submissions, based on the same parameters and one additional constraint: the Ministry's own estimation of the available resource envelope. This process reveals two forms of imbalance: (i) imbalance between overall expenditure requirements and available resources; and (ii) imbalance between the individual oblast's authorized expenditure and its "own" revenue forecast. A bargaining process ensues which involves:
(i) bringing oblast expenditure submissions within the overall resource envelope; and (ii) allocating first the regulating taxes, then the envelope of republican subventions, among oblasts. From this process comes: (i) each oblast's authorized expenditure; (ii) the sharing rates for the regulating taxes; and (iii) the amount of subvention (if any) per oblast. The Ministry then consolidates its revised oblast budgets with a draft republican budget to form a draft state budget.

Box 7.3: Preparation of Territorial Budgets

Stage 1: The draft lower tier budgets

Conceptually, though not necessarily chronologically, the first stage of the budget process takes the form of rayons and oblasts preparing draft budgets for the following year. For each service, they are obliged to estimate their expenditure under each of 11 standard headings, based on norms and incremental factors. As well as spending figures, the rayons and oblasts also include in their draft budgets their estimates of their revenue from the relevant nationwide taxes and from taxes and nontax revenues. Estimates of receipts from the nationwide taxes are based on the assumption that rayons and oblasts will continue to receive their present shares and that present tax rates will continue. When the rayons have completed their draft budgets, they send them to their parent oblasts. These parent oblasts then prepare consolidated draft budgets which show their own spending plans and revenue forecasts plus all the spending plans and revenue forecasts of their subordinate rayons. This "bottom-up" process was used in the communist period, but was not used in 1992 and 1993 because of a flight of experienced personnel. The process was resumed in 1994.

Stage 2: The Ministry of Finance budgets

By around September or October, these consolidated draft oblast budgets are submitted to the Division of Territorial Budgets at the Ministry of Finance. By this time, however, the Division will have prepared its own individual budgets for each of the oblasts, covering both revenues and expenditures. These budgets are prepared by the Division in the light of the revenues that it expects will be raised from local taxes and local non-tax revenues, the shares of nationwide taxes that it thinks can be afforded to lower tiers, and its perceived spending needs of each oblast. Currently, the Division is unlikely to adjust its budgets very much in the light of the draft budgets submitted by the oblasts, and this explains why the oblasts and rayons may not expend much effort in preparing their draft budgets. When any minor adjustments to the budgets prepared by the Division of Territorial Budgets have been made, they are sent to the Consolidated Economics Division of the Ministry of Finance. There, they are consolidated with the republican budget to form a draft state budget. This is then considered by the Council of Ministers, Parliament, and the President. Substantial modifications may be made at this stage.

Stage 3: The approved budgets

Eventually, an approved budget is sent back to the Consolidated Economics Division of the Ministry of Finance. This Division then divides the approved budget between the Republic and the oblasts. The share available for the oblasts is then divided among the oblasts by the Division of Territorial Budgets; at this stage, this Division is usually subject to intense lobbying by some oblasts. The amount available for the oblasts is typically less than the amount submitted by the Division of Territorial Budgets in Stage 2. The procedure for allocating this smaller amount is broadly that unavoidable items of spending, such as wages, are not cut, while other items are cut proportionally all around. As well as determining the total approved sending for each oblast, the Division of Territorial Budgets also approves final estimates of each oblast's revenues from taxes and non-tax revenues, and it then adjusts each oblast's tax shares and/or its subventions to ensure that each can finance its approved spending. The oblasts then prepare detailed budgets showing how they propose to allocate their available funds among themselves and their subordinate rayons, a process in which they face intense lobbying by their subordinate rayons. However, oblasts apparently try to allocate their funds among their subordinate rayons in a way that ensures reasonably comparable service levels among them.

Stage 4: Detailed allotments

The oblasts also make proposals about how to allocate the funds available for their own activities among their service headings. They are not obliged to follow the division of spending among their major service groups as outlined in the approved budgets sent to them by the Ministry of Finance; still less are they obliged to follow the spending suggested by the norms for individual parts of these service groups. But in practice they would be unlikely to change the spending among the main groups very much, for a cut in spending on item X in favor of more on item Y might cause the Ministry of Finance to allow less for X next year while not allowing more for Y. The Constitution requires each oblast to submit its proposed budget to its locally elected oblast maslikhat (assembly) for approval, but it seems that this amounts to little more than the oblast seeking approval to spend all the money that has been allocated to it.

In turn, the rayons also make proposals about how to allocate their available funds among their service headings. As with the oblasts, the rayons would be more likely to change the allocation within groups than among groups. They also have to submit their proposed budgets to their local maslikhats. The maslikhats seem to have little power, though it is unclear just how little power they have.

The actual rayon budgets are then submitted to the oblasts who prepare actual consolidated budgets. These are in turn submitted to the Ministry of Finance. This second process of submitting budgets upward is essentially intended only so that the Ministry can check that the approved budgets are legal. The period between the time when the Ministry notifies the oblasts of their approved budgets and when the oblasts and rayons determine their actual budgets and submit them for checking can be some months.

7.47   Subsequently, the President and Council of Ministers agree upon an approved state budget, and the Ministry of Finance then divides the approved spending between the Republic and the different oblasts. It also finalizes the republican-oblast tax shares of the four shared taxes and it finalizes subvention levels to ensure that each oblast can finance its approved expenditure. Oblast administrations in turn divide their budgets among themselves and their subordinate rayons. Again, the oblasts finalize the tax shares of the shared taxes and finalize the subvention levels to each rayon to ensure that each can finance its approved expenditure.

7.48   To some extent, the ongoing fiscal crisis has resulted in increasing discretion in the fiscal decisions of oblast and rayon administrations. As, in the final analysis, the expenditure requirements emerging from the application of norms and incremental factors now systematically exceed authorized expenditures, oblasts and rayons in practice enjoy a degree of appreciation in apportioning the resulting shortfall across the organization and categories of expenditure charged to their budgets. It is understood, however, that some categories of expenditures need to be fully budgeted for (personnel and medicine, for example) and that the local room for appreciation needs to remain within the bounds of what is tolerable by higher authorities.

Equalization

7.49   It has been said that the present budget system sought to equalize the level of services across the territory of the Republic ("needs equalization"). The question remained as to whether it was succeeding in this. Tentative evidence presented below would tend to indicate that it succeeds reasonably well.

7.50   It is notoriously hard to measure service levels. In fact, it is hard even to find indicators of service levels. But some indication of varying service levels for the health service might be found in the numbers of doctors and nurses per 100,000 population in each oblast. These figures are shown in Table 7.14. The table also shows that the coefficient of variation for doctors was 33.2 in 1993 while for nurses it was 11.4. The coefficient of variation is a unit-free measure of dispersion that shows the standard deviation as a percentage of the mean. If there were identical numbers of doctors and nurses per 100,000 citizens in each area, then both the standard deviations and the coefficients of variation would be zero. The fact that the coefficients of variation are not zero does not necessarily imply that there are sharp variations in health service levels: it could reflect variations in needs.

7.51   It seems worth comparing these coefficients with those in another country which does seek comparable service levels in each area. Scotland was chosen as a useful comparison because it might be expected to have somewhat higher coefficients of variation than Kazakstan. This is partly because Scotland's health districts have somewhat smaller populations than Kazakstan's oblasts and partly because Scotland has some island districts with small populations which might secure relatively high numbers of medical staff. Thus if Scotland's coefficients of variation were lower than Kazakstan's, this might be taken as pointing to uneven standards in Kazakstan.

Table 7.14: Numbers of Doctors and Nurses
(per 100,000 population, 1993)

OBLAST	DOCTORS PER 100,000 INHABITANTS (1)	COLUMN (1) AS A PERCENT OF THE MEAN (2)	NURSES PER 100,000 INHABITANTS (3)	COLUMN (3) AS A PERCENT OF THE MEAN (4)
Akmola	47.2	121.5	109.9	98.5
Aktyubinsk	48.5	124.9	108.8	97.5
Almaty	22.3	57.4	86.1	77.2
Atyrau	37.9	97.6	114.6	102.7
East Kazakstan	37.8	97.3	120.2	107.8
Zhambyl	29.7	76.5	109.7	98.3
Zhezkazgan	38.0	97.8	133.7	119.9
West Kazakstan	35.4	91.1	102.4	91.8
Karaganda	51.6	132.9	119.3	106.9
Kzyl-Orda	36.1	92.9	144.1	129.2
Kokshetau	31.6	81.4	107.7	96.5
Kostanai	29.3	75.4	99.9	89.6
Mangystau	40.3	103.8	112.8	101.1
Pavlodar	36.0	92.7	113.6	101.8
North Kazakstan	32.3	83.2	98.4	88.2
Semipalatinsk	48.3	124.4	111.6	100.0
Taldykorgan	30.4	78.3	102.0	91.4
Turgai	31.8	81.9	114.7	102.8
South Kazakstan	27.8	71.6	99.0	88.7
Almaty	84.5	217.6	122.6	109.9
Mean	38.8	-	111.6	-
Standard Deviation	12.9	-	12.5	-
Coefficient of Variation	33.2	-	11.4	-

Source: Annual Regional Statistics of Kazakstan, 1993 (1994), 248 and 250.

7.52   The fact that not all the coefficients of variation in Scotland are higher than those in Kazakstan suggests that there may be at most relatively modest variations in service levels in Kazakstan. Table 7.15 gives the data for Scotland's health districts. The coefficients of variation for all doctors and for general practitioners are respectively 19 and 25; these figures are appreciably lower than those for doctors in Kazakstan. On the other hand, the coefficient of variation for nurses in Scotland is 16 which is appreciably higher than the figure for Kazakstan.

**Table 7.15: Numbers of Doctors, General Practitioners, and Nurses in Scotland
(per 100,000 population, 1992)**

AREA	DOCTORS PER 100,000 INHABITANTS (1)	COLUMN (1) AS A PERCENT OF THE MEAN (2)	GPS[1] PER 100,000 INHABITANTS (3)	COLUMN (3) AS A PERCENT OF THE MEAN (4)	NURSES PER 100,000 INHABITANTS (5)	COLUMN (5) AS A PERCENT OF THE MEAN (6)
Argyll & Clyde	160	89.1	75	89.6	1089	94.7
Ayrshire & Arran	156	86.9	71	84.8	904	78.6
Borders	160	89.1	78	93.2	1107	96.3
Dumfries & Galloway	179	99.7	86	102.7	1294	112.5
Fife	141	78.6	65	77.6	975	84.8
Forth Valley	161	89.7	73	87.2	1304	113.4
Grampian	192	107.0	69	82.4	1176	102.3
Greater Glasgow	266	148.2	72	86.0	1481	128.8
Highland	205	114.2	103	123.0	1150	100.0
Lanarkshire	144	80.2	60	71.7	922	80.2
Lothian	227	126.5	74	88.4	1198	104.2
Orkney	168	93.6	138	164.8	1151	100.1
Shetland	140	78.0	102	121.8	961	83.6
Tayside	217	120.9	71	84.8	1514	131.7
Western Isles	176	98.1	119	142.1	1022	88.9
Mean	179	-	84	-	1150	-
Standard Deviation	34	-	21	-	181	-
Coefficient of Variation	19	-	25	-	16	-

[1] Includes general, assistant, associate, and trainee general practitioners.
Source: Scottish Health Statistics 1993, The National Health Service in Scotland (1993), 164 and 166.

D. Creation of Local Governments

Rationale for Decentralization

7.53   Before presenting options for reform, it is useful to note the main arguments for having a system of democratic local government. This is taken to be a system of local government in which local authorities are accountable to local electorates through the democratic process. This accountability can take a number of forms. For example, local assemblies may appoint and oversee local administrators, or some local administrators may also be elected.

7.54   A major reason for having a system of democratic local government stems from the fact that preferences among the population may vary between areas.[17/] Preferences may vary over the total levels of local public spending and local taxes, over the allocation of local public spending between different activities, and over the actual nature of these activities. Decentralization allows public interventions to adjust to these differences in preferences. A second common, but less convincing, argument for local governments is that they offer a larger menu of public interventions from which citizens can pick and choose: if citizens dislike local choices, they also have the freedom to "vote-with-their-feet" and move to a more acceptable locality. There is, however, little international evidence, other than perhaps in exceptional cases such as the United States, of such type of behavior.

7.55   In brief, the creation of local government would permit a differentiation in the nature and level of public services across the territory of the Republic. It would allow local populations to restructure the existing supply of services according to locally perceived priorities within clearly defined budget constraints.

7.56   There are other advantages of local government. For example, the existence of local authorities, each operating its own services, would make it more likely that experiments and innovation will be carried out. In addition, the fact that decisions over some services would be carried out locally rather than centrally would make it easier for a central government to concentrate on the remaining public functions. Conceivably, this may be one factor that helps to explain why, among OECD countries, those with the greatest decentralization of tax revenues seem also to be those with the most successful macroeconomic performance: it is possible that those central governments which devolve the greatest amount of decisionmaking are consequently also those that are best able to concentrate on successful macroeconomic policies.[18/]

7.57   Once the need for decentralization is admitted, there remain many administrative questions to be solved before the creation of local governments is begun. The first order of business is to define the administrative framework under which local governments will operate, the nature of their authority, the level at which decentralization is to take place, the field of responsibility of local authorities, the situation of their personnel, and the form of the state oversight over local authorities. Once these parameters are defined, local government does not need to come into being overnight; it may instead be the result of an evolutionary process.

7.58   The remainder of the present section seeks to delineate the major administrative options in the design of a decentralization policy in Kazakstan. Taking into account the fundamental principles established by the Constitution, it is suggested: (i) that administrative decentralization would best be initiated by transforming the present localities into urban or rural municipalities; and (ii) that such municipalities might over time take over most of the assignments of the present territorial administrations within their jurisdictions. This devolution process might be tailored so as to proceed in tandem with the assertion of an autonomous management capacity at the local level. On this basis,

---

[17/]   For a sober economic assessment of decentralization policies, see Vito Tanzi, "Fiscal Federalism and Decentralization: A Review of Some Efficiency and Macroeconomic Aspects," *Annual Conference on Development Economics 1995*, World Bank, 1996.

[18/]   For an examination of the relationship between decentralized tax power and macroeconomic success, see David King, "Australian Reform Option: A European View," in D.J. Collins (ed.), *Vertical Fiscal Balance*, Australian Tax Foundation (Sydney, 1993), 265-300, especially 286-91.

Section E examines possible funding arrangements for the new local governments as well as for the remaining state territorial administrations.

Delegation or Devolution

7.59   There are two ways to involve the populations in those decisions which concern them most directly: through delegation of authority, or through devolution or transfer of authority.[19/] The delegation of authority is a technique of administrative organization. In this case, the state delegates parts its own authority to territorial bodies, possibly elected. Within the limits defined by the delegation of authority, territorial bodies receiving a delegation of state authority have discretion in executing their mandate in consideration of local circumstances. The autonomy provided under a delegation of authority is necessarily limited on at least four counts: (i) the responsibilities of the state which are being delegated are restrictively defined; (ii) delegated bodies remain within the state itself, which assumes the legal responsibility for their acts; (iii) these bodies are also placed in a hierarchical situation vis-à-vis the source of their delegation; and (iv) the latter can, under defined circumstances, repeal the delegation and/or overturn a decision made by a subordinate body.

7.60   Under a system of devolution of authority, there is no such hierarchical link. The bodies benefiting from such devolution (i.e., "local governments") have an exclusive authority in the matters transferred to them. In matters under their authority, they assume responsibility for their acts both politically vis-à-vis the local populations, and legally vis-à-vis third parties, including the state itself. Whereas delegation of authority may go to bodies whether they are elected or not, a territorial jurisdiction organized as local government would require the following:

(i)   A representative body to make decisions and to control their implementation, as well as an executive body to carry out decision

(ii)   A legal status allowing it to face the legal responsibility of its decisions, to defend its interests in court, to contract, to own property and to exercise ownership rights.

The authority of the state vis-à-vis bodies of local government is limited to circumstances explicitly defined: generally the control over the legality of local decisions, and also in some countries -- but rather more controversially -- the preservation of the "common good." This authority is exercised not through hierarchical channels but through "tutelage."

7.61   The Constitution of Kazakstan envisages the use of both mechanisms: Articles 85 through 88 define the system of delegation of state authority or "territorial state administration," whereas Article 89 determines the conditions for a devolution of authority to local governments or "local self-administration [...] exercised directly through elections as well as through representative and other bodies of local self-administration [...] established by law." At the moment, however, only the first mechanism is in place, as was described in Section B. This section will outline suggestions for reforming territorial administration which bring into play both constitutional notions.

[19/]   Both delegations and devolution can have a territorial dimension, but also a functional one. In the latter case, the state may delegate its own authority to a separate legal body which it creates or organizes (for instance, through the transformation of a departmental enterprise into a joint stock company). Only the case of territorial delegations or devolution is discussed in this part of the report.

Level of Decentralization

7.62   The first question to address in designing a decentralization policy is to define the number of tiers that should be involved. All OECD countries have at least one basic tier of local government; some also have a second tier, intermediary between the state and the basic tier. But a few have more, and those countries that have more than two tiers (for example, Belgium) commonly struggle with problems of conflicts of responsibilities, redundancies of functions and services. Two tiers should be considered an upper limit for Kazakstan. In practice, it would probably be sensible to start with only one.

7.63   Indeed, Article 89 of the Constitution reserves local self-administration to "rural and urban jurisdictions covering territories on which groups of population live compactly" (i.e., to localities as defined in para. 7.4). For reasons of minimum size of a jurisdiction, it is probably advisable that only localities of national importance (cities), oblast (towns), or rayon importance (townships) should qualify, at least initially, to be transformed into municipalities. Lower-level localities would remain subadministrative levels, as currently. So as not to disenfranchise the countryside from local self-administration, it might be advisable to review the current status of rural rayons and determine whether many of them are not sufficiently populated to qualify as localities, and to serve as a basis for the creation of rural municipalities.

7.64   From an economic viewpoint, it would appear that the largest critical impact of local government should be expected at this lower level. This is the level at which public services are in direct and day-to-day contact with the population (particularly through schools and general health care) and at which therefore they are thus likely to form well-grounded preferences regarding the nature and level of services they receive, and to participate actively in the definition of policies or, for that matter, in the mobilization of resources to support these policies.

7.65   Such a system would result in a geographical organization of the country, which is not uncommon among countries with vast and sparsely populated territories. In many such countries, local government jurisdictions may often not cover the entire national territory, but may be limited to areas with sufficient population to justify the establishment of specific public services, as well as to generate a sufficient fiscal capacity to operate them (the maintenance of rural roads, for example, may be well within the means of sufficiently populated rural jurisdictions, but may become unaffordable where settlements are few and far between). In such a system, localities are incorporated into municipalities and, so to speak, carved out of larger territorial jurisdictions. Such is the case in the United States (where municipalities are incorporated within state counties), in Tunisia (where municipalities are incorporated from the territory of délégations générales, themselves part of gouvernorats), in Morocco (communes within cercles), and Algeria (communes within wilayas).

7.66   At some stage in the process, Kazakstan may consider introducing a second tier of local government at the level of regions (as defined in para. 7.4). The Constitution leaves open the possibility of a devolution of authority in specified matters to oblast (and rural rayon) maslikhats (Art. 86). But such decentralization could only be limited, as these representative bodies would not have their own executives. They might entrust territorial administrations with the execution of tasks under maslikhat authority (Art. 89), but these administrations would remain entirely part of the national executive. The situation of the maslikhats would then be similar to that of the conseils généraux in French departements before the 1981 decentralization. The creation of decentralized executives within oblasts would probably require amending the Constitution.

7.67   When possibly designing a second tier of decentralization, care should be taken to ensure a functional specialization for each tier of government. The functional role of the basic tier is to provide the services which require a close contact with the population. The criterion is a socioeconomic one: access to service. In contrast, the functional role of an intermediary tier is to provide services which for technical reasons (size of infrastructures or services) have a regional catchment area and to coordinate and support the activities of lower tiers (intermunicipality networks or teacher training, for example).

Box 7.4: Decentralization in Poland

After World War II, Poland had adopted a three-tier, unitary public administration system essentially identical to the one that existed before 1939. The country was divided into 17 voivodships, 330 *powiats* (intermediate-level administrations), and, at the local level, 704 towns and 2,993 *gminy* (municipalities). The administrative structures had little decision-making autonomy, but were considered local subdivisions of the central power. Substantive power rested with the party, with the state administration relegated to the role of an executive machine. In June 1975, the *powiats* were abolished, with their administrative functions shifted to the voivodships. By the end of the 1980s, voivodships had achieved considerable independence from the central government. Deconcentration reforms during the 1980s essentially transferred authority within an integrated administrative system. Lower administrative levels remained subject to central control.

The administrative, territorial and fiscal structure of Poland was fundamentally transformed, starting in 1990. A Law on Local Self-Government was passed on March 22, 1990, which gives local governments (gminy, now numbering nearly 2,500) legally protected autonomy. It also grants local governments responsibility for all public matters of local significance not legally reserved for other units. Specifically, the Law gives local governments varying degrees of authority over housing, health services, water supply and sanitation, kindergarten and primary education, public order and fire protection, and spatial organization, land use, and environmental protection. This authority ranges from full devolution to gminy of financing and delivery responsibilities, to delegation from the central to local governments of delivery responsibilities.

The Law on Local Self-Government also states that:
-     Local governments are to be held accountable to their constituents through free elections and local budget execution is to be audited by regional accounting offices.
-     National laws may delegate to gminy the delivery of certain "mandated tasks" (such as social assistance programs) for which the central government provides financing and guidelines for coverage and service levels.
-     Local governments are autonomous for budget formulation and implementation, but the Ministry of Finance will allocate general subsidies on the basis of objective criteria.
-     Gminy may form associations for the joint provision of services (river basin management association, for example) or for purposes of representation (as with voivodship-level associations of gminy).

This framework separated the local budgets from the central budget and simplified the public finance system by abolishing extrabudgetary arrangements and by linking financing with assigned tasks. The acts also incorporated voivodship budgets in the central budget and eliminated the voivodship share of enterprise taxes.

In July 1990, 254 regional offices (*rejony*) were established to support the general administrative work of voivodships, especially with regard to rural gminy. One rejon usually contains three to twelve gminy. Gminy have their own administrative support units called *solectwo*, with the responsibilities of these units defined by gmina councils.

The initial legislation provided for phasing in the decentralization of some large expenditure items, most notably primary education and water supply and sanitation.

Source: Luca Barbone and James F. Hicks, "Local and Intergovernmental Finances in Poland," in *Decentralization of the Socialist State*, R. Bird, R. Ebel and C. Wallich (eds.), World Bank, 1995.

Figure 7.1

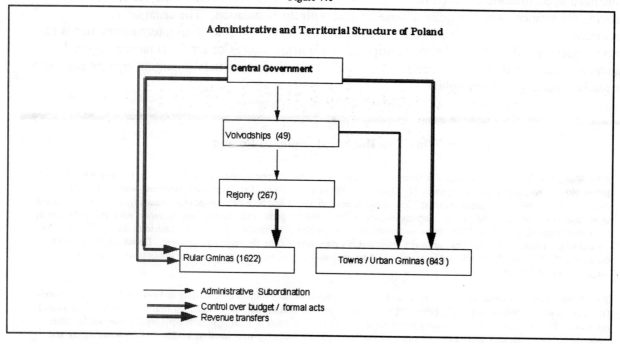

Administrative and Territorial Structure of Poland

Central Government

Voivodships (49)

Rejony (267)

Rular Gminas (1622)

Towns / Urban Gminas (843)

→ Administrative Subordination
⇒ Control over budget / formal acts
⟹ Revenue transfers

Field of Responsibility

7.68   The range of functions carried out by Kazakstan's localities is extensive but is fairly conventional by OECD standards (see paras. 7.22-27 above). Over time, most of these functions might be transferred to municipalities. Given the fairly conventional list of local authority activities in Kazakstan, a wholesale reform could involve immediately handing all current local activities over to the oversight of maslikhats rather than that of the central government, with perhaps roads being added to this and most transfers and subsidies being placed under central responsibility. A more cautious approach might be preferred, however. For example, current activities of territorial administrations within the localities could be split into two groups and municipal maslikhats could be made responsible for one initial group, as described in para. 7.71. Extra functions could be transferred to the maslikhats over time. This might be the simplest cautious approach.

7.69   Among the current expenditure items in the budgets of localities, three warrant further consideration. First, the range of subsidies given under the heading of social security and welfare should be examined. If these subsidies are retained, then they should be considered as essentially a form of redistribution. Redistribution is considered to be an activity that should be carried out in a more-or-less uniform way, and therefore is essentially a matter of central policies. It is not easy to give much discretion over redistribution to local authorities, because an authority that raised its taxes on the rich in order to give more help to the poor would tend to drive the rich out and attract the poor. In time, its redistribution policies might become unsustainable. As internal population movements become more frequent, there could well be difficulties if localities were to introduce significant variations in their transfer payment levels. Thus, most of these payments should probably remain a national responsibility.

7.70   Second, localities do not have responsibility over road building and maintenance in their areas, yet these are very common local functions in OECD countries. Minor roads could well be entrusted to localities. And third, localities and rural rayons provide most of general education and health services. In OECD countries, all or part of these services are often handled by central governments.

7.71   This transfer of responsibility to municipalities does not need to happen overnight. It may instead be the result of an evolutionary process. This devolution process might be tailored so as to proceed in tandem with the development of an autonomous management capacity, as well as democratic practices, at the local level. The phasing of decentralization to local authorities may be based on the following three criteria: (i) degree of externalities associated with the public services provided; (ii) economies of scale in furnishing them; and (iii) institutional capacity to manage them. The process could start with those activities which exhibit low externalities and low economies of scale, and are not excessively demanding in terms of management capacity. Another consideration would be to limit the rearrangement of administrative assignments among levels of jurisdiction to a minimum in order to avoid unnecessary disruption. With these criteria in mind, the authorities may want to begin by devolving a limited set of responsibilities to new municipalities, starting, for example, with urban infrastructures (e.g., water, district heat, street lighting, sanitation, and public transportation), kindergarten, culture and recreation, and some social services. Such a package would represent about 1.5 percent of GDP. In a second phase, the responsibility for local roads, and some of the health services, could be transferred to the municipalities. Further along in the process, the authorities would consider the desirability of decentralizing some or all general education.

7.72   The responsibilities of local government need not be limited. The Constitution determines that local governments will be competent in matters of local significance for the population. These matters need not be specifically defined. Indeed, many European countries (including Germany, France, Portugal, Spain, and Italy) strive to let their local governments adjust as closely as possible to local priorities by giving them a general competence for all local matters. The latter competence is understood to include all functions not exercised by a higher authority. Most countries add to this a number of mandatory assignments (matched by commensurate resources), such as hygiene, sanitation, fire protection, local roads, or public transportation. In the case of Kazakstan, such mandatory assignments may vary between urban municipalities (e.g., garbage collection) and rural ones (e.g., regulation of agricultural activities).

7.73   However, one concrete aspect of the transformation of localities into municipalities is that the latter would not be subject to the system of norms. Obviously, the national laws would continue to define general rules in certain matters applicable across the country -- or to entrust the government with formulating them -- (school curricula, for example). And obviously local governments would be subject to national laws. But in the discharge of their duties in the fields where exclusive authority has devolved to them by law, it would be up to the maslikhat, not the state, to define the norms applicable in their jurisdictions.

Interaction between Local and State Services within Territorial Jurisdictions

7.74   The emergence of local governments within localities should not necessarily lead to a duplication of administrative structures within local jurisdictions with the new municipalities, on the one hand, and the remaining state territorial administrations, on the other. There could remain integrated state/local administrations under the authority of the local akim, but accountable to two different authorities (state or local maslikhat) for two separate sets of matters. As concerns the head of administration, it is not uncommon in other countries that he would have dual responsibility, being both the representative of the state and the head of the local authority (of which he is the executive).[20] This is indeed the case in most countries influenced by the Napoleonic administrative law. A similar system would appear to be in line with the provisions of the Constitution of Kazakstan regarding the heads of territorial administration.

7.75   In this dual capacity, the head of administration could be head of: (i) the services which, either during the transition or permanently, would remain part of the state territorial administration within his jurisdiction; as well as (ii) local government services. This system of "integrated field services" is also common to many countries. In addition to being simple to design, it facilitates coordination of and cooperation among public activities within the jurisdiction.

7.76   In such a system, the head of administration would be in charge of executing two separate budgets: the national budget in the jurisdiction and the local government budget as approved by the local maslikhat. This procedure does not represent any particular difficulty, as will be seen in the next section.

Local Personnel

7.77   In the field of personnel management, as in other fields, one of the implications of the devolution policy is that the state would stop subjecting local payrolls to national norms and limits. Each municipality would have its own personnel and would make its own employment decisions. It would, however, still be the state's responsibility to define the general framework for local civil service.

7.78   A comparative study of local civil service rules would indicate that the latter come broadly under three categories: open regime, unified regime, and integrated regime.

  (i)   Open Regime (e.g., the former Soviet Union): Each local government employs its own personnel under contract. The advantage of this system is that all personnel are recruited locally and that it ensures a high degree of loyalty. The disadvantage is that it reduces the mobility of public employees and their career perspectives. It is therefore difficult for smaller entities to attract good personnel.

  (ii)   Unified Regime (e.g., Ireland, Jamaica, Sri Lanka): Local governments employ their own personnel under statutory rules for all local civil servants defined at the national level. The advantage of this system is the harmonization of employment and salary systems, which makes it possible to organize careers and mobility across local governments, while limiting the risk of cronyism. The disadvantage of the system is that it necessitates a central management of staff rules and possibly cumbersome coordination procedures among local governments.

---

[20]   He can either be appointed by the state, as its representative and head of the local jurisdiction (as in Belgium), or he can be elected by the jurisdiction and in this position can exercise some state functions (as in France).

(iii)   Integrated Regime (e.g., the Netherlands): Local governments employ their own personnel under specific provisions of single statutory rules for all civil servants, national or local. The advantage of the system is that it facilitates the mobility of staff between the state and local governments. The disadvantage is a lower level of loyalty of local personnel and more complex civil service management at the state level.

7.79   The unified regime would appear to fit the needs of Kazakstan best, at least as concerns the employment of administrative personnel. This regime leaves sufficient autonomy to local governments while allowing the state to harmonize employment conditions and provide special measures for local governments which are either smaller or whose jurisdictions are weak in human resources. However, if the option were taken of maintaining a single administrative structure within municipalities, the local civil service regime would need to be closely coordinated with the state regime, to avoid any feeling of discrimination between state and local civil servants working within municipalities. As was suggested for the state civil service itself, temporary or manual workers could continue to be employed under local contracts.

E. Funding Local Governments and Territorial Administrations

7.80   Fiscal decentralization is a corollary of administrative decentralization. There cannot be fiscal decentralization without local government, nor can there be local government without fiscal decentralization. The relationship between the two is sequential, however. The options available for fiscal decentralization can only be meaningfully discussed once the strategic directions are taken in terms of administrative decentralization. This section therefore elaborates on the developments presented above and explores their implication for fiscal management. It first discusses the process of separating state from local finances, then turns to reviewing the possible sources of finance for the new municipalities. Finally, it returns to some parallel suggestions for reforming the remaining territorial budgets.

Budgetary Arrangements

7.81   As far as the budget is concerned, the outcome on the budget side of the devolution policy discussed above would be to introduce a clear distinction between two types of budgets: the budget of the state and the budgets of municipal governments. To differentiate this new situation from the existing one (state, republican, and territorial budgets), the rest of the chapter will use the terms "national" and "municipal" budgets to characterize the proposed arrangements. The former would cover all of the fiscal activities of the state in matters of general interest, whether administered by central or territorial state administrations, and the others would encompass the fiscal activities of local governments within their sphere of responsibilities. Each of these categories of budget would be regulated by its own organic law.

7.82   Both budgets may be executed by municipalities, at least during the transitory period in which currently state functions are gradually transferred to new municipalities.[21/] It has been suggested (see paras. 7.74 to 7.76) that it might be advisable to maintain a single administrative structure within

---

[21/]   Obviously the national budget would also be executed directly within municipal jurisdictions by the field services of state administrations.

municipalities under the authority of the akim, rather than running two administrations in parallel (one state, one local). The local functions (and services) would come under the municipal budgets, whereas the state functions (and the services which deliver them) performed by municipal administrations would come under the national budget. In this context, the head of administration would at the same time be chief authorizing officer for the municipal budget and would be delegated the execution of the relevant appropriations of the national budget. The latter system is further described in paras 7.117 and 7.118, following a discussion of the possible sources of funding for municipalities.

Resources of Local Governments

7.83   Newly created local governments would require their own funding resources, independent from those of the national budget. A range of options is available involving fees, taxes, loans, and grants. Their potential role is discussed below. It should be underscored from the start that, in the evolutionary scenario presented above, the magnitude of local government's financing requirements will expand only over time, as the process of devolution unfolds and local government responsibilities grow. Therefore, not all the decisions regarding the ultimate composition of this funding need to be taken immediately. Indeed, in the course of the devolution process, the country's revenue outlook is bound to undergo substantial changes as a result of the ongoing economic transformation as well as the development of tax bases and collection capacities. Forms of revenue which today would seem minor may become buoyant in two to three years' time. A fundamental principle will need to remain unchanged through the process, however: that there should be no devolution of responsibility without a commensurate resource transfer. It would appear that, at least in the initial years of establishing local governments, the best part of their resources could come from a combination of tax income (the current local taxes plus some share of, or surcharge on, the personal income tax) and equalizing grants. The first section below briefly considers fees (or user charges), while the following sections consider the other three possible sources (loans, taxes, and grants).

Fees

7.84   It should not be expected that fee finance could be relied on substantially. In recent years, there has been an extensive debate in OECD countries about fees in local government. One attractive feature of fees is that they allow users to be confronted with the cost of services and deter them from consuming when the costs exceed the benefits. Another attraction is that they make the heaviest users of services pay the most. On the other hand, with many services, such as health, there is usually a desire for everyone to benefit irrespective of ability to pay. The result is that in practice OECD countries have made little progress in terms of actually implementing additional fees.

7.85   One obvious candidate for fee-based financing might be health services. In principle, these services could be financed wholly through fees, so that all citizens would need insurance policies. In this scenario, the main role of the government sector might be in ensuring that the poor are helped with the cost of insurance, and this role, being redistributive, might be left to the central government.

7.86   Aside from this possible example of health, there are few government services that can be wholly financed through fees. Rather, the reason why governments are involved in the provision of these services (rather than leaving provision to the market) is that there are arguments for relying chiefly on tax finance. For example, education is financed through taxes to ensure that all children have reasonably equal access; roads are financed through taxes because it would be costly to have tollbooths on all roads; homes for the mentally handicapped are financed through taxes because this group may have no income; and recreation and culture are often subsidized out of taxes in the hope of encouraging people to make greater use of these facilities.

7.87   Consequently, extending the use of fees is typically more a question of seeing if fees could be used for small parts of services. Thus there might be fees for the medical prescription part of the health budget, there could be fees for police attendance at football matches, and there could be full fees for food at kindergartens. The tight budget constraints that Kazakstan's localities will face suggest the need for a detailed study of the possible introduction and extension of fees.

Loans

7.88   Loans are generally considered the best form of finance for capital spending by local authorities. The reason is that when an authority purchases capital equipment or a building, it acquires an asset that will benefit citizens for years to come; thus, it seems right that all citizens over this period should help meet the cost, and a loan that must be gradually repaid enables this to be done as taxes are levied each year to help meet these repayments. On the other hand, loans are generally considered unsuitable for current spending, since current spending benefits only those citizens resident in the year concerned, and it seems fair that they meet the full cost through taxes rather than that some of the cost is shifted onto future citizens through loans.

7.89   If local authorities are required to finance capital spending out of taxes, they might in fact undertake little capital spending. The full cost of capital spending falls on current citizens, yet they receive only a small proportion of the benefits and thus may be reluctant to finance such spending. A classic example of this problem occurs in Australia, where local authorities have to resurface roads out of tax receipts and the result is a very low level of capital spending. Indeed, on the basis of present trends, it seems that the average Australian road will be resurfaced only once a century.

7.90   Thus, the case for arranging for Kazakstan's local authorities to borrow is based on the arguments that loans are the correct method of finance for capital spending and that they are a necessary method if capital spending is to be at adequate levels. Admittedly, Kazakstan's local authorities might initially face some difficulties in trying to borrow at reasonable interest rates, especially if they had little control over their tax rates and thus had an uncertain ability to repay their debts. There may be a case for them to combine to form a single borrowing agency which would in turn lend to them; if this agency were to become a trusted source, it could thus enjoy low borrowing rates.

7.91   A final point to note about borrowing is that most countries limit local authority borrowing for macroeconomic reasons, mainly to ensure that there is not an excessive amount of loan-financed spending. This responsibility should be exercised by the Ministry of Finance. Some formula may be used to apportion the permitted borrowing between authorities.

Taxes versus Grants

7.92   For current spending where fees cannot be used, there is a choice between taxes and grants. Most OECD countries combine both, as Table 7.16 shows. Ignoring loan receipts, OECD subcentral governments have revenues equal to 17.6 percent of GDP. Some 43 percent of their nonloan revenues comes from taxes (7.6 percent of GDP) and 39 percent from grants (6.8 percent of GDP);

the rest comes from other sources. However, Table 7.16 oversimplifies the revenue position because the figures shown for taxes include local taxes at locally set rates, local taxes at centrally set rates, and tax-sharing revenues.[22]

7.93   Local taxes at locally set rates have two advantages: they enable local authorities to raise or reduce their spending in line with local wishes, and they are genuine local revenue sources -- that central governments usually allow local authorities to spend more or less as they wish. In contrast, none of the other tax sources allows local authorities to vary their revenues. The issue of locally set tax rates, however, goes beyond the freedom to meet local wishes. If local authorities have no control over their tax rates and hence no control over their total revenues, they may have little incentive to spend efficiently because they can always blame any shortcomings in their services on the limited funds available. Once they have some control over the funds available, this excuse weakens considerably.

Table 7.16: State and Local Revenues in Selected OECD Countries[1] (as percentages of GDP)

COUNTRY	YEAR	TAXES (%)	GRANTS (%)	OTHER[2] (%)	TOTAL (%)
Denmark	1990	15.0	13.7	3.3	32.0
Canada	1989	15.3	7.5	3.8	26.6
Sweden	1990	16.3	4.8	3.5	24.6
Switzerland	1980	12.5	5.1	5.6	23.2
Finland	1990	9.9	7.5	3.9	21.3
Norway	1990	9.6	8.1	2.5	20.2
(West) Germany	1990	11.1	4.1	4.7	19.9
United States	1990	9.2	5.4	4.9	19.5
Australia	1990	6.3	7.2	5.3	18.8
Austria	1990	9.0	4.9	4.1	18.0
Netherlands	1990	1.1	11.9	2.2	15.2
Italy	1989	0.8	10.6	1.4	12.8
United Kingdom	1990	2.5	7.3	2.6	12.4
Ireland	1990	0.9	8.6	2.8	12.3
France	1990	4.1	3.1	1.8	9.0
Spain	1990	4.3	2.1	1.1	7.5
Belgium	1990	2.0	3.3	0.5	5.8
Mean for Countries		7.6	6.8	3.2	17.6

[1] Iceland and Luxembourg are omitted because they have populations below 500,000. Greece, Japan, New Zealand, Portugal, and Turkey are omitted because comparable data are not available.

[2] Excluding loan finance, which is omitted in OECD statistics.

Sources: Revenue Statistics of OECD Member Countries: 1965-91, OECD (Paris, 1992), 92, 206-229 and 242-253; and *Revenue Statistics of OECD Member Countries: 1965-93* OECD (1994), 253.

---

[22]   Unfortunately, OECD data do not allow the tax revenues to be divided into these different categories.

7.94   If the case for some local discretion over tax rates is accepted, there remains the question of how much is needed. Answering this question involves a trade-off between two orders of considerations: local accountability and equalization. It should be clearly understood first that local discretion over revenues is typically limited in OECD countries. In these countries, local governments with discretion over the rates of taxes raising even 20 or 30 percent of their resources would be considered reasonably autonomous. Subcentral governments with no discretion over their local tax rates are rare in OECD, although such is the case, for example, with the Länder in Germany and it is also virtually true of the municipalities in Portugal. Indeed, it is sometimes argued that so long as local authorities can vary the rate of one tax, no matter how small, they can still control their total revenue, and this is all that matters. But it is important to avoid a very low level of locally set taxes, as relying on a single small local tax produces a "gearing" problem. If a local authority receives, for example, only 10 percent of its revenue from a locally set tax, then even a doubling of its tax rates will have only a modest impact on its revenues and service levels. Electors might complain if huge increases in local tax rates led to little impact on services. If a degree of autonomy over revenues is to be granted, it needs to be sufficiently large for it to be meaningfully exercised.

7.95   However, before discretion over local tax rates is allowed, it would be desirable to tackle the problem of heavily concentrated tax revenues. The most obvious solution to the problem of heavily concentrated tax shares is to reform the ways in which the taxes concerned are levied. But reforming every tax would be a huge undertaking, and it is unlikely that there would be enthusiasm for this so soon after the implementation of the 1995 tax reform. Even if there was such enthusiasm, practical solutions might not be readily available.

7.96   A more modest two-part solution would seem to be as follows. First, some taxes could be selected for local use; care should be taken with their administration to ensure that their revenues are allocated reasonably. Secondly, the remaining resources would come under the form of subventions. This seems an attractive solution: if a country wants a measure of local autonomy combined with a measure of central influence, then a system in which most or all areas receive some grants, but none relying too extensively on grants, seems appropriate.

Choice of Local Taxes

7.97   In deciding which taxes might most usefully be assigned as local taxes, it is helpful to consider the OECD experience. Table 7.17 shows that the highest yielding subcentral taxes in the OECD are taxes on income and taxes on property. It is possible for these taxes to be levied by one or more tiers of local government and also by the central government, each setting its own tax rate. In cases where more than one tier uses a tax, there can still, for convenience, be a single tax machinery. Quite often the central government will administer the tax collection. And quite often it will determine the tax base, thus leaving local authorities discretion over nothing but the tax rate.

Table 7.17: State and Local Tax Yields in Selected OECD Countries[1]
(as percentages of GDP)

COUNTRY	INCOME TAXES (%)	PROPERTY TAXES (%)	SALES TAXES (%)	OTHER TAXES (%)	TOTAL TAXES (%)
Sweden	17.0	-	0.1	-	17.1
Canada	5.9	4.1	4.6	1.1	15.7
Denmark	14.3	1.0	-	-	15.3
Switzerland	9.6	1.6	0.1	0.4	11.7
(West) Germany	7.4	1.0	2.4	0.4	11.2
Finland	9.6	0.1	-	-	9.7
Norway	8.4	0.9	-	0.4	9.7
Austria	4.3	0.5	3.4	1.3	9.5
United States	2.4	3.1	3.3	0.7	9.5
Japan	4.5	2.0	0.6	0.4	7.5
Australia	-	2.8	0.9	2.9	6.6
Spain	0.7	1.6	1.3	0.6	4.2
France	0.6	1.3	0.2	2.0	4.1
Belgium	1.7	-	-	0.5	2.2
New Zealand	-	2.1	-	0.1	2.2
Portugal	0.5	0.7	0.7	0.1	2.0
Turkey	0.9	0.1	0.8	0.1	1.9
United Kingdom	-	-	-	1.3	1.3
Italy	0.5	-	0.2	0.5	1.2
Netherlands	-	0.7	-	0.3	1.0
Ireland	-	0.9	-	-	0.9
Greece	-	-	0.1	0.3	0.4
Unweighted Mean	4.0	1.1	0.9	0.6	6.6

[1] Iceland and Luxembourg are omitted because they have populations under 500,000.
Source: Derived from *Revenue Statistics of OECD Member Countries: 1965-93*, OECD (Paris, 1994), 197 and 199.

7.98   Kazakstan already has a tax on individual incomes and it has taxes on land and buildings. Table 7.7 has shown that the individual income tax and the land tax between them make up about 28 percent of the resources of territorial budgets. If local spending on transfers and welfare subsidies were to be reduced, then this figure would rise, possibly to over 35 percent. The only drawback is that the state might want to retain some use of the individual income tax so that it could vary its tax rate for macroeconomic stabilization purposes. Certainly no OECD countries allocate the whole of their individual income tax revenues to local authorities, although Sweden comes very close. Nevertheless, so long as local authorities were allowed to levy the bulk of the individual income tax at locally set rates, and were also allowed to set the rates of the local property and land taxes, they would seem to have a reasonably acceptable degree of local tax rate control. It is hoped, also, that income tax receipts will grow with the economy and will result in greater autonomy.

7.99   The following paragraphs briefly discuss local property and income taxes. They also look at other possible local taxes.

7.100   *Property taxes*. Property taxes on land and buildings have many advantages: (i) they fall on all residents;[23] (ii) they fall on businesses that receive benefits from some local services; (iii) their yield is fairly certain; (iv) the subject of taxation cannot easily migrate; and (v) evasion is hard. But their potential yield is limited as they relate only loosely to ability to pay and thus seem unfair if levied at a high rate. Few countries have had property tax yields in excess of 2 percent of GDP.

7.101   *Local taxes on incomes*. Because property tax yields are limited, countries where local authorities have substantial fiscal autonomy invariably make use chiefly of local individual income taxes. These have high potential yields and are usually levied on residents. It is useful to levy the tax on residents, partly to ensure reasonably even per capita tax yields and partly to ensure that people pay taxes to the areas in which they are entitled to vote. Although the income tax is not, at the moment, levied on a residence basis, it could be converted to this system more easily than could other taxes. The income tax is currently withheld at the source by enterprises and therefore is assigned on the basis of enterprise location. However, when state or private firms pay the withheld amount, they fill in special forms that provide information about their employees, and this could be used for tax assignment. Furthermore, since November 15, 1995, every resident has started to be enrolled for the purpose of the property tax and is receiving a Taxpayer Registration Number. This identification number together with the employers' information could serve as a basis for managing residence information, without requiring taxpayers to file tax returns.

7.102   A possible drawback to a local income tax is that many people may have incomes so low that they are exempt. If a local income tax were the only local tax, then low income people might vote for better services knowing they would not have to contribute to them through higher taxes. Thus, there is a case for not relying on a local individual income tax alone but for having at least one other tax, such as a property tax, which impinges on all people.

7.103   Finally, national authorities might be reluctant, and this is legitimate, to relinquish control over the income tax. Other than being a revenue source, the personal income tax is also an important instrument of macroeconomic policy, through its impact on the distribution of income or on savings patterns. Allowing local governments to raise income tax *surcharges* (within nationwide limits) would appear to offer the best compromise between these national and local claims.

7.104   Countries with local individual income taxes usually also have local profit taxes, although with these there are always problems with allocating the profits of multiarea enterprises among the areas in which they have plants or branches. An advantage of a local profit tax is that it raises some income from businesses which, as was noted, usually benefit from some local services. However, in a country like Kazakstan where spending at the rayon level is devoted chiefly to health, education, and social welfare, it might be that a business contribution through a local business property tax would be a sufficient contribution from businesses and thus that it would be possible to avoid the administrative complications of a local profit tax.

---

[23] This is clearly the case when property taxes are levied on property occupiers. It is less clearly the case when property taxes are levied on property owners, for it may seem that the tax on a rented property is paid by the landlord who may not live in the area where the property is located; but in fact the tax will be in part -- often in large part -- shifted forward to the tenant in the form of a higher rent.

7.105 *Local taxes on expenditure*. Taxes on expenditure, such as VAT or excise duties, are rarely used locally. They are certainly unacceptable if they are levied on an origin basis (that is, where products are made), because that would result in a few rich areas and many poor ones. They are considerably better as local taxes if they are levied on a destination basis (that is, where things are bought). It is very difficult to administer satisfactorily a VAT on a destination basis, but it is possible to administer excise taxes on such a basis. However, even destination-based excise taxes can have problems if they are used as local taxes with locally set rates. The main problem is that it may be difficult for local authorities to raise their tax rates because, if they do so, they will tend to lose shoppers to other areas. For this reason they would typically not be used to finance municipalities.[24/]

7.106 *Local taxes on natural resources*. Local taxes on natural resources, such as the fixed rents tax, are very rare in OECD countries. A major problem is that their revenues tend to be highly concentrated in a few areas. Indeed, such areas are sometimes tempted to consider secession. Another problem is that the yields of these taxes may be very erratic, which would make it difficult for local authorities to forecast their future revenues. Thus, if it were thought politically feasible, Kazakstan should probably try to use the fixed rents tax solely as a source of funds for the national budget.

Grants

7.107 *Grants and external benefits*. One reason for the use of grants is to subsidize local authorities which provide services that benefit nonresidents. When deciding how much to spend on these services, local authorities may ignore the benefits of the services to nonresidents and may therefore spend too little on them. The most commonly cited examples of such services are major roads provided by small authorities through which the roads pass. In such a case, however, determining the correct degree of subsidy for each area is a very complex task, and, ideally, each area would be given a different level of grant which might well lead to complaints from the areas with the lowest subsidies. Arguably, it is best to avoid these problems. This could be done by giving local

---

[24/] However, taxes on expenditures might be more readily used to fund an intermediary tier of decentralization at the oblast level, if and when such a level is created. There are at least two possibilities:

One possibility would be for the oblasts to use some excise taxes as locally set taxes, perhaps having some constraints over the range of permitted tax rates. The point here is that the huge size of the oblasts might make it possible for the oblasts to set their own rates without having much effect on shopping patterns. Perhaps the main limitation here is that there might have to be some similarity between the tax rates set in the city of Almaty and those set in the oblast of Almaty. Also, there might be problems if in due course oblasts were to be reduced in size, a possibility that was mentioned above. It might seem a daunting task to devise new arrangements for one or more excise duties to ensure that their revenues were collected on a destination basis. But it might be possible to simulate destination-based excise taxes by using the arrangements adopted by the Australian states. According to the Australian Constitution, the states are not allowed to levy excise taxes. But in practice they issue licenses to retailers of liquor, petrol, and tobacco products and they make these license fees proportional to sales. As territorial authorities in Kazakstan issue permits to all enterprises, the permit fee system might be adapted to form a quasi-excise tax on the destination principle with little or no local discretion over tax rates. Of course, if these modified license fees raised substantial sums, then it would be appropriate for the central government to reduce its excise tax rates. But it might well wish to continue raising some money from this source so that the central rates could be changed from time to time for purposes of macroeconomic stabilization.

The impossibility of allocating VAT shares on a destination basis makes it unsuitable as a locally set tax and unsuitable as a conventional shared tax. Perhaps the best arrangement would be for its revenues to be left with the national budget. If it was desired to allocate VAT revenues to local authorities, it might be best for them all to be given an equal per capita sum, as is the case with the Länder in both Austria and Germany.

government only roads of local importance, and leaving to the Republic all the roads of national importance. This arrangement would avoid the need for such grants.

7.108 *Grants for revenue sharing and equalization.* Aside from handling externalities, grants can be used for two purposes:

(i) *Revenue sharing*, i.e., to correct vertical imbalances (that is, to help local authorities when between them they have inadequate tax revenues to meet their expenditure assignments); or

(ii) *Equalization*, i.e., to correct horizontal imbalances, arising from:

Difference in needs: where the characteristics of the jurisdictions (e.g., size, population, age structure, public health) give rise to different levels of public service requirements

Difference in resources: where the revenue bases are unevenly spread across the various jurisdictions.

Usually a system of general grants handles both revenue sharing and equalization simultaneously. Indeed, most OECD countries make some formal efforts to use general grants for revenue sharing and equalization purposes. The United States is the most notable exception.

7.109 Countries can seek to equalize difference in needs, difference in resources, or both. At one extreme, a simple system can be used, as in Portugal and Spain, where each area is given a large equal per capita sum and where there are also modest additional payments for areas with special needs, such as many kilometers of roads in relation to population. At the other extreme, there can be *full equalization of differences in resources and needs*, as in the United Kingdom and Sweden. Here the government works out (A) how much money each area would have to spend to finance its services at standard levels, and (B) how much tax revenue each area would raise if it levied its taxes at standard tax rates. Then the government gives each area a grant equal to (A-B). Areas can in fact set their own tax rates rather than the standard rates, and thus they can supply services at levels of their own choosing rather than at the standard levels and yet receive the same grant whatever tax rates and service levels they adopt.

7.110 *Full equalization in Kazakstan.* At present Kazakstan seems to pursue full equalization within the context of the national budget, except that (in effect) it makes all areas actually adopt the standard tax rates and standard service levels. The way in which equalization currently operates in Kazakstan is shown in Table 7.18. The spending needs of each oblast, shown in column *(1)*, are taken to be given by their budgets. Column *(2)* gives the total tax yield in each oblast. Where this yield exceeds the oblast's spending needs, some of its tax yield is 'lost' to the republican budget as the oblast is allowed to keep less than 100 percent of the revenues of the regulating taxes; the lost tax amounts are shown in column *(3)*. Where the total tax yield is below the oblast's spending needs, the oblast receives a grant or subvention; these payments are shown in column *(4)*. Thus, each oblast ends up with the revenue shown in column *(5)* which is equal to its spending needs, and so each oblast can provide services at the standard levels used in assessing those needs. For convenience, the service levels in an oblast can be expressed in index form as a ratio of the actual level to the standard level, found by relating actual revenue and spending -- shown in column *(6)* -- to spending needs -- shown in column *(1)*. In the present situation, each area's actual spending equals its spending needs, so each area has a service level index of 1.00.

Table 7.18: Equalization of Difference in Needs and Resources, 1995

OBLAST	EXPEND. (tenge 000s) (1)	TAX YIELD (tenge 000s) (2)	TAX LOST (tenge 000s) (3)	SUBVENTION (tenge 000s) (4)	NET RECEIPTS (tenge 000s) (5)	REVENUE (tenge 000s) (6)	SERVICE LEVEL INDEX (7)
Akmola	4,609.7	5,859.4	-1,249.7	0.0	-1,249.7	4,609.7	1.00
Aktyubinsk	4,598.0	6,300.4	-1,702.4	0.0	-1,702.4	4,598.0	1.00
Almaty	5,292.4	2,495.2	0.0	2,797.2	2,797.2	5,292.4	1.00
Atyrau	2,812.3	5,775.0	-2,962.7	0.0	-2,962.7	2,812.3	1.00
East Kazakstan	6,554.7	5,812.3	0.0	742.4	742.4	6,554.7	1.00
Zhambyl	4,709.8	2,617.8	0.0	2,092.0	2,092.0	4,709.8	1.00
Zhezkazgan	2,986.1	3,339.2	-353.1	0.0	-353.1	2,986.1	1.00
West Kazakstan	4,109.5	3,060.1	0.0	1,049.4	1,049.4	4,109.5	1.00
Karaganda	7,568.8	9,962.7	-2,393.9	0.0	-2,393.9	7,568.8	1.00
Kzyl-Orda	5,085.4	1,527.1	0.0	3,558.3	3,558.3	5,085.4	1.00
Kokshetau	3,795.1	2,520.3	0.0	1,274.8	1,274.8	3,795.1	1.00
Kostanai	5,469.2	8,374.3	-2,905.1	0.0	-2,905.1	5,469.2	1.00
Mangystau	2,349.5	3,996.1	-1,646.6	0.0	-1,646.6	2,349.5	1.00
Pavlodar	5,221.0	9,187.7	-3,966.7	0.0	-3,966.7	5,221.0	1.00
North Kazakstan	3,501.6	2,366.2	0.0	1,135.4	1,135.4	3,501.6	1.00
Semipalatinsk	6,145.5	3,070.6	0.0	3,074.9	3,074.9	6,145.5	1.00
Taldykorgan	3,699.1	1,151.8	0.0	2,547.3	2,547.3	3,699.1	1.00
Turgai	1,882.4	859.2	0.0	1,023.2	1,023.2	1,882.4	1.00
South Kazakstan	9,537.3	6,785.7	0.0	2,751.6	2,751.6	9,537.3	1.00
Almaty	7,957.7	18,920.0	-10,962.3	0.0	-10,962.3	7,957.7	1.00
Total/Mean	97,885.1	103,981.1	-28,142.5	22,046.5	-6,096.0	97,885.1	1.00

7.111 *Securing full equalization through grants.* The Kazakstan scheme of full equalization within the state budget is highly practicable. It could be extended to the new local government budgets, in a similar fashion as the United Kingdom and Sweden use grants to achieve full equalization among local governments *without imposing a uniform level of services*. Local governments are able to alter their tax rates and thus raise or lower their revenues and service levels. The crucial point is that they would have equal service levels if they chose to set the same standard tax rates. However, such a scheme may require, if tax yields vary widely across the country, the use of typically unpopular negative grants. Both Sweden and the United Kingdom have avoided such a situation by maintaining local taxes sufficiently low.[25] In terms of making an equalization scheme acceptable, there is something to be said for having fewer local taxes, and hence making most or all areas eligible for positive grants.

7.112 Alternatively, grant schemes may seek to equalize differences in resources or differences in needs alone. The next two paragraphs illustrate the impact that each of such schemes would have on

---

[25] In fact, the situation in Sweden is not exactly as implied here. One or two areas with exceptionally high tax yields enjoy a favorable position and can have standard service levels combined with low tax rates.

service levels across oblasts if the national budget were to be constructed on that basis. The results obtained should be considered a first approximation. A more refined analysis would require simulating their impact at the level of localities and taking into account only those resources which will have been designated for municipal budgets. The overall impression, however, is unlikely to change: any such scheme would cause a substantial divergence in service levels across the country.

7.113 *Equalizing resource differences alone.* It would be possible to equalize only differences in resources. In this case, the situation would be as shown in Table 7.19, assuming that a mixture of positive and negative grants were used. Here, the ultimate aim would be to secure equal per capita revenues in each oblast, and the scheme would accept the fact that areas with high needs would end up with lower service levels (or higher tax rates) than those with low needs. Column *(1)* shows each oblast's population. Columns *(2)* and *(3)* show their spending needs and total tax revenues as taken from Table 7.18. Column *(4)* shows the grant receipts which are designed to ensure that the final tax plus grant revenues given in column *(5)* result in equal per capita revenues, as shown in column *(6)*. Equal per capita revenues mean that some areas have more than they need for spending at the column *(2)* levels while others have less, so service levels vary. The index in column *(7)* ranges from 1.30 to 0.69, a ratio of about 1.9:1. This would be the range if all areas set the same tax rates. It may be doubtful whether this range would be politically acceptable.

Table 7.19: The Effect of Equalizing Differences in Resources Alone, 1995

OBLAST	POPULATION (000s) (1)	EXPEND. (tenge 000s) (2)	TAX YIELD (tenge 000s) (3)	GRANTS (tenge 000s) (4)	REVENUE (tenge 000s) (5)	REV. PER HEAD (tenge 000s) (6)	SERVICE LEVEL INDEX (7)
Akmola	869.6	4,609.7	5,859.4	-813.9	5,045.5	5,802.0	1.09
Aktyubinsk	760.2	4,598.0	6,300.4	-1,889.7	4,410.7	5,802.0	0.96
Almaty	962.9	5,292.4	2,495.2	3,091.6	5,586.8	5,802.0	1.06
Atyrau	457.7	2,812.3	5,775.0	-3,119.4	2,655.6	5,802.0	0.94
East Kazakstan	961.0	6,554.7	5,812.3	-236.5	5,575.8	5,802.0	0.85
Zhambyl	1,052.6	4,709.8	2,617.8	3,489.4	6,107.2	5,802.0	1.30
Zhezkazgan	493.4	2,986.1	3,339.2	-476.5	2,862.7	5,802.0	0.96
West Kazakstan	674.3	4,109.5	3,060.1	852.2	3,912.3	5,802.0	0.95
Karaganda	1,305.5	7,568.8	9,962.7	-2,388.1	7,574.6	5,802.0	1.00
Kzyl-Orda	606.3	5,085.4	1,527.1	1,990.7	3,517.8	5,802.0	0.69
Kokshetau	674.9	3,795.1	2,520.3	1,395.5	3,915.8	5,802.0	1.03
Kostanai	1,082.5	5,469.2	8,374.3	-2,093.6	6,280.7	5,802.0	1.15
Mangystau	338.5	2,349.5	3,996.1	-2,032.1	1,964.0	5,802.0	0.84
Pavlodar	965.9	5,221.0	9,187.7	-3,583.5	5,604.2	5,802.0	1.07
North Kazakstan	620.6	3,501.6	2,366.2	1,234.5	3,600.7	5,802.0	1.03
Semipalatinsk	839.2	6,145.5	3,070.6	1,798.5	4,869.1	5,802.0	0.79
Taldykorgan	737.9	3,699.1	1,151.8	3,129.5	4,281.3	5,802.0	1.16
Turgai	313.2	1,882.4	859.2	958.0	1,817.2	5,802.0	0.97
South Kazakstan	1,969.2	9,537.3	6,785.7	4,639.7	11,425.4	5,802.0	1.20
Almaty	1,185.4	7,957.7	18,920.0	-12,042.3	6,877.7	5,802.0	0.86
Total/Mean	16,870.8	97,885.1	103,981.1	-6,096.0	97,885.1	5,802.0	1.00

7.114 *Equalizing needs differences alone*. Alternatively, it would be possible to equalize only differences in needs. In this case, the situation would be as shown in Table 7.20, assuming again that a mixture of positive and negative grants was used. As in Table 7.19, columns *(1)*, *(2)*, and *(3)* show the oblasts' populations, spending needs, and tax revenues. As their per capita spending needs vary, so areas with high or low per capita needs get respectively high or low per capita grants. The grant payments are shown in column *(4)*. These grants are calculated so that the additional per capita tax revenue that each area requires (that is, the gap between its per capita spending needs and its per capita grant) in order to secure spending at the standard level is the same everywhere, as shown in column *(5)*. Each area's combined revenue from taxes and grants is shown in column *(6)*, and the result is a huge range of service levels, as shown in column *(7)*. The range is from 2.46 to 0.08, a ratio of over 30:1. It is inconceivable that this range would be politically acceptable. If Kazakstan were ever to contemplate abandoning resource equalization, it would have to take prior steps to rearrange tax revenues so that they are much more equally distributed in relation to population.

Table 7.20: The Effect of Equalizing Differences in Needs Alone, 1995

OBLAST	POPULATION (000s) *(1)*	EXPEND. (tenge 000s) *(2)*	TAX YIELD (tenge 000s) *(3)*	GRANTS (tenge 000s) *(4)*	(2)-(4) PER HEAD (tenge 000s) *(5)*	REVENUE (tenge 000s) *(6)*	SERVICE LEVEL INDEX *(G)*
Akmola	869.6	4,609.7	5,859.4	-749.9	6,163.4	5,109.5	1.11
Aktyubinsk	760.2	4,598.0	6,300.4	-87.4	6,163.4	6,213.0	1.35
Almaty	962.9	5,292.4	2,495.2	-642.3	6,163.4	1,852.9	0.35
Atyrau	457.7	2,812.3	5,775.0	-8.7	6,163.4	5,766.3	2.05
East Kazakstan	961.0	6,554.7	5,812.3	631.7	6,163.4	6,444.0	0.98
Zhambyl	1,052.6	4,709.8	2,617.8	-1,777.8	6,163.4	840.0	0.18
Zhezkazgan	493.4	2,986.1	3,339.2	-55.0	6,163.4	3,284.2	1.10
West Kazakstan	674.3	4,109.5	3,060.1	-46.5	6,163.4	3,013.6	0.73
Karaganda	1,305.5	7,568.8	9,962.7	-477.4	6,163.4	9,485.3	1.25
Kzyl-Orda	606.3	5,085.4	1,527.1	1,348.5	6,163.4	2,875.6	0.57
Kokshetau	674.9	3,795.1	2,520.3	-364.6	6,163.4	2,155.7	0.57
Kostanai	1,082.5	5,469.2	8,374.3	-1,202.6	6,163.4	7,171.7	1.31
Mangystau	338.5	2,349.5	3,996.1	263.1	6,163.4	4,259.2	1.81
Pavlodar	965.9	5,221.0	9,187.7	-732.2	6,163.4	8,455.5	1.62
North Kazakstan	620.6	3,501.6	2,366.2	-323.4	6,163.4	2,042.8	0.58
Semipalatinsk	839.2	6,145.5	3,070.6	973.2	6,163.4	4,043.8	0.66
Taldykorgan	737.9	3,699.1	1,151.8	-848.9	6,163.4	302.9	0.08
Turgai	313.2	1,882.4	859.2	-48.0	6,163.4	811.2	0.43
South Kazakstan	1,969.2	9,537.3	6,785.7	-2,599.5	6,163.4	4,186.2	0.44
Almaty	1,185.4	7,957.7	18,920.0	651.6	6,163.4	19,571.6	2.46
Total/Mean	16,870.8	97,885.1	103,981.1	-6,096.1	6,163.4	97,885.0	1.00

7.115 *Equalization in the future*. Given the very different resources among areas, it is hard to envisage Kazakstan ending resource equalization. And given a history of establishing needs in each area, it is hard to see the country abolishing needs equalization. It seems likely, then, that the country will continue to use reasonably full equalization. Although some economists are wary of full equalization, it should be said that such system seeks only to ensure that people paying equal tax rates in different areas can enjoy similar service levels. This secures equity between areas and eliminates incentives for people to move to areas with high resources or low needs which would otherwise have low tax rates. Moreover, full equalization merely replicates the situation that applies to national services, since these are financed by uniform tax rates in all areas and should normally be supplied at equal levels (relative to needs) in all areas.

7.116 If equalization is to continue, there is a case for checking the system of assessing spending needs. The present budgets rely only loosely on any assessed norms, and the old USSR norms may not measure needs accurately. As was discussed earlier, these norms seem to rely as much on indirect factors (such as numbers of hospital beds) as on direct factors (such as numbers of sick people). Apparently new norms are in preparation. While these are being prepared, Kazakstan might wish to learn from countries with experience in estimating spending needs (e.g., the United Kingdom, Sweden).

Resources of Territorial Administrations

7.117 A number of services will in any case remain within the realm of state territorial administrations, particularly oblast services. The services should continue to be funded by general resources, as they are at the moment. However, it is hoped that the state will soon be able to assert its authority sufficiently over tax collection to do away with the incredibly cumbersome system of revenue earmarking to the more than 300 territorial budgets. It was noted above (i) that this system did not serve any visible purpose as far as ex ante resource allocation was concerned, since territorial expenditure envelopes were determined more or less independently (see paras. 7.45-7.48), but (ii) that it provided a powerful incentive for territorial administrations to cooperate in the collection of national taxes, by linking ex post their spending capacity to the tax performance of their jurisdiction. Unfortunately, not only is this practice unwieldy to administer but it also creates serious rigidities in the execution of the budget, as it parcels out fiscal resources in so many purses.

7.118 As tax collection becomes more reliable, it would become feasible to restore the unity of the national budget (i.e., minus the budgets of local governments) and fund state territorial administrations through normal budget appropriations. A measure of autonomy may, however, be retained in favor of territorial administration, through a system of delegation of spending authority, as is explained below.

7.119 In line with the country's administrative organization, the national budget would consolidate all fiscal revenues (except those assigned to municipal budgets) and appropriate resources for all state functions, by ministerial administration and by categories of expenditure. Each ministerial appropriation would cover the expenditures of both central and territorial administrations within that particular sector. To facilitate the review and execution of these appropriations at the territorial level, however, budget appropriations would also be regrouped into territorial fascicles consolidating in one document all national budget appropriations to be executed by state territorial administrations. At the preparation stage, the proposed appropriations could be reviewed by the relevant territorial authorities, taking into account the overall balance of priorities within their jurisdiction. At the execution stage, these fascicles would serve as a basis for a delegation of spending authority from each and all ministers to the relevant heads of administration. Under such delegation, the heads of administration would retain full administrative authority over the execution of the national budget by the state territorial departments under them, the latter remaining, however, under the technical supervision of national ministries. Such an arrangement would not represent a dramatic departure from current procedures, but rather it would put fiscal practices in line with existing administrative arrangements within the state administration. It would, however, allow a considerably more effective and transparent deployment of fiscal resources according to national priorities.

F. Conclusions

7.120   This chapter has made the case: (i) that decentralization could powerfully contribute to the necessary restructuring of government services, by bringing structural decisions closer to beneficiaries and by allowing a geographical differentiation of public interventions; and (ii) that such decentralization should best be, at least initially, in favor of future urban and rural municipalities. Decentralization can be designed as an evolutionary process, in which the actual devolution of administrative and fiscal responsibilities is tailored to the development of management and fiscal capacities -- as well as democratic practices -- at the local level. The above discussions also noted that this policy could be made compatible with the maintenance of a high degree of equalization across jurisdictions, if the authorities so wish. Finally, the chapter indicated how the proposed approach, rather than weakening the state, would actually allow it to assert its authority over national policies, expressed in a single national budget.

7.121   A first objective of the reform of territorial administration would therefore be the creation of local governments in 287 urban localities as well as perhaps 200-400 rural localities. This process would involve the following steps:

-    Defining by law the fundamental principles for the administration of municipalities, including legal status, powers, personnel system, scope and nature of state tutelage ("Law on Self-Government") as well as for municipal budgets ("Organic Law of Municipal Budgets").

-    Giving localities the dual status of state and local jurisdiction and maintaining territorial and municipal administrations within the jurisdiction under the single authority of the jurisdiction's akim.

-    Devolving to their maslikhat exclusive administrative authority over an initial set of responsibilities, starting, for instance, with urban infrastructures (e.g., water, district heat, street lighting, sanitation, and public transportation), kindergarten, culture and recreation, and some social services. Such package would represent about 1.5 percent of GDP. In a second phase, municipalities could be transferred the charge of local roads, and some of the health services. Further along in the process, the authorities would consider the desirability of decentralizing all or part of general education.

-    Initially assigning to the new municipalities the current "local" taxes and allowing them to impose a surcharge on the personal income tax. Municipalities would be free to set the rates (not the base) of these taxes at their own discretion, within limits defined at the national level. New tax resources would be identified over time as the devolution process unfolds.

- Establishing a system of equalizing grants from the national budget to municipal ones.

7.122 A second objective would be to clarify the role of remaining territorial administrations by the following actions:

- Specifying the delegations of state authority under which they operate.

- As national authority over tax administration strengthens, unifying the national budget by eliminating the present system of earmarking "regulating" taxes, and funding territorial administrations through normal appropriations from the national budget, over which territorial administration would receive a delegation of budget authority from national ministries.

CHAPTER VIII. FUNDING EDUCATION AND HEALTH

A. Introduction

8.1   The ongoing fiscal crisis has placed all public expenditures in Kazakstan under enormous pressure. Its impact, however, is being felt differently across and within sectors. Since they are predominantly financed through public sources, education and health services are two areas in which this fiscal shock has had some of the most significant effects. Real resource flows to these sectors are at almost a third of their 1990 levels. Resource disparities among regions are also growing. In the absence of any major change in the cost effectiveness of service delivery, the sustainability of past health and education achievements is now at issue. In view also of their share in public expenditures (25 percent) and government employment (70 percent), these two sectors remain priority areas for expenditure rationalization.

8.2   This chapter focuses on ways of prioritizing resource use within the two sectors in order to maintain basic service provision and achieve the highest educational and health impact per tenge spent. The review below will highlight two current sources of structural inefficiencies. In education, student to teacher ratios range well below those observed in comparable countries. This situation stems from the current funding arrangements which serve to maintain in existence marginal facilities and from excessively diversified curricula. In health, expenditure patterns show an undue reliance on hospital-based in-patient treatment, which absorbs the lion's share of available resources at the expense of outpatient treatment and ambulatory services. Despite resource shortages, these service patterns have remained largely unchanged in recent years.

8.3   The necessary consolidation of delivery systems -- and the downsizing of facilities and personnel -- will require changes in both sector policies (curricula, protocols, etc.) and funding arrangements, with a move toward capitation funding and a greater autonomy for facility managers. The introduction of a compulsory medical insurance system from 1996 may assist in this process. Many issues regarding, inter alia, the competition between providers and the financial stability of the scheme still need to be resolved, however, before the proposed system can be satisfactorily implemented.

8.4   This chapter first takes stock, in Section B, of recent developments in health and education. Section C reviews the funding arrangements for education and health, and Section D discusses the regional distribution of responsibilities and budgetary resources in these two sectors. Section E then reviews the main patterns of education and health services, highlighting where the main structural deficiencies lie as well the priorities for reform, including the potential role of the proposed compulsory medical insurance scheme.

B. Recent Developments in Education and Health

Education and Health Status

8.5   The achievements of the Soviet health and education system in Kazakstan are considerable. Basic indicators of human welfare in the country at the beginning of the 1990s were impressive and compared favorably with the average performance for countries in the medium range of human development according to the UN Human Development Index (see Table 8.1).

Table 8.1: International Comparison of Basic Health and Education Indicators

	KAZAKSTAN	TURKEY	CHINA	HIGH HUMAN DEVELOPMENT COUNTRIES (Average)	MEDIUM HUMAN DEVELOPMENT COUNTRIES (Average)	LOW DEVELOPMENT COUNTRIES (Average)
Life expectancy at birth (1992), years	69	66.7	70.5	74.1	68	55.8
Adult literacy rates (1992), percent	97.5	81.9	80	97.3	80.4	47.4
Mean years of schooling (1992), years	5	3.6	5	9.8	4.8	2
Real GDP per capita PPP $ (1991)	4,490	4,840	2,946	14,000	3,420	1,170

Source: UNDP Human Development Report, 1994.

8.6   Social indicators have been deteriorating since the beginning of the decade, however, especially in health (see Table 8.2). This decline is due in part to the declining effectiveness of the basic social service delivery system in the context of severe fiscal pressures, and is also due in part to changes in the underlying risk factors and other determinants of health and education status including poverty levels, structure of the labor market, diet, transition stress, etc. Whereas a sustained improvement in health and education status will ultimately depend on the resumption of growth in the economy and the distribution of the gains across the population, it will be important to utilize scarce public resources effectively to maintain access to and quality of basic services during the transition.

Table 8.2: Mortality Rates in Kazakstan, 1990 and 1993

	1990	1995
Mortality rate (per 000 population)	7.7	10.0
Infant mortality rate (per 000 live births)	26.4	26.1

Source: UNDP Kazakstan Human Development Report, 1995.

Box 8.1: Social Expenditure Data: Sources and Limitations

The analysis in this chapter is based on information on actual budgetary expenditures. Planned expenditures can be misleading since approved allocations are revised several times over the course of the year and disbursement patterns do not necessarily reflect allocations, especially in the current budgetary crisis. The main data sources were made available by the Ministry of Finance and consist of expenditure execution records for health and education sectors, by major facility levels, for the 21 oblast-level territorial budgets for the years 1992 to 1994. In addition, expenditure execution data from the republican health and education budgets have been utilized. Furthermore, the comparison of recent expenditure levels with the pre-transition or early transition periods is based on summary budget execution data for the consolidated state budgets (i.e., combining republican and territorial budgets) for 1990 and 1991. Finally, these fiscal data are combined with physical data on the network of facilities to determine the relationships between expenditure levels on the one hand and service and utilization patterns on the other.

The structure of budget execution data reported to the MOF places certain constraints on the type of analysis that is possible, especially concerning the analysis of territorial budgets below the aggregated oblast level. Thus, for example:

- Expenditures for hospitals cannot be broken down between oblast city hospital and central rayon hospital.

- Expenditures cannot be broken down by types of service provided within a single facility level, which makes it difficult to estimate unit costs (e.g., expenditure proportions allocated for inpatient versus outpatient services within hospitals could not be estimated) or to establish a firm categorization of expenditures among primary, secondary, or tertiary levels of services, especially within the health budget.

- Expenditure data from different levels of territorial budgets do not lend themselves easily to a breakdown between urban and rural regions.

The analysis concerns only *budgetary expenditures,* and does not, for the most part, address expenditures on health and education undertaken by enterprises. The differential fiscal impact of divestiture of social assets on territorial budgets across the country, is thus an issue which remains largely beyond the scope of this review.

Sectoral Impact of the Fiscal Crisis

8.7   Public spending on both health and education has declined to an unsustainably low level. Public expenditure on social sectors as a share of current GDP is widely used as a summary measure of the appropriateness of aggregate resource allocation levels within a country. On that score, spending on education dropped from about 7 percent of GDP in the early 1990s to less than 3 percent of GDP in 1994, while spending on health was cut back from about 3-4 percent of GDP to about 2 percent of GDP in 1994 (see Table 8.3). By 1994, Kazakstan's resource flows to education and health services as a share of GDP ranged well below those in OECD countries as well as in some middle-income countries in the region (see Table 8.4).

Table 8.3: Evolution of Health and Education Budgets, 1990-1994

	1990	1991	1992	1993	1994
Total budget expenditures as percent of GDP[1]	36.2	44.2	31.4	23.7	19.2
Consolidated revenues and grants as percent of GDP			38.9	39.6	22.8
Education as percent of total budget expenditures[1]	*18*	*17*	*11*	*19*	*16*
Health as percent of total budget expenditures[1]	*9*	*10*	*7*	*11*	*10*
Education expenditures as percent of GDP	6.6	7.6	3.6	4.6	2.9
Health expenditures as percent of GDP	3.3	4.2	2.1	2.5	2.0
Territorial education expenditures as percent of total education	71	82	82	81	83
Territorial health expenditures as percent of total health	95	95	94	90	86

[1] Total budget expenditures excluding extrabudgetary funds and quasi-fiscal operations.
Sources: MOF, GOK, World Bank staff estimates.

Table 8.4: Education and Health Spending in Selected Countries
(as percentages of GDP)

	KAZAKSTAN 1994	KYRGYZ REPUBLIC 1994	TURKEY 1992	RUSSIA 1994	UNITED STATES 1992	OECD AVERAGE 1992
Health	2.0	3.9	4.1	4.0	13.6	8.1
Education	3.0	n.a.	n.a.	3.4 (1992)	5.5	n.a.

Note: Figures for FSU countries are for public spending as a percentage of GDP, while figures for other countries are for public and
   private expenditures. Given the dominance of public social spending in the FSU, however, the public spending ratios to
   GDP are broadly comparable to the total spending ratios of the comparator countries.
Sources: Kazakstan, Kyrgyz Republic, Russia, World Bank staff estimates. Turkey, OECD: G. Schieber, et al., "Health System
   Performance in OECD Countries," *Health Affairs*, Fall 1994.

8.8   The picture is even bleaker if one looks at the evolution of the resources available to the health
and education sectors in constant tenge and per population (see Table 8.5). According to this
measure, *overall public expenditures in 1994 are below one-third of the pretransition levels in 1990.*
Resources available per capita in education spending declined to a third of 1990 levels, while in health
they were down to about 40 percent of pretransition levels. In current U.S. dollar terms, this is
equivalent to a very low per capita public expenditure of US$22 for education and only US$15 for
health in 1994. This compares in the case of health to US$149 in Egypt, US$185 in Turkey, US$374
in Jordan, and US$1,500 per capita on average in OECD countries.[1]

8.9   The dramatic decline in health and education expenditures does not reflect a lower priority
given to those sectors, but rather the burden of the overall fiscal crisis. The fiscal impact of the
transition has taken the form of declines in total revenues and public expenditures, as evidenced by
their large declines as a share of GDP (see Table 8.3). But the brunt of the adjustment does not seem

---

[1]   Jeni Klugman and George Schieber, *A Survey of Health Reform in Central Asia*, World Bank Technical Paper No. 344, December 1996.

their large declines as a share of GDP (see Table 8.3). But the brunt of the adjustment does not seem to have been disproportionately borne by the health and education sectors (see Table 8.3). A steep decline in the share of health and education in the overall budget is seen in 1992, the year of independence, but the two sectors appear to have received a higher priority once again from 1992 onward. As a consequence, *total* (republican plus territorial) health and education budgetary expenditure appears to have *more or less maintained their share of total public* expenditures between 1990 and 1994.

Table 8.5: Real Resources of Education and Health Sectors, 1991-1994[a]
(per capita and in constant tenge, as a percent of 1990 level)

	1991	1992	1993	1994
		(as of 1990 levels)		
Total Budget Expenditures[b]	107	91	60	31
Education (total)	101	57	57	29
Health (total)	111	66	62	39
Education (republican)	63	35	37	17
Health (republican)	109	77	127	102
Education (territorial)	117	66	65	34
Health (territorial)	111	66	59	35

Notes: [a] Expenditures deflated by CPI average for year; base year = 1990; estimates as percent of 1990.
      [b] Total budgetary expenditures excluding extrabudgetary funds and quasi-fiscal operations.
Source: World Bank staff estimates.

8.10 The adjustment to real resource decline has been different among levels of budgets *within* each sector (see Table 8.5). Expenditures on republican education institutions have experienced the greatest decline in real terms per capita since 1990 (to only 17 percent of 1990 levels). Expenditures on republican health facilities appear to have been maintained in full, while real per capita declines in local health spending are equivalent to declines in overall public expenditures. This implies that the relatively lower real declines in total health expenditures noted above actually reflect the *protection of republican facilities rather than of territorial health facilities*. Since republican health facilities generally include the most specialized and research-oriented facilities, a preliminary conclusion is that tertiary rather than primary or secondary health services have received a priority for scarce funds within the health sector.

C. Funding Arrangements

Sources of Funding

8.11 At present, health and education services in Kazakstan are provided predominantly by the public sector. The bulk[2] of health and education services through the public provision system is meant to be free of charge to the user. In practice, however, there appears to be a long tradition of

---

[2] Some nonessential health services (e.g., orthodontics, acupuncture, massage, etc.) are not free. In the kindergarten sector, publicly funded facilities have the right to set user fees, albeit with ceilings on the levels of cost-sharing permitted.

informal in-kind payments to public providers (e.g., doctors, teachers) of these services. In recent times of fiscal crisis, when wages to medical and education personnel are often in arrears, regional studies[3] and anecdotal evidence indicate that these types of private expenditures have increased significantly. In addition, certain services which are technically meant to be free of charge, such as drugs, textbooks, and meals, are often fully or partly directly purchased by individuals. There is also evidence of the recent emergence of private providers of education and health services that are financed by out-of-pocket direct payments from users.[4] Such private provision is still relatively uncommon.

8.12   Some health services and kindergarten services have historically also been financed by employers (public enterprises and state farms). In education, enterprise financing was largely focused on kindergartens (and vocational institutions), while in health, enterprises and farms provided funding for polyclinics, ambulatories, sanatoria, etc. In some urban rayons where an enterprise is the sole or major employer, enterprise withdrawal of financing for education or health services could lead to considerable stress on municipal resources. In practice, ongoing divestment of social assets is often seen to be partial (e.g., the enterprise may continue to pay for the utilities or the wages of the divested facility).

The Role of Norms

8.13   In the context of fiscal stringency, the relevance of the normative framework for budgeting has become ambiguous (see Chapters III through V). Under the Soviet system of budgetary planning, which is still partially in place, financial resources would be allocated in strict relation to physical norms such as numbers of beds, visits, cubic size of a facility, etc. Reporting systems were thus geared towards collecting information on the "network of facilities and personnel" which would indicate by formula the amount of resources for which facilities were eligible. The role of sector ministries in planning in this context would be to negotiate with *Gosplan* state investments in physical capacity. Taking "objective" physical norms as a given, the major "planning" decisions revolved more around building sectoral capacities and less around ways to achieve objectives in the health and education status of the population through cost-effective resource allocation. Norms thus introduced perverse incentives into sectoral planning as well as sclerosis in the management of scarce budgetary resources.

8.14   At present, sector agencies continue to prepare and submit budgets based on norms or incremental coefficients, while knowing full well that they ultimately will receive considerably less than that. Despite this lack of funding, sector agencies are likely to downsize facilities and services for which they seek funding -- the common wisdom being that any effort at rationalization will be self-defeating. There are a number of known instances in which sector authorities have reported downsizing (e.g., numbers of beds) to bring physical capacities and line-item expenditures in rough correspondence with ratios dictated by norms, given the available funding levels, only to see their budgetary allocations for the following year cut on the grounds of having this smaller physical

---

[3]   See, for example, "Zdrav Reform," draft report on household medical expenditures in Shimkent, South Kazakstan (May 1995).

[4]   Private financing of services is direct or out-of-pocket in nature. In health, there was an experiment in 1992-93 in pooled private financing through a voluntary private insurance scheme in South Kazakstan. The scheme suffered a demise due to allegations of corruption of the officials who ran the operations.

capacity. Sectoral facilities reporting attempts to economize may, in effect, be penalized by the financing system.

Autonomy in Budget Execution

8.15   In the current weakened normative framework, sectoral authorities and facilities have adopted a variety of expedients to cope with the funding crisis. During the Soviet period, the 18-line budgeting (and execution system) was reported to have been enforced in fairly strict accordance with norms. Nowadays, across regions (and not only for health and education expenditures), local authorities are reported to accommodate the shortage of funds by accumulating arrears on certain expenditure chapters (particularly utilities) once the budget allocations for a period are exhausted; in the next period, the arrears are paid off, and new arrears are run up by the end of the period. Arrears are not legally permitted and are accommodated with some additional allocations only on a case-by-case basis (for example, in an unforeseeable shortfall in revenues). Another measure commonly adopted by facilities and local authorities is reported to be that of *virement*, whereby the relevant authority reallocates expenditures between categories differently from the amounts allocated in the budget. Again, this procedure is not permitted technically under the existing expenditure system, but is reported to be widely practiced (see Chapter V).

8.16   *Facility authorities and local authorities may thus have greater autonomy in executing budgets than would appear to be the case at first glance.* This autonomy is, however, more a result of the need to respond to the current fiscal crisis than of a system which encourages and enables local or facility management authorities to undertake planned rationalization of the structure of services.[5]

8.17   Although the perverse incentives for resource use created by norms has weakened in these times of financial crisis, there is an urgent need to institute explicit reform in payment mechanisms to create sustained incentives for efficient resource use in a sector. As has been mentioned, some initiatives are already developing: for example, the Ministry of Health is advocating that resources be allocated to facilities *on the basis of capitation* (specifically, on a per patient enrolled basis) rather than on the basis of capacity, such as number of beds or normative numbers of visits. The Ministry of Economy is advocating greater autonomy for sector institutions *in reallocation of resources across expenditure items*.

8.18   Both objectives could be best achieved by first *incorporating* sectoral facilities into statutory bodies with management autonomy. This would allow facility managers to use financial and administrative management procedures different from those applied within the state sector (see Chapters I and IV for a broader discussion of the incorporation of public entities). Facilities could then be funded partially or fully through operating subsidies, calculated on a per capita basis (e.g., per patient in health, or per student in education). Depending on the degree of control which government authorities want to retain, these subsidy programs could be differentiated by medical protocols, education levels and programs, etc.

---

[5]   This perception gains support from at least two features. First, in recent years the Ministry of Finance has released funding to both education and health in five-day tranches (i.e., the amounts allocated for a five-day period) and monitors whether the reported expenditures conform to stipulated priorities for each sector: wages, drugs, and office expenditures for health, wages and office expenditures for education. This measure is intended to prevent local sectoral authorities from exercising *virement* to encroach on priority expenditures. Second, attempts to rationalize physical capacity are not clearly rewarded, as was mentioned earlier.

Role of Sectoral Administrations

8.19   The obsolescence of norms and the collapse of sectoral investments have left sectoral authorities bereft of their pervious role in sectoral planning. As a striking consequence, neither the central sectoral Ministries of Education and Health nor the relevant oblast and rayon sectoral departments actually exercise even the rather weak authority they previously had in planning for their respective service areas. It is the Ministry of Finance and the local oblast and rayon departments of finance that have the key information pooling and decisionmaking roles.

8.20   A further complicating factor is the multiple jurisdiction over some health and education facilities by different departments or ministries. For example, 23 republican departments had educational institutions subordinated to them. These institutions are often intended for employees of the other ministries and their families, and/or sometimes offer highly specialized services. Whatever the situation, they are not systematically included in the overall planning of education sector objectives or resource use.

8.21   The fragmentation of planning authority also contributes to the duplication of services and excess capacity. These different channels of subordination, which are vertically separate, result in a multiplication of establishments with underutilized resources (diagnostic laboratories, libraries, etc.). These dually subordinated institutions can often provide higher standards of service than mainstream sector institutions because they receive resources, in cash or in kind, from more than one source.

8.22   The formulation of a sectoral policy framework for education and health in Kazakstan is critical in order to set priorities in terms of sector objectives and to indicate the rationalization of the service structures necessary to meet these objectives. A priority for planning sectoral policy is thus to eliminate dual supervisory roles and consolidate responsibilities for administrative and technical supervision of sectoral institutions under the Ministries of Education and Health, and their territorial counterparts, and to have them financed exclusively from their budgets. Furthermore, in order to enable sectoral planning of reform and resource needs, the Ministries of Education and Health should be put clearly in charge of developing and managing all expenditure programs for all education and health institutions that are not specifically transferred to future local governments (see Chapter VII), whatever their levels of administrative subordination.

D. Territorial Aspects

8.23   The provision of health and education is mainly the charge of territorial administrations. Nevertheless, the Soviet system sought to maintain a degree of interregional equalization (see Chapter VII). The current financial instability, however, has led to growing inequalities in the allocation of education and health resources across oblasts.

Administrative Structure

8.24   The vast majority of health and education services are subordinated to territorial administrations. Consequently, in 1994 territorial budgets executed about 83 percent of state education expenditures and about 86 percent of state health expenditures (see Table 8.3). As has been noted in Chapters I and VII, the allocation of social facilities among different levels of budgets is not based on a clear functional typology. Similar service levels can thus be replicated across budgetary levels. Hospitals, polyclinics, ambulatory institutions, sanitary-epidemiological stations, etc., can be financed through republican and territorial health budgets. Similarly, in education, preschool institutions, schools, vocational-technical schools, higher education institutions, etc., may be funded through any level of budget. The level of the budget financing a particular institution is usually determined by one of the two following factors:

(i) The *catchment area* of the services it provides. Thus, republican hospitals accept referrals from across the country, while central rayon hospitals provide services to the population of the rayon in which they are situated. There are exceptions, however. For example, there are several ambulatory and polyclinic institutions financed under the republican health budget which serve only the population in their immediate locality. However, the tuberculosis center charged to the budget of Kostanai oblast, although it was used to service the entire Soviet Union, is a reverse example. In practice, most republican budget financed service institutions are located in and around the city and oblast of Almaty, while institutions subordinated to territorial administrations are distributed throughout the territories.

(ii) The *degree of specialization* of the services it provides. Although all budgets finance primary, secondary, and tertiary services, in general the republican budget finances the more specialized and research-oriented establishments in health and education sectors, while the territorial budgets finance progressively less specialized institutions.

Regional Allocation of Resources

8.25 Whatever equality in the actual allocation of resources per capita was achieved in the Soviet period, the current trend is toward increased inequity across oblast territories. In the Soviet system, the distribution of service institutions throughout the country was intended to ensure the population's equitable access to health care and education. The strict application of norms to resource allocation was intended also to ensure similar service quality across regions. At present, however, the weak relevance of the normative structure, local differences in revenue generation capacity, and the constrained ability of the state to redistribute, have all undermined previous regional equity in resource allocation and service levels.

8.26 The equalization of resources across oblasts can be examined through an analysis of the territorial budget execution for health and education.[6] Tables 8.6 and 8.7 provide an estimate of the growing inequality, as measured by the coefficient of variation in the distribution of education and health expenditures per capita across oblasts for the period 1992 to 1994. The closer the value of the coefficient is to zero, the less is the variation (i.e., greater resource equality) in the per capita expenditures across the oblasts. These two tables show that the said coefficient almost *doubled* between 1992 and 1994, indicating growing inequities in resource distribution.

---

[6] The collected data do not permit an analysis for the pretransition period, but allow changes during transition to be monitored.

Table 8.6: Regional Distribution of Territorial Education Expenditures, 1992-1994
(per capita, in current prices)

OBLAST	1992	AS % OF MEAN	1993	AS % OF MEAN	1994	AS % OF MEAN
	(ruble)		(tenge)		(tenge)	
Aktyubinsk	1826.90	0.93	51.40	0.92	728.20	1.15
Almaty	1572.50	0.80	64.10	1.14	617.10	0.97
East Kazakstan	1806.50	0.92	51.80	0.93	705.50	1.11
Atyrau	2332.50	1.19	65.90	1.18	1546.90	2.44
Zhambyl	1588.50	0.81	43.70	0.78	478.10	0.75
Zhezkazgan	2456.20	1.26	51.10	0.91	808.70	1.28
Karaganda	2218.50	1.13	47.20	0.84	524.50	0.83
Kzyl-Orda	1859.40	0.95	84.20	1.50	727.40	1.15
Kokshetau	2191.30	1.12	64.40	1.15	648.20	1.02
Kostanai	2523.50	1.29	50.30	0.90	589.60	0.93
Mangystau	2361.40	1.21	70.80	1.26	959.40	1.51
Pavlodar	2106.10	1.08	60.40	1.08	487.60	0.77
North Kazakstan	2079.30	1.06	64.40	1.15	486.00	0.77
Semipalatinsk	1884.20	0.96	59.00	1.05	637.20	1.01
Taldykorgan	1915.30	0.98	50.50	0.90	480.20	0.76
Turgai	2756.40	1.41	75.10	1.34	645.90	1.02
West Kazakstan	2257.10	1.15	59.70	1.07	551.70	0.87
Akmola	1953.80	1.00	60.10	1.07	527.40	0.83
South Kazakstan	1627.80	0.83	52.10	0.93	608.90	0.96
City of Almaty	1404.00	0.72	41.30	0.74	682.40	1.08
City of Leninsk	na	na	117.40	2.10	1068.00	1.68
Kazakstan	**1955.40**	**1.00**	**56.00**	**1.00**	**634.00**	**1.00**
Standard Deviation	354.90		16.63		248.99	
Coefficient of Variation	0.18		0.30		0.39	

Source: World Bank staff estimates based on Local Budget Execution data, MOF, GOK.

Table 8.7: Regional Distribution of Territorial Health Expenditures, 1992-1994
(per capita, in current prices)

OBLAST	1992	AS % OF MEAN	1993	AS % OF MEAN	1994	AS % OF MEAN
	(ruble)		(tenge)		(tenge)	
Aktyubinsk	1172.30	0.82	29.80	0.83	444.20	0.96
Almaty	1049.00	0.73	32.50	0.91	393.40	0.85
East Kazakstan	1571.00	1.10	36.50	1.02	550.70	1.19
Atyrau	1408.80	0.99	34.20	0.96	901.90	1.95
Zhambyl	1151.70	0.81	27.00	0.76	308.30	0.67
Zhezkazgan	1852.60	1.30	36.00	1.01	662.70	1.43
Karaganda	1831.80	1.28	36.40	1.02	496.30	1.07
Kzyl-Orda	1413.90	0.99	57.20	1.60	553.60	1.20
Kokshetau	1560.90	1.09	39.40	1.10	476.50	1.03
Kostanai	1739.00	1.22	34.30	0.96	485.50	1.05
Mangystau	1589.60	1.11	38.10	1.07	552.90	1.19
Pavlodar	1612.10	1.13	40.60	1.14	341.60	0.74
North Kazakstan	1450.60	1.01	38.60	1.08	363.80	0.79
Semipalatinsk	1255.40	0.88	35.00	0.98	475.90	1.03
Taldykorgan	1182.40	0.83	28.70	0.80	291.00	0.63
Turgai	1533.80	1.07	44.00	1.23	426.60	0.92
West Kazakstan	1483.00	1.04	33.50	0.94	376.30	0.81
Akmola	1615.50	1.13	39.80	1.11	337.40	0.73
South Kazakstan	1074.10	0.75	30.20	0.85	395.60	0.85
City of Almaty	1455.00	1.02	39.80	1.11	704.60	1.52
City of Leninsk	n.a.	n.a.	39.70	1.11	686.00	1.48
Kazakstan	**1430.17**	**1.00**	**35.70**	**1.00**	**462.70**	**1.00**
Standard Deviation	238.45		6.41		152.81	
Coefficient of Variation	0.17		0.18		0.33	

Source: World Bank staff estimates based on Local Budget Execution data, MOF, GOK.

8.27   This dispersion process would appear to proceed rather randomly, which compounds the difficulties facing territorial sector and financial authorities in planning service levels or service quality. Indeed, the rank correlation between real social expenditures per capita and per oblast is very weak over the period (see Table 8.8). The rank correlation coefficient range between 1992 and 1993, and 1993 and 1994, lies between a low of 0.25 and a high of 0.44. This low correlation over time may indicate that expenditures depend more on the varying ability of individual oblast administrations to mobilize resources (i.e., revenues and subventions) from year to year rather than on any sustained policy divergence across oblasts. In any case, past rankings of oblasts in terms of actual social expenditure levels do not seem to be a very good indicator at present for future oblast level sector expenditures.

Table 8.8: Evolution of Social Expenditure Per Capita and Per Oblast
(in constant 1992 prices)

OBLAST	EDUCATION				HEALTH			
	1993/1992	1994/1992	CORRELATION COEFFICIENT FOR REAL P/C EXPENDITURES BETWEEN		1993/1992	1994/1992	CORRELATION COEFFICIENT FOR REAL P/C EXPENDITURES BETWEEN	
			1992:1993	1993:1994			1992:1993	1993:1994
Aktyubinsk	1.01	0.66			0.91	0.63		
Almaty	1.46	0.65			1.11	0.62		
East Kazakstan	1.03	0.65			0.83	0.58		
Atyrau	1.01	1.10			0.87	1.06		
Zhambyl	0.98	0.50			0.84	0.44		
Zhezkazgan	0.74	0.55			0.70	0.59		
Karaganda	0.76	0.39			0.71	0.45		
Kzyl-Orda	1.62	0.65			1.45	0.65		
Kokshetau	1.05	0.49			0.90	0.51		
Kostanai	0.71	0.39			0.71	0.46		
Mangystau	1.07	0.67			0.86	0.58		
Pavlodar	1.03	0.38			0.90	0.35		
North Kazakstan	1.11	0.39			0.95	0.42		
Semipalatinsk	1.12	0.56			1.00	0.63		
Taldykorgan	0.94	0.42			0.87	0.41		
Turgai	0.98	0.39			1.03	0.46		
West Kazakstan	0.95	0.41			0.81	0.42		
Akmola	1.10	0.45			0.88	0.35		
South Kazakstan	1.15	0.62			1.01	0.61		
City of Almaty	1.05	0.81			0.98	0.80		
City of Leninsk	n.a.	n.a.			n..a.	n.a.		
Kazakstan	1.03	0.54	0.44	0.37	0.89	0.54	0.25	0.40

Source: World Bank staff estimates based on Local Budget Execution data, MOF, GOK.

E. Patterns of Services

8.28   The collapse of financing in the education and health sectors should have given a strong impetus to the search for efficiency gains in the sectors. It has not. To date, as this section makes clear, inherited patterns of services have hardly changed. These patterns must change, however, if access to, and quality of, basic services are to be maintained.

Priorities by Facility Levels

Education

8.29   Expenditure on education in Kazakstan appropriately emphasizes primary and secondary education levels, rather than tertiary or vocational training levels (see Table 8.9). The financing of general education schools (including primary, incomplete secondary, and secondary education levels) is primarily the task of territorial budgets. Vocational-technical training and preschool levels come second and third among the priorities of territorial budgets (see Table 8.10). The pattern appears to be more or less uniform across oblasts. The republican education budget emphasizes expenditures on tertiary education, as is to be expected given the structure of responsibilities (see Table 8.11).

Table 8.9: Total Education Expenditures by Facility Levels, 1992-1994
(percentage shares)

	1992	1993	1994
Preschool	4.3	12.1	12.1
Schools	52.3	48.2	46.8
Boarding Schools	5.8	5.1	6.6
Extramural	4.4	3.8	3.7
Vocational-Technical (PTUs, Technikums, etc.)	12.7	13.1	14.3
Higher Education	13.4	13.3	11.9
Other Institutions	4.8	3.4	3.2
Textbooks	0.3	0.3	1.0
State Capital Expenditures	2.0	0.8	0.2
Total	100.0	100.0	100.0

Note: Total expenditure includes republican and territorial education budget expenditure.
Sources: World Bank staff estimates based on Local and Republican Budget Execution data, MOF, GOK.

8.30   In comparison with 1992, the main change to note is the tripling in the proportion of territorial education expenditures on preschool or kindergartens, mainly at the expense of schools (see Table 8.9). This reflects the ongoing process of divestiture of kindergartens on the part of enterprises and the increased pressure that this has placed on territorial budgets. Indeed, it costs about 3.5 times more to keep a child in kindergarten than in lower secondary school.

8.31   Although the majority of expenditures is on compulsory general education in schools (plus preschool), the continuing significant expenditures for vocational training in Kazakstan are a cause for concern. A major orientation of the education system in the Soviet period was toward producing shop-floor technicians to meet pre-identified labor needs of enterprises. The vocational training institutes were often cofinanced by enterprises which were potential employers of the graduates, and the curriculum was narrowly tailored to the needs of the enterprise. A parallel situation existed in the higher education sector. For graduates to adapt to a labor market that requires more flexibility, it is necessary to ensure that the continuing significant allocation for vocational and higher training from budgetary sources is no longer focused on narrow specializations. New curricula will be necessary to provide technical training that will permit graduates to be more flexible in responding to local labor market conditions and in finding employment among state-owned enterprises and the private sector.

Table 8.10: Territorial Education Expenditures by Facility Levels and Oblast, 1994
(percentage shares)

Territorial Budgets	Preschool Institutions	Schools	Boarding Schools	Extra-curricular Activities	Vocational-Technical Institutions	Higher Education Institutions	Methodological Training	Centralized Construction, Repair, Accounting	Textbooks	Capital Investments on all Facilities	Total
Aktyubinsk	12.63	59.06	6.37	4.45	13.49	0.00	2.31	1.68	0.02	0.00	100.00
Almaty	15.09	59.98	7.04	4.95	8.87	0.00	2.62	1.25	0.20	0.00	100.00
East Kazakstan	11.21	60.09	6.79	3.62	13.15	0.00	1.93	2.11	1.03	0.09	100.00
Atyrau	16.03	57.13	8.15	4.09	7.99	0.31	2.12	2.31	0.00	1.86	100.00
Zhambyl	15.24	60.64	5.45	4.00	9.90	0.00	2.37	1.61	0.57	0.21	100.00
Zhezkazgan	9.64	59.56	5.41	4.26	15.28	0.06	2.40	1.35	2.03	0.00	100.00
Karaganda	12.11	44.67	9.90	5.40	23.80	0.00	1.31	2.16	0.12	0.54	100.00
Kzyl-Orda	19.40	56.93	5.06	5.34	10.41	0.00	1.46	1.29	0.11	0.00	100.00
Kokshetau	11.79	64.55	5.06	2.86	11.88	0.00	1.66	1.76	0.32	0.11	100.00
Kostanai	8.24	56.24	12.97	3.72	16.07	0.06	1.53	1.16	0.02	0.00	100.00
Mangystau	19.43	52.62	2.22	3.10	16.76	0.00	4.27	1.56	0.04	0.00	100.00
Pavlodar	12.80	55.51	6.56	5.55	14.51	0.00	2.56	2.10	0.16	0.26	100.00
North	12.56	55.07	11.22	3.70	13.15	0.00	2.34	1.80	0.15	0.00	100.00
Semipalatinsk	12.32	60.34	6.06	4.29	13.28	0.00	1.48	1.55	0.68	0.00	100.00
Taldykorgan	11.37	62.44	6.08	4.58	11.90	0.00	1.97	1.63	0.02	0.00	100.00
Turgai	9.89	50.01	4.19	4.55	23.89	0.01	3.90	2.85	0.00	0.70	100.00
West Kazakstan	8.62	56.11	8.65	2.93	18.80	0.01	1.36	1.19	0.04	2.27	100.00
Akmola	13.64	56.08	6.30	4.25	13.99	0.00	1.84	1.35	2.54	0.00	100.00
South Kazakstan	11.29	54.18	8.03	5.50	15.80	0.35	1.53	1.35	1.94	0.04	100.00
City of Almaty	24.25	46.69	10.89	2.90	13.16	0.00	0.65	1.14	0.31	0.00	100.00
City of Leninsk	40.90	38.19	0.00	9.15	4.95	0.00	3.03	1.62	0.00	2.17	100.00
Kazakstan	13.79	55.88	7.49	4.32	14.02	0.07	1.91	1.62	0.60	0.30	100.00

Notes: 1. Numbers are percentage of row total.
2. Schools include daytime, night shift, distance and special schools.
3. Boarding schools include special regime and orphan houses.
4. Vocational-Technical schools include PTUs, Technikums.
5. Methodological training includes propaganda/methodological and professional development institutes.
6. Textbooks include purchases for all facilities.

Source: World Bank staff estimates based on Local Budget Execution data, MOF, GOK.

Table 8.11: Republican Education Expenditure by Facility Levels, 1994
(percentage shares)

FACILITY LEVEL	% OF EXPENDITURES
Preschool	4.4
Schools	4.2
Boarding Schools	2.5
Extramural	0.9
Vocational-Technical	15.8
Higher Education	67.5
Other Institutions	1.5
Textbooks for All Institutions	3.1
Total	100.0

Source: World Bank staff estimates based on Republican Budget Education data, MOF, GOK.

8.32   In sum, greater cost effectiveness in the education sector is likely to be achieved through improved effectiveness within each level of education (as discussed in the next section) more than through large shifts in resources from one education level to another.

Health

8.33   Priorities within the health budget appear to be less appropriate. The overwhelming emphasis of both territorial and republican health budgets is on the hospital sector (see Tables 8.12, 8.13, and 8.14). The pattern holds true across oblasts[7] and has not changed between 1992 and 1994. It is consistent with the pattern of health expenditures elsewhere in the FSU, in the Central Asian republics, and in Russia. Although hospitals do provide outpatient services through attached polyclinics,[8] the bulk of hospital expenditures is for in-patient care. By contrast, polyclinics and ambulatories, which are the main institutions providing services on an ambulatory basis, have to be satisfied with from 6 to 8 percent of total health spending. Even including expenditures on outpatient care by hospitals, total ambulatory treatment probably would not account for more than 11 percent of the total health budget. It is, however, well-established in international experience that, for a broad range of treatments, service delivery is more cost-effective in ambulatory settings than through in-patient care. The current emphasis on in-patient care over ambulatory and primary care institutions in the expenditure pattern clearly suggests structural inefficiency in the health delivery system of Kazakstan.

---

[7]   It can be noted that the oblast level territory spending the lowest share of health resources on hospitals is the City of Almaty. This is because the population of Almaty City has ready access to the republican hospitals which are concentrated in the city. The low share of hospitals in Almaty City's health expenditures is thus not due to a more efficient structure of health services.

[8]   Hence aggregate hospital expenditures overestimate the extent of in-patient financing.

Table 8.12: Total Health Expenditures by Facility Levels, 1992-1994
(percentage shares)

FACILITY LEVEL	1992	1993	1994
Hospitals	73.6	71.7	73.1
Polyclinics	6.1	6.8	6.5
Ambulatory and Polyclinic Institutions	1.1	1.0	0.8
Public Health Units	4.1	5.1	4.5
Other health activities	14.0	14.9	14.8
State capital investment	1.0	0.5	0.2
Total	100.0	100.0	100.0

Source: World Bank staff estimates based on Local and Republican Budget Execution data, MOF, GOK.

Table 8.13: Territorial Health Expenditure by Facility Levels and by Oblast, 1994
(percentage shares)

OBLAST	HOSPITALS	POLYCLINICS	OTHER AMBULATORY AND POLYCLINIC INSTITUTIONS	PUBLIC HEALTH UNITS	OTHER	CAPITAL INVESTMENT ON ALL FACILITIES	TOTAL
Aktyubinsk	80.45	3.77	1.48	3.51	10.79	0.00	100.00
Almaty	65.20	2.95	0.81	3.80	27.23	0.00	100.00
East Kazakstan	81.39	3.20	1.15	4.08	10.18	0.00	100.00
Atyrau	86.02	4.46	1.38	2.64	5.25	0.24	100.00
Zhambyl	83.67	6.21	1.35	4.07	4.70	0.00	100.00
Zhezkazgan	80.61	5.49	0.85	3.23	9.82	0.00	100.00
Karaganda	72.80	5.62	0.27	3.56	17.45	0.30	100.00
Kzyl-Orda	77.60	8.97	1.07	4.87	7.50	0.00	100.00
Kokshetau	77.98	4.13	1.71	4.96	11.22	0.00	100.00
Kostanai	80.39	5.21	0.58	4.30	9.31	0.21	100.00
Mangystau	73.12	9.20	0.40	5.43	11.84	0.00	100.00
Pavlodar	71.92	5.97	0.93	4.39	15.62	1.18	100.00
North	81.82	3.39	1.43	3.28	10.08	0.00	100.00
Semipalatinsk	76.44	10.02	1.09	2.46	9.99	0.00	100.00
Taldykorgan	82.69	3.47	1.37	4.06	7.08	1.32	100.00
Turgai	77.61	7.21	0.60	6.55	7.98	0.04	100.00
West Kazakstan	74.96	7.14	1.22	6.77	9.85	0.06	100.00
Akmola	78.29	5.72	1.05	4.56	9.18	1.19	100.00
South Kazakstan	77.67	6.13	1.35	3.78	11.08	0.00	100.00
City of Almaty	45.73	15.46	0.00	2.86	35.95	0.00	100.00
City of Leninsk	59.44	14.19	0.00	6.04	5.89	14.45	100.00
Kazakstan	74.32	6.71	0.93	3.91	13.86	0.28	100.00

Note: Numbers are percentage of row total.
Source: World Bank staff estimates based on Local Budget Execution data, MOF, GOK.

Table 8.14: Republican Health Expenditures by Facility Levels, 1994
(percentage shares)

FACILITY LEVEL	1994
Hospitals	65.4
Polyclinics	5.2
Other Ambulatory and Polyclinic Institutions	0.2
Public Health Units	8.5
Other Health Activities	20.7
Total	**100.0**

Source: World Bank staff estimates based on Republican Budget Execution data, MOF, GOK.

8.34   This excessive emphasis on hospitalization is further borne out by a comparison of the basic indicators of in-patient capacity for Kazakstan, OECD countries, and middle- and low-income countries of the region (see Table 8.15). On all counts (i.e., rate of admission into hospitals, average length of stay in hospitals, and beds/population) the health sector appears to have placed a comparatively heavier emphasis on in-patient care. Many diseases which are treated on an outpatient basis in other countries are treated through in-patient care in Kazakstan, and, once admitted, patients are often kept for longer periods than is the case outside of the FSU.

Table 8.15: Availability and Use of Health Care in Selected Countries, 1992 and 1994

	KAZAKSTAN[1/] 1994	UZBEKISTAN[2/] 1994	RUSSIA[3/] 1994	TURKEY 1992	OECD AVERAGE 1992
In-patient Admission (% of population)	18.0	19.3	21.0	5.5	16.2
Average Length of Stay (days)	16.8	14.3	17.0	6.8	14.4
Physicians/000 Population	3.7	3.4	3.9	0.9	2.5
In-patient Beds/000 Population	12.4	8.8	12.2	2.4	8.4

Sources: 1. Kazakstan: Annual Report of the Ministry of Health, 1994.
   2. Uzbekistan: *A Survey of Health Reform in Central Asia*, World Bank Technical Paper No. 344, December 1996.
   3. Russia: Medical Equipment Project, Staff Appraisal Report, World Bank, 1996
   4. Turkey and OECD: G.J. Schieber and al. *Health System Performance in OECD Countries*, Health Affairs, 1994

8.35   The bias of health expenditures toward non-cost-effective forms of treatment is also evident in the underfunding of the rural ambulatory and polyclinic network. Ambulatories and polyclinics provide basic primary services throughout rural areas and were traditionally cofinanced by rayon administrations and collective farms during the Soviet period. Since the early 1990s, however, reductions in the contributions of collective and state farms to ambulatory and polyclinic care financing have been widely reported. The proportion of health resources allocated to ambulatory and polyclinic facilities from budgetary sources does not appear to have been increased to compensate for this.

8.36   This primary service network is under serious financial stress. Indeed, there are reports that ambulatory and polyclinic facilities are closing in many regions throughout the country owing to lack of salary financing and a dearth of equipment and/or medical supplies. Yet strengthening ambulatory and polyclinic facilities (rather than hospitals) through the provision of equipment and essential drugs could be a highly cost-effective way to maintain basic health services in rural areas.

8.37   Major recommendations to improve the cost-effectiveness of the health service delivery system would thus include that medical protocols emphasizing ambulatory care be introduced where appropriate, and that incentives for cost-effective resource use by medical care providers be introduced through payment systems which place responsibility on the provider for any gap between established compensation rates and actual cost of treatment. In an initial phase, primary physician groups and hospitals could be funded by payments calculated on the basis of a capitated fund (i.e., funds that cover basic services for the number of enrolled patients), allocations which the facility managers could operate with flexibility. These measures essentially imply a bottom-up strategy for the rationalization of expenditure away from in-patient care. The expected impact is that more treatment will be undertaken in cost-effective ambulatory institutions and through ambulatory protocols. The rate of specialist referrals, the rate of hospital admissions, and the average length of hospital stay would be expected to decline gradually as the demand for costly and lengthy inpatient treatment is reduced. The savings from the reduction in inpatient capacity through ward/facility and staff rationalization could be reinvested to strengthen the primary care sector.

Priorities by Nature of Expenditure

8.38   The structure of expenditures in the two sectors was also examined with respect to the proportions allocated to investment versus recurrent costs, and with respect to the priorities within recurrent costs.

Investment

8.39   Expenditures are currently devoted essentially to operating existing facilities rather than to the creating new capacity. State capital investments declined as a percentage of territorial expenditures on education (see Table 8.16) and health (see Table 8.12) over the period 1992-94. This would seem to be an appropriate strategy given the current resource constraints and given the extensive distribution of facilities that already exist.

Table 8.16: Territorial Education Expenditure by Economic Nature, 1993-1994
(percentage shares)

EXPENDITURE ARTICLES	1993	1994
Wages and Salaries	46.52	41.95
Payroll Contribution	11.10	9.35
Utilities, etc.	15.90	19.86
Business Trips	0.12	0.16
Scholarships	1.28	1.77
Meals	4.53	5.76
Compensation of Meal Expenses	1.80	0.98
Equipment and Supplies	1.90	1.36
Soft Supplies	0.70	0.69
Repair and Rehabilitation	3.88	4.58
Other	11.37	13.25
State Capital Investments	0.90	0.29
Total	100.0	100.0

Source: World Bank staff estimates based on Local Budget Execution data, MOF, GOK.

Table 8.17: Territorial Health Expenditure by Economic Nature, 1992-1994
(percentage shares)

EXPENDITURE ARTICLES	1992	1993	1994
Wages and Salaries	32.93	35.56	29.61
Payroll Contribution	11.25	10.31	7.45
Utilities, etc.	21.32	21.50	24.29
Business Trips	0.23	0.28	0.25
Meals	11.82	10.52	12.57
Medicine and Bandages	7.03	9.87	14.84
Equipment	5.94	4.71	3.62
Soft Supplies	2.30	1.27	0.88
Repair and Rehabilitation	5.92	4.24	5.07
Other	1.27	1.76	1.42
Total	100.0	100.0	100.0

Note: State capital investments are not included.
Source: World Bank staff estimates based on Local Budget Execution data, MOF, GOK.

Recurrent Costs

8.40   Recurrent expenditures in the health and education sectors are heavily concentrated in two areas: wages/salaries (plus mandatory payroll contributions) and utilities. Together, they constitute over 70 percent of expenditures (recurrent plus investment) on educational establishments under territorial budgets in 1994, and over 60 percent of expenditures on health facilities under territorial supervision in the same year.[9] Nonwage/utilities recurrent costs for consumables are at minimal levels. Furthermore, the very low expenditure share on textbooks is of concern, because of its impact on the quality of education provided as well as its impact on accessibility.[10] Increased private expenditures in this regard have compensated only partially. It is noted further that republican education institutions appear to have relatively better provision in terms of textbooks (3.1 percent of republican education expenditures in 1994) than do territorial education facilities (0.6 percent of territorial education spending in 1994). In health, the main area of concern is the low share to pharmaceuticals and medical supplies (Article 10).[11] The lack of availability of drugs in the public health system contributes to ineffective hospitalizations where length of stay is often substituted for effective treatment.

Adjustment in Quality of Outputs

8.41 The most striking feature, however, in the recent evolution of health and education expenditure patterns is their structural inertia in the face of the fiscal crisis. A basic determinant of the structure of the health and education sectors is the Soviet system of resource allocation on the basis of norms related to physical capacity, as has been mentioned. The continued application of norms to questions of resource adjustments has deprived institutions of any incentives to reduce capacity (because they cannot retain any savings), to use capacity in more cost-effective ways (for the same reason), or to report capacity reductions (because future allocations may be reduced on the basis of physical norms). As a consequence, the burden of adjustment to lower real resources is mostly in terms of the lower quality of outputs.

Adjustment in Education

8.42 Little adjustment has taken place in *education*. In fact, the number of teachers employed in day schools has actually increased during the period (see Figure 8.1), while resources dropped abruptly. Part of the reason for this increase is the recent efforts to establish schools where instruction is in Kazak rather than in Russian. This has led to a continuation of low student-teacher ratios in primary/secondary schools. Indeed, student-teacher ratios in schools and in higher education institutions in Kazakstan are even lower than in the better endowed OECD countries (see Table 8.18). The low ratios are suggestive of low efficiency in the education system in that too great a share of resources is spent on salaries and not enough is spent on the teaching materials and equipment which would make teaching more effective.

---

[9] The share of wages in territorial budget health expenditures actually declined in 1994, which may reflect closures of beds and staffing positions as discussed below.

[10] The expenditure for textbooks is aggregated for all public education facilities and reported as a separate activity under the territorial and republican education expenditure classifications.

[11] The share of health expenditures for pharmaceuticals has actually increased over 1992-94, but the expenditure levels still translate to only about US$1.90 per capita in 1994.

Figure 8.1: Number of Teachers in Daytime Schools, 1985-1995
(in thousands at the beginning of the school year)

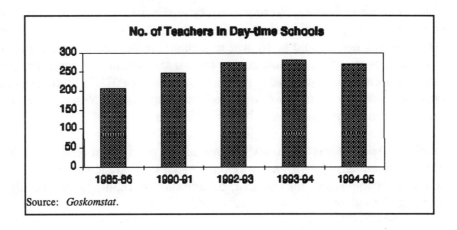

Source: *Goskomstat.*

Table 8.18: Student/Staff Ratios in Selected Countries

STUDENT:STAFF RATIOS	KAZAKSTAN (1994)	UNITED KINGDOM (1992)	GERMANY (1992)	TURKEY (1992)	OECD (1992)
Primary/secondary schools					
student:teacher	8.8:1	20.6/15.2	19.6/16.2	29:3/23.4	18.5/14.6
student:all staff	6.1:1				

Sources: 1. Kazakstan - World Bank staff estimates based on Network of Facilities and Personnel data, MOF
2. Other countries - OECD, *Education at a Glance*, Paris, 1995.

8.43   The low overall student-teacher ratios are symptomatic of two features of the Soviet education system. A first source of the problem resides in the methods of resource allocation within education. Resources are currently allocated on the basis of "class-complexes" (i.e., notional class sizes rather than actual student enrollment). The logic of using class complexes stems from the size of the country and the disparities in population density. In densely populated areas such as Almaty, for example, there are 35-40 students in a class, whereas in a small village in the rural areas there may be only 5-7 students in a class. To account for this difference, the budget takes into consideration average class size and calculates all associated expenditures. The result is a "class complex" which is applied uniformly per grade level across the country, independent of actual class sizes. Whatever rationale is offered for justifying such calculations, it creates an incentive for keeping open "marginal" classrooms and courses with low enrollment whether in schools, vocational institutions or higher educational establishments. The funding mechanism also imposes restrictions on reallocation between line items, as has been noted earlier, resulting in disincentives to change amounts or combinations of inputs.

8.44   A second factor resulting in low student-teacher ratios in vocational and higher education institutions is the excessive focus of the Soviet education system on specialization as mentioned earlier. The curricula were thus often burdened with numerous narrow courses which required specialist teaching staff.

8.45 Priorities which emerge in considering the downsizing of education facilities while protecting educational outcome thus include:

(i) *Capitation-based funding.* Resource allocation decisions could be shifted to a *capitation-based funding mechanism* (on a per student basis) or the application of the class-complex norm could be limited to a class size beyond a certain ratchet level. Classes or entire schools below such a critical size should be closed or merged with larger establishments (especially relevant for rural areas). Capitation grants to programs would additionally encourage bottom-up closure of unnecessary specializations in vocational and higher education.

(ii) *Increased teaching loads in schools.* In schools, per student recurrent costs could be reduced by *increasing teaching workloads* in addition to increasing class sizes. This could be accomplished, for example, by introducing multitopic and multigrade teaching methods in low density areas.

(iii) *Improved relevance of vocational and higher education.* The relevance of higher and vocational training needs to be improved by *developing curricula and teaching methods* for areas which are in demand in the changing labor market (e.g., business, management, computer science, language). While a shift to capitation funding should induce facilities to eventually close specializations for which there is falling demand, some specializations (and institutions) can already be identified as redundant.

(iv) *Improved textbook supplies.* There is a need to maintain learning achievements and support changes in curricula and teaching methods by increasing the supply and quality of textbooks.

8.46 Most of the reforms outlined above are expected to lead to lower net demand for teachers. Salaries for teachers remaining in employment would need to be increased, however, to reflect increased workloads and new requirements in qualifications. The net impact of the reforms on recurrent costs is thus uncertain, but the *cost-effectiveness of* the education system is likely to be *improved* in that programs with the greatest returns will be supported through a more judicious combination of teaching effort, curricula and materials.

Adjustment in Health

8.47 In the *health sector*, some efforts have been made by facility managers to reduce in-patient capacity by reducing the number of beds. Between 1993 and 1994, the number of beds per 10,000 population declined across all oblasts and the number of doctors' positions (which are associated with the number of beds) also fell (see Figure 8.2). These reductions in capacity amount to about 8 percent in the case of beds and 4 percent in the case of doctors. While these rationalization efforts are commendable, they are not commensurate with the challenge at hand, namely, the decline by almost two-thirds, of real resources per capita available to the sector from the beginning of the 1990s. This suggests that the adjustment is in terms of quality of services delivered rather than in capacity.[12] Thus, while access to services is nominally relatively unaffected, quality and effective coverage are greatly reduced.

---

[12] A separate point is that the volume of utilization of services may also have declined because of deteriorating quality. In the health sector, this takes the form of patients not coming in to use health institutions, or coming in at later stages of illness, at which point treatment is much more costly.

Figure 8.2: Evolution in Numbers of Doctors and Beds, 1993-1994
(per 10,000)

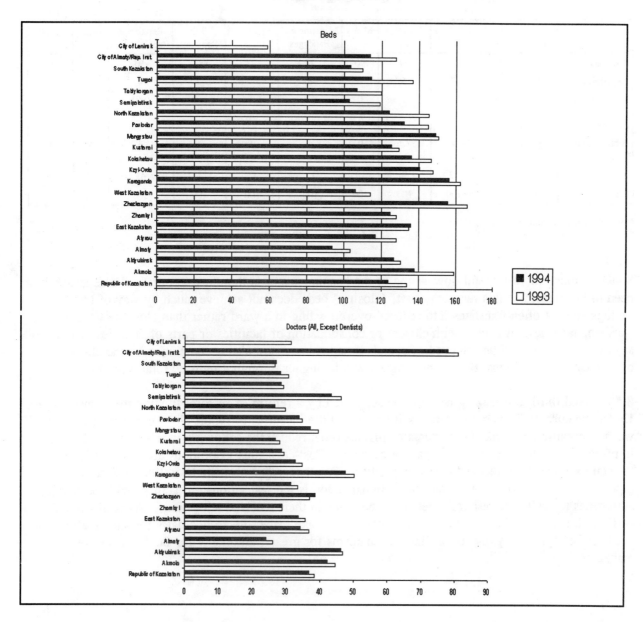

Source: Annual Report of the MOH, 1994, GOK.

8.48   A profile of expenditures by major facility categories for territorial spending in 1994 further reinforces this impression of inertia. Not unexpectedly, given the structure of aggregate health spending, hospitals continue to dominate most categories (see Table 8.19). The low proportion of expenditures on equipment and pharmaceuticals incurred by ambulatory facilities indicates that the relatively poorly funded ambulatory service sector continues to have poor access to those resources that would improve its diagnostic and treatment capacity.

Table 8.19: Territorial Health Expenditures by Economic Category and by Facility Level, 1994
(percentage shares)

	Wage Bill	Payroll Tax	Utilities, etc.	Business Trips	Meals	Medicine and Bandages	Equipment	Soft Supplies	Repair and Rehabilitation	Other	Total
Hospitals	71	71	75	67	90	78	77	88	50	53	75
Polyclinics	10	10	7	6	0	6	4	2	4	6	7
Ambulatory and Polyclinic Facilities	2	2	1	1	0	0.4	0.05	0.3	0.01	0.03	1
Public Health Units	5	6	4	17	0	4	4	1	3	5	4
Other	12	11	13	9	10	12	16	8	43	35	14
Total	100	100	100	100	100	100	100	100	100	100	100

Note: Numbers are column percentages.
Source: World Bank staff estimates based on Local Budget Execution data, MOF, GOK.

8.49   A much more forceful downsizing of the hospital sector is therefore in order. Three issues need to be stressed in this respect. First, "closing" beds does not achieve much by way of real savings since it often translates into reduced overcrowding in a ward rather than closure of entire wards or facilities. It is only with closure or consolidation of facilities or parts of facilities that savings in utilities will be achieved. Second, if bed closures are also accompanied by the elimination of medical staff positions, the savings impact will be higher through a reduced total wage bill.

8.50   And third, downsizing needs to be supported by a reform of sectoral funding mechanisms. Under the current financing system, facilities have little incentive to report closure of beds (let alone wards), because territorial departments of finance often reduce the following year's budget allocation in proportion to the reduction in inpatient capacity. Cost-conscious institutions are thus not allowed to retain savings from reduced excess capacity.[13] Another major obstacle to institutionalizing this type of incentive for bottom-up capacity rationalization is the restrictions on facility and local budget authorities to reallocate resources between line items in their received allocations. As is discussed earlier, although reallocation between line items does take place, the ad hoc basis for such reallocation needs to be replaced by institutionalized mechanisms for greater autonomy for facility resource managers.

---

[13]   The Ministry of Health reports that in order to remove the disincentive to cut excess capacity, the Ministry of Finance had issued instructions to the Department of Finance at oblast and rayon levels not to enforce capacity-related cutbacks in budgetary allocations. The instruction was issued as a recommendation rather than a requirement, however, leaving the decision to the discretion of local financial authorities, and the outcome essentially unclear.

Proposed Compulsory Medical Insurance

Main Features

8.51   The Compulsory Medical Insurance scheme (CMI) attempts to address some of the issues raised earlier regarding the use of health resources. The scheme, created by a Presidential Decree of June 15, 1995, covers all citizens of the Republic of Kazakstan and came fully into force in April 1996. The declared purpose of the CMI is to raise additional revenues for health financing in Kazakstan and to promote more efficient resource-use patterns. The basic program of services appears to be focused on high priority diseases and emphasizes ambulatory care. It is also intended to encourage competition between, and cost-management by, providers in their delivery of diagnostic and treatment services. The CMI may be a positive step toward achieving the highest health payoffs at the lowest cost. But a large number of fundamental issues remain to be elaborated before the CMI can meet its stated objectives.

8.52   The CMI establishes new relations between four actors in the insurance process: the fund, the insurer (the employer or local administration, depending on the category of population), the patient, and the provider of medical services (public or private, holding a license). Key features of the scheme are as follows.

-    *Funding.* The CMI is funded by a premium collected in the form of an employer's payroll tax contribution. The state budget pays premiums for the officially unemployed, pensioners, and students, while the self-employed pay their own premiums. These contributions are not additional to the existing 30 percent social security contribution to the Pension Fund and the Social Insurance Fund, but will rather come from a reallocation of its proceeds. There is a 10 percent allocation of the payroll tax collected as premiums for the CMI (i.e., 3 percent of total payroll).

-    *Coverage.* Each territorial CMI Fund is responsible for a so-called Basic Package of Health Services on behalf of employed persons (notionally funded by employer contributions) and "socially protected groups" (notionally funded from a Ministry of Finance budget contribution). The package includes comprehensive "free" care for children under 14 and pregnant women, plus emergency in-patient care (including drugs) at general hospitals, and outpatient and ambulatory care (excluding drugs) for other adults. At the oblast level, facilities will be designated either as providing "basic" services, or as remaining under oblast/municipal control (e.g., current oblast specialist hospitals).

-    *Service delivery.* Providers of medical services would render free medical services to patients according to the basic CMI program. The CMI Fund would contract services from licensed public and private providers on an equivalent payment basis. Local departments of health would license local providers of health services. The Fund would sign agreements with both the insurer and the provider of medical services. The territorial CMI Fund will contract with "basic service" provider units on a cost per case basis for in-patient care and a capitation basis for outpatient care to provide specified service volumes (initially using block contracts in most cases). Such a contract-based provider payment mechanism should, it is hoped, provide incentives and freedom for individual providers to improve operating efficiency and quality.

-   *Financial management.* The Fund is meant to be a nonprofit institution. Its finances would consist of a development fund (for the maintenance of the Fund itself) and an insurance reserve fund (for the compensation of CMI expenditures). The Fund would invest its reserves in state bonds and make deposits in banks. As far as the development fund is concerned, the Fund would be accountable to the State Committee for Financial Control; the insurance reserve fund would be jointly accountable to the Committee mentioned above, the Ministry of Health, and the Ministry of Finance.

-   *Transitory financing arrangements.* Since it will take time for the new system to consolidate its financial base, the assumption is that, for a substantial period of time, the Fund will also be financed from the general budget. General revenue thus finances both oblast health departments and territorial CMI Funds, with the share going to each negotiated by oblast, but the rough division being 45 and 55 percent to the CMI Funds and the Ministry of Health, respectively. The Ministry of Finance has stated its intention to index current levels of the health budget to inflation for the next two years (1996, 1997) and to treat funds from collected premiums as additional to budgetary financing for the health sector.[14/] On the basis of the CMI performance for these two years, decisions would be made regarding the need for budgetary allocations for subsequent years.

Outstanding Issues

8.53   Whereas the broad operating principles of the CMI appear clear, many issues remain to be addressed, including the following:

-   *Access.* Certain significant groups of the population fall outside the insurance-based "Basic Package," namely the self-employed, and unemployed individuals who do not qualify as members of a "socially protected" group. Such persons will be able to purchase policies from the Fund as individuals, at a price which is currently being set (but which is likely to be quite a substantial sum in relation to average incomes). Should they choose not to buy a policy, or be unable to afford an individual policy, these groups will pay on a fee-for-service basis when they require Basic Package service items. They will, however, be entitled to services from the so-called "Guaranteed Volume of Services," which will continue to be provided by oblast health departments from their general budgetary allocations.[15/]

-   *Overconsumption.* Little progress has been made toward preventing an excessive demand for medical care on the part of patients. As in the current system, patients are not directly responsible for payments for basic medical services. By initiating provider payments on a capitated basis, however, the system would provide incentives

---

[14/]   In this interim period, part of the budgetary financing allocated to the health sector would not be channeled through the Fund, but instructions have not yet been issued on the proportion to be administered through the current financing system.

[15/]   The Guaranteed Volume of Services includes elective/planned inpatient care at general hospitals, more specialized care, and population-based public health activities. In theory, oblast health departments will also contract with provider units to promote efficiency.

to facilities and practices to effectively use referrals and ambulatory procedures, to avoid exceeding the capitated payment for which they are responsible.

- *Financial stability.* The credibility of the new CMI will depend critically on its ability to raise revenues and set compensation levels at amounts that cover the basic program. Given artificially determined historical cost information (as per norms), there is likely to be a period of transition when cost and payment rates will be poorly estimated. To determine actuarial risk and appropriate premium levels (bearing in mind that tariffs and service packages will be modified at the oblast territorial level), national health accounts will need to be developed to provide appropriate and timely information on utilization and cost patterns.

    The actual collection of the CMI contributions is also an issue. Of the oblasts that are already experimenting with different models of a CMI Fund, the most elaborated model is to be found in the central province of Zhezkazgan. In this oblast, a CMI contribution rate of 5.5 percent has been imposed since July 1995, and the licensing of providers has begun. In the first few months, however, only about a quarter of the assessed contributions had been collected.

    Also, by including the CMI contribution within the existing social security contribution without increasing the contribution rate, medical insurance would in effect have to be financed at the expense of other social insurance components: pensions and social benefits (work accidents, maternity leave, etc.). This might be difficult given the depressed level of these benefits.

- *Competition.* A continued lack of competition may blunt the incentives for health providers to deliver cost-effective care. Individuals (with some exceptions, such as the self-employed) would not have freedom in choosing the provider of their medical services and insurers might tend to remain with the provider that rendered medical services before the introduction of the CMI. For example, local administrations might continue to register students with the University Polyclinic, while workers might be registered with the polyclinics previously run by the enterprise employing them. Hence, providers might not be in direct competition with each other and the service delivery market might be segmented, with differences coexisting in the quality of services provided. To overcome this, it would be necessary to introduce the right of individuals (not just insurers) to enroll with providers of their choice. The importance of introducing adequate quality assurance schemes to protect service standards and consumer choice also needs to be stressed.[16]

- *Public health.* Some health resources may be retained outside of the CMI Fund and in the health budget, owing to a legitimate concern that the Fund may fail to protect resources for public health services (e.g., infectious diseases). The feasibility of pooling budgetary and insurance resources under the CMI Fund could be explored after the start-up of the national Fund in order to cut down administrative costs. This

---

[16] It is necessary to note, however, that devising and enforcing these systems can often be a lengthy process.

could be attempted in the context of a legally enforceable protection ("ring-fencing") of resources for health services that have a public goods dimension.

- *Coordination.* The complementary and interdependent nature of the Basic Package and Guaranteed Volume make it inevitable that many facilities will be funded from both CMI Funds and local authorities. This situation emphasizes the vital importance of developing strong partnerships between funding agencies, and the need to develop a strong planning function as the means of working in partnership.

8.54 The stakes are high in the introduction of a CMI, and so are the risks. A previous experiment in South Kazakstan in 1993 collapsed amid allegations of fraud. A second (and national) failure may terminally condemn a potentially worthwhile idea. In these circumstances, it is recommended that authorities evaluate all experiences of the oblast models currently in operation and engage in broad-based consultations with users (institutional and individual), providers, administrators and politicians before making any final implementation decisions.

F. Conclusions

8.55 The health and education sectors are facing a severe financing crisis which threatens both the coverage and the quality of services provided by the two sectors. Reductions in capacity have not kept pace with reductions in real resources, with the consequence that while access to services is nominally relatively unaffected, quality and effective coverage are greatly reduced. This crisis is the reflection of the overall fiscal situation rather than of a lower priority given to the sectors. As the resources envelopes of the sectors are unlikely to expand again quickly, the current focus of policies should be on promoting a more efficient use of public resources (i.e., the achievement of the greatest gain in educational and health outcomes at a given cost).

8.56 The emphasis in *education* expenditures on general primary and secondary education is appropriate. But student to teacher ratios are very low by international standards in schools as well as in higher education institutions. The overall number of teachers in schools actually increased over the last few years despite reduced resources to the sector. The overall low student-teacher ratios result from: (i) a funding mechanism (based on "class complexes") designed to maintain all classrooms open however marginal they may be; and (ii) an excessive specialization in curricula, particularly in vocational and higher education institutions. Both institutions as well as training programs need to be reduced and/or consolidated.

8.57 The priorities emerging from the analysis are as follows:

(i) The introduction of capitation funding on a per student basis or by limiting the application of the class-complex norm to beyond a minimum threshold level. This would facilitate consolidation of classes and institutions in the school sector and closure of specializations for which enrollment is declining in higher education.

(ii) Increase in teaching loads in schools, including through the introduction of multitopic and multigrade teaching methods in low density areas.

(iii)   In vocational and higher education institutions, the development of curricula in high growth skill areas (e.g., business, management, computer science, languages), accompanied by closure of narrow specializations with little demand.

(iv)   Improvements in the supply and quality of textbooks.

8.58   In *health*, the resource allocation patterns show a bias toward in-patient and tertiary care. In contrast, the ambulatory and polyclinic network which provides outpatient care in rural areas is under serious financial stress, with severe implications for both the equity and cost-effectiveness of health spending. A main underlying factor is the reliance on physical norms and the inducement they create for expanding in-patient capacity without providing incentives for providers to make efficient cost-management decisions.

8.59   Priority should be given to shifting treatment to cost-effective ambulatory institutions, where appropriate. Recommendations to rationalize resource allocation patterns to cost-effective uses and to encourage the sustainability of cost-effective practices include the following:

(i)   Introducing medical protocols emphasizing ambulatory care where appropriate.

(ii)   Strengthening diagnostic and treatment capacity at the level of ambulatory and polyclinic institutions and devoting to them a higher proportions of health spending.

(iii)   Introducing funding mechanisms on a per patient basis (i.e., funds to cover agreed treatment packages for the number of enrolled patients).

8.60   Rationalization could be stimulated by *incorporating* sectoral facilities into *statutory bodies with management autonomy*. These statutory bodies could then be funded partially or fully through operating subsidies, calculated on a per capita basis (e.g., per patient in health, or per student in education). Depending on the degree of control which the government authorities want to retain, these subsidy programs could be differentiated by medical protocols, education levels and programs.

8.61   In this context, the CMI may be a positive step toward achieving the highest health payoffs for a given cost. But a number of fundamental issues still remain to be carefully considered before the CMI can be satisfactorily implemented. They concern: (i) problems of access to basic services for certain social groups; (ii) the need to protect those services which have a "public good" nature; (iii) the uncertain financial stability of the financing arrangements; (iv) the lack of competition in the proposed scheme; and (v) the need for close coordination and strategic partnership between CMI Fund and the Ministry of Health at all levels. It is thus recommended that the authorities review and evaluate oblast experiments with the CMI and engage in broad-ranging consultations as they elaborate the implementation procedures for the CMI.

8.62   The expected impact of the above measures would be a decline in the rate of hospital admissions, and average lengths of stay would be expected to decline gradually as the demand for costly and lengthy inpatient treatment is reduced. This decline should be accompanied by the closure of entire facilities or wards, rather than by the decommissioning of beds, which may not produce much in terms of actual savings. It is also important to recognize that the implementation of such measures as new protocols, facility conversion-consolidation-closure, staff retraining will require significant up front capital investments.

8.63   The structural adjustments proposed here cannot accommodate the current atomization of responsibilities over the sectors: they will require a strong leadership. In order to make possible the sectoral planning of reform and resource needs, all education and health facilities which are not specifically transferred to future municipalities (see Chapter VII) should be brought under the sole jurisdiction of the education and health ministries and their territorial counterparts. Similarly, as was argued in Chapter IV, the Ministries of Health and Education should be put firmly in charge of programming and managing all national expenditures in their respective sectors.

Annex I. OVERVIEW OF MAJOR TAXES

1.   The following paragraphs give some details of the nationwide taxes whose revenues accrue in whole or part to the lower tiers. They also give some details of the three genuine local taxes. The descriptions relate to the 1995 tax decree regulations. In the case of the nationwide taxes, the descriptions include a discussion of the factors that determine the amount of tax that is raised in each jurisdiction and the reasons for the highly uneven distribution of tax revenues across territorial jurisdictions.

Income tax

2.   *Tax on individual incomes*. This is applied to earned income, real capital gains (with taxpayers' principal residences exempt), and investment income (with interest on state securities exempt). For earned income and capital gains, each individual's taxable income is set equal to his or her actual income minus the minimum wage and also minus a further amount equal to the minimum wage for each person dependent on that individual. Taxable income is taxed on a progressive scale from 5 percent on the first 10 minimum wages, 10 percent on the next 10 minimum wages, 15 percent on the next 10, 20 percent on the next 10, 30 percent on the next 10, and 40 percent on any excess. Investment income is taxed at 15 percent.

3.   The tax on earned incomes is withheld by employers from employees' gross wages and is paid to the employers' tax offices. Likewise, the tax on interest and dividends is withheld by the enterprises making the payments and is paid to the enterprises' tax offices.

4.   *The profit tax on business incomes*.   This is a profit tax with a rate of 30 percent. There is a lower 10 percent rate for businesses where land is the main production asset. Each enterprise's tax is paid to the tax office in the area where it is registered.

Value added tax (VAT)

5.   VAT is levied at 20 percent. The few exemptions include leasing land or buildings, financial services, stamps, services provided by specified nonprofit organizations, and funeral services. In essence, VAT is charged whenever purchases are made. The enterprise making the sale has to collect the tax from the purchaser and send it to the tax authorities. But in calculating its VAT liability, each business may deduct from the amount due on its sales the amount it has paid on its purchases. Alternatively, it may be seen as paying the full amount on its sales and simultaneously asking for a refund of the payments made on its purchases.

Excise taxes

6.   There are excise taxes on the producers of the following items:

    (i)   Alcoholic drinks
    (ii)   Tobacco products
    (iii)   Sturgeon, salmon and their roe
    (iv)   Gold, platinum and silver jewelry
    (v)   Hides and clothes made with leather or fur

(vi)   Objects made out of crystal

(vii)   Gasoline (except aviation fuel) and diesel fuel

(viii)   Firearms

(ix)   Automobiles.

Each item is taxed at a rate determined by the Council of Ministers.

Rental Payments

7.   Enterprises exploiting mineral resources are liable to three types of payment, namely:

(i)   So-called "bonuses" or fees which are payable on a one-off basis when permission is granted to explore, when deposits are found, and at certain stages of extraction

(ii)   Royalties which cover the rights to use the subsurface in the course of extraction

(iii)   An excess profits tax which is payable in favorable market conditions.

Rental payments are levied only in six resource rich oblasts.

Land tax

8.   This is levied by rayons on most land. The decree specifies three main categories of taxed land, and associated tax rates, as shown below:

(i)   Agricultural land is taxed between 0.25 and 105.00 tenge per hectare depending on its quality

(ii)   Land with inhabited localities is taxed at 0.20 tenge per m^2 if it is occupied by residences and between 0.25 and 15.00 tenge per m^2 otherwise, the rates depending on which town or other settlement the land is in

(iii)   Land used for industrial, transportation, communication, defense, and other (similar) purposes is taxed between 25 and 3,000 tenge per hectare depending on its quality, the steeply progressive scale being intended to encourage industry to settle on sites with poor quality land.

9.   The decree also allows rayons to change the tax rates by 20 percent of the specified amounts. However, the aim of this provision is not to give the rayons discretion over their tax revenues. Rather it is to let them adjust the rates on individual plots where the usual rates would seem harsh or generous. Thus, the rates on agricultural land may be altered "depending on the location of a land lot" and "the sufficiency of its water supply." The rates in inhabited localities may be adjusted depending on factors such as "the accessibility of the land lot for transport, the architectural and artistic or landscape value of the buildings, the environmental, microclimatic, sanitary and hygienic conditions' and 'the liability of the territory to destructive impacts of natural calamities." The rates on land used for industry, etc., may be varied on the basis of factors such as "the location of the land lot" and "the availability of communications."

10.   The list of land types subject to tax shows that the exemptions include several types of land that are exempt in many other countries, including land used for embassies and consulates, religious buildings and cemeteries, and parks and historical monuments. But there are also exemptions for categories that most countries would tax, such as land used for education, nonprofit enterprises, and government buildings. If local self-administration is established, it would be useful to apply this local tax also to central government buildings.

Tax on motor vehicles

11.   This is levied on most road vehicles, the main exemptions being agricultural vehicles, vehicles for disabled persons, vehicles for heroes of the Soviet Union, and vehicles belonging to the National Bank of Kazakstan. The rates depend on the type of vehicle and are expressed as percentages of the minimum wage for each kilowatt of power. The rates include 1.0 percent for motorcycles and scooters, 4.0 percent for trucks, and 8.0 percent for cars and buses.

Property tax

12.   This is levied on homes and also on capital goods valued at 600 or more tenge (except for vehicles) used by businesses. Apparently the data on business assets are supplied by enterprises from their own records. Homeowners are taxed at 0.1 percent of their property values and pay in a single annual installment, while business owners are taxed at 0.5 percent and pay in four quarterly installments. The scope of the tax on businesses is wider than in most OECD countries. A 1983 OECD survey found that assets beyond buildings were taxed only in the case of one of Japan's three property taxes and in the case of the property tax in Turkey.[1]

Nontax revenues

13.   As was noted earlier, three so-called taxes in the new tax decree are not discussed in detail by that decree. These are business registration fees, fees to perform specific activities, and auction fees. As these so-called taxes are more in the way of fees than charges, they are best regarded as sources of non-tax revenue. They are intended to replace a plethora of levies which disappeared on 1 July 1995, but at present it is unclear exactly how many of the activities previously subject to levies will be so subject in future.[2]

Other levies

14.   The new tax decree covers all the compulsory taxes administered by the Tax Inspectorate, but it ignores some other compulsory levies which resemble taxes and which are administered by local authorities, typically rayons. The most significant in revenue terms are the so-called "state duties," which roughly correspond to stamp duties on items such as legal fees and visa fees. There are also some very low-yielding levies which include water charges on irrigation users and logging fees.

---

[1]   OECD, Taxes on Immovable Property (Paris, 1983), p. 41.

[2]   The levies that disappeared on 1 July 1995 included a number of fees and 12 so-called taxes. The fees included levies on people registering as producers (both enterprises and others), on people detained in "sobering-up houses," on people supplied with passports, and on people whose cars were detained for inspection. The 12 taxes were on construction, advertising, sales of businesses, compulsory contributions to special activities such as street improvements, parking, peddlers, clothing used for advertising, auctions, TV shows, home registrations, licenses to sell liquor, and lotteries.

Statistical Annex

Contents

TABLE 1-1. Population and Labor Force (thousands)

Population or labor group	1980	1985	1986	1987	1988	1989	1990	1991	1992	1993	1994	1995
Total population a/	14,824	15,696	15,865	16,065	16,268	16,456	16,618	16,721	16,892	16,913	16,870	16,607
Males	7,141	7,568	7,656	7,761	7,869	7,970	8,057	8,116	8,204	8,218	8,199	8,068
Females	7,683	8,128	8,209	8,304	8,399	8,486	8,561	8,605	8,688	8,695	8,671	8,539
Urban population	7,968	8,757	8,896	9,068	9,243	9,394	9,523	9,634	9,713	9,655	9,491	9,270
Rural population	6,856	6,939	6,969	6,997	7,025	7,062	7,095	7,087	7,179	7,258	7,379	7,337
Population under working age	5,131	5,327	5,384	5,443	5,507	5,556	5,573	5,559	5,575	5,533	5,467	5,334
Working-age population b/	8,189	8,687	8,763	8,873	8,971	9,082	9,175	9,226	9,335	9,356	9,359	9,231
Population over working age	1,504	1,682	1,718	1,749	1,790	1,818	1,870	1,936	1,982	2,024	2,044	2,042
Economically Active Population, in non-working age	227	254	253	232	226	226	230	229	230	265	217	..
Above working age	213	242	242	222	216	216	218	218	219	244	203	..
Below working age	14	12	11	10	10	10	12	11	11	21	14	..
Total labor resources	8,360	8,854	8,935	9,016	9,113	9,203	9,262	9,331	9,368	9,380	9,241	9,153
Total employment	6,640	7,136	7,208	7,295	7,400	7,467	7,563	7,494	7,356	6,926	6,579	6,548
State sector employees	6,225	6,719	6,789	6,846	6,862	6,789	5,912	5,686	5,231	4,486	..	..
Leased enterprise employees	..	..	..	..	..	..	484	673	344	168	..	..
Joint-stock company employees	..	..	..	..	..	..	8	15	251	508	..	..
Economic association employees	..	..	..	..	..	..	121	127	12	..	..	..
Social organization employees	..	..	..	..	..	..	37	52	33	25	..	..
Joint venture employees	..	..	..	..	..	..	..	7	7	13	..	..
Collective farm workers	276	279	276	274	264	254	260	258	268	247	..	..
Cooperative workers	..	..	..	5	42	..	241	185	98	43	..	..
Individual labor activities	..	..	..	..	..	..	12	..	24	12	..	..
Private subsidiary agricultural workers	137	136	142	162	221	230	275	310	337	349	..	..
Private agricultural workers	..	..	..	..	..	..	..	..	39	49	..	..
Students	810	791	777	773	772	770	759	763	734	701	671	625
Religious workers	..	..	..	..	..	..	..	..	..	..	3	3
Working age population not employed in the national economy	910	927	949	948	941	966	940	1,074	1,064	1,715	1,988	1,976
Housewives	..	..	..	..	..	..	..	..	..	..	..	..
Military personnel	..	..	..	..	..	..	..	..	..	..	..	..
Unemployed (registered)	..	..	..	..	..	..	..	4	34	37	54	98
Unemployed (not registered)	..	..	..	..	..	..	..	..	..	..	483	710
Labor force	..	..	..	..	..	..	..	7,498	7,390	6,963	7,118	7,360

a/ Data at the beginning of the year.
b/ Working age includes women aged 16-54 and men aged 16-59.

Source: State Committee of Statistics.

TABLE 1-2. Employment by Sector, Annual Average (thousands)

Sector	1980	1985	1986	1987	1988	1989	1990	1991	1992	1993	1994	1995
Material sphere	4,838	5,177	5,203	5,270	5,343	5,341	5,405	5,307	5,187	4,752	4,673	4,687
Agriculture and forestry	1,561	1,662	1,655	1,695	1,733	1,676	1,726	1,754	1,794	1,759	1,419	1,445
Agriculture	1,545	1,646	1,640	1,680	1,718	1,662	1,713	1,740	1,781	1,746	1,408	1,434
Forestry	16	16	16	15	15	14	14	14	13	13	11	10
Industry and construction	2,072	2,218	2,245	2,279	2,336	2,420	2,447	2,304	2,230	1,925	1,683	1,452
Industry	1,410	1,520	1,532	1,541	1,563	1,562	1,539	1,533	1,490	1,305	1,201	1,088
Construction	662	699	713	738	773	857	908	771	740	620	482	364
Other	1,205	1,297	1,303	1,297	1,275	1,245	1,232	1,249	1,163	1,068	1,571	1,790
Transport of goods 1/	558	606	607	591	561	509	510	508	484	448	551	507
Road Maintenance	..	..	..	..	..	..	..	..	..	..	..	..
Communication servicing material production	..	..	..	..	..	..	..	..	..	..	..	..
Wholesale trade 2/	549	576	577	577	576	563	561	551	533	482	847	1,035
Retail trade and catering	..	..	..	..	..	..	..	..	..	..	..	..
Material supply	..	..	..	..	..	..	..	..	..	..	..	..
Procurement	..	..	..	..	..	..	..	..	..	..	..	..
Information and computing services	17	20	22	27	26	23	21	20	14	11	10	7
Other sectors	81	95	97	102	113	150	140	170	132	127	164	243
Nonmaterial sphere	1,802	1,959	2,005	2,025	2,057	2,126	2,158	2,187	2,169	2,174	1,721	1,711
Transport 3/	206	222	222	213	209	197	194	192	180	136	..	..
Communication	..	..	..	..	..	..	..	..	..	..	..	..
Housing 4/	227	246	248	257	267	294	292	289	283	283	270	275
Public utilities and personal services	..	..	..	..	..	..	..	..	..	..	..	..
Health care, social security, and sports	351	393	402	412	428	446	456	465	481	429	429	417
Education 5/	693	754	774	798	820	1,001	1,022	1,036	871	837	827	818
Culture and art	..	..	..	..	..	..	..	..	..	..	..	..
Science and research	149	154	157	144	140	..	..	..	124	79	..	..
Credit 6/	38	41	40	40	40	40	39	42	46	54	49	50
Insurance	..	..	..	..	..	..	..	..	..	..	..	..
General administration and defense	138	149	162	161	153	148	155	163	184	132	145	148
Private nonprofit institutions serving households (other nonmaterial)	..	..	..	..	..	..	..	..	..	224	3	3
Other, material and nonmaterial spheres	3,007	3,256	3,308	3,322	3,332	3,371	3,390	3,436	3,332	3,242	3,292	3,501
Total employment	6,640	7,136	7,208	7,295	7,400	7,467	7,563	7,494	7,356	6,926	6,394	6,398

1/ Includes road maintenance and communication.

2/ Includes retail trade, catering, material supply and procurement.

3/ Includes communication.

4/ Includes public utilities and personal services.

5/ Includes culture and art, science and research in selected years.

6/ Includes insurance.

Source: State Committee of Statistics.

TABLE 1-3a. State Workers and Employees by Sector on January 1, 1995 (thousands)

Sector	Total	Workers	Employees
Material sphere	3,868	3,450	1,010
Agriculture and forestry	1,121	928	193
Agriculture	1,108	918	190
Forestry	13	10	3
Industry and construction	1,687	1,330	357
Industry	1,195	941	254
Construction	492	389	103
Other	1,060	783	277
Transport of goods	497	386	111
Road maintenance	..	..	..
Communication servicing material production	79	56	23
Wholesale trade	..	..	..
Retail trade and catering	294	215	79
Material supply	59	40	19
Procurement	39	28	11
Information and computing services	10	6	8
Other sectors	82	81	38
	1,060		
Nonmaterial sphere	1,763	584	1,179
Transport	..	..	..
Communication	..	..	..
Housing	252	183	69
Public utilities and personal services	..	..	..
Health care, social security, and sports	425	148	277
Education	732	173	559
Culture and art	93	27	66
Science and research	77	30	47
Credit	52	5	47
Insurance	..	..	..
General administration and defense	132	18	114
Private nonprofit institutions serving households	..	..	..
Other, material and nonmaterial spheres	1,763	584	1,179
Total	5,631	4,034	2,189

Source: State Committee of Statistics.

TABLE 1-3b. State Workers and Employees by Sector on January 1, 1996 (thousands)

Sector	Total	Workers	Employees
Material sphere	3,471	2,865	606
Agriculture and forestry	1,208	1,083	125
Agriculture	1,198	1,076	122
Forestry	10	7	3
Industry and construction	1,393	1,134	259
Industry	1,049	867	182
Construction	344	267	77
Other	870	648	222
Transport of goods	403	323	80
Road maintenance	..	..	..
Communication servicing material production	81	54	27
Wholesale trade	202	151	51
Retail trade and catering	21	18	3
Material supply	44	30	14
Procurement	27	20	7
Information and computing services	6	2	4
Other sectors	86	50	36
Nonmaterial sphere	1,523	490	1,033
Transport			
Communication	..	..	..
Housing	..	..	..
Public utilities and personal services	168	110	58
Health care, social security, and sports	36	30	6
Education	383	130	253
Culture and art	644	163	481
Science and research	65	20	45
Credit	36	10	26
Insurance	47	6	41
General administration and defense	..	..	..
Private nonprofit institutions serving households	144	21	123
	..	..	..
Other, material and nonmaterial spheres	2,393	1,138	1,255
Total	4,994	3,355	1,639

Source: State Committee of Statistics.

TABLE 1-4. Labor Force Participation Rate by Age Group

Year and indicator	All age groups	0-15	16-19	20-24	25-29	30-34	35-39	40-44	45-49	50-54	55-59	60-64	Over 65
1989 Census													
Total population (thousands)	16,456	5,551	1,140	1,346	1,544	1,364	1,130	697	751	836	586	592	927
Labor force (thousands)	7,825	7	430	1,064	1,413	1,286	1,078	666	703	696	307	118	57
Labor force participation rate (percent)	47.55	0.13	37.72	79.05	91.52	94.28	95.40	95.55	93.61	83.25	52.39	19.93	6.15
Male population (thousands)	7,970	2,809	592	680	773	681	557	341	357	400	270	235	279
Labor force, Males (thousands)	4,155	5	254	565	748	669	546	334	346	371	220	68	29
Labor force participation rate (percent)	52.13	0.18	42.91	83.09	96.77	98.24	98.03	97.95	96.92	92.75	81.48	28.94	10.39
Female population (thousands)	8,486	2,742	548	666	771	683	573	356	394	436	316	357	648
Labor force, Females (thousands)	3,670	2	176	499	665	617	532	332	357	325	87	50	28
Labor force participation rate (percent)	43.25	0.07	32.12	74.92	86.25	90.34	92.84	93.26	90.61	74.54	27.53	14.01	4.32
1979 Census													
Total population (thousands)	..	..	..	..	..	..	..	..	..	..	..	..	..
Labor force (thousands)	..	..	..	..	..	..	..	..	..	..	..	..	..
Labor force participation rate (percent)	..	..	..	..	..	..	..	..	..	..	..	..	..
Male population (thousands)	..	..	..	..	..	..	..	..	..	..	..	..	..
Labor force, Males (thousands)	..	..	..	..	..	..	..	..	..	..	..	..	..
Labor force participation rate (percent)	..	..	..	..	..	..	..	..	..	..	..	..	..
Female population (thousands)	..	..	..	..	..	..	..	..	..	..	..	..	..
Labor force, Females (thousands)	..	..	..	..	..	..	..	..	..	..	..	..	..
Labor force participation rate (percent)	..	..	..	..	..	..	..	..	..	..	..	..	..

Source: State Committee of Statistics.

TABLE 1-5. Registered Unemployment (thousands; end of month)

Year and month		Total	Males	Females	Receiving benefits
1992	January	4.5	..	..	1.2
	February	6.7			2.3
	March	9.2	2.9	6.3	3.6
	April	11.8	..	..	5.0
	May	13.6			6.2
	June	15.8	4.2	11.6	7.7
	July	19.6	..	..	10.2
	August	22.4			12.3
	September	25.0	6.9	18.1	13.5
	October	28.2	..	..	15.1
	November	30.6			16.7
	December	33.7	8.6	25.1	18.2
1993	January	35.6	..	..	17.7
	February	37.2			17.8
	March	39.3	11.5	27.8	18.5
	April	40.6	..	..	19.2
	May	39.4			18.6
	June	37.6	11.3	26.3	17.6
	July	37.3	..	..	16.9
	August	36.8			16.6
	September	37.2	10.4	26.8	15.5
	October	39.1	..	..	14.8
	November	39.8			14.8
	December	40.5	12.1	28.4	15.4
1994	January	42.9	..	..	16.0
	February	46.7			17.8
	March	48.1	17.5	30.6	18.5
	April	50.8	..	..	20.8
	May	51.1			21.0
	June	52.2	18.7	33.5	21.8
	July	53.6	..	..	23.5
	August	56.2			25.2
	September	60.0	20.5	39.5	26.7
	October	62.5	..	..	27.6
	November	66.7			29.8
	December	70.1	24.7	45.4	33.2
1995	January	75.4	..	..	36.0
	February	82.8			41.6
	March	85.7	32.9	52.8	44.6
	April	90.3	..	..	48.3
	May	92.5			49.2
	June	95.8	36.9	58.9	49.4
	July	98.3	..	..	52.3
	August	103.1			54.0
	September	108.4	42.3	66.1	56.1
	October	116.1	..	..	58.9
	November	127.8			65.0
	December	139.6	55.7	83.9	73.5
1996	January	157.7	..	..	84.8
	February	186.5			102.9
	March	205.7	84.8	120.9	116.7
	April	225.9	..	..	134.2

Source: State Committee of Statistics.

TABLE 2-1. Gross Domestic Product at Current Prices (millions of national currency)

Sector of origin or expenditure category	1990	1991	1992	1993	1994	1995
		(mill. rubles)			(mill. tenge)	
Gross domestic product by sector of origin						
Agriculture and forestry	..	..	252,253	3,451	63,155	113,483
Agriculture	..	..	252,163	3,436	62,895	..
Forestry	..	..	90	15	261	..
Industry and construction	..	..	405,357	10,781	159,661	336,598
Industry	..	..	339,740	8,297	116,641	260,498
Construction	..	..	65,617	2,484	43,020	76,100
Other	..	..	370,804	13,684	213,262	506,237
Transport	..	..	63,378	1,384	43,280	79,699
Road maintenance	..	..	..	..	..	..
Communication	..	..	5,393	184	4,003	12,854
Wholesale trade	..	..	..	..	..	..
Retail trade and catering	..	..	19,863	1,345	63,755	182,543
Material supply	..	..	19,503	734	5,016	..
Procurement	..	..	4,821	298	1,775	..
Information and computing services	..	..	487	29	272	..
Other sectors of material production	..	..	4,419	..	..	..
Housing	..	..	..	378	20,263	74,888
Public utilities and personal services	..	..	6,934	149	19,600	..
Health care, social security,				349	6,891	16,350
and sports	..	..	11,686	718	113	..
Education	..	..	24,119	139	10,376	29,889
Culture and art	..	..	1,177	131	3,258	7,657
Science and research	..	..	852	4,536	861	1,648
Credit	..	..	169,678	29	27,810	13,309
Insurance	..	..	2,477	467	73	..
General administration and defense	..	..	17,382	684	6,531	13,224
Private nonprofit institutions serving households	..	..	18,635	684	6,618	..
Imputed service charge of financial intermediaries	..	..	..	0	-20,690	..
Other (incl. Geology)					13,457	74,177
Total gross value added (GVA)	..	..	1,028,414	23,957	436,078	956,318
Taxes on production and imports (TOPI)	..	..	..	2,881	21,442	36,185
Taxes on products	..	..	..	2,827	21,442	36,185
Other taxes on production (OTOP)	..	..	..	54	..	..
Taxes on imports	..	..	..	..	..	..
Subsidies on production and imports (SOPI)	..	..	..	..	..	..
Subsidies on products	..	..	..	..	7,603	..
Other subsidies on production (OSOP)	..	..	..	..	..	..
Subsidies on imports	..	..	..	..	..	..
Total GDP at factor cost (GVA-OTOP+OSOP)	..	..	1,019,664	23,957	436,078	956,318
Net Indirect taxes (TOPI - SOPI)	..	..	193,952	2,881	13,839	36,185
Total GDP at market prices	44,369	74,215	1,213,616	26,838	449,917	992,503
Gross domestic product by expenditure category						
Consumption	..	..	..	15,323	377,583	..
Private consumption	..	..	..	11,593	335,439	..
Government consumption	..	..	..	3,730	42,144	..
Gross domestic investment	..	..	..	13,197	96,243	..
Gross fixed investment	..	..	..	5,952	85,345	..
Change in stocks	..	..	..	7,245	10,898	..
Resource balance (net exports of GNFS)	..	..	..	-1,682	-23,909	..
Exports of goods and nonfactor services	..	..	..	8,881	145,866	..
Imports of goods and nonfactor services	..	..	..	10,563	169,775	..

Source: State Committee of Statistics.

TABLE 2-1a. Distribution of Gross Domestic Product by Origin and Expenditure at Current Prices (percent)

Sector of origin or expenditure category	1990	1991	1992	1993	1994	1995
Gross domestic product by sector of origin						
Agriculture and forestry	..	..	20.8	12.9	14.0	11.4
Agriculture	..	..	20.8	12.8	14.0	..
Forestry	..	..	0.0	0.1	0.1	..
Industry and construction	..	..	33.4	40.2	35.5	33.9
Industry	..	..	28.0	30.9	25.9	26.2
Construction	..	..	5.4	9.3	9.6	7.7
Other	..	..	30.6	51.0	47.4	51.0
Transport	..	..	5.2	5.2	9.6	8.0
Road maintenance	..	..	..	..	..	..
Communication	..	..	0.4	0.7	0.9	1.3
Wholesale trade	..	..	..	..	..	..
Retail trade and catering	..	..	1.6	5.0	14.2	18.4
Material supply	..	..	1.6	2.7	1.1	0.0
Procurement	..	..	0.4	1.1	0.4	0.0
Information and computing services	..	..	0.0	0.1	0.1	0.0
Other sectors of material production	..	..	0.4	..	..	..
Housing	..	..	..	1.4	4.5	7.5
Public utilities and personal services	..	..	0.6	0.6	4.4	0.0
Health care, social security, and sports	..	..	1.0	1.3	0.0	..
Education	..	..	2.0	2.7	2.3	3.0
Culture and art	..	..	0.1	0.5	0.7	0.8
Science and research	..	..	0.1	0.5	0.2	0.2
Credit	..	..	14.0	16.9	6.2	1.3
Insurance	..	..	0.2	0.1	0.0	..
General administration and defense	..	..	1.4	1.7	1.5	1.3
Private nonprofit institutions serving households	..	..	1.5	2.5	1.5	..
Imputed service charge of financial intermediaries	..	..	..	0.0	-4.6	..
Other	..	..	..	..	3.0	7.5
Total gross value added	..	..	84.7	104.0	96.9	96.4
Total GDP at factor cost	..	..	84.0	89.3	96.9	96.4
Net indirect taxes	..	..	16.0	10.7	3.1	3.6
Total GDP at market prices	100.0	100.0	100.0	100.0	100.0	100.0
Gross domestic product by expenditure category						
Consumption	..	..	..	57.1	83.9	..
Private consumption	..	..	..	43.2	74.6	..
Government consumption	..	..	..	13.9	9.4	..
Gross domestic investment	..	..	..	49.2	21.4	..
Gross fixed investment	..	..	..	22.2	19.0	..
Change in stocks	..	..	..	27.0	2.4	..
Resource balance (net exports of GNFS)	..	..	..	-6.3	-5.3	..
Exports of goods and nonfactor services	..	..	..	33.1	32.4	..
Imports of goods and nonfactor services	..	..	..	39.4	37.7	..

Source: State Committee of Statistics.

TABLE 2-5. Net Material Product at Current Prices (millions of national currency units)

Sector of origin or expenditure category	1980	1985	1986	1987	1988	1989	1990	1991	1992	1993
Net material product by sector of origin					(rubles)					(tenge)
Agriculture and forestry	5,338	6,818	8,283	8,066	9,214	10,461	13,962	22,862	255,739	4,304
Agriculture	5,327	6,797	8,262	8,044	9,189	10,435	13,937	22,810	255,634	4,279
Forestry	12	22	22	22	25	26	25	52	105	25
Industry and construction	9,759	11,353	10,872	11,260	11,605	11,277	12,341	33,786	455,074	11,822
Industry	6,672	7,627	6,680	6,915	6,762	5,659	7,003	24,764	390,254	9,253
Construction	3,087	3,727	4,192	4,345	4,843	5,618	5,338	9,022	64,820	2,569
Other sectors of material production	5,475	4,982	5,114	4,870	5,900	6,259	7,056	10,185	129,193	5,225
Transport of goods	1,775	2,177	2,229	2,275	2,433	2,481	3,083	5,420	62,498	2,186
Road maintenance	..	57	34	66	68	43	56	85	..	..
Communication servicing material production	..	82	86	95	104	110	118	161	4,673	180
Wholesale trade	..	92	101	81	109	113	125	140	..	..
Retail trade and catering	1,069	1,119	1,195	1,041	1,230	1,368	1,477	2,542	29,348	1,385
Material supply	266	365	411	389	377	384	439	1,020	25,917	993
Procurement	344	444	434	424	507	399	460	594	5,938	434
Information and computing services	..	30	48	54	60	83	94	76	532	30
Other sectors	2,021	616	578	446	1,012	1,278	1,205	147	287	17
Foreign trade income	..	..	..	..	..	..	..	..	418	..
Net material product	20,572	23,153	24,270	24,197	26,719	27,997	33,359	66,833	840,424	21,351
By expenditure category:										
Consumption	17,500	21,548	21,804	22,480	23,880	25,833	28,453	63,097	667,788	15,323
Personal consumption	15,129	18,466	18,744	19,113	20,378	22,185	24,442	47,633	579,334	11,593
Consumption of government institutions	1,818	2,273	2,343	2,567	2,679	2,797	3,008	14,747	60,806	0
General government and scientific institutions	553	809	717	800	823	851	1,003	717	27,648	0
Investment (accumulation)	6,200	9,900	9,100	8,307	8,500	8,728	11,693	22,481	324,971	8,422
Fixed capital	4,200	5,300	5,700	6,035	5,100	5,326	5,594	5,139	242,731	1,217
Changes in inventories and other	2,000	4,600	3,400	2,272	3,400	3,402	6,099	17,342	82,240	7,245
Losses	..	..	..	582	..	792	969	660	9,013	..
Net exports	-3,128	-8,295	-6,634	-7,172	-5,662	-7,355	-7,756	-19,405	-161,348	..
memo:										
Consumption	17,500	21,548	21,804	22,480	23,880	25,833	28,453	63,097	667,788	15,323
Private consumption	15,129	18,466	18,744	19,113	20,378	22,185	24,442	47,633	579,334	11,593
Social consumption	2,371	3,082	3,060	3,367	3,502	3,648	4,011	15,464	88,454	3,730

Source: State Committee of Statistics.

TABLE 2-5a. Distribution of Net Material Product by Origin and Expenditure at Current Prices (percent)

Sector of origin or expenditure category	1980	1985	1986	1987	1988	1989	1990	1991	1992	1993
Net material product by sector of origin										
Agriculture and forestry	25.9	29.4	34.1	33.3	34.5	37.4	41.9	34.2	30.4	20.2
Agriculture	25.9	29.4	34.0	33.2	34.4	37.3	41.8	34.1	30.4	20.0
Forestry	0.1	0.1	0.1	0.1	0.1	0.1	0.1	0.1	0.0	0.1
Industry and construction	47.4	49.0	44.8	46.5	43.4	40.3	37.0	50.6	54.1	55.4
Industry	32.4	32.9	27.5	28.6	25.3	20.2	21.0	37.1	46.4	43.3
Construction	15.0	16.1	17.3	18.0	18.1	20.1	16.0	13.5	7.7	12.0
Other	26.6	21.5	21.1	20.1	22.1	22.4	21.2	15.2	15.4	24.5
Transport of goods	8.6	9.4	9.2	9.4	9.1	8.9	9.2	8.1	7.4	10.2
Road maintenance	..	0.2	0.1	0.3	0.3	0.2	0.2	0.1	..	..
Communication servicing material production	..	0.4	0.4	0.4	0.4	0.4	0.4	0.2	0.6	0.8
Wholesale trade	..	0.4	0.4	0.3	0.4	0.4	0.4	0.2	..	..
Retail trade and catering	5.2	4.8	4.9	4.3	4.6	4.9	4.4	3.8	3.5	6.5
Material supply	1.3	1.6	1.7	1.6	1.4	1.4	1.3	1.5	3.1	4.7
Procurement	1.7	1.9	1.8	1.8	1.9	1.4	1.4	0.9	0.7	2.0
Information and computing services	..	0.1	0.2	0.2	0.2	0.3	0.3	0.1	0.1	0.1
Other sectors of material production	9.8	2.7	2.4	1.8	3.8	4.6	3.6	0.2	0.0	0.1
Foreign trade income	..	..	..	..	..	..	..	..	0.0	..
Total net material product	100.0	100.0	100.0	100.0	100.0	100.0	100.0	100.0	100.0	100.0
Net material product by expenditure category										
Consumption	85.1	93.1	89.8	92.9	89.4	92.3	85.3	94.4	79.5	71.8
Personal consumption	73.5	79.8	77.2	79.0	76.3	79.2	73.3	71.3	68.9	54.3
Consumption of govt. institutions serving households	8.8	9.8	9.7	10.6	10.0	10.0	9.0	22.1	7.2	0.0
General government and scientific institutions	2.7	3.5	3.0	3.3	3.1	3.0	3.0	1.1	3.3	0.0
Investment (accumulation)	30.1	42.8	37.5	34.3	31.8	31.2	35.1	33.6	38.7	39.4
Fixed capital	20.4	22.9	23.5	24.9	19.1	19.0	16.8	7.7	28.9	5.7
Changes in inventories and other	9.7	19.9	14.0	9.4	12.7	12.2	18.3	25.9	9.8	33.9
Losses	..	..	..	2.4	..	2.8	2.9	1.0	1.1	..
Net exports	-15.2	-35.8	-27.3	-29.6	-21.2	-26.3	-23.3	-29.0	-19.2	..
memo:										
Consumption	85.1	93.1	89.8	92.9	89.4	92.3	85.3	94.4	79.5	71.8
Private consumption	73.5	79.8	77.2	79.0	76.3	79.2	73.3	71.3	68.9	54.3
Social consumption	11.5	13.3	12.6	13.9	13.1	13.0	12.0	23.1	10.5	17.5

Source: State Committee of Statistics.

TABLE 2-6. Net Material Product by Origin and Expenditure at Constant Prices (millions of national currency)

Sector of origin or expenditure category	1980	1985	1986	1987	1988	1989	1990	1991	1992	1993
Net material product by sector of origin						(rubles)				
Agriculture and forestry	4,546	7,365	8,586	8,066	8,765	7,812	8,768	6,612	6,635	..
Agriculture	4,534	7,343	8,565	8,044	8,739	7,786	8,743	6,561	6,594	..
Forestry	12	22	22	22	26	25	25	51	41	..
Industry and construction	10,492	11,459	10,796	11,260	11,927	12,306	10,410	8,972	6,557	..
Industry	7,048	7,571	6,911	6,915	6,956	7,053	5,582	5,351	4,494	..
Construction	3,444	3,887	3,884	4,345	4,970	5,253	4,828	3,621	2,063	..
Other	5,186	4,947	4,909	4,870	5,554	6,099	6,161	6,143	5,177	..
Transport of goods	1,859	2,177	2,229	2,275	2,433	2,449	2,546	3,601	3,081	..
Road maintenance	..	57	34	66	68	42	52	64	..	..
Communication servicing material production	..	82	86	95	104	107	114	123	106	..
Wholesale trade	..	87	93	81	100	116	129	74	..	..
Retail trade and catering	907	1,085	1,072	1,041	1,117	1,234	1,336	1,187	996	..
Material supply	455	380	362	389	336	481	361	600	517	..
Procurement	222	437	417	424	330	393	462	303	309	..
Information and computing services	..	30	48	54	60	82	94	75	62	..
Other sectors of material production	1,743	611	569	446	1,006	1,196	1,067	116	106	..
Foreign trade income	..	..	..	..	..	..	..	..	9	..
Total net material product	20,426	23,833	24,248	24,197	26,258	26,237	25,991	22,130	19,043	..
Net material product by expenditure category										
Consumption	16,945	21,819	21,898	22,480	23,850	24,542	24,890	..	..	..
Personal consumption	14,620	18,743	18,843	19,113	20,352	20,951	21,116	..	..	..
Consumption of govt. institutions serving households	1,778	2,274	2,343	2,567	2,673	2,750	2,824	..	..	..
General government and scientific institutions	547	801	712	800	825	841	950	..	..	..
Investment (accumulation)	6,208	9,474	9,409	8,307	8,747	8,088	8,973	..	..	..
Fixed capital	4,503	5,670	5,731	6,035	5,090	4,771	4,143	..	..	..
Changes in inventories and other	1,706	3,803	3,678	2,272	3,657	3,316	4,830	..	..	..
Losses and discrepancy	..	..	..	582	..	742	755	..	..	..
Net exports	-3,106	-8,539	-6,628	-7,172	-5,564	-6,893	-6,043	..	..	..
memo:										
Consumption	16,945	21,819	21,898	22,480	23,850	24,542	24,890	..	..	..
Private Consumption	14,620	18,743	18,843	19,113	20,352	20,951	21,116	..	..	..
Social Consumption	2,325	3,076	3,055	3,367	3,498	3,590	3,774	..	..	..
Discrepancy in production	-203	-63	43	0	-12	-20	-653	-404	-665	..
Discrepancy in expenditure	..	..	..	..	..	..	..	..	..	..
Discrepancy production-ex	175	1,016	-388	0	-788	-262	-3,236	..	..	..

Source: State Committee of Statistics.

TABLE 2-6a. Growth Rate of Net Material Product by Origin and Expenditure at Constant Prices (percent)

Sector of origin or expenditure category	1986	1987	1988	1989	1990	1991	1992	1993
Growth rate by sector of origin								
Agriculture and forestry	16.6	-6.1	8.7	-10.9	12.2	-24.6	0.3	..
Agriculture	16.6	-6.1	8.6	-10.9	12.3	-25.0	0.5	..
Forestry	1.4	1.8	14.9	-0.4	-3.5	109.2	-19.8	..
Industry and construction	-5.8	4.3	5.9	3.2	-15.4	-13.8	-26.9	..
Industry	-8.7	0.1	0.6	1.4	-20.9	-4.1	-16.0	..
Construction	-0.1	11.8	14.4	5.7	-8.1	-25.0	-43.0	..
Other	-0.8	-0.8	14.0	9.8	1.0	-0.3	-15.7	..
Transport of goods	2.4	2.1	6.9	0.6	4.0	41.4	-14.4	..
Road maintenance	-40.0	93.3	2.4	-38.4	26.1	22.8	..	..
Communication servicing material production	4.6	10.5	9.8	2.2	7.2	8.0	-14.4	..
Wholesale trade	6.8	-12.8	24.0	16.0	10.5	-42.5	..	..
Retail trade and catering	-1.3	-2.9	7.3	10.4	8.3	-11.2	-16.1	..
Material supply	-4.8	7.4	-13.6	43.2	-25.0	66.3	-13.8	..
Procurement	-4.6	1.7	-22.3	19.3	17.6	-34.5	2.0	..
Information and computing services	59.7	11.7	12.5	36.3	14.2	-20.2	-17.4	..
Other sectors of material production	-7.0	-21.6	125.5	18.9	-10.8	-89.1	-8.2	..
Foreign trade income	..	..	..	..	..	..	..	..
Total net material product	1.7	-0.2	8.5	-0.1	-0.9	-14.9	-14.0	..
Growth rate by expenditure category								
Consumption	0.4	2.7	6.1	2.9	1.4	..	..	..
Personal consumption	0.5	1.4	6.5	2.9	0.8	..	..	..
Consumption of govt. institutions serving households	3.0	9.6	4.1	2.9	2.7	..	..	..
General government and scientific institutions	-11.1	12.3	3.1	1.9	13.0	..	..	..
Investment (accumulation)	-0.7	-11.7	5.3	-7.5	10.9	..	..	..
Fixed capital	1.1	5.3	-15.7	-6.3	-13.2	..	..	..
Changes in inventories and other	-3.3	-38.2	61.0	-9.3	45.6	..	..	..
Losses and discrepancy	..	..	..	..	1.7	..	..	..
Net Exports	-22.4	8.2	-22.4	23.9	-12.3	..	..	..
memo:								
Consumption	0.4	2.7	6.1	2.9	1.4	..	..	..
Private Consumption	0.5	1.4	6.5	2.9	0.8	..	..	..
Social Consumption	-0.7	10.2	3.9	2.7	5.1	..	..	..
Discrepancy in production	-167.8	-100.0	..	60.4	3,183.5	-38.1	64.7	..
Discrepancy in expenditure	..	..	..	..	..	..	..	..
Discrepancy production-ex	-138.2	-100.0	..	-66.8	1,136.0	..	..	..

Source: State Committee of Statistics.

TABLE 2-6b. Implicit Price Deflators for Net Material Product by Origin and Expenditure (percent)

Sector of origin or expenditure category	1980	1985	1986	1987	1988	1989	1990	1991	1992	1993
Price deflators by sector of origin										
Agriculture and forestry	117.4	92.6	96.5	100.0	105.1	133.9	159.2	345.8	3,854.6	..
Agriculture	117.5	92.6	96.5	100.0	105.1	134.0	159.4	347.7	3,877.1	..
Forestry	100.0	100.0	100.0	100.0	98.0	102.4	102.0	101.4	255.3	..
Industry and construction	93.0	99.1	100.7	100.0	97.3	91.6	118.6	376.6	6,939.8	..
Industry	94.7	100.7	96.7	100.0	97.2	80.2	125.5	462.8	8,683.4	..
Construction	89.6	95.9	107.9	100.0	97.4	106.9	110.6	249.1	3,141.6	..
Other	105.6	100.7	104.2	100.0	106.2	102.6	114.5	165.8	2,495.7	..
Transport of goods	95.5	100.0	100.0	100.0	100.0	101.3	121.1	150.5	2,028.4	..
Road maintenance	..	100.0	100.0	100.0	100.0	103.1	106.0	131.4	..	..
Communication servicing material production	..	100.0	100.0	100.0	100.0	103.5	103.5	130.3	4,425.6	..
Wholesale trade	..	106.4	109.1	100.0	108.4	97.4	97.2	189.8	..	..
Retail trade and catering	117.9	103.1	111.5	100.0	110.1	110.8	110.5	214.2	2,947.2	..
Material supply	58.5	95.9	113.4	100.0	112.2	79.8	121.7	170.0	5,013.2	..
Procurement	154.9	101.4	104.0	100.0	153.7	101.5	99.6	196.1	1,922.2	..
Information and computing services	..	100.0	100.0	100.0	99.7	101.1	100.3	101.6	860.8	..
Other sectors of material production	115.9	100.8	101.5	100.0	100.6	106.8	112.9	127.0	269.6	..
Foreign trade income	..	..	..	..	..	..	..	..	4,413.3	..
Total net material product	100.7	97.1	100.1	100.0	101.8	106.7	128.3	302.0	4,413.3	..
Price deflators by expenditure category										
Consumption	103.3	98.8	99.6	100.0	100.1	105.3	114.3	..	..	..
Personal consumption	103.5	98.5	99.5	100.0	100.1	105.9	115.7	..	..	..
Consumption of govt. institutions serving households	102.2	100.0	100.0	100.0	100.2	101.7	106.5	..	..	..
General government and scientific institutions	101.1	101.0	100.7	100.0	99.8	101.2	105.5	..	..	..
Investment (accumulation)	99.9	104.5	96.7	100.0	97.2	107.9	130.3	..	..	..
Fixed capital	93.3	93.5	99.5	100.0	100.2	111.6	135.0	..	..	..
Changes in inventories and other	117.2	120.9	92.4	100.0	93.0	102.6	126.3	..	..	..
Losses and discrepancy	..	..	..	100.0	..	106.7	128.3	..	..	..
Net exports	100.7	97.1	100.1	100.0	101.8	106.7	128.3	..	..	..
memo:										
Consumption	103.3	98.8	99.6	100.0	100.1	105.3	114.3	..	..	..
Private Consumption	103.5	98.5	99.5	100.0	100.1	105.9	115.7	..	..	..
Social Consumption	102.0	100.2	100.2	100.0	100.1	101.6	106.3	..	..	..

Source: State Committee of Statistics.

TABLE 2-6c. Growth of Implicit Price Deflators for Net Material Product by Origin and Expenditure (percent)

Sector of origin or expenditure category	1986	1987	1988	1989	1990	1991	1992	1993
Growth rates of price deflators by sector of origin								
Agriculture and forestry	4.2	3.7	5.1	27.4	18.9	117.1	1,014.8	..
Agriculture	4.2	3.7	5.1	27.5	18.9	118.1	1,015.1	..
Forestry	0.0	0.0	-2.0	4.4	-0.4	-0.6	151.8	..
Industry and construction	1.6	-0.7	-2.7	-5.8	29.4	217.6	1,742.9	
Industry	-4.0	3.5	-2.8	-17.5	56.4	268.9	1,776.2	..
Construction	12.6	-7.3	-2.6	9.8	3.4	125.3	1,161.0	..
Other	3.5	-4.0	6.2	-3.4	11.6	44.8	1,405.3	..
Transport of goods	0.0	0.0	0.0	1.3	19.5	24.3	1,247.6	..
Road maintenance	0.0	0.0	0.0	3.1	2.8	24.0	..	..
Communication servicing material production	0.0	0.0	0.0	3.5	0.0	25.9	3,296.1	..
Wholesale trade	2.6	-8.3	8.4	-10.1	-0.2	95.3		..
Retail trade and catering	8.1	-10.3	10.1	0.7	-0.3	93.8	1,276.2	..
Material supply	18.2	-11.8	12.2	-28.9	52.6	39.7	2,848.8	..
Procurement	2.5	-3.8	53.7	-33.9	-2.0	97.0	880.2	..
Information and computing services	0.0	0.0	-0.3	1.5	-0.8	1.3	747.1	..
Other sectors of material production	0.8	-1.5	0.6	6.2	5.7	12.5	112.4	..
Foreign trade income	..	..	..	..	..	..	..	..
Total net material product	3.0	-0.1	1.8	4.9	20.3	135.3	1,361.4	..
Growth rates of price deflators by expenditure category								
Consumption	0.8	0.4	0.1	5.1	8.6	..	..	..
Personal consumption	1.0	0.5	0.1	5.8	9.3	..	..	..
Consumption of govt. institutions serving households	0.0	0.0	0.2	1.5	4.7	..	..	..
General government and scientific institutions	-0.3	-0.7	-0.2	1.4	4.3	..	..	..
Investment (accumulation)	-7.4	3.4	-2.8	11.1	20.8	..	..	..
Fixed capital	6.4	0.5	0.2	11.4	20.9	..	..	..
Changes in inventories and other	-23.6	8.2	-7.0	10.3	23.1	..	..	..
Losses and discrepancy	..	..	..	..	20.3	..	..	..
Net exports	3.0	-0.1	1.8	4.9	20.3	..	..	..
memo:								
Consumption	0.8	0.4	0.1	5.1	8.6	..	..	..
Private Consumption	1.0	0.5	0.1	5.8	9.3	..	..	..
Social Consumption	0.0	-0.2	0.1	1.5	4.6	..	..	..

Source: State Committee of Statistics.

TABLE 2-7. Depreciation by Sector at Current Prices (millions of national currency)

Sector	1980	1985	1986	1987	1988	1989	1990	1991	1992	1993	1994
					(rubles)					(tenge)	
Material sphere	4,132	5,715	6,290	6,940	6,901	7,261	7,256	4,211	11,430	4,130	307,890
Agriculture and forestry	1,271	1,600	1,682	2,059	1,836	1,874	1,914	1,198	2,549	750	55,130
Agriculture	1,268	1,596	1,678	2,054	1,832	1,870	1,908	1,192	2,535	746	55,114
Forestry	3	4	4	5	4	4	6	6	14	4	16
Industry and construction	2,182	2,897	3,249	3,296	3,515	3,720	3,673	2,064	5,552	2,592	189,196
Industry	1,839	2,425	2,730	2,736	2,915	3,102	3,038	1,646	5,010	2,384	168,003
Construction	343	472	519	560	600	618	635	418	542	208	21,193
Other	679	1,218	1,359	1,585	1,550	1,667	1,669	949	3,329	788	63,564
Transport of goods	385	822	946	1,183	1,124	1,288	1,238	657	2,358	556	47,251
Road maintenance	16	24	26	27	30	29	33	36	..	..	..
Communication servicing material production	14	19	25	26	31	32	35	32	198	57	6,193
Wholesale trade	120	151	160	173	154	140	149	85	322	45	3,620
Retail trade and catering	..	..	..	..	..	..	..	..	..	..	..
Material supply	64	98	98	78	81	86	94	72	217	48	3,449
Procurement	73	81	82	85	112	70	97	47	206	82	2,877
Information and computing services	..	17	19	10	10	14	15	13	17	..	174
Other sectors	7	6	3	3	8	8	8	7	11	..	..
Nonmaterial sphere	1,349	1,940	1,998	1,987	2,129	2,176	2,282	1,340	5,571	186	13,602
Transport	151	364	352	235	291	228	283	48	..	..	..
Communication	4	56	60	65	70	75	58	35	..	..	..
Housing	608	764	798	801	846	893	960	625	3,521	73	184
Public utilities and personal services	154	198	208	221	242	266	290	205	662	5	7,152
Health care, social security, and sports	75	97	100	104	120	123	125	75	255	..	..
Education	164	196	207	253	238	254	240	150	557	..	..
Culture and art	49	59	62	80	84	85	60	36	160	..	..
Science and research	61	94	103	110	112	121	135	95	140	..	..
Credit	..	..	..	..	..	..	..	..	..	..	..
Insurance	..	..	..	..	..	..	..	..	..	..	..
General administration and defense	..	..	..	..	..	..	..	..	..	..	..
Private nonprofit institutions serving households	83	112	108	118	126	131	131	71	276	..	..
Other, material and nonmaterial spheres	2,028	3,158	3,357	3,572	3,679	3,843	3,951	2,289	8,900	974	77,166
Total depreciation	5,481	7,655	8,288	8,927	9,030	9,437	9,538	5,551	17,001	4,316	321,492

Source: State Committee of Statistics.

TABLE 2-7a. Sector Shares of Depreciation (percent)

Sector	1980	1985	1986	1987	1988	1989	1990	1991	1992	1993	1994
Material sphere	75.4	74.7	75.9	77.7	76.4	76.9	76.1	75.9	67.2	95.7	95.8
Agriculture and forestry	23.2	20.9	20.3	23.1	20.3	19.9	20.1	21.6	15.0	17.4	17.1
Agriculture	23.1	20.8	20.2	23.0	20.3	19.8	20.0	21.5	14.9	17.3	17.1
Forestry	0.1	0.1	0.0	0.1	0.0	0.0	0.1	0.1	0.1	0.1	0.0
Industry and construction	39.8	37.8	39.2	36.9	38.9	39.4	38.5	37.2	32.7	60.1	58.8
Industry	33.6	31.7	32.9	30.6	32.3	32.9	31.9	29.7	29.5	55.2	52.3
Construction	6.3	6.2	6.3	6.3	6.6	6.5	6.7	7.5	3.2	4.8	6.6
Other	12.4	15.9	16.4	17.8	17.2	17.7	17.5	17.1	19.6	18.3	19.8
Transport of goods	7.0	10.7	11.4	13.3	12.4	13.6	13.0	11.8	13.9	12.9	14.7
Road maintenance	0.3	0.3	0.3	0.3	0.3	0.3	0.3	0.6	..	..	..
Communication servicing material production	0.3	0.2	0.3	0.3	0.3	0.3	0.4	0.6	1.2	1.3	1.9
Wholesale trade	2.2	2.0	1.9	1.9	1.7	1.5	1.6	1.5	1.9	1.0	1.1
Retail trade and catering	..	..	..	..	..	..	..	..	..	..	..
Material supply	1.2	1.3	1.2	0.9	0.9	0.9	1.0	1.3	1.3	1.1	1.1
Procurement	1.3	1.1	1.0	1.0	1.2	0.7	1.0	0.8	1.2	1.9	0.9
Information and computing services	..	0.2	0.2	0.1	0.1	0.1	0.2	0.2	0.1	..	0.1
Other sectors	0.1	0.1	0.0	0.0	0.1	0.1	0.1	0.1	0.1	..	..
Nonmaterial sphere	24.6	25.3	24.1	22.3	23.6	23.1	23.9	24.1	32.8	4.3	4.2
Transport	2.8	4.8	4.2	2.6	3.2	2.4	3.0	0.9	..	..	..
Communication	0.1	0.7	0.7	0.7	0.8	0.8	0.6	0.6	..	..	..
Housing	11.1	10.0	9.6	9.0	9.4	9.5	10.1	11.3	20.7	1.7	0.1
Public utilities and personal services	2.8	2.6	2.5	2.5	2.7	2.8	3.0	3.7	3.9	0.1	2.2
Health care, social security, and sports	1.4	1.3	1.2	1.2	1.3	1.3	1.3	1.4	1.5	..	..
Education	3.0	2.6	2.5	2.8	2.6	2.7	2.5	2.7	3.3	..	..
Culture and art	0.9	0.8	0.7	0.9	0.9	0.9	0.6	0.6	0.9	..	..
Science and research	1.1	1.2	1.2	1.2	1.2	1.3	1.4	1.7	0.8	..	..
Credit	..	..	..	..	..	..	..	..	..	..	..
Insurance	..	..	..	..	..	..	..	..	..	..	..
General administration and defense	..	..	..	..	..	..	..	..	..	..	..
Private nonprofit institutions serving households	1.5	1.5	1.3	1.3	1.4	1.4	1.4	1.3	1.6	..	..
Other, material and nonmaterial spheres	37.0	41.3	40.5	40.0	40.7	40.7	41.4	41.2	52.3	22.6	24.0
Total depreciation	100.0	100.0	100.0	100.0	100.0	100.0	100.0	100.0	100.0	100.0	100.0

Source: State Committee of Statistics.

TABLE 2-10. Gross Social Product by Sector at Current Prices

Sector	1980	1985	1986	1987	1988	1989	1990	1991	1992	1993
					(mill. rubles)					(mill. tenge)
Gross social product by sector										
Agriculture and forestry	10,850	14,239	16,383	16,362	17,338	18,142	22,283	36,218	427,702	7,728
Agriculture	10,833	14,207	16,352	16,330	17,301	18,105	22,248	36,123	427,528	7,701
Forestry	18	32	32	33	36	38	35	95	174	27
Industry and construction	29,833	38,146	38,146	40,797	41,938	43,416	43,764	102,925	1,575,692	27,398
Industry	23,308	29,811	29,541	31,542	32,105	32,339	33,624	85,959	1,370,037	23,144
Construction	6,526	8,335	8,605	9,256	9,833	11,078	10,140	16,966	205,656	4,254
Other	7,340	7,897	8,037	7,969	9,081	9,516	10,630	15,467	308,274	8,836
Transport of goods	3,052	3,921	4,028	4,123	4,258	4,341	5,130	8,085	143,130	3,285
Road maintenance	..	495	425	497	518	543	569	264	7,649	0
Communication servicing material production	75	113	119	130	140	150	160	233	7,060	214
Wholesale trade	96	114	125	122	139	146	158	216	6,548	..
Retail trade and catering	1,257	1,464	1,552	1,459	1,670	1,837	2,004	3,434	48,977	1,722
Material supply	314	428	490	462	450	467	546	1,995	63,858	1,331
Procurement	494	628	600	593	726	550	631	840	28,745	594
Information and computing services	..	76	76	83	98	120	143	134	1,078	37
Other sectors of material production	2,052	659	624	499	1,083	1,363	1,289	267	1,228	1,653
Total gross social product	48,024	60,281	62,566	65,128	68,357	71,075	76,676	154,611	2,311,667	43,962
Sector shares of gross social product (percent)										
Agriculture and forestry	22.6	23.6	26.2	25.1	25.4	25.5	29.1	23.4	18.5	17.6
Agriculture	22.6	23.6	26.1	25.1	25.3	25.5	29.0	23.4	18.5	17.5
Forestry	0.0	0.1	0.1	0.1	0.1	0.1	0.0	0.1	0.0	0.1
Industry and construction	62.1	63.3	61.0	62.6	61.4	61.1	57.1	66.6	68.2	62.3
Industry	48.5	49.5	47.2	48.4	47.0	45.5	43.9	55.6	59.3	52.6
Construction	13.6	13.8	13.8	14.2	14.4	15.6	13.2	11.0	8.9	9.7
Other	15.3	13.1	12.8	12.2	13.3	13.4	13.9	10.0	13.3	20.1
Transport of goods	6.4	6.5	6.4	6.3	6.2	6.1	6.7	5.2	6.2	7.5
Road maintenance	..	0.8	0.7	0.8	0.8	0.8	0.7	0.2	0.3	0.0
Communication servicing material production	0.2	0.2	0.2	0.2	0.2	0.2	0.2	0.2	0.3	0.5
Wholesale trade	0.2	0.2	0.2	0.2	0.2	0.2	0.2	0.1	0.3	..
Retail trade and catering	2.6	2.4	2.5	2.2	2.4	2.6	2.6	2.2	2.1	3.9
Material supply	0.7	0.7	0.8	0.7	0.7	0.7	0.7	1.3	2.8	3.0
Procurement	1.0	1.0	1.0	0.9	1.1	0.8	0.8	0.5	1.2	1.4
Information and computing services	..	0.1	0.1	0.1	0.1	0.2	0.2	0.1	0.0	0.1
Other sectors of material production	4.3	1.1	1.0	0.8	1.6	1.9	1.7	0.2	0.1	3.8
Total gross social product	100.0	100.0	100.0	100.0	100.0	100.0	100.0	100.0	100.0	100.0

Source: State Committee of Statistics.

TABLE 2-11. Material Input by Sector at Current Prices (millions of national currency)

Sector	1980	1985	1986	1987	1988	1989	1990	1991	1992	1993
					(mill. rubles)					(mill. tenge)
Material input by sector										
Agriculture and forestry	5,512	7,421	8,100	8,296	8,123	7,681	8,321	13,356	171,963	3,505
Agriculture	5,506	7,411	8,090	8,286	8,112	7,669	8,311	13,313	171,894	3,503
Forestry	6	10	10	10	11	12	11	43	69	2
Industry and construction	20,074	26,792	27,273	29,537	30,334	32,139	31,424	69,139	1,120,618	16,583
Industry	16,636	22,184	22,861	24,626	25,343	26,680	26,621	61,195	979,783	14,807
Construction	3,438	4,608	4,413	4,911	4,991	5,459	4,803	7,944	140,835	1,776
Other	1,866	2,915	2,923	3,098	3,181	3,258	3,574	5,282	178,662	2,523
Transport of goods	1,330	1,744	1,799	1,848	1,825	1,859	2,047	2,665	83,442	1,321
Road maintenance	..	438	391	431	450	501	513	179	4,839	0
Communication servicing material production	23	31	33	35	35	41	42	72	2,387	42
Wholesale trade	15	22	23	41	28	30	33	76	3,004	0
Retail trade and catering	269	345	357	419	442	472	527	892	23,173	416
Material supply	48	63	79	73	73	83	107	975	37,941	539
Procurement	150	184	166	169	219	151	171	246	22,807	188
Information and computing services	..	46	28	30	38	37	49	58	546	7
Other sectors of material production	31	42	47	52	71	85	85	120	523	10
Total material input	27,452	37,128	38,296	40,931	41,637	43,077	43,318	87,777	1,471,243	22,611
Sector shares of material input (percent)										
Agriculture and forestry	20.1	20.0	21.2	20.3	19.5	17.8	19.2	15.2	11.7	15.5
Agriculture	20.1	20.0	21.1	20.2	19.5	17.8	19.2	15.2	11.7	15.5
Forestry	0.0	0.0	0.0	0.0	0.0	0.0	0.0	0.0	0.0	0.0
Industry and construction	73.1	72.2	71.2	72.2	72.9	74.6	72.5	78.8	76.2	73.3
Industry	60.6	59.7	59.7	60.2	60.9	61.9	61.5	69.7	66.6	65.5
Construction	12.5	12.4	11.5	12.0	12.0	12.7	11.1	9.1	9.6	7.9
Other	6.8	7.9	7.6	7.6	7.6	7.6	8.2	6.0	12.1	11.2
Transport of goods	4.8	4.7	4.7	4.5	4.4	4.3	4.7	3.0	5.7	5.8
Road maintenance	..	1.2	1.0	1.1	1.1	1.2	1.2	0.2	0.3	0.0
Communication servicing material production	0.1	0.1	0.1	0.1	0.1	0.1	0.1	0.1	0.2	0.2
Wholesale trade	0.1	0.1	0.1	0.1	0.1	0.1	0.1	0.1	0.2	0.0
Retail trade and catering	1.0	0.9	0.9	1.0	1.1	1.1	1.2	1.0	1.6	1.8
Material supply	0.2	0.2	0.2	0.2	0.2	0.2	0.2	1.1	2.6	2.4
Procurement	0.5	0.5	0.4	0.4	0.5	0.4	0.4	0.3	1.6	0.8
Information and computing services	..	0.1	0.1	0.1	0.1	0.1	0.1	0.1	0.0	0.0
Other sectors of material production	0.1	0.1	0.1	0.1	0.2	0.2	0.2	0.1	0.0	0.0
Total material input	100.0	100.0	100.0	100.0	100.0	100.0	100.0	100.0	100.0	100.0

Source: State Committee of Statistics.

TABLE 2-14. Change in Stocks by Sector at Current Prices

Sector	1980	1985	1986	1987	1988	1989	1990	1991	1992	1993	1994
Change in stocks by sector											(mill. tenge)
Agriculture and forestry	..	..	..	..	..	..	..	..	..	2,587	32,351
Agriculture	..	..	..	..	..	..	..	..	..	2,587	32,347
Forestry	..	..	..	..	..	..	..	..	..	..	4
Industry and construction	..	..	..	..	..	..	..	..	..	10,539	110,763
Industry	..	..	..	..	..	..	..	..	..	9,594	102,895
Construction	..	..	..	..	..	..	..	..	..	945	7,868
Other	..	..	..	..	..	..	..	..	..	6,496	40,964
Transport of goods	..	..	..	..	..	..	..	..	..	983	6,346
Road maintenance	..	..	..	..	..	..	..	..	..	..	..
Communication servicing material production	..	..	..	..	..	..	..	..	..	35	1,541
Wholesale trade	..	..	..	..	..	..	..	..	..	..	..
Retail trade and catering	..	..	..	..	..	..	..	..	..	1,837	15,332
Material supply	..	..	..	..	..	..	..	..	..	1,635	7,251
Procurement	..	..	..	..	..	..	..	..	..	1,047	7,447
Information and computing services	..	..	..	..	..	..	..	..	..	..	12
Other sectors of material production	..	..	..	..	..	..	..	..	..	..	..
Total change in stocks	..	..	..	..	..	..	..	..	..	19,622	184,078
Sector shares of change in stocks(percent)											
Agriculture and forestry	..	..	..	..	..	..	..	..	..	13.2	17.6
Agriculture	..	..	..	..	..	..	..	..	..	13.2	17.6
Forestry	..	..	..	..	..	..	..	..	..	..	0.0
Industry and construction	..	..	..	..	..	..	..	..	..	53.7	60.2
Industry	..	..	..	..	..	..	..	..	..	48.9	55.9
Construction	..	..	..	..	..	..	..	..	..	4.8	4.3
Other	..	..	..	..	..	..	..	..	..	33.1	22.3
Transport of goods	..	..	..	..	..	..	..	..	..	5.0	3.4
Road maintenance	..	..	..	..	..	..	..	..	..	..	..
Communication servicing material production	..	..	..	..	..	..	..	..	..	0.2	0.8
Wholesale trade	..	..	..	..	..	..	..	..	..	..	..
Retail trade and catering	..	..	..	..	..	..	..	..	..	9.4	8.3
Material supply	..	..	..	..	..	..	..	..	..	8.3	3.9
Procurement	..	..	..	..	..	..	..	..	..	5.3	4.0
Information and computing services	..	..	..	..	..	..	..	..	..	..	0.0
Other sectors of material production	..	..	..	..	..	..	..	..	..	..	..
Total change in stocks	..	..	..	..	..	..	..	..	..	100.0	100.0

Source: State Committe of Statistics.

TABLE 3-1. Balance of Payments Summary at Current Prices (millions of U.S. dollars)

Item	1992	1993	1994	1995
Exports of goods and services				
(including workers' remittances)	4,197.0	3,449.0	3,307.5	5,261.2
Exports of goods and nonfactor services	4,197.0	3,449.0	3,307.5	5,261.2
Merchandise (FOB)	4,197.0	3,449.0	3,285.3	5,196.7
Nonfactor services	..	..	22.2	64.5
Imports of goods and nonfactor services	4,335.0	4,243.6	4,110.3	5,691.7
Merchandise (FOB)	4,100.0	4,107.0	4,055.0	5,419.1
Nonfactor services	235.0	136.6	55.3	272.6
Resource balance	-138.0	-794.6	-802.8	-430.5
Net factor income	-175.0	-19.6	-51.1	-146.7
Factor receipts	..	..	..	34.9
Factor payments	175.0	19.6	51.1	181.6
Total interest DUE	175.0	19.6	42.7	102.0
Other factor payments and discrepancy	..	..	8.4	79.6
Net current transfers	168.0	55.0	97.4	59.0
Current receipts	168.0	55.0	97.4	59.0
Workers remittances	..	..	..	..
Other current transfers	168.0	55.0	97.4	59.0
Current payments	..	..	..	..
Current account balance before official grants	-145.0	-759.2	-756.5	-518.2
Official capital grants	..	..	..	..
Current account balance after official grants	-145.0	-759.2	-756.5	-518.2
Long Term Capital Inflows	-105.0	1,075.8	1,678.7	404.7
Direct investment	100.0	473.0	819.5	858.9
Net long term borrowing	-205.0	602.8	851.3	506.7
Disbursements	233.0	803.5	905.8	624.7
Repayments	438.0	200.7	54.5	118.0
Other long-term inflows (net)	..	..	7.9	-960.9
Adjustment to Scheduled Debt Service	..	..	..	..
Debt service not paid	..	..	..	..
Interest not paid	..	..	..	..
Principal not paid	..	..	..	..
Arrears reductions/prepayments(-)	..	..	..	..
Total Other items (Net)	-339.0	49.4	-711.2	239.6
Net short-term capital	..	..	..	..
Capital flows n.e.i. (incl. exceptional financing)	8.0	280.0	-400.3	535.3
Errors and omissions	-347.0	-230.6	-310.9	-295.7
of which Migrant transfers	..	..	-1,179.1	-380.6
Changes in net reserves (- is increase)	589.0	-366.0	-211.0	-126.0
Net credit from IMF	0.0	88.0	192.4	141.1
Reserve changes n.e.i.	589.0	-454.0	-403.4	-267.1
Gross reserves (excluding gold)	n.a.	454.0	857.4	1,124.5
Gross reserves (including gold)	n.a.	735.0	1,287.4	1,697.5
Annual average exchange rate (LCU/US$)	..	2.8	36.0	61.3

Source: National Bank of Kazakstan.

TABLE 3-2. Exchange Rates

	1980	1985	1986	1987	1988	1989	1990	1991	1992
				(rubles per dollar)					
Official Exchange Rate 1/	..	..	..	0.6328	0.6080	0.6274	0.5856	0.5819	..

	1992		1993		1994		1995		1996	
	Daily average rate	End-period rate	Daily average rate	End-period rate	Daily average rate	End-period rate	Daily average rate	End-period rate	Daily average rate	End-period rate
				Official Exchange Rates 2/						
				(rubles per dollar)						
January	110.0	110.0	461.7	572.0	..	..	..	..	..	..
February	104.8	90.0	572.0	593.0	..	..	..	..	..	..
March	92.3	100.0	658.7	684.0	..	..	..	..	..	..
April	100.0	100.0	756.3	823.0	..	..	..	..	..	..
May	95.3	85.0	911.0	1024.0	..	..	..	..	..	..
June	88.5	100.0	1080.0	1060.0	..	..	..	..	..	..
July	138.3	161.2	1025.0	987.0	..	..	..	..	..	..
August	167.9	205.0	985.8	992.5	..	..	..	..	..	..
September	217.4	254.0	1073.0	1169.0	..	..	..	..	..	..
October	344.7	398.0	1188.0	1184.0	..	..	..	..	..	..
November	423.5	447.0	..	..	..	..	..	..	..	..
December	414.6	414.5	..	..	..	..	..	..	..	..
				(tenge per dollar)						
January	..	..	..	..	9.28	10.71	55.43	56.82	64.30	64.80
February	..	..	..	..	11.56	11.58	58.67	59.70	65.20	65.30
March	..	..	..	..	16.95	19.84	60.49	61.20	65.22	65.10
April	..	..	..	..	25.35	29.92	61.30	62.75	65.50	65.95
May	..	..	..	..	35.65	40.73	63.11	63.40	65.44	66.80
June	..	..	..	..	41.72	43.29	63.54	63.35	..	..
July	..	..	..	..	44.66	45.33	62.62	61.00	..	..
August	..	..	..	..	45.69	46.16	56.69	58.00	..	..
September	..	..	..	..	47.04	48.00	59.91	59.90	..	..
October	..	..	..	..	48.62	49.55	61.48	62.20	..	..
November	..	..	4.7	4.7	50.96	52.10	63.35	63.90	..	..
December	..	..	5.92	6.31	53.47	54.26	63.97	63.95	..	..

1/ Annual average.

2/ As determined by the Central Bank of Russia (CBR). The official rate of exchange in Kazakstan has been pegged to the CBR market rate since July 1992 till October 1993. In November 1993 Kazakstan introduced its own currency, the tenge (1 tenge = 500 rubles).

Sources: National Bank of Kazakstan.

TABLE 3-5. Geographical Distribution of Extrarepublic Trade (millions of current U.S. dollars)

	EXPORTS						IMPORTS					
	1990	1991	1992	1993	1994	1995	1990	1991	1992	1993	1994	1995
TOTAL TRADE	1,402.0	928.0	1,450.7	1,534.0	1,095.0	2,173.3	1,490.0	584.0	565.5	471.6	515.0	663.7
INDUSTRIAL COUNTRIES	647.0	357.0	835.2	985.7	809.0	..	556.0	253.0	182.9	252.1	340.0	..
Australia	..	..	0.5	20.6	30.0	..	..	..	..	6.7	1.0	..
Austria	..	..	50.2	32.4	11.0	..	..	..	30.3	21.5	16.0	..
Belgium	..	..	10.9	12.6	16.0	..	..	..	..	8.3	9.0	..
Denmark	..	..	3.0	8.2	5.0	..	..	..	..	0.7	1.0	..
Finland	..	..	42.7	9.3	1.0	..	..	..	25.0	4.7	4.0	..
France	..	..	18.5	6.7	5.0	..	..	..	7.4	8.6	21.0	..
Germany	..	..	123.1	131.0	65.0	..	..	..	19.0	76.3	125.0	..
Iceland	..	..	..	..	..	..	..	..	..	..	..	..
Ireland	..	..	0.2	4.9	4.0	..	..	..	..	..	..	..
Italy	..	..	40.2	83.8	24.0	..	..	..	29.8	20.7	37.0	..
Japan	..	..	48.9	36.9	31.0	..	..	..	4.1	3.6	8.0	..
Netherlands	..	..	52.2	49.1	42.0	..	..	..	1.0	1.2	4.0	..
Norway	..	..	2.8	..	4	..	..	..	..	..	..	..
Spain	..	..	1.3	14.2	1.0	..	..	..	..	0.2	..	..
Sweden	..	..	150.5	91.5	5.0	..	..	..	9.9	2.2	8.0	..
Switzerland	..	..	104.1	174.7	345.0	..	..	..	15.0	17.8	40.0	..
United Kingdom	..	..	26.3	96.9	87.0	..	..	..	23.2	18.9	17.0	..
United States	..	..	100.1	145.3	121.0	..	..	..	6.4	38.5	42.0	..
Others 1/	..	..	59.7	67.6	12.0	..	..	..	11.8	22.2	7.0	..
DEVELOPING COUNTRIES	617.0	354.0	615.5	548.3	286.0	..	875.0	330.0	382.6	219.5	175.0	..
Africa	2.0	1.0	..	0.8	1.0	..	0.0	1.0	..	..	..	..
Asia	102.0	101.0	285.9	280.6	144.0	..	182.0	121.0	235.3	115.1	106.0	..
Afghanistan	..	..	3.8	2.5	1.0	..	..	..	2.4	0.7	..	..
China, People's Rep.	..	..	237.0	172.2	85.0	..	..	..	212.6	80.1	46.0	..
India	..	..	0.7	2.9	1.0	..	..	..	9.2	13.4	9.0	..
Korea	..	..	12.6	45.5	22.0	..	..	..	1.7	8.5	14.0	..
Korea, Dem. People's Rep.	..	..	17.7	22.1	3.0	..	..	..	8.5	0.4	3.0	..
Mongolia	..	..	3.1	0.3	1.0	..	..	..	..	0.6	..	..
Viet Nam	..	..	..	0.6	2.0	..	..	..	..	..	..	..
Others	..	..	11.0	34.5	29.0	..	..	..	0.9	11.4	34.0	..
Europe	430.0	191.0	235.8	257.3	129.0	..	337.0	79.0	78.0	97.1	68.0	..
Bulgaria	..	..	17.4	21.6	9.0	..	..	..	2.2	4.1	5.0	..
Czechoslovakia	..	..	80.5	48.5	25.0	..	..	..	2.8	47.7	18.0	..
Czech Repulic	..	..	..	18.5	14.0	..						..
Slovakia	..	..	..	30.0	11.0	..						..
Hungary	..	..	21.7	36.5	12.0	..	..	..	27.4	23.1	14.0	..
Poland	..	..	48.6	36.9	13.0	..	..	..	8.5	3.6	1.0	..
Romania	..	..	4.9	1.5	9.0	..	..	..	5.0	1.7	8.0	..
Turkey	..	..	16.2	55.9	40.0	..	..	..	4.6	15.1	17.0	..
Yugoslavia	..	..	13.9	1.4	1.0	..	..	..	27.0	0.4	..	..
Others 2/	..	..	32.6	6.5	20.0	..	..	..	..	1.4	4.0	..
Latin America and Caribbean	49.0	6.0	22.4	2.7	1.0	..	348.0	125.0	29.1	4.3	..	..
Cuba	47.0	6.0	18.9	..	..	..	316.0	115.0	29.0	3.5	..	..
Others	2.0	0.0	3.5	2.7	1.0	..	32.0	10.0	0.1	0.8	..	..
Middle East	34.0	55.0	71.4	6.9	11.0	..	8.0	4.0	40.2	3.0	1.0	..
Egypt	..	..	..	0.2	..	..	..	..	..	..	..	..
Iraq	..	..	..	..	..	..	..	..	..	..	..	..
Libya	..	..	..	..	..	..	..	..	..	..	..	..
Syrian Arab Republic	..	..	..	0.7	..	..	..	..	..	..	..	..
Others 3/	..	..	71.4	6.0	11.0	..	..	..	40.2	3.0	1.0	..

1/ Includes Canada, New Zealand, Greece, Luxembourg, and Portugal.   2/ Includes Cyprus and Malta.
3/ Includes Bahrain, Iran, Jordan, Kuwait, Lebanon, Oman, Qatar, Saudi Arabia, United Arab Emirates, and Yemen, Rep. of.

Sources: State Committee of Statistics.

TABLE 3-5a. Geographical Distribution of Extrarepublic Trade (percentage of total trade)

	EXPORTS					IMPORTS				
	1990	1991	1992	1993	1994	1990	1991	1992	1993	1994
TOTAL TRADE	100.0	100.0	100.0	100.0	100.0	100.0	100.0	100.0	100.0	100.0
INDUSTRIAL COUNTRIES	46.1	38.5	57.6	64.3	73.9	37.3	43.3	32.3	53.5	66.0
Australia	..	..	0.0	1.3	2.7	..	..	..	1.4	0.2
Austria	..	..	3.5	2.1	1.0	..	..	5.4	4.6	3.1
Belgium	..	..	0.8	0.8	1.5	..	..	..	1.8	1.7
Denmark	..	..	0.2	0.5	0.5	..	..	..	0.1	0.2
Finland	..	..	2.9	0.6	0.1	..	..	4.4	1.0	0.8
France	..	..	1.3	0.4	0.5	..	..	1.3	1.8	4.1
Germany	..	..	8.5	8.5	5.9	..	..	3.4	16.2	24.3
Iceland	..	..	..	..	..	..	..	..	..	..
Ireland	..	..	0.0	0.3	0.4	..	..	..	..	..
Italy	..	..	2.8	5.5	2.2	..	..	5.3	4.4	7.2
Japan	..	..	3.4	2.4	2.8	..	..	0.7	0.8	1.6
Netherlands	..	..	3.6	3.2	3.8	..	..	0.2	0.3	0.8
Norway	..	..	0.2	..	0.4	..	..	..	..	..
Spain	..	..	0.1	0.9	0.1	..	..	..	0.0	..
Sweden	..	..	10.4	6.0	0.5	..	..	1.8	0.5	1.6
Switzerland	..	..	7.2	11.4	31.5	..	..	2.7	3.8	7.8
United Kingdom	..	..	1.8	6.3	7.9	..	..	4.1	4.0	3.3
United States	..	..	6.9	9.5	11.1	..	..	1.1	8.2	8.2
Others 1/	..	..	4.1	4.4	1.1	..	..	2.1	4.7	1.4
DEVELOPING COUNTRIES	44.0	38.1	42.4	35.7	26.1	58.7	56.5	67.7	46.5	34.0
Africa	0.1	0.1	..	0.1	0.1	0.0	0.2	..	..	..
Asia	7.3	10.9	19.7	18.3	13.2	12.2	20.7	41.6	24.4	20.6
Afghanistan	..	..	0.3	0.2	0.1	..	..	0.4	0.1	..
China, People's Rep.	..	..	16.3	11.2	7.8	..	..	37.6	17.0	8.9
India	..	..	0.0	0.2	0.1	..	..	1.6	2.8	1.7
Korea	..	..	0.9	3.0	2.0	..	..	0.3	1.8	2.7
Korea, Dem. People's Rep.	..	..	1.2	1.4	0.3	..	..	1.5	0.1	0.6
Mongolia	..	..	0.2	0.0	0.1	..	..	..	0.1	..
Viet Nam	..	..	..	0.0	0.2	..	..	..	..	..
Others	..	..	0.8	2.2	2.6	..	..	0.2	2.4	6.6
Europe	30.7	20.6	16.3	16.8	11.8	22.6	13.5	13.8	20.6	13.2
Bulgaria	..	..	1.2	1.4	0.8	..	..	0.4	0.9	1.0
Czechoslovakia	..	..	5.5	3.2	2.3	..	..	0.5	10.1	3.5
Czech Republic	..	..	0.0	1.2	1.3					
Slovakia	..	..	0.0	2.0	1.0					
Hungary	..	..	1.5	2.4	1.1	..	..	4.8	4.9	2.7
Poland	..	..	3.4	2.4	1.2	..	..	1.5	0.8	0.2
Romania	..	..	0.3	0.1	0.8	..	..	0.9	0.4	1.6
Turkey	..	..	1.1	3.6	3.7	..	..	0.8	3.2	3.3
Yugoslavia	..	..	1.0	0.1	0.1	..	..	4.8	0.1	0.0
Others 2/	..	..	2.2	0.4	1.8	..	..	..	0.3	0.8
Latin America and Caribbean	3.5	0.6	1.5	0.2	0.1	23.4	21.4	5.1	0.9	..
Cuba	3.4	0.6	1.3	..	..	21.2	19.7	5.1	0.7	..
Others	0.1	0.0	0.2	0.2	0.1	2.1	1.7	0.0	0.2	..
Middle East	2.4	5.9	4.9	0.4	1.0	0.5	0.7	7.1	0.6	0.2
Egypt	..	..	..	0.0	0.0	..	..	..	..	..
Iraq	..	..	..	..	..	..	..	..	..	..
Libya	..	..	..	..	..	..	..	..	..	..
Syrian Arab Republic	..	..	..	0.0	..	..	..	..	..	..
Others 3/	..	..	4.9	0.4	1.0	..	..	7.1	0.6	0.2

1/ Includes Canada, New Zealand, Greece, Luxembourg, and Portugal.   2/ Includes Cyprus and Malta.

3/ Includes Bahrain, Iran, Jordan, Kuwait, Lebanon, Oman, Qatar, Saudi Arabia, United Arab Emirates, and Yemen, Rep. of.

Source: Table 3-5.

TABLE 3-6. Geographical Distribution of Interrepublic Trade at Domestic Prices, 1990-94 1/

	EXPORTS					IMPORTS				
	1990	1991	1992	1993	1994	1990	1991	1992	1993 2/	1994
	(millions of current: rubles; tenge)					(millions of current: rubles; tenge)				
TOTAL TRADE	8,445.0	13,744.9	342,020.8	4,716.2	61,491.0	14,317.0	13,219.6	346,941.5	5,196.9	30,337.0
Armenia	65.0	103.9	453.9	1.3	1.0	235.0	35.1	123.9	7.5	7.0
Azerbaijan	296.0	140.8	5,876.4	150.9	1,220.0	284.0	290.5	3,423.8	30.6	256.0
Belarus	379.0	621.8	8,957.7	234.2	1,580.0	728.0	340.3	14,238.4	154.0	576.0
Estonia	57.0	96.0	186.0	1.0	92.0	101.0	46.8	..	13.7	4.0
Georgia	85.0	77.2	408.7	9.3	8.0	367.0	54.3	..	20.1	23.0
Kazakstan	..	..	..	..	..	..	..	..	..	..
Kyrgyz Republic	358.0	476.5	8,073.4	107.4	1,349.0	268.0	544.3	9,312.8	69.0	277.0
Latvia	102.0	232.3	900.0	9.6	732.0	238.0	63.6	..	25.1	64.0
Lithuania	81.0	179.2	1,949.6	24.3	803.0	180.0	106.8	..	34.4	35.0
Moldova	76.0	146.9	1,112.3	16.8	87.0	156.0	43.9	210.6	41.4	33.0
Russia	4,276.0	8,515.2	246,702.5	3,285.3	48,372.0	9,074.0	8,719.7	257,721.8	3,684.7	27,098.0
Tajikistan	269.0	342.2	3,699.7	67.7	377.0	318.0	174.5	1,445.3	26.1	55.0
Turkmenistan	217.0	208.4	9,519.2	99.9	443.0	79.0	264.5	9,829.5	245.8	35.0
Ukraine	731.0	1,338.7	33,637.8	381.7	3,177.0	1,505.0	1,669.1	37,930.9	378.7	1,098.0
Uzbekistan	1,453.0	1,265.8	20,543.6	326.8	3,250.0	784.0	866.2	12,704.5	465.8	776.0
Statistical Discrepancy	..	..	..	..	..	..	..	..	..	..
	(percentage of total trade)					(percentage of total trade)				
TOTAL TRADE	100.0	100.0	100.0	100.0	100.0	100.0	100.0	100.0	100.0	100.0
Armenia	0.8	0.8	0.1	0.0	0.0	1.6	0.3	0.0	0.1	0.0
Azerbaijan	3.5	1.0	1.7	3.2	2.0	2.0	2.2	1.0	0.6	0.8
Belarus	4.5	4.5	2.6	5.0	2.6	5.1	2.6	4.1	3.0	1.9
Estonia	0.7	0.7	0.1	0.0	0.2	0.7	0.4	..	0.3	0.0
Georgia	1.0	0.6	0.1	0.2	0.0	2.6	0.4	..	0.4	0.1
Kazakstan	..	..	..	..	..	..	..	..	..	..
Kyrgyz Republic	4.2	3.5	2.4	2.3	2.2	1.9	4.1	2.7	1.3	0.9
Latvia	1.2	1.7	0.3	0.2	1.2	1.7	0.5	..	0.5	0.2
Lithuania	1.0	1.3	0.6	0.5	1.3	1.3	0.8	..	0.7	0.1
Moldova	0.9	1.1	0.3	0.4	0.1	1.1	0.3	0.1	0.8	0.1
Russia	50.6	62.0	72.1	69.7	78.7	63.4	66.0	74.3	70.9	89.3
Tajikistan	3.2	2.5	1.1	1.4	0.6	2.2	1.3	0.4	0.5	0.2
Turkmenistan	2.6	1.5	2.8	2.1	0.7	0.6	2.0	2.8	4.7	0.1
Ukraine	8.7	9.7	9.8	8.1	5.2	10.5	12.6	10.9	7.3	3.6
Uzbekistan	17.2	9.2	6.0	6.9	5.3	5.5	6.6	3.7	9.0	2.6
Statistical Discrepancy	..	..	..	..	..	..	..	..	..	..

1/ Data for 1990 represents total trade; for 1991-93 it represents produsers' goods only.
2/ In addition to the data presented in this table, in 1993 Kazakstan also imported 139.3 mill. $US of electrical and energy goods from the Kyrgyz Republic (25.6 mill. $US), Turkmenistan (79.6 mill. $US) and from Uzbekistan (34 mill. $US).

Sources: State Committee of Statistics.

TABLE 3-6a. Geographical Distribution of Interrepublic Trade, 1995

(millions of current U.S. dollars)

	1995	
	EXPORTS	IMPORTS
TOTAL TRADE	2,801.2	2,606.2
Armenia	0.2	2.7
Azerbaijan	22.4	24.9
Belarus	57.5	79.8
Estonia	15.7	6.8
Georgia	0.3	2.2
Kazakstan	..	..
Kyrgyz Republic	73.3	28.4
Latvia	33.2	11.5
Lithuania	120.8	18.0
Moldova	2.5	5.6
Russia	2,102.6	1,834.1
Tajikistan	40.8	11.4
Turkmenistan	51.1	230.6
Ukraine	121.4	86.7
Uzbekistan	159.5	263.5
Statistical Discrepancy	..	..
TOTAL TRADE	100.0	100.0
Armenia	0.0	0.1
Azerbaijan	0.8	1.0
Belarus	2.1	3.1
Estonia	0.6	0.3
Georgia	0.0	0.1
Kazakstan	..	..
Kyrgyz Republic	2.6	1.1
Latvia	1.2	0.4
Lithuania	4.3	0.7
Moldova	0.1	0.2
Russia	75.1	70.4
Tajikistan	1.5	0.4
Turkmenistan	1.8	8.8
Ukraine	4.3	3.3
Uzbekistan	5.7	10.1
Statistical Discrepancy	..	..

Sources: State Committee of Statistics.

TABLE 5-1. Evolution of the Consolidated Budget, 1992-95

(in millions of tenge, current prices)

	Budget				Extra-budgetary				Consolidated			
	1992	1993	1994	1995	1992	1993	1994	1995	1992	1993	1994	1995
1. Current Operations:												
Current Revenues and Grants	595	5,769	82,331	189,969	371	4,208	28,362	76,600	943	9,977	110,693	256,442
Direct Taxes	184	2,081	24,272	61,097	279	2,907	19,592	68,773	463	4,988	43,864	129,870
Indirect Taxes	338	2,500	31,623	52,335	36	336	2,264	0	374	2,836	33,887	52,335
Non-Tax Revenues	21	1,188	26,375	74,238	33	629	6,506	0	54	1,817	32,881	74,238
Grants	42	0	61	0	10	336	0	0	52	336	61	0
Intragovernmental Transfers	10	0	0	2,300	13	0	0	7,827	:	:	:	:
Current Expenditures	600	5,404	69,417	192,114	267	3,068	39,694	73,675	844	8,472	109,111	255,662
Consumption	424	4,691	52,347	149,259	15	460	4,394	8,528	439	5,151	56,741	157,786
Interest Payments	54	39	7,838	1,407	:	:	10,400	:	54	39	18,238	1,407
Domestic Debt	0	36	7,405	-434	:	:	10,400	:	0	36	17,805	-434
External Debt	54	3	433	1,841	54	:	:	:	54	3	433	1,841
Transfers to Households	73	303	3,099	8,688	198	1,914	18,275	62,847	271	2,217	21,374	71,535
Transfers to ROW	0	0	1,622	0	10	0	0	0	10	0	1,622	0
Subsidies 1/	36	371	4,511	24,978	34	694	6,625	2,300	70	1,065	11,136	24,978
Intragovernmental Transfers	13	0	0	7,827	10	0	0	:	:	:	:	:
Budgetary Savings	-5	365	12,914	-2,145	104	1,140	-11,332	2,925	99	1,505	1,582	780
2. Capital Operations:												
Capital Revenues (Privatization Fund)	:	:	:	:	:	:	:	:	:	:	:	:
Capital Revenue Transfers Received	1	784	1,459	7,233	:	:	:	:	1	784	1,459	7,233
Total Capital Expenditures	162	1,360	26,193	28,155	115	1,110	7,230	-5,960	277	2,470	33,423	22,196
Net Lending and Participation	0	405	12,631	17,724	115	1,110	7,230	-5,960	115	1,515	19,861	11,764
Total Public Sector Investment	162	955	13,562	10,432	0	0	0	0	162	955	13,562	10,432
Capital Revenue Transfers Made	:	:	:	:	:	:	:	:	:	:	:	:
3. Budget Deficit	-166	-211	-11,820	-23,067	-11	30	-18,562	8,885	-177	-181	-30,382	-14,182
4. Financing	166	211	11,820	23,067	11	-30	18,562	-8,885	177	181	30,382	14,182
Domestic	63	35	2,217	2,754	11	-30	18,562	-8,885	74	5	20,779	-6,131
Banking System	-50	-171	17,087	13,697	0	-129	-481	6,313	-50	-300	16,606	20,010
Other Domestic (residual)	113	206	-14,870	-10,943	11	99	19,043	-15,198	124	305	4,173	-26,141
External	103	176	9,603	20,313	0	0	0	0	103	176	9,603	20,313
Memorandum item:												
GDP (mill. tenge)	2,427	26,838	464,454	1,086,000	2,427	26,838	464,454	1,086,000	2,427	26,838	464,454	1,086,000

1/ Subsidies in 1995 include adjustment for transfers to households.

Source: Ministry of Finance, IMF and World Bank staff estimates.

TABLE 5-2. Evolution of the Consolidated Budget, 1992-95
(in percent of GDP at current prices)

	Budget				Extra-budgetary				Consolidated			
	1992	1993	1994	1995	1992	1993	1994	1995	1992	1993	1994	1995
1. Current Operations:												
Current Revenues and Grants	24.5	21.5	17.7	17.5	15.3	15.7	6.1	7.1	38.9	37.2	23.8	23.6
Direct Taxes	7.6	7.8	5.2	5.6	11.5	10.8	4.2	6.3	19.1	18.6	9.4	12.0
Indirect Taxes	13.9	9.3	6.8	4.8	1.5	1.3	0.5	0.0	15.4	10.6	7.3	4.8
Non-Tax Revenues	0.9	4.4	5.7	6.8	1.4	2.3	1.4	0.0	2.2	6.8	7.1	6.8
Grants	1.7	0.0	0.0	0.0	0.4	1.3	0.0	0.0	2.1	1.3	0.0	0.0
Intragovernmental Transfers	0.4	0.0	0.0	0.2	0.5	0.0	0.0	0.7	..	..	..	..
Current Expenditures	24.7	20.1	14.9	17.7	11.0	11.4	8.5	6.8	34.8	31.6	23.5	23.5
Consumption	17.5	17.5	11.3	13.7	0.6	1.7	0.9	0.8	18.1	19.2	12.2	14.5
Interest Payments	2.2	0.1	1.7	0.2	..	..	2.2	..	2.2	0.1	3.9	0.2
Domestic Debt	0.0	0.1	1.6	0.0	..	..	2.2	..	0.0	0.1	3.8	0.0
External Debt	2.2	0.0	0.1	0.2	..	..	..	..	2.2	0.0	0.1	0.2
Transfers to Households	3.0	1.1	0.7	0.8	8.2	7.1	3.9	5.8	11.2	8.3	4.6	6.6
Transfers to ROW	0.0	0.0	0.3	0.0	0.4	0.0	0.0	0.0	0.4	0.0	0.3	0.0
Subsidies 1/	1.5	1.4	1.0	2.3	1.4	2.6	1.4	0.0	2.9	4.0	2.4	2.3
Intragovernmental Transfers	0.4	0.0	0.0	0.2	0.5	0.0	0.0	0.7	..	..	..	..
Budgetary Savings	-0.2	1.4	2.8	-0.2	4.3	4.2	-2.4	0.3	4.1	5.6	0.3	0.1
2. Capital Operations:												
Capital Revenues (Privatization Fund)	0.0	..	..	..	..	..	..	..	0.0	2.9	0.3	0.7
Capital Revenue Transfers Received	..	2.9	0.3	0.7	..	..	..	..	..	..	..	..
Total Capital Expenditures	6.7	5.1	5.6	2.6	4.7	4.1	1.6	-0.5	11.4	9.2	7.2	2.0
Net Lending and Participation	0.0	1.5	2.7	1.6	4.7	4.1	1.6	-0.5	4.7	5.6	4.3	1.1
Total Public Sector Investment	6.7	3.6	2.9	1.0	0.0	0.0	0.0	0.0	6.7	3.6	2.9	1.0
Capital Revenue Transfers Made	..	..	..	..	..	..	..	..	..	..	..	..
3. Budget Deficit	-6.8	-0.8	-2.5	-2.1	-0.5	0.1	-4.0	0.8	-7.3	-0.7	-6.5	-1.3
4. Financing	6.8	0.8	2.5	2.1	0.5	-0.1	4.0	-0.8	7.3	0.7	6.5	1.3
Domestic	2.6	0.1	0.5	0.3	0.5	-0.1	4.0	-0.8	3.0	0.0	4.5	-0.6
Banking System	-2.1	-0.6	3.7	1.3	0.0	-0.5	-0.1	0.6	-2.1	-1.1	3.6	1.8
Other Domestic (residual)	4.7	0.8	-3.2	-1.0	0.5	0.4	4.1	-1.4	5.1	1.1	0.9	-2.4
External	4.2	0.7	2.1	1.9	0.0	0.0	0.0	0.0	4.2	0.7	2.1	1.9

1/ Subsidies in 1995 include adjustment for transfers to households.
Source: Ministry of Finance, IMF and World Bank staff estimates.

TABLE 6-1. Monetary Survey (end of period)

	1991	1992	1993	1994	1995
	(billions of rubles)		(millions of tenge)		
National Bank					
Net Foreign Assets	15	-230	3,667	49,243	63,143
Net International Reserves	0	..	3,836	49,203	63,115
Other Net Foreign Assets	15	-230	-168	40	28
Net Domestic Assets	30	529	254	-17,346	895
Credit to Government (net)	15	2	-322	17,362	32,841
Credit to Banks	31	652	5,847	11,655	7,365
Credit to the Economy	0	38	756	762	385
Other Assets (net)	-16	-163	-6,028	-47,124	-39,695
Liabilities	45	299	3,921	31,898	64,038
Currency outside NBK	14	148	2,319	20,592	48,643
Reserves	4	46	521	717	505
Other Deposits	27	105	1,081	10,589	14,890
Banking System					
Net Foreign Assets	15	-78	-520	-924	64,453
International Reserves of NBK	0	34	3,836	49,203	63,115
Other Net Foreign Assets	15	-112	-4,356	-50,127	1,338
Net Domestic Assets	72	504	7,255	55,932	48,284
Credit to Government (net)	10	-25	-350	16,255	33,556
Credit to the Economy	58	986	15,561	110,269	64,841
Other Assets (net)	4	-457	-7,956	-70,593	-50,112
Liabilities	87	426	6,735	55,007	112,737
Currency in Circulation	14	147	2,272	20,255	47,998
Deposits	73	279	4,463	34,752	64,739

Source: National Bank of Kazakstan and the International Monetary Fund staff estimates.

TABLE 7-1. Agricultural Production (millions of current national currency)

Item	1980	1985	1986	1987	1988 (mill. rubles)	1989	1990	1991	1992	1993 (mill. tenge)	1994
Total gross agricultural production	10,832	14,207	16,352	16,330	17,549	18,105	21,797	35,749	407,006	14,932	223,255
Crops	..	..	..	..	7,332	6,259	8,672	12,379	145,320	9,826	146,641
Grains	..	..	..	..	..	..	..	..	..	5,178	66,518
Potatoes	..	..	..	..	..	..	..	..	..	1,083	27,436
Vegetables	..	..	..	..	..	..	..	..	..	971	15,167
Fruits (excluding grapes)	..	..	..	..	..	..	..	..	..	105	1,402
Grapes	..	..	..	..	..	..	..	..	..	37	350
Tobacco	..	..	..	..	..	..	..	..	..	35	47
Cotton	..	..	..	..	..	..	..	..	..	235	399
Sugarbeets	..	..	..	..	..	..	..	..	..	158	991
Oilseeds	..	..	..	..	..	..	..	..	..	..	..
Other	..	..	..	..	..	..	..	..	..	..	..
Animal husbandry	..	..	..	..	10,217	11,845	13,124	23,370	261,686	5,106	76,614
Livestock	..	..	..	..	..	..	..	..	..	..	..
Cattle	..	..	..	..	..	..	..	..	..	2,681	44,380
Pigs	..	..	..	..	..	..	..	..	..	417	7,411
Sheep and goats	..	..	..	..	..	..	..	..	..	979	11,609
Poultry	..	..	..	..	..	..	..	..	..	615	9,388
Other	..	..	..	..	..	..	..	..	..	414	3,827
Milk	..	..	..	..	..	..	..	..	..	1,280	26,854
Eggs	..	..	..	..	..	..	..	..	..	277	5,852
Wool	..	..	..	..	..	..	..	..	..	274	3,800
Other livestock	..	..	..	..	..	..	..	..	..	2,199	33,521
Agricultural services	..	..	..	..	..	..	..	..	..	..	..
Material inputs	5,506	7,411	8,090	8,286	8,076	7,669	8,068	13,313	122,735	4,510	101,581
Crops	..	..	..	..	..	..	..	..	..	..	..
Animal husbandry	..	..	..	..	..	..	..	..	..	..	..
Agricultural services	..	..	..	..	..	..	..	..	..	..	..
Net material product, by type of output	5,327	6,797	8,262	8,044	9,472	10,435	13,729	22,436	284,271	10,423	121,674
Crops	..	..	..	..	..	..	..	..	..	..	..
Animal husbandry	..	..	..	..	..	..	..	..	..	..	..
Agricultural services	..	..	..	..	..	..	..	..	..	..	..

Source: State Committee of Statistics.

TABLE 7-2. Agricultural Production in Constant Rubles (millions of 1983 national currency)

Item	1980	1985	1986	1987	1988	1989	1990	1991	1992	1993	1994 (mill. tenge) 1/
Total gross agricultural production	14,135	13,832	15,578	15,169	15,833	14,678	15,673	14,041	14,158	13,424	111,627
Crops	6,399	5,878	6,804	6,138	6,339	4,934	6,118	4,883	5,811	5,120	73,320
Grains	..	..	3,427	3,272	2,781	2,468	3,690	1,689	3,834	2,845	33,259
Potatoes	..	..	408	395	432	341	444	410	491	439	13,718
Vegetables	..	..	363	374	415	400	366	307	320	415	7,584
Fruits (excluding grapes)	..	..	221	146	167	92	190	77	109	61	701
Grapes	..	..	74	66	43	23	65	31	29	19	175
Tobacco	..	..	42	41	37	25	24	24	20	21	24
Cotton	..	..	230	211	219	224	236	207	171	142	1,992
Sugarbeets	..	..	88	91	67	61	58	37	66	43	495
Oilseeds	..	..	43	55	65	51	70	45	70	44	606
Other	..	..	1,908	1,487	2,113	1,249	975	2,056	701	1,071	14,766
Animal husbandry	7,736	7,954	8,774	9,031	9,494	9,744	9,555	9,158	8,347	8,304	38,307
Livestock	..	..	5,375	5,557	5,832	5,985	5,817	5,520	4,941	4,867	20,054
Cattle	..	..	2,589	2,713	2,936	2,968	2,857	2,705	2,487	2,511	8,763
Pigs	..	..	703	739	759	804	816	775	623	586	3,705
Sheep and goats	..	..	1,202	1,213	1,293	1,299	1,259	1,203	1,128	1,134	3,904
Poultry	..	..	557	568	591	622	616	573	422	345	1,768
Other	..	..	324	324	253	292	269	264	281	241	1,914
Milk	..	..	2,008	2,064	2,118	2,213	2,246	2,211	2,096	2,220	13,427
Eggs	..	..	392	401	402	407	401	390	341	315	2,926
Wool	..	..	919	922	938	952	933	904	835	816	1,900
Other livestock	..	..	80	87	204	187	158	133	134	86	..
Agricultural services	..	..	..	..	..	..	..	..	..	..	..
Material inputs	..	..	..	..	..	..	..	..	..	..	..
Crops	..	..	..	..	..	..	..	..	..	..	..
Animal husbandry	..	..	..	..	..	..	..	..	..	..	..
Agricultural services	..	..	..	..	..	..	..	..	..	..	..
Net material product by type of output	..	..	..	..	..	..	..	..	..	..	..
Crops	..	..	..	..	..	..	..	..	..	..	..
Animal husbandry	..	..	..	..	..	..	..	..	..	..	..
Agricultural services	..	..	..	..	..	..	..	..	..	..	..

1/ In 1994 prices.
Source: State Committee of Statistics.

TABLE 7-3. Production and Average Yield of Major Agricultural Crops

Crop	1980	1985	1986	1987	1988	1989	1990	1991	1992	1993	1994	1995
Production (thousands of tons)												
Grain - Cleanweight	25,930	22,694	26,562	25,721	20,970	18,797	28,488	11,992	29,772	21,631	16,454	9,505
Winter wheat	1,357	935	1,328	2,255	1,354	1,452	1,966	1,298	1,743	1,934	884	622
Spring wheat	16,191	13,256	15,415	13,853	10,808	9,332	14,231	5,591	16,542	9,651	8,168	5,868
Coarse grain	..	..	..	..	..	..	..	..	24,040	18,342	10,560	
Rye	129	144	394	364	587	784	889	506	568	889	264	84
Corn	414	598	505	477	561	479	442	330	368	355	234	136
Winter barley	122	85	99	135	91	54	118	105	125	119	25	19
Spring barley	6,283	6,277	7,481	7,274	6,216	5,673	9,185	3,307	9,337	7,790	5,472	2,189
Oats	691	570	656	490	372	283	681	265	831	906	822	250
Millet	385	446	424	593	637	534	1,077	287	562	294	130	39
Rice	613	671	634	654	686	651	653	590	543	479	283	183
Flax	..	..	..	..	..	..	..	..	..	..	..	..
Oilseeds	126	129	139	182	216	167	230	155	235	172	184	162
Sunflowerseed	100	93	83	117	139	105	141	108	122	107	97	97
Soybeans	8	18	35	45	41	33	33	16	12	6	6	4
Other	18	18	21	20	36	29	56	31	101	59	81	61
Cotton (raw)	358	305	333	312	325	315	324	291	252	200	208	223
Cotton fiber	..	10	11	10	10	10	10	9	..	..	..	..
Sugarbeets	2,223	1,901	1,721	1,804	1,321	1,188	1,134	726	1,276	925	433	371
Potatoes	2,238	2,197	2,137	2,066	2,260	1,783	2,324	2,143	2,570	2,296	2,040	1,720
Pulses	135	119	159	154	141	118	176	75	148	108	52	29
Vegetables	1,134	1,085	1,211	1,190	1,354	1,254	1,136	955	985	808	781	780
Fruit	257	133	386	209	276	118	301	98	169	85	100	97
Grapes	172	69	158	141	94	48	139	66	62	40	37	68
Other	85	64	228	68	182	70	162	32	107	..	..	..
Corn (silage and greenchop)	25,576	33,170	27,870	31,130	28,347	19,851	44,104	14,238	24,748	19,202	15,837	4,404
Hay	16,114	16,805	18,275	19,538	18,747	18,477	17,150	13,401	16,416	16,132	15,679	11,332
Average yield (kilograms per hectare)												
Grain	1,020	900	1,080	1,050	860	790	1,220	530	1,320	1,000	790	500
Winter wheat	1,090	940	1,250	1,950	1,480	1,320	1,640	1,080	1,430	1,500	890	780
Spring wheat	1,020	870	1,060	980	770	700	1,110	460	1,310	800	700	500
Coarse grain	1,100	1,000	1,200	1,100	900	900	1,300	600	1,500	1,100	890	580
Rye	490	630	910	740	1,020	1,080	1,160	900	910	1,500	820	480
Corn	4,300	4,450	4,250	4,030	4,090	3,580	3,440	2,720	2,910	3,000	2,080	1,580
Winter barley	1,320	1,270	1,180	2,160	2,140	1,860	2,240	1,600	2,060	1,900	970	870
Spring barley	1,050	930	1,130	1,070	890	840	1,390	500	1,650	1,100	910	460
Oats	1,400	1,620	1,460	1,010	1,060	690	1,780	520	1,820	1,700	1,280	510
Millet	460	540	610	880	910	690	1,380	340	560	600	360	160
Rice	4,680	4,710	4,920	4,910	5,090	4,890	5,250	4,980	4,490	4,300	2,760	1,930
Flax	..	..	..	..	..	..	..	..	..	..	..	..
Oilseeds	770	600	720	760	720	590	860	510	510	400	420	320
Sunflowerseed	970	900	870	1,120	1,140	800	1,030	570	410	400	430	290
Soybeans	690	1,260	1,100	1,200	1,470	1,340	1,440	940	1,080	1,000	920	770
Other	..	..	..	..	..	..	..	..	..	..	..	..
Cotton (raw)	2,830	2,340	2,590	2,440	2,540	2,640	2,710	2,500	2,250	1,800	1,870	2,030
Cotton fiber	..	760	840	750	790	830	850	810	..	..	..	..
Sugarbeets	28,500	26,400	27,900	32,000	31,610	26,690	25,990	15,900	15,000	13,500	8,340	910
Potatoes	11,700	11,510	11,200	10,830	11,200	8,570	11,290	9,890	10,400	9,400	9,350	8,350
Pulses	990	710	970	840	770	690	1,110	500	1,060	900	490	440
Vegetables	16,700	16,100	17,900	16,500	16,900	15,620	15,440	12,100	11,400	10,600	10,390	10,060
Fruit	3,840	1,840	5,360	2,960	3,790	1,610	4,190	1,460	2,220	1,200	1,490	1,430
Grapes	8,340	3,280	7,740	7,320	4,990	2,560	8,050	3,850	3,680	2,500	2,380	4,610
Other	..	..	..	..	..	..	..	..	..	..	..	..
Corn (silage and greenchop)	11,000	13,500	11,500	13,500	13,100	9,100	19,300	7,200	11,000	9,600	9,710	5,400
Hay	..	..	..	..	..	..	..	..	..	..	..	..

Source: State Committee of Statistics.

TABLE 7-4. Main Aggregates of Animal Husbandry

Type of livestock or product	1980	1985	1986	1987	1988	1989	1990	1991	1992	1993	1994
Livestock (thousands of heads)											
Cattle	8,693	9,165	9,528	9,672	9,752	9,818	9,757	9,592	9,576	9,347	8,073
of which: Cows	2,985	3,087	3,161	3,207	3,273	3,327	3,368	3,490	3,623	3,687	3,397
Pigs	3,093	2,968	3,221	3,237	3,188	3,262	3,224	2,976	2,591	2,445	1,983
Sheep and goats	35,208	35,485	36,408	36,388	36,498	36,222	35,661	34,556	34,420	33,133	24,235
of which: Goats	678	838	883	918	953	979	983	997	1,044	1,095	897
Horses	1,300	1,455	1,533	1,540	1,581	1,619	1,626	1,666	1,704	1,777	1,636
Other	..	..	..	..	..	..	..	..	..	..	..
Animal husbandry products											
Meat (thousands of tons)	1,069	1,133	1,300	1,399	1,493	1,573	1,560	1,524	1,258	1,312	1,048
Beef	465	506	580	632	689	727	710	724	596	662	..
Pork	195	185	219	245	255	273	286	274	217	194	..
Lamb	231	221	253	258	279	289	286	270	243	275	..
Poultry	126	166	191	198	201	210	201	185	139	114	..
Other	52	55	57	67	70	74	77	72	62	67	..
Milk (thousands of tons)	4,597	4,763	5,040	5,185	5,321	5,563	5,642	5,555	5,265	5,577	5,128
Eggs (millions)	3,369	3,803	4,097	4,189	4,202	4,253	4,185	4,075	3,565	3,288	2,772
Wool (thousands of tons)	104	98	106	106	108	110	198	104	96	95	79

Source: State Committee of Statistics.

TABLE 7-5. Agricultural Production by Type of Ownership (millions of local currency, constant prices)

Ownership category	1980	1985	1986	1987	1988	1989	1990	1991	1992	1993	1994	1995
					(millions of 1983 rubles)						(mill. of 1994 tenge)	
Total agricultural production	14,135	13,832	15,578	15,169	15,833	14,678	15,673	14,041	14,063	13,424	111,627	85,014
Crops	6,399	5,878	6,804	6,138	6,339	4,934	6118	4,883	5,716	5,120	73,320	57,857
Animal husbandry	7,736	7,954	8,774	9,031	9,494	9,744	9,555	9,158	8,347	8,304	38,307	27,157
Collective farms (kolkhoz)	1,719	1,571	1,673	1,786	1,805	1,744	1,690	1,405	1,390	1,204	44,727	34,006
Crops	899	834	837	914	894	838	819	630	741	616	35,102	26,525
Animal husbandry	820	737	836	872	911	906	871	775	649	588	9,625	7,481
State farms	9,088	8,590	10,015	9,385	9,681	8,449	9,349	7,876	7,424	6,936	23,999	17,853
Crops	4,883	4,493	5,338	4,665	4,800	3,551	4,631	3,611	4,067	3,618	18,597	13,747
Animal husbandry	4,205	4,097	4,677	4,720	4,881	4,898	4,718	4,265	3,357	3,318	5,402	4,106
Other state enterprises	150	221	246	223	246	233	234	198	355	2	742	850
Crops	82	100	121	85	102	88	93	86	186	2	742	850
Animal husbandry	68	121	125	138	144	145	141	112	169	..	..	..
Private plots	3,178	3,450	3,644	3,775	4,101	4,252	4,400	4,512	4,689	5,062	40,126	30,605
Crops	535	451	508	474	543	457	575	545	626	768	17,478	13,466
Animal husbandry	2,643	2,999	3,136	3,301	3,558	3,795	3,825	3,967	4,063	4,294	22,648	17,139
Private farms	..	..	..	..	..	..	..	50	205	220	2,033	1,700
Crops	..	..	..	..	..	..	..	11	97	116	1,402	1,173
Animal husbandry	..	..	..	..	..	..	..	39	108	104	631	527

Source: State Committee of Statistics.

TABLE 7-6. Summary/Employment in Agriculture (in thousands)

	1980	1985	1986	1987	1988	1989	1990	1991	1992	1993	1994	1995
Total	1,545	1,646	1,640	1,680	1,718	1,662	1,713	1,740	1,781	1,821	1,406	1,432
Collective farms	276	279	276	274	264	254	260	258	268	247	229	725
State farms	1,112	1,176	1,172	1,177	1,156	1,102	1,092	1,082	1,047	1,015	803	356
Temporary workers	19	47	40	41	42	26	26	26	34	20	..	..
Labor on private plots	137	136	142	162	221	230	275	310	337	349	..	..
New Private Cooperatives	..	..	..	..	..	..	9	11	5	5	..	..
Private farms	..	..	..	..	..	..	1	5	39	49	69	102
Other	..	8	10	24	35	50	23	48	51	136	305	249

Source: State Committee of Statistics.

TABLE 7-7. Farm Activities: Main Indicators

1980	Total	Collective farms (kolhozes)	State farms (sovhozes)	Other (state farms)	Private plots	Private farms
Number of farms	..	397	2,077	..	..	..
Gross Output (million 1983 rubles)	14,135	1,719	9,088	150	3,178	..
Fixed Capital (billion 1984 rubles)	9	0	..	..	..	..
Profits (billion 1983 rubles)	0	..	..	..	..	..
Number of loss-making farms	..	147	1,091	..	..	..
Production (thousand tons)						
Grain	27,506	3,610	23,665	214	17	..
Sugar beets	2,223	1,004	1,208	11	..	..
Sunflowers	100	45	48	0	7	..
Flax	..	..	..	..	..	..
Potatoes	2,238	107	835	61	1,235	..
Vegetables	1,134	160	544	34	396	..
Meat	1,069	96	600	10	363	..
Milk	4,597	552	2,107	36	1,902	..
Eggs (millions)	3,369	22	2,063	13	1,271	..
Cattle (thousand heads)	8,693	917	5,506	131	2,139	..
Cows	2,985	283	1,528	17	1,157	..
Pigs	3,093	432	1,904	84	673	..
Sheep, goats	35,208	5,235	25,921	360	3,692	..
Poultry	48,092	730	27,113	252	19,997	..

1985	Total	Collective farms (kolhozes)	State farms (sovhozes)	Other (state farms)	Private plots	Private farms
Number of farms	..	388	2,140	..	..	..
Gross Output (million 1983 rubles)	13,832	1,571	8,591	221	3,449	..
Fixed Capital (billion 1984 rubles)	11	0	..	..	..	..
Profits (billion 1983 rubles)	0	..	..	..	..	..
Number of loss-making farms	..	191	1,142	..	..	..
Production (thousand tons)						
Grain	24,164	2,977	20,877	291	19	..
Sugar beets	1,901	745	1,133	23	..	..
Sunflowers	93	46	43	0	4	..
Flax	0	..	..	..	..	..
Potatoes	2,197	117	879	70	1,131	..
Vegetables	1,085	184	574	40	287	..
Meat	1,133	91	652	29	361	..
Milk	4,763	542	2,099	50	2,072	..
Eggs (millions)	3,803	17	2,533	9	1,244	..
Cattle (thousand heads)	9,165	960	5,607	184	2,414	..
Cows	3,087	286	1,518	37	1,246	..
Pigs	2,968	357	1,846	236	529	..
Sheep, goats	35,485	4,911	25,592	480	4,502	..
Poultry	55,436	651	35,373	302	19,110	..

TABLE 7-7. Farm Activities: Main Indicators, cont'd.

1986	Total	Collective farm (kolhozes)	State farms (sovhozes)	Other (state farms)	Private plots	Private farms
Number of farms	..	388	2,119	..	..	..
Gross Output (million 1983 rubles)	15,578	1,673	10,015	246	3,644	..
Fixed Capital (billion 1984 rubles)	11	0	..	..	..	..
Profits (billion 1983 rubles)	0	..	..	..	..	..
Number of loss-making farms	..	79	685	..	..	..
Production (thousand tons)						
Grain	28,306	3,549	24,387	352	18	..
Sugar beets	1,721	672	1,031	18	..	..
Sunflowers	83	41	38	0	4	..
Flax	0	..	..	..	..	..
Potatoes	2,137	110	816	77	1,134	..
Vegetables	1,211	211	663	42	295	..
Meat	1,300	114	769	27	390	..
Milk	5,040	582	2,258	54	2,146	..
Eggs (millions)	4,097	20	2,816	7	1,254	..
Cattle (thousand heads)	9,528	984	5,801	180	2,563	..
Cows	3,161	287	1,539	31	1,304	..
Pigs	3,221	382	2,007	269	563	..
Sheep, goats	36,408	4,992	26,152	358	4,906	..
Poultry	57,542	667	37,428	344	19,103	..

1987	Total	Collective farm (kolhozes)	State farms (sovhozes)	Other (state farms)	Private plots	Private farms
Number of farms	..	386	2,143	..	..	..
Gross Output (million 1983 rubles)	15,169	1,786	9,385	223	3,775	..
Fixed Capital (billion 1984 rubles)	12	0	..	..	..	..
Profits (billion 1983 rubles)	0	..	..	..	..	..
Number of loss-making farms	..	85	645	..	..	..
Production (thousand tons)						
Grain	27,444	3,589	23,544	292	19	..
Sugar beets	1,804	683	1,121	..	..	..
Sunflowers	117	59	54	0	4	..
Flax	0	..	..	..	..	..
Potatoes	2,066	109	782	64	1,111	..
Vegetables	1,190	224	646	33	287	..
Meat	1,399	122	830	28	419	..
Milk	5,185	600	2,321	39	2,225	..
Eggs (millions)	4,189	19	2,907	7	1,256	..
Cattle (thousand heads)	9,672	995	5,872	161	2,644	..
Cows	3,207	286	1,525	33	1,363	..
Pigs	3,237	397	2,016	270	554	..
Sheep, goats	36,388	5,004	25,921	337	5,126	..
Poultry	57,667	489	37,829	270	19,079	..

TABLE 7-7. Farm Activities: Main Iindicators, cont'd.

1 9 8 8	Total	Collective farm (kolhozes)	State farms (sovhozes)	Other (state farms)	Private plots	Private farms
Number of farms	..	399	2,125	..	..	..
Gross Output (million 1983 rubles)	15,833	1,805	9,681	246	4,101	..
Fixed Capital (billion 1984 rubles)	13	0	..	..	..	..
Profits (billion 1983 rubles)	0	..	..		..	..
Number of loss-making farms	..	54	517	..	..	..
Production (thousand tons)						
Grain	22,560	3,006	19,276	257	21	..
Sugar beets	1,312	489	823	..	..	..
Sunflowers	139	67	66	3	3	..
Flax	0	..	..	..	..	..
Potatoes	2,260	124	857	62	1,217	..
Vegetables	1,354	247	709	43	355	..
Meat	1,493	128	871	31	463	..
Milk	5,321	624	2,357	48	2,292	..
Eggs (millions)	4,202	14	2,916	10	1,262	..
Cattle (thousand heads)	9,752	990	5,791	168	2,803	..
Cows	3,273	288	1,506	38	1,441	..
Pigs	3,188	352	1,959	280	597	..
Sheep, goats	36,498	4,896	25,606	512	5,484	..
Poultry	58,436	693	37,728	419	19,596	..

1 9 8 9	Total	Collective farm (kolhozes)	State farms (sovhozes)	Other (state farms)	Private plots	Private farms
Number of farms	..	400	2,119	..	..	..
Gross Output (million 1983 rubles)	14,678	1,744	8,449	233	4,252	..
Fixed Capital (billion 1984 rubles)	14	0	..	..	..	..
Profits (billion 1983 rubles)	0	..	..	..	..	..
Number of loss-making farms	..	13	242	..	..	..
Production (thousand tons)						
Grain	20,356	3,027	17,052	258	19	..
Sugar beets	1,188	432	755	1	..	..
Sunflowers	105	51	49	2	3	..
Flax	0	..	..	..	..	..
Potatoes	1,783	103	661	59	960	..
Vegetables	1,254	235	628	41	350	..
Meat	1,573	131	915	33	494	..
Milk	5,563	639	2,411	50	2,463	..
Eggs (millions)	4,253	15	2,921	10	1,307	..
Cattle (thousand heads)	9,818	985	5,725	186	2,922	..
Cows	3,327	289	1,488	39	1,511	..
Pigs	3,262	377	1,970	290	625	..
Sheep, goats	36,222	4,723	24,958	544	5,997	..
Poultry	59,286	771	38,246	478	19,791	..

TABLE 7-7. Farm Activities: Main Indicators, cont'd.

1 9 9 0	Total	Collective farm (kolhozes)	State farms (sovhozes)	Other (state farms)	Private plots	Private farms
Number of farms	..	402	2,118	..	..	324
Gross Output (million 1983 rubles)	15,673	1,690	9,349	234	4,400	..
Fixed Capital (billion 1984 rubles)	13	0	..	..	..	..
Profits (billion 1983 rubles)	0	..	..	..	..	..
Number of loss-making farms	..	4	73	..	..	..
Production (thousand tons)						
Grain	31,249	3,581	27,217	426	18	7
Sugar beets	1,134	390	744	..	..	..
Sunflowers	141	70	66	2	3	..
Flax	0	..	..	..	..	..
Potatoes	2,324	109	914	55	1,246	..
Vegetables	1,136	191	523	31	391	..
Meat	1,560	126	880	33	520	1
Milk	5,642	629	2,387	48	2,578	..
Eggs (millions)	4,185	16	2,843	6	1,320	..
Cattle (thousand heads)	9,757	958	5,606	175	3,013	5
Cows	3,368	282	1,467	39	1,578	2
Pigs	3,224	358	1,938	263	664	1
Sheep, goats	35,661	4,527	24,136	587	6,360	51
Poultry	59,899	586	38,777	539	19,997	..

1 9 9 1	Total	Collective farm (kolhozes)	State farms (sovhozes)	Other (state farms)	Private plots	Private farms
Number of farms	..	408	2,120	..	..	3,333
Gross Output (million 1983 rubles)	14,041	1,659	7,622	198	4,512	50
Fixed Capital (billion 1984 rubles)	13	0	..	..	..	..
Profits (billion 1983 rubles)	0	..	..	..	..	..
Number of loss-making farms	..	26	272	..	..	..
Production (thousand tons)						
Grain	13,274	1,991	11,013	204	25	41
Sugar beets	726	282	442	2	..	..
Sunflowers	108	51	53	1	3	..
Flax	0	..	..	..	..	..
Potatoes	2,143	82	708	47	1,304	2
Vegetables	955	156	407	25	365	2
Meat	1,524	121	845	30	525	3
Milk	5,555	589	2,230	52	2,681	3
Eggs (millions)	4,075	15	2,752	4	1,304	..
Cattle (thousand heads)	9,592	913	5,280	171	3,195	33
Cows	3,490	277	1,438	44	1,716	15
Pigs	2,976	287	1,751	234	698	6
Sheep, goats	34,556	4,311	22,270	593	6,950	432
Poultry	59,932	613	39,358	292	19,659	10

TABLE 7-7. Farm Activities: Main Indicators, cont'd.

1 9 9 2	Total	Collective farm (kolhozes)	State farms (sovhozes)	Other (state farms)	Private plots	Private farms
Number of farms	..	452	2,055	..	9,262	..
Gross Output (million 1983 rubles)	14,158	1,390	7,424	355	4,784	205
Fixed Capital (billion 1984 rubles)	7	0	..	..	..	..
Profits (billion 1983 rubles)	0	..	..	..	..	..
Number of loss-making farms	..	30	299	..	..	..
Production (thousand tons)						
Grain	33,427	3,774	28,069	1,062	16	506
Sugar beets	1,276	498	726	22	5	25
Sunflowers	122	53	61	5	2	1
Flax	0	..	..	..	..	..
Potatoes	2,570	88	695	46	1,711	30
Vegetables	985	143	359	44	379	60
Meat	1,258	96	581	28	544	9
Milk	5,265	505	1,813	68	2,856	23
Eggs (millions)	3,565	9	2,229	2	1,324	1
Cattle (thousand heads)	9,576	907	4,940	208	3,452	69
Cows	3,623	271	1,345	59	1,918	30
Pigs	2,591	179	1,516	171	713	12
Sheep, goats	34,420	4,485	20,422	967	7,767	779
Poultry	52,733	222	32,877	154	19,075	405

1 9 9 3	Total	Collective farm (kolhozes)	State farms (sovhozes)	Other (state farms)	Private plots	Private farms
Number of farms	..	445	2,079	..	..	..
Gross Output (million 1983 rubles)	..	..	..	..	..	..
Fixed Capital (billion 1984 rubles)	..	..	..	..	..	..
Profits (billion 1983 rubles)	..	..	..	..	..	..
Number of loss-making farms	..	157	1,132	..	..	..
Production (thousand tons)						
Grain	21,631	2,854	16,253	1,932	17	575
Sugar beets	843	276	264	245	24	34
Sunflowers	86	40	36	6	3	1
Flax	..	..	..	..	..	..
Potatoes	2,296	76	440	90	1,627	64
Vegetables	808	92	181	43	452	39
Meat	1,258	..	..	..	..	..
Milk	5,548	..	..	..	..	..
Eggs (millions)	3,376	..	..	..	..	..
Cattle (thousand heads)	9,347	817	3,884	164	3,802	88
Cows	3,687	250	1,137	51	2,045	39
Pigs	2,445	143	1,281	123	805	14
Sheep, goats	34,208	4,159	16,974	598	8,523	828
Poultry	52,591	..	..	..	..	..

TABLE 7-7. Farm Activities: Main Indicators, cont'd.

1994	Total	Collective farm (kolhozes)	State farms (sovhozes)	Other (state farms)	Private plots	Private farms
Number of farms	..	434	764	2,182	349,000	22,401
Gross Output (million 1983 rubles)	..	..	..	..	..	..
Fixed Capital (billion 1984 rubles)	..	..	..	..	..	..
Profits (billion 1983 rubles)	..	..	..	..	..	..
Number of loss-making farms	..	..	..	..	..	..
Production (thousand tons)						
Grain	16,454	1,907	4,822	269	464	438
Sugar beets	469	143	99	4	34	34
Sunflowers	97	43	18	4	5	2
Flax	..	..	..	..	..	..
Potatoes	2,040	39	177	27	1,611	15
Vegetables	781	71	87	17	498	15
Meat	1,048	..	..	..	..	..
Milk	5,128	..	..	..	..	..
Eggs (millions)	2,772	..	..	..	..	..
Cattle (thousand heads)	8,073	653	3,535	134	3,654	97
Cows	3,397	249	875	39	2,005	46
Pigs	1,983	97	525	100	767	11
Sheep, goats	25,132	2,748	7,503	378	7,967	692
Poultry	38,239	..	10,981	1,251	18,522	405

Source: State Committee of Statistics.

TABLE 8-1. Industrial Production by Sector (millions of current national currency)

Sector	1980	1985	1986	1987	1988 (mill. rubles)	1989	1990	1991	1992	1993	1994 (mill. tenge)	1995 1/
All industry	23,308	29,041	30,418	31,763	33,037	34,151	34,738	85,436	1,301,988	22,951	340,993	642,881
Heavy industry	..	18,902	19,988	20,858	21,664	22,241	22,235	48,302	1,063,511	18,499	286,905	..
Fuel and energy	..	3,791	4,046	4,199	4,343	4,449	4,521	10,627	375,263	6,902	139,105	..
Electricity	..	1,334	1,396	1,434	1,492	1,632	1,797	4,141	121,309	3,302	64,535	105,212
Fuels	..	2,457	2,650	2,765	2,851	2,817	2,724	6,486	253,954	3,600	74,570	143,533
Ferrous and nonferrous metallurgy	..	5,044	5,237	5,416	5,622	5,744	5,728	12,670	360,120	5,491	81,585	166,746
Chemicals and petrochemical industry	..	1,732	1,894	2,054	2,216	2,270	2,259	5,390	99,447	925	12,611	23,293
Machinery and metalworking	..	3,162	3,390	3,440	3,532	3,629	3,568	6,571	71,020	2,281	24,821	37,248
Forestry, woodworking, and pulp and paper ind.	..	827	876	935	952	961	964	1,788	2,016	541	3,563	4,766
Construction materials	..	1,761	1,830	1,943	2,018	2,067	1,990	4,200	51,842	1,193	13,995	18,598
Light industry	..	4,707	4,780	4,907	5,131	5,329	5,402	15,798	83,673	1,323	12,906	16,480
Textiles	..	2,754	2,900	2,988	3,125	3,293	3,299	11,008	58,125	838	8,439	10,611
Clothing	..	1,357	1,306	1,332	1,381	1,403	1,459	3,235	15,486	273	2,685	2,776
Leather and shoes	..	587	565	578	616	624	635	1,541	7,545	208	1,740	..
Food processing	..	5,432	5,650	5,998	6,242	6,581	7,101	21,336	154,804	3,128	41,182	69,678
Processed food	..	2,007	2,004	2,105	2,173	2,231	2,275	4,900	56,505	1,120	15,314	24,246
Meat and dairy products	..	2,373	2,662	2,917	3,024	3,161	3,189	13,730	87,255	1,424	17,416	22,560
Fish	..	185	184	183	187	181	177	384	2,282	68	1,054	1,475

1/ For 1995 includes production of the household sector.

Source: State Committee of Statistics.

TABLE 8-2. Industrial Production in Constant Rubles and Growth in Production by Sector

Sector	1980	1985	1986	1987	1988	1989	1990	1991	1992	1993	1994	1995
Industrial production						(millions of national currency)						
All Industry	21,770	30,094	31,599	33,036	34,196	35,036	35,042	34,727	29,934	21,725	312,550	..
Heavy Industry	..	20,023	21,199	22,120	22,842	23,221	22,781	22,508	20,054	17,139	255,012	..
Fuel and energy	2,808	4,950	5,270	5,465	5,542	5,572	5,444	7,414	6,970	5,554	101,856	..
Electricity	879	1,655	1,725	1,796	1,792	1,888	1,868	1,851	1,736	1,902	22,196	..
Fuels	1,929	3,295	3,545	3,669	3,750	3,684	3,576	5,580	5,251	3,652	79,660	
Ferrous and nonferrous metallurgy	3,424	5,022	5,202	5,344	5,566	5,662	5,463	5,394	5,038	5,491	86,500	
Chemicals and petrochemicals	970	1,732	1,898	2,057	2,221	2,273	2,258	1,565	1,144	925	13,036	
Machinery building and metalworking	2,139	3,155	3,402	3,484	3,557	3,637	3,572	3,622	2,727	2,272	24,805	
Forestry, woodworking, and pulp and paper	561	815	870	923	941	959	960	797	563	530	3,562	
Construction materials	1,372	1,754	1,812	1,924	2,005	2,056	1,980	2,000	1,662	1,193	13,995	
Light industry	3,926	4,741	4,832	4,968	5,204	5,399	5,483	5,620	4,440	1,324	12,914	..
Textiles	2,323	2,756	2,905	2,992	3,132	3,291	3,295	3,255	2,556	838	8,439	..
Clothing	1,146	1,376	1,338	1,374	1,434	1,465	1,532	1,769	1,380	273	2,692	
Leather and shoe	452	273	271	279	295	319	318	351	275	208	1,740	
Food industry	4,566	5,330	5,568	5,948	6,150	6,416	6,778	6,371	4,785	3,263	44,624	..
Processed foods	1,710	1,931	1,908	2,022	2,091	2,151	2,135	1,986	1,636	1,176	16,581	..
Meat and dairy products	2,017	2,349	2,669	2,943	3,061	3,207	3,233	3,013	1,986	1,503	19,584	..
Fish	159	182	191	195	197	190	187	206	164	68	1,054	..
Growth in production by sector						(in percent)						
All industry			5.0	4.5	3.5	2.5	0.0	-0.9	-13.8	-14.8	-28.1	-7.9
Heavy industry			5.9	4.3	3.3	1.7	-1.9	-1.2	-10.9	-15.7	-21.5	..
Power and fuels			6.5	3.7	1.4	0.5	-2.3	36.2	-6.0	-11.5	-14.5	..
Electricity			4.2	4.1	-0.2	5.4	-1.1	-0.9	-6.2	-4.4	-15.2	-1.9
Fuels			7.6	3.5	2.2	-1.8	-2.9	56.0	-5.9	-14.8	-14.0	-12.3
Ferrous and nonferrous metallurgy			3.6	2.7	4.2	1.7	-3.5	-1.3	-6.6	-15.9	-20.6	11.0
Chemicals and petrochemicals			9.6	8.4	8.0	2.3	-0.7	-30.7	-26.9	-44.6	-26.9	3.4
Machinery and metalworking			7.8	2.4	2.1	2.2	-1.8	1.4	-24.7	-14.7	-24.4	-32.9
Forestry, woodworking, and pulp and paper			6.7	6.1	2.0	1.9	0.1	-17.0	-29.4	-8.7	-44.9	-45.0
Construction materials			3.3	6.2	4.2	2.5	-3.7	1.0	-16.9	-26.8	-57.1	-31.3
Light industry			1.9	2.8	4.8	3.7	1.6	2.5	-21.0	11.7	-44.3	-59.8
Textiles			5.4	3.0	4.7	5.1	0.1	-1.2	-21.5	-12.2	-39.7	-55.7
Clothing			-2.8	2.7	4.4	2.2	4.6	15.5	-22.0	-4.3	-54.9	-84.9
Leather and shoe			-0.7	3.0	5.7	8.1	-0.3	10.3	-21.7	-17.4	-56.3	..
Food industry			4.5	6.8	3.4	4.3	5.6	-6.0	-24.9	-11.7	-26.1	-20.7
Processed foods			-1.2	6.0	3.4	2.9	-0.7	-7.0	-17.6	-15.6	-18.8	-39.7
Meat and dairy products			13.6	10.3	4.0	4.8	0.8	-6.8	-34.1	-12.7	-31.6	-36.1
Fish			4.9	2.1	1.0	-3.6	-1.6	10.2	-20.2	-1.3	-23.2	-27.5

Note: Data for 1993-94 in millions of current tenge. Growth rates for 1993-95 based on physical units.

Source: State Committee of Statistics.

TABLE 8-3. Electricity Production and Consumption (billions of kilowatt-hours)

Source of electricity or type of consumption	1980	1985	1986	1987	1988	1989	1990	1991	1992	1993	1994
Domestic production	..	81	85	88	88	90	87	86	83	77	64
Thermal	..	76	80	83	81	82	80	79	76	70	55
Hydro	..	5	5	6	7	7	7	7	7	7	9
Nuclear	..	..	..	..	..	..	..	..	..	..	..
Imports	..	22	23	24	25	27	31	31	30	27	27
Inter-republic	..	..	..	..	..	..	..	..	..	..	..
Extra-republic	..	..	..	..	..	..	..	..	..	..	..
Total supply	..	103	108	112	114	117	119	117	112	104	91
Domestic consumption	..	92	95	100	102	104	105	102	97	73	77
Industry and construction	..	57	59	62	64	64	64	60	55	39	36
Agriculture	..	11	11	11	12	12	14	14	15	12	10
Transport	..	5	5	6	6	6	6	6	6	5	4
Other sectors	..	11	11	12	12	12	12	13	13	8	8
Households	..	..	..	..	..	..	..	..	..	9	9
Losses	..	8	8	8	8	8	8	8	9	9	10
Exports	..	12	13	13	12	13	14	15	15	15	14
Interrepublic	..	..	..	..	..	..	..	..	..	..	..
Extrarepublic	..	..	..	..	..	..	..	..	..	..	..
Total consumption	..	103	108	112	114	117	119	117	112	104	91

State Committee of Statistics.

TABLE 8-4. Industrial Production by Commodities
(volume in units indicated)

	Unit	1980	1985	1986	1987	1988	1989	1990	1991	1992	1993	1994	1995
Electricity Production	MKW	61,530	81,263	85,095	88,490	88,417	89,657	87,379	85,984	81,293	76,121	65,126	65,700
Coal	TT	115,375	130,816	137,799	142,053	143,087	138,355	131,443	130,382	127,000	112,000	104,000	83,200
Oil	TT	..	22,800	..	..	..	..	25,800	26,600	25,800	23,000	20,300	20,500
Natural Gas	MM3	4,314	5,456	5,824	6,311	7,134	6,710	7,114	7,885	8,113	6,685	4,490	5,900
Iron Ore	TT	25,763	22,977	23,630	24,224	24,342	23,764	23,846	21,993	17,700	13,100	10,500	15,100
Cast Iron	TT	4,710	4,932	4,890	4,797	4,940	5,279	5,226	4,953	4,666	3,552	2,436	2,600
Steel	TT	5,967	6,155	6,496	6,555	6,766	6,831	6,754	6,377	6,063	4,558	2,968	3,000
Rolled Steel	TT	4,114	4,448	4,566	4,580	4,874	5,011	4,955	4,660	4,426	3,489	2,322	2,100
Coke (6% Humidity)	TT	4,321	4,100	4,237	4,191	4,169	4,137	3,711	3,404	3,166	2,494	1,696	1,811
Metal Cutting Machine Tools	U	3,017	2,848	2,630	2,155	2,214	2,307	2,578	2,389	1,629	1,193	377	..
Excavators	U	1,803	1,877	1,843	1,045	570	578	710	618	312	210	32	..
Bulldozers	U	8,863	13,670	14,504	15,220	14,810	15,308	13,328	10,288	3,494	4,234	695	521
Tractors	U	..	54,550	..	..	..	..	41,050	34,131	13,414	5,643	1,987	1,800
Primary Oil Processing	TT	11,381	13,917	17,555	18,149	17,603	18,406	17,854	18,002	16,866	14,778	11,775	..
Sulphuric Acid	TT	1,891	1,671	1,850	2,008	2,063	1,896	3,151	2,815	2,349	1,179	681	694
Fertilizers	TT	1,262	1,430	1,520	1,603	1,737	1,705	1,656	1,516	880	304	126	197
Artificial Fibers	T	19,268	21,007	23,552	23,352	21,834	20,568	17,406	11,280	8,500	1,900	800	..
Tires	TU	..	1,452	..	..	..	..	2,633	3,029	2,880	1,784	263	..
Cement	TT	..	7,549	..	..	..	..	8,301	7,575	6,436	3,963	2,033	1,772
Building Bricks	M	1,989	1,947	2,055	2,268	2,354	2,468	2,285	2,146	1,971	1,303	753	414
Ferro-Concrete Construction	T M3	6,067	6,575	6,824	7,535	7,747	7,717	7,504	7,221	5,450	3,604	1,590	874
Sheets of Asbestos	MU	591	643	652	668	681	691	722	721	688	559	136	159

Source: State Committee of Statistics.

TABLE 8-4a. Industrial Production by Commodities
(index: 1985 = 100)

	1980	1985	1986	1987	1988	1989	1990	1991	1992	1993	1994	1995
Electricity Production	75.7	100.0	104.7	108.9	108.8	110.3	107.5	105.8	100.0	93.7	80.1	80.8
Coal	88.2	100.0	105.3	108.6	109.4	105.8	100.5	99.7	97.1	85.6	79.5	63.6
Oil	..	100.0	..	..	..	..	113.2	116.7	113.2	100.9	89.0	89.9
Natural Gas	79.1	100.0	106.8	115.7	130.8	123.0	130.4	144.5	148.7	122.5	82.3	108.1
Iron Ore	112.1	100.0	102.8	105.4	105.9	103.4	103.8	95.7	77.0	57.0	45.7	65.7
Cast Iron	95.5	100.0	99.2	97.3	100.2	107.0	106.0	100.4	94.6	72.0	49.4	52.7
Steel	96.9	100.0	105.5	106.5	109.9	111.0	109.7	103.6	98.5	74.0	48.2	48.7
Rolled Steel	92.5	100.0	102.7	103.0	109.6	112.7	111.4	104.8	99.5	78.4	52.2	47.2
Coke (6% Humidity)	105.4	100.0	103.3	102.2	101.7	100.9	90.5	83.0	77.2	60.8	41.4	44.2
Metal Cutting Machine Tools	105.9	100.0	92.3	75.7	77.7	81.0	90.5	83.9	57.2	41.9	13.2	..
Excavators	96.1	100.0	98.2	55.7	30.4	30.8	37.8	32.9	16.6	11.2	1.7	..
Bulldozers	64.8	100.0	106.1	111.3	108.3	112.0	97.5	75.3	25.6	31.0	5.1	3.8
Tractors	..	100.0	..	..	..	..	75.3	62.6	24.6	10.3	3.6	3.3
Primary Oil Processing	81.8	100.0	126.1	130.4	126.5	132.3	128.3	129.4	121.2	106.2	84.6	..
Sulphuric Acid	113.2	100.0	110.7	120.2	123.5	113.5	188.6	168.5	140.6	70.5	40.8	41.6
Fertilizers	88.3	100.0	106.3	112.1	121.5	119.2	115.8	106.0	61.5	21.2	8.8	13.8
Artificial Fibers	91.7	100.0	112.1	111.2	103.9	97.9	82.9	53.7	40.5	9.0	3.8	..
Tires	..	100.0	..	..	..	..	181.3	208.6	198.3	122.9	18.1	..
Cement	..	100.0	..	..	..	..	110.0	100.3	85.3	52.5	26.9	23.5
Building Bricks	102.2	100.0	105.5	116.5	120.9	126.8	117.4	110.2	101.2	66.9	38.7	21.3
Ferro-Concrete Construction	92.3	100.0	103.8	114.6	117.8	117.4	114.1	109.8	82.9	54.8	24.2	13.3
Sheets of Asbestos	91.8	100.0	101.4	103.9	105.9	107.4	112.3	112.1	106.9	87.0	21.1	24.8

Source: Table 8-4.

TABLE 8-6. Energy Balance, 1995 (natural units)***

	Coal	Oil	Gas	Nuclear/hydro/ and electric power	Heat	Total
	TT	TT	MM3	MKWh	TKcal	
Indigenous Production	83,271.0	17,931.9	5,915.8	66,659.4	82,875.5	..
Imports	1,192.6	678.5	91,209.0	7,392.7	..	..
Exports	12,950.8	11,249.4	2,565.5	..	..	..
Intl. Marine Bunkers	..	..	..	..	..	..
Stock Change	..	..	..	..	..	..
Total energy requirements	..	..	..	..	..	..
Returns and Transfers	..	..	..	..	..	..
Statistical Differences	..	..	..	..	..	..
Gas Works	..	..	..	..	..	..
Petroleum Refineries	..	..	..	..	..	..
Liquefaction	..	..	..	..	..	..
Public Service Electricity	..	..	..	..	..	..
Autoproducers of Electr.	..	..	..	..	..	..
Other Transformation	..	..	..	..	..	..
Own Use	..	..	..	..	..	..
Distrib. and Transf. Losses	..	..	..	..	..	..
Total final consumption	60,974.1	10,858.0	7,516.3	53,495.9 1/	49,816.2 1/	..
Total industry	52,990.4	..	5,747.5	27,174.9	21,079.8	..
Iron and Steel	..	..	..	9,446.3	2,524.7	..
Chemical and Petrochemical	..	..	..	3,205.4	3,992.5	..
(of which: Petrochemical Feedstocks)	..	..	..	..		
Non-Ferrous Metals	..	..	..	7,522.5	5,805.5	..
Non-Metallic Minerals	..	..	..	..	..	..
Transp. Equip. and Machinery	..	..	..	..	..	..
Mining and Quarrying	..	..	..	..	..	..
Food and Tobacco	..	..	..	915.4	1,507.1	..
Paper, Pulp and Printing	..	..	..	..	..	..
Wood and Wood Products	..	..	..	..	..	..
Construction Materials	..	..	..	822.2	910.8	..
Textile and Leather	..	..	..	..	..	..
Unspecified	..	..	..	..	..	..
Total transport	1,169.6	..	283.5	3,992.3	2,234.5	..
Air	..	..	..	79.8	..	..
Road	..	..	..	300.5	..	..
Rail	..	..	..	2,987.0	..	..
Internal Navigation	..	..	..	11.4	..	..
Unspecified	..	..	..	..	..	..
Total other	..	..	..	..	..	
Agriculture	3,485.4	..	230.4	..	..	..
Commerce	90.6	..	5.4	..	..	..
Public Services	..	..	..	..	..	..
Residential	..	..	..	1,602.0	11,785.0	..
Unspecified	..	..	..	8,099.3	18,797.6	..
Non-Energy Use	..	..	..	..	..	..
Memo Items:						
Electricity Generated (mill. KWh)	64,581.0	..	..	..	..	..
Public	..	..	..	..	..	..
Autoproducers	..	..	..	..	..	..

*** TT=thous. tons, MKWh=mill. KWh, MM3=mill. m3, TKcal=thous. Kcal.
1/ Enterprises of Kazakstan State Energy Complex.
Source: Goskomstat.

TABLE 8-7. Energy Balance Sheet (in TJ)

	1980	1985	1986	1987	1988	1989	1990	1991	1992	1993	1994
Domestic sources	106,088	114,222	..	..	..	..	220,068	..	..	..	..
Coal	73,383	82,152	..	..	..	..	85,408	..	..	..	..
Other solid fuels	..	..	..	..	..	..	..	..	..	..	..
Liquid fuel	26,677	32,661	..	..	..	..	36,922	..	..	..	..
Other 1/	6,028	-591	..	..	..	..	97,738	..	..	..	..
Imports	48,365	50,554	..	..	..	..	74,044	..	..	..	..
Liquid fuel	10,129	14,764	..	..	..	..	26,538	..	..	..	..
Gas	11,791	6,958	..	..	..	..	13,005	..	..	..	..
Other primary energy	26,445	28,832	..	..	..	..	34,501	..	..	..	..
Exports	66,128	71,250	..	..	..	..	82,342	..	..	..	..
Liquid fuel	19,305	27,700	..	..	..	..	28,569	..	..	..	..
Gas	4,891	2,579	..	..	..	..	4,660	..	..	..	..
Other primary energy	41,932	40,971	..	..	..	..	49,113	..	..	..	..
Change in stocks	-1,324	1,269	..	..	..	..	-8,931	..	..	..	..
Domestic use of primary energy 2/	87,001	94,795	..	..	..	..	202,839				
For electricity and heat energy generation (including hydro- and nuclear power)	37,491	45,519	..	..	..	..	45,987	..	..	..	..
For other purposes of which:	49,510	49,276	..	..	..	..	156,852	..	..	..	..
By industry	13,253	13,241	..	..	..	..	15,783	..	..	..	..
By agriculture	4,423	4,429	..	..	..	..	3,565	..	..	..	..
By households	5,074	5,749	..	..	..	..	8,248	..	..	..	..

1/ Incl. primary energy equivalent for the energy production in WPS and NPS.

2/ Visible consumption = domestic sources + import - export + or - change in stocks.

Source: State Committee of Statistics.

TABLE 8-7a. Energy Balance Sheet (in natural units)

	1991	1992	1993	1994	1995
Domestic sources	180,605.9	175,263.8	154,359.3	139,493.3	119,161.3
Coal (thous. tons)	130,382.0	126,536.0	111,880.0	104,625.0	83,271.0
Other solid fuels	..	..	..	..	
Liquid fuel (thous. tons)	42,338.8	40,615.2	35,793.9	30,380.4	29,974.5
Other (thous. tons)	7,885.1	8,112.6	6,685.4	4,487.9	5,915.8
Imports	..	..	..	..	..
Oil and condensed gas (thous. tons)	12,134.0	11,547.0	8,683.7	1,835.5	..
Gas (mill. m3)	5,171.0	14,282.1	9,772.3	7,173.1	..
Other primary energy	..	..	..	..	..
Exports	..	..	..	..	..
Oil and condensed gas (thous. tons)	19,732.0	18,174.3	13,696.8	9,444.8	..
Gas (mill. m3)	4,167.0	3,915.0	3,450.5	1,635.5	..
Other primary energy	..	..	..	..	..
Change in stocks	..	..	..	..	..
Domestic use of primary energy	..	..	..	..	..
For electricity and heat energy generation (boiler/stove fuel thous. tons)	48,496.7	50,756.8	..	..	..
For other purposes	..	..	..	..	..
of which:					
By industry (thous. tons)	42,551.9	45,842.0	..	..	..
By agriculture (thous. tons)	2,990.4	2,120.0	..	..	..
By households	..	..	..	..	..

Source: State Committee of Statistics.

TABLE 9-1. Producer and Consumer Prices

		Producer prices (% change monthly)	Consumer prices (% change monthly)
1994	January	44.9	42.6
	February	34.9	24.2
	March	29.5	17.4
	April	82.8	31.8
	May	37.2	33.8
	June	45.7	45.9
	July	35.8	25.4
	August	13.2	13.3
	September	16.8	9.7
	October	13.1	20.1
	November	3.0	14.2
	December	4.5	10.2
1995	January	5.9	8.9
	February	5.5	6.7
	March	5.1	5.1
	April	4.3	3.2
	May	0.4	2.7
	June	1.2	2.3
	July	1.9	2.9
	August	6.7	2.1
	September	-2.2	2.4
	October	3.7	4.1
	November	1.6	4.4
	December	0.6	3.6
1996	January	3.6	4.1
	February	3.0	2.5
	March	0.4	1.7
	April	1.0	3.0
1994	I		
	II	235.9	117.1
	III	121.8	99.2
	IV	35.3	50.1
1995	I	16.0	28.8
	II	10.5	11.8
	III	6.6	7.7
	IV	5.7	10.9
1996	I	6.8	10.5
1995		231.2	247.0

Source: State Committee of Statistics.

TABLE 9-3. Monthly Nominal Wages by Sector

Sector	1980	1985	1986	1987	1988	1989	1990	1991	1992	1993	1994	1995
Nominal wages					(current rubles)						(current tenge)	
Economywide	167.0	186.5	192.7	199.3	214.6	233.6	265.4	440.8	4,625.0	127.5	1,725.7	4,786.0
Material sphere	..	201.0	..	..	..	..	287.0	467.0	5,100.0	138.0	1,960.1	5,432.0
Industry	188.0	212.4	218.0	223.5	244.6	266.6	296.0	534.3	6,161.0	170.5	2,800.5	7,792.0
Electricity	178.0	204.0	206.0	214.0	242.0	268.0	316.0	737.0	8,555.0	270.4	4,862.0	12,281.0
Fuels	303.0	339.0	344.0	355.0	382.0	409.0	456.0	825.0	11,636.0	295.0	4,892.0	10,659.0
Metallurgy (ferrous and nonferrous)	237.0	256.0	264.0	269.0	297.0	326.0	350.0	657.0	10,088.0	224.7	3,819.0	11,562.0
Machinery and metalworking	186.0	224.0	229.0	228.0	249.0	273.0	303.0	508.0	4,450.0	126.0	1,894.0	5,203.0
Chemicals and petrochemicals	199.0	231.0	239.0	244.0	272.0	291.0	315.0	587.0	6,241.0	139.1	2,638.0	7,153.0
Forestry, woodworking and paper and pulp	177.0	200.0	204.0	208.0	234.0	248.0	278.0	462.0	4,214.0	116.8	1,500.0	4,121.0
Construction materials	185.0	208.0	214.0	224.0	240.0	265.0	292.0	495.0	5,122.0	144.6	2,160.0	6,248.0
Light industry	138.0	160.0	162.0	166.0	187.0	203.0	224.0	406.0	3,547.0	114.9	1,378.0	3,658.0
Textiles	153.0	189.0	191.0	194.0	216.0	236.0	261.0	504.0	4,562.0	129.1	1,581.0	4,423.0
Clothing	124.0	136.0	138.0	144.0	164.0	176.0	194.0	329.0	2,613.0	92.4	1,198.0	2,774.0
Leather and shoes	150.0	180.0	181.0	183.0	203.0	221.0	248.0	441.0	3,250.0	123.4	1,156.0	3,251.0
Food processing	155.0	170.0	176.0	188.0	205.0	219.0	244.0	447.0	4,820.0	146.8	1,851.0	4,754.0
Meat and dairy	165.0	179.0	185.0	194.0	212.0	224.0	251.0	501.0	5,255.0	152.0	1,742.0	4,355.0
Fish	162.0	169.0	177.0	185.0	204.0	225.0	239.0	375.0	3,172.0	99.8	1,472.0	4,050.0
Other industry	145.0	165.0	168.0	175.0	193.0	208.0	248.0	495.0	4,745.0	144.0	2,491.0	5,647.0
Construction	206.0	233.8	240.3	249.7	276.0	304.6	330.3	536.1	5,727.0	170.4	2,660.1	7,850.0
Agriculture	167.0	197.5	210.9	217.2	225.3	243.8	292.4	413.6	5,001.0	170.5	1,038.2	2,392.0
Transport	206.0	220.6	226.0	234.7	255.1	272.7	302.7	492.8	5,797.0	181.6	2,407.7	6,808.0
Communications	134.0	145.1	146.9	156.3	185.0	197.8	227.5	388.9	3,726.0	119.8	1,821.4	5,875.0
Trade (retail and wholesale)	125.0	137.0	139.8	140.4	149.3	168.9	212.6	354.0	3,349.0	100.6	1,395.6	3,350.0
Other	107.0	121.2	126.3	136.5	143.8	160.5	176.1	293.2	3,531.0	92.4	1,353.4	4,058.0
Nonmaterial sphere	..	141.0	..	..	..	..	203.0	356.0	2,853.0	93.0	1,158.1	3,538.0
Municipal services	130.0	141.7	143.9	148.2	164.1	178.3	198.9	336.7	3,283.0	101.7	1,728.7	4,628.0
Science, research and development	183.0	202.8	212.6	220.8	260.9	292.5	320.2	476.0	4,459.0	119.3	1,469.9	4,483.0
Education	125.0	139.2	143.7	156.0	161.9	171.9	182.1	319.0	2,484.0	80.6	892.6	2,933.0
Culture	102.0	105.4	106.4	109.3	117.6	129.4	161.1	285.4	2,011.0	70.0	774.9	2,342.0
Arts	115.0	120.0	122.3	125.8	130.7	141.2	169.5	297.5	2,160.0	68.1	748.0	2,233.0
Health care, social security, sports	121.0	125.2	127.2	134.4	140.9	158.2	178.0	351.8	2,199.0	66.2	797.2	2,675.0
Banking, finance, credit, insurance	144.0	158.2	168.9	173.3	175.8	202.0	354.2	742.7	8,340.0	288.1	4,179.2	10,967.0
Government	148.0	154.5	160.7	173.2	197.2	228.2	334.7	474.2	4,665.0	139.4	1,775.0	4,475.0
Nominal wage index Economywide	100.0	111.7	115.4	119.3	(1980=100) 128.5	139.9	158.9	264.0	2,769.5	(1993=100) 100.0	1,353.5	3,753.7
Material sphere	..	..	..	..	..	..	..	..	..			
Industry	100.0	113.0	116.0	118.9	130.1	141.8	157.4	284.2	3,277.1	100.0	1,642.5	4,570.1
Electricity	100.0	114.6	115.7	120.2	136.0	150.6	177.5	414.0	4,806.2	100.0	1,798.1	4,541.8
Fuels	100.0	111.9	113.5	117.2	126.1	135.0	150.5	272.3	3,840.3	100.0	1,658.3	3,613.2
Metallurgy (ferrous and nonferrous)	100.0	108.0	111.4	113.5	125.3	137.6	147.7	277.2	4,256.5	100.0	1,699.6	5,145.5
Machinery and metalworking	100.0	120.4	123.1	122.6	133.9	146.8	162.9	273.1	2,392.5	100.0	1,503.2	4,129.4
Chemicals and petrochemicals	100.0	116.1	120.1	122.6	136.7	146.2	158.3	295.0	3,136.2	100.0	1,896.5	5,142.3
Forestry, woodworking and paper and pulp	100.0	113.0	115.3	117.5	132.2	140.1	157.1	261.0	2,380.8	100.0	1,284.2	3,528.3
Construction materials	100.0	112.4	115.7	121.1	129.7	143.2	157.8	267.6	2,768.6	100.0	1,493.8	4,320.9
Light industry	100.0	115.9	117.4	120.3	135.5	147.1	162.3	294.2	2,570.3	100.0	1,199.3	3,183.6
Textiles	100.0	123.5	124.8	126.8	141.2	154.2	170.6	329.4	2,981.7	100.0	1,224.6	3,426.0
Clothing	100.0	109.7	111.3	116.1	132.3	141.9	156.5	265.3	2,107.3	100.0	1,296.5	3,002.2
Leather and shoes	100.0	120.0	120.7	122.0	135.3	147.3	165.3	294.0	2,166.7	100.0	936.8	2,634.5
Food processing	100.0	109.7	113.5	121.3	132.3	141.3	157.4	288.4	3,109.7	100.0	1,260.9	3,238.4
Meat and dairy	100.0	108.5	112.1	117.6	128.5	135.8	152.1	303.6	3,184.8	100.0	1,146.1	2,865.1
Fish	100.0	104.3	109.3	114.2	125.9	138.9	147.5	231.5	1,958.0	100.0	1,474.9	4,058.1
Other industry	100.0	113.8	115.9	120.7	133.1	143.4	171.0	341.4	3,272.4	100.0	1,729.9	3,921.5
Construction	100.0	113.5	116.7	121.2	134.0	147.9	160.3	260.2	2,780.1	100.0	1,561.1	4,606.8
Agriculture	100.0	118.3	126.3	130.1	134.9	146.0	175.1	247.7	2,994.6	100.0	608.9	1,402.9
Transport	100.0	107.1	109.7	113.9	123.8	132.4	146.9	239.2	2,814.1	100.0	1,325.8	3,748.9
Communications	100.0	108.3	109.6	116.6	138.1	147.6	169.8	290.2	2,780.6	100.0	1,520.4	4,904.0
Trade (retail and wholesale)	100.0	109.6	111.8	112.3	119.4	135.1	170.1	283.2	2,679.2	100.0	1,387.3	3,330.0
Other	100.0	113.3	118.0	127.6	134.4	150.0	164.6	274.0	3,300.0	100.0	1,464.7	4,391.8
Nonmaterial sphere	..	..	..	..	..	..	..	..	..			
Municipal services	100.0	109.0	110.7	114.0	126.2	137.2	153.0	259.0	2,525.4	100.0	1,699.8	4,550.6
Science, research and development	100.0	110.8	116.2	120.7	142.6	159.8	175.0	260.1	2,436.6	100.0	1,232.1	3,757.8
Education	100.0	111.4	115.0	124.8	129.5	137.5	145.7	255.2	1,987.2	100.0	1,107.4	3,639.0
Culture	100.0	103.3	104.3	107.2	115.3	126.9	157.9	279.8	1,971.6	100.0	1,107.0	3,345.7
Arts	100.0	104.3	106.3	109.4	113.7	122.8	147.4	258.7	1,878.3	100.0	1,098.4	3,279.0
Health care, social security, sports	100.0	103.5	105.1	111.1	116.4	130.7	147.1	290.7	1,817.4	100.0	1,204.2	4,040.8
Banking, finance, credit, insurance	100.0	109.9	117.3	120.3	122.1	140.3	246.0	515.8	5,791.7	100.0	1,450.6	3,806.7
Government	100.0	104.4	108.6	117.0	133.2	154.2	226.1	320.4	3,152.0	100.0	1,273.3	3,210.2

Source: State Committee of Statistics.

TABLE 10-1. Money Income and Expenditure of the Population (millions of current national currency)

	1980	1985	1986	1987	1988	1989	1990	1991	1992	1993	1994	1995
					(mill. rubles)						(mill. tenge)	
INCOME												
LABOR INCOME	14,548	17,796	18,253	18,950	20,548	23,160	26,697	44,478	455,361	7,824	83,870	215,064
Regular Wages	12,863	15,424	15,961	16,585	18,056	20,206	23,033	37,654	301,293	6,960	74,443	199,770
of which: Wages paid by Cooperatives	..	..	..	..	116	684	1,167	1,712	20,496	496	399	99
Other Wages and Compensations	459	530	538	547	630	742	850	1,945	10,281	243	3,253	9,167
Income paid by Collective Farms	465	564	572	606	618	614	702	1,701	8,919	210	..	448
Income from Sale of Farm Products	761	1,278	1,182	1,212	1,244	1,598	2,112	3,178	134,868	411	6,174	5,679
TRANSFER RECEIPTS	2,644	3,491	3,734	3,928	4,447	4,611	5,606	16,231	97,712	2,819	37,732	74,923
Pensions and Allowances	1,812	2,399	2,575	2,693	2,861	3,012	3,430	13,467	81,340	1,802	23,453	74,923
Scholarships	147	153	153	159	167	166	184	546	2,878	52	675	..
Income from the Financial System (Insurance, Interest, etc.)	421	657	641	700	946	795	1,286	1,329	9,598	263	1,992	..
Other Income	264	282	365	376	473	638	706	889	3,896	702	11,612	..
TOTAL INCOME	17,192	21,287	21,987	22,878	24,995	27,771	32,303	60,709	553,073	10,643	121,602	289,987
EXPENDITURE												
PURCHASES	14,244	17,236	17,594	18,375	19,671	21,366	24,039	41,237	297,461	5,487	69,470	121,454
Retail Goods	12,809	15,515	15,731	16,365	17,383	18,945	21,512	35,591	261,209	4,601	50,633	67,710
Services	1,435	1,721	1,863	2,010	2,288	2,421	2,527	5,646	36,252	886	18,837	53,744
Rent and Utilities	433	557	598	626	656	693	667	760	7,688	180	7,073	..
Transport and Communications	686	794	872	939	1,023	1,064	1,113	1,860	18,581	634	9,016	..
Health and Other Services	316	370	394	442	556	586	636	2,300	9,723	42	2,748	..
Cooperatives	..	..	..	3	53	78	111	725	260	30	..	..
TRANSFERS AND SAVINGS	2,442	3,253	3,659	3,922	4,373	5,139	6,349	11,011	120,010	2,105	34,452	139,304
Taxes, Fees, Dues and Other	1,858	2,415	2,536	2,653	2,901	3,256	3,864	4,715	45,252	1,272	9,207	34,646
Savings	418	616	932	1,054	1,244	1,692	2,274	6,061	74,735	830	4,703	7,717
Other	166	222	191	215	228	191	211	235	23	3	20,542	96,941
TOTAL EXPENDITURE	16,685	20,489	21,253	22,297	24,044	26,505	30,388	52,248	417,471	7,592	103,922	260,757
INCOME less EXPENDITURE	507	798	734	581	951	1,266	1,915	8,461	135,602	3,051	17,680	29,230

Sources: State Committee of Statistics.

TABLE 11-1. Capital Investment by State Enterprises and Organizations by Sector (millions of current national currency)

Sector	1980	1985	1986	1987	1988	1989	1990	1991	1992	1993	1994	1995
					(mill. rubles)						(mill. tenge)	
Material sphere	6,347	7,321	7,550	8,032	8,903	9,037	8,660	11,840	160,850	2,956	29,765	50,666
Agriculture and forestry	2,154	2,321	2,396	2,330	2,460	2,535	2,656	4,576	65,160	865	2,808	2,304
Agriculture excluding forestry	2,154	2,312	2,387	2,320	2,451	2,525	2,646	4,553	65,003	859	2,771	2,267
Forestry	..	9	9	10	9	10	10	23	157	6	37	37
Industry and construction	3,116	3,868	4,001	4,531	5,213	5,193	4,635	6,108	84,688	1,831	19,689	32,322
Industry	2,904	3,590	3,709	4,146	4,689	4,586	4,032	5,544	81,646	1,797	19,609	32,136
Construction	212	278	292	385	524	607	603	564	3,042	34	80	186
Other , material sphere	1,077	1,132	1,153	1,171	1,230	1,309	1,369	1,156	11,002	260	7,268	16,040
Transport of goods	828	888	916	911	939	1,047	1,091	755	8,169	210	5,338	6,000
Road maintenance	..	..	..	..	..	..	..	..	..	..	..	..
Communication servicing material production	73	112	115	136	149	149	150	189	1,137	18	1,724	9,964
Wholesale trade	98	79	76	72	84	83	87	140	913	8	..	..
Retail trade and catering	..	..	..	..	..	..	..	..	..	..	37	20
Material supply	..	..	..	..	..	..	..	..	..	..	23	27
Procurement	78	53	46	52	58	30	41	72	783	24	129	24
Information and computing services	..	..	..	..	..	..	..	..	..	..	..	..
Other sectors	..	..	..	..	..	..	..	..	..	..	17	5
Nonmaterial sphere	2,236	2,610	2,849	3,453	3,338	3,622	3,481	5,050	68,205	1,206	11,492	16,114
Transport	..	..	..	..	..	..	..	..	..	..	..	..
Communication	..	..	..	..	..	..	..	..	..	..	..	..
Housing	1,176	1,513	1,643	2,090	2,134	2,144	2,167	3,210	41,296	738	6,100	8,210
Public utilities and personal services	..	..	..	..	..	347	388	680	11,180	197	2,033	4,949
Health care, social security, physical culture, and sports	..	..	..	..	..	160	150	280	4,051	69	674	1,503
Education	..	..	..	..	..	396	361	666	8,526	134	613	647
Culture and art	..	..	..	..	..	49	50	99	1,076	17	146	480
Science and scientific services	..	..	..	..	..	..	..	9	48	..	1	..
Credit	..	..	..	..	..	..	..	..	..	..	..	..
Insurance	..	..	..	..	..	..	..	..	..	..	..	..
General administration and defense	..	..	..	..	..	..	..	..	..	..	..	..
Private nonprofit institutions serving households	..	..	..	..	..	..	..	..	..	..	..	..
Other, material and nonmaterial spheres	3,313	3,742	4,002	4,624	4,568	4,931	4,850	6,206	79,207	1,466	18,760	32,154
Total capital investment	8,583	9,931	10,399	11,485	12,241	12,659	12,141	16,890	229,055	4,162	41,257	66,780

Source: State Committee of Statistics.

TABLE 11-2. Capital Investment Financing by Type of Enterprise (millions of current national currency)

Type of enterprise	1980	1985	1986	1987	1988	1989	1990	1991	1992	1993	1994	1995
					(mill. rubles)						(mill. tenge)	
State enterprises 1/	8,583	9,931	10,399	11,485	12,241	12,659	12,142	16,891	229,055	4,162	41,257	66,780
Cooperatives	115	154	183	189	212	236	309	287	2,139	31	..	..
Private sector	43	75	82	126	200	190	225	465	5,898	406	3,991	10,367
Other sources	307	335	343	341	344	369	383	1,104	24,217	917	35,697	71,442
of which:												
Mixed ownership within Kazakstan	..	..	..	..	..	..	..	..	..	..	16,694	47,474
Mixed ownership of Kazakstan and foreign capital	..	..	..	..	..	..	..	..	..	..	17,903	21,869
Foreign capital	..	..	..	..	..	..	..	..	..	..	150	1,139
Small and private enterprises	..	..	..	..	..	..	..	..	..	..	829	835
Social and regional organizations	..	..	..	..	..	..	..	..	..	..	121	125
Total capital investment	9,048	10,495	11,007	12,141	12,997	13,454	13,059	18,747	261,309	5,516	80,945	148,589

1/ Including infrastructure investment.

Source: State Committee of Statistics.

TABLE 11-3. Stocks at End of Year by Sector (millions of current national currency)

Sector	1980	1985	1986	1987	1988	1989	1990	1991	1992	1993	1994	1995
					(mill. rubles)						(mill. tenge)	
Material Sphere	14,161	20,013	19,063	18,820	19,426	19,862	23,429	40,272	668,972	21,016	202,059	328,390
Agriculture and forestry	4,848	7,302	9,046	9,964	10,536	10,009	9,811	14,633	137,110	2,899	35,250	65,235
Agriculture	4,848	7,302	9,046	9,964	10,536	10,009	9,811	14,633	137,110	2,899	35,246	65,223
Forestry	..	..	..	..	..	..	..	..	..	..	4	12
Industry and construction	6,468	9,623	6,790	6,611	6,702	7,500	8,077	19,771	363,573	11,751	122,514	212,676
Industry	3,667	5,304	5,552	5,484	5,496	6,230	6,598	17,185	332,948	10,706	113,601	193,552
Construction	2,801	4,319	1,238	1,128	1,206	1,269	1,478	2,586	30,625	1,045	8,913	19,124
Other	2,846	3,089	3,227	2,245	2,188	2,354	5,541	5,868	168,288	6,366	44,295	50,479
Transport of goods	265	434	381	382	417	448	517	975	13,791	1,051	7,397	16,768
Road maintenance	..	..	..	..	..	..	..	..	..	..	..	..
Communication servicing material production	31	40	50	47	52	56	61	141	869	37	1,578	1,466
Wholesale trade	..	..	..	..	..	..	..	..	..	..	..	..
Retail trade and catering	..	..	..	..	..	..	..	..	..	2,012	17,344	17,479
Material supply	899	1,150	1,209	432	462	587	638	2,722	59,371	1,926	9,177	9,116
Procurement	1,651	1,465	1,587	1,383	1,258	1,263	4,325	2,030	94,257	1,340	8,787	5,567
Information and computing services	..	..	..	..	..	..	..	..	..	..	12	83
Other sectors	..	..	..	..	..	..	..	..	..	..	..	..
Nonmaterial sphere	464	919	651	634	603	1,417	1,460	3,493	6,744	1,019	4,054	8,148
Transport	..	..	..	..	..	..	..	..	..	..	..	..
Communication	..	..	..	..	..	..	..	..	..	..	..	..
Housing	..	..	..	..	..	..	..	131	2,455	285	1,060	3,731
Public utilities and personal services	139	216	225	218	206	219	218	312	1,657	32	108	445
Health care, social security, physical culture and sports	..	..	..	..	..	..	..	..	..	..	..	..
Education	..	..	..	..	..	..	..	..	..	..	..	..
Culture and art	..	..	..	..	..	..	..	..	..	..	..	..
Science and scientific services	186	343	..	..	..	..	..	204	2,631	46	776	1,030
Credit	..	..	..	..	..	..	..	..	..	..	..	..
Insurance	..	..	..	..	..	..	..	..	..	..	..	..
General administration and defense	..	..	..	..	..	..	..	..	..	..	..	..
Private nonprofit institutions serving households	..	..	..	..	..	..	..	..	..	..	..	..
Other, material and nonmaterial spheres	3,310	4,008	3,877	2,878	2,791	3,771	7,001	9,362	175,032	7,385	48,349	58,627
Total stocks at end of year	18,151	26,277	24,507	23,867	24,354	25,839	30,280	48,759	766,665	22,035	206,113	336,538

Source: State Committee of Statistics.

TABLE 11-4. Change in Stocks by Type and by Economic Sector (millions of current national currency)

Type of stock or sector	1980	1985	1986	1987	1988	1989	1990	1991	1992	1993	1994	1995
											(mill. tenge)	
Change in stocks by type of stock	..	..	..	..	..	..	..	..	..	19,622	184,078	130,425
Raw materials	..	..	..	..	..	..	..	..	..	5,142	86,168	86,876
Unfinished production	..	..	..	..	..	..	..	..	..	1,034	13,311	14,619
Outlay in progress	..	..	..	..	..	..	..	..	..	2,048	119,972	74,242
Finished production, goods	..	..	..	..	..	..	..	..	..	5,697	62,996	11,608
Other stocks	..	..	..	..	..	..			..	7,749	21,603	17,322
Change in stocks												
Material sphere	..	..	..	..	..	..	..	..	..	18,663	181,043	126,331
Agriculture and forestry	..	..	..	..	..	..	..	..	..	2,587	32,351	29,985
Agriculture	..	..	..	..	..	..	..	..	..	2,587	32,347	29,977
Forestry	..	..	..	..	..	..	..	..	..	..	4	8
Industry and construction	..	..	..	..	..	..	..	..	..	10,539	110,763	90,162
Industry	..	..	..	..	..	..	..	..	..	9,594	102,895	79,951
Construction	..	..	..	..	..	..	..	..	..	945	7,868	10,211
Other	..	..	..	..	..	..	..	..	..	5,537	37,929	6,184
Transport of goods	..	..	..	..	..	..	..	..	..	983	6,346	9,371
Road maintenance	..	..	..	..	..	..	..	..	..	..	..	..
Communication servicing material production	..	..	..	..	..	..	..	..	..	35	1,541	-112
Wholesale trade	..	..	..	..	..	..	..	..	..	..	..	..
Retail trade and catering	..	..	..	..	..	..	..	..	..	1,837	15,332	135
Material supply	..	..	..	..	..	..	..	..	..	1,635	7,251	-61
Procurement	..	..	..	..	..	..	..	..	..	1,047	7,447	-3,220
Information and computing services	..	..	..	..	..	..	..	..	..	..	12	71
Other sectors	..	..	..	..	..	..	..	..	..	..	..	..
Nonmaterial Sphere	..	..	..	..	..	..	..	..	..	959	3,035	4,094
Transportation	..	..	..	..	..	..	..	..	..	..	..	..
Communication	..	..	..	..	..	..	..	..	..	..	..	..
Housing	..	..	..	..	..	..	..	..	..	273	775	2,671
Public utilities and personal services	..	..	..	..	..	..	..	..	..	27	73	357
Health care, social security, physical culture and sports	..	..	..	..	..	..	..	..	..	..	..	..
Education	..	..	..	..	..	..	..	..	..	..	..	..
Culture and art	..	..	..	..	..	..	..	..	..	..	..	..
Science and scientific services	..	..	..	..	..	..	..	..	..	41	730	254
Credit	..	..	..	..	..	..	..	..	..	..	..	..
Insurance	..	..	..	..	..	..	..	..	..	..	..	..
General administration and defense	..	..	..	..	..	..	..	..	..	..	..	..
Private nonprofit institutions serving households	..	..	..	..	..	..	..	..	..	..	..	..
Other, material and nonmaterial spheres	..	..	..	..	..	..	..	..	..	6,496	40,964	10,278
Total change in stocks	..	..	..	..	..	..	..	..	..	19,622	184,078	130,425

Source: State Committee of Statistics.

TABLE 11-5. Work in Progress in Construction (millions of current national currency)

	1980	1985	1986	1987	1988	1989	1990	1991	1992	1993	1994	1995
			(mill. rubles)								(mill. tenge)	
Material Sphere	..	..	..	..	..	..	..	12,324	87,289	2,103	120,683	238,644
Agriculture including forestry	..	..	..	..	..	..	..	2,464	16,291	358	12,319	16,193
Agriculture excluding forestry	..	..	..	..	..	..	..	2,458	16,239	333	12,240	16,106
Forestry	..	..	..	..	..	..	..	6	52	25	79	87
Industry, total	..	..	..	..	..	..	..	8,917	63,651	1,585	96,299	202,024
Industry, other	..	..	..	..	..	..	..	8,191	61,405	1,561	94,904	199,353
Construction	..	..	..	..	..	..	..	726	2,246	24	1,395	2,671
Other, material sphere	..	..	..	..	..	..	..	943	7,347	160	12,065	20,427
Transportation of goods	..	..	..	..	..	..	..	578	5,694	147	9,087	14,826
Maintenance of roads	..	..	..	..	..	..	..					
Communication servicing material production	..	..	..	..	..	..	..	142	712	14	2,131	4,753
Wholesale trade	..	..	..	..	..	..	..	..	..	..	..	..
Retail trade and catering	..	..	..	..	..	..	..	74	327	5	374	431
Material supply	..	..	..	..	..	..	..	37	263	3	77	142
Procurement	..	..	..	..	..	..	..	36	350	12	274	171
Information and computing services	..	..	..	..	..	..	..	..	..	..	..	..
Other branches of material production	..	..	..	..	..	..	..	69	..	27	122	104
Nonmaterial Sphere	..	..	..	..	..	..	..	4,514	45,637	1,052	41,423	57,790
Transportation	..	..	..	..	..	..	..	..	..	..	..	..
Communication	..	..	..	..	..	..	..	..	..	..	..	..
Housing	..	..	..	..	..	..	..	2,543	25,433	590	12,299	17,412
Public utilities and personal services	..	..	..	..	..	..	..	841	8,525	197	13,240	16,331
Health care, social security, physical culture and sports	..	..	..	..	..	..	..	372	3,072	78	7,178	15,598
Education	..	..	..	..	..	..	..	530	5,845	121	4,270	7,259
Culture and art	..	..	..	..	..	..	..	106	924	18	912	1,189
Science and scientific services	..	..	..	..	..	..	..	3	50	..	2	1
Credit	..	..	..	..	..	..	..	..	..	..	..	..
Insurance	..	..	..	..	..	..	..	..	..	..	..	..
General administration and defense	..	..	..	..	..	..	..	..	..	..	..	..
Private nonprofit institutions serving households	..	..	..	..	..	..	..	..	..	..	..	..
								4,395	43,849	1,004	37,901	57,790
Other, material and nonmaterial spheres	..	..	..	..	..	..	..	5,457	52,984	1,212	53,488	78,217
Total Work-in-progress in Construction	..	..	..	..	..	..	..	16,838	132,926	3,155	162,106	296,434

Source: State Committee of Statistics.

Distributors of World Bank Publications

Prices and credit terms vary from country to country. Consult your local distributor before placing an order.

ARGENTINA
Oficina del Libro Internacional
Av. Cordoba 1877
1120 Buenos Aires
Tel: (54 11) 815-8354
Fax: (54 11) 815-8156

AUSTRALIA, FIJI, PAPUA NEW GUINEA, SOLOMON ISLANDS, VANUATU, AND WESTERN SAMOA
D.A. Information Services
648 Whitehorse Road
Mitcham 3132
Victoria
Tel: (61) 3 9210 7777
Fax: (61) 3 9210 7788
E-mail: service@dadirect.com.au
URL: http://www.dadirect.com.au

AUSTRIA
Gerold and Co.
Weihburggasse 26
A-1011 Wien
Tel: (43 1) 512-47-31-0
Fax: (43 1) 512-47-31-29
URL: http://www.gerold.co/at.online

BANGLADESH
Micro Industries Development
Assistance Society (MIDAS)
House 5, Road 16
Dhanmondi R/Area
Dhaka 1209
Tel: (880 2) 326427
Fax: (880 2) 811188

BELGIUM
Jean De Lannoy
Av. du Roi 202
1060 Brussels
Tel: (32 2) 538-5169
Fax: (32 2) 538-0841

BRAZIL
Publicações Tecnicas Internacionais Ltda.
Rua Peixoto Gomide, 209
01409 Sao Paulo, SP.
Tel: (55 11) 259-6644
Fax: (55 11) 258-6990
E-mail: postmaster@pt.uol.br
URL: http://www.uol.br

CANADA
Renouf Publishing Co. Ltd.
5369 Canotek Road
Ottawa, Ontario K1J 9J3
Tel: (613) 745-2665
Fax: (613) 745-7660
E-mail: http// renouf@fox.nstn.ca
URL: http://www.fox.nstn.ca/~renouf

CHINA
China Financial & Economic
Publishing House
8, Da Fo Si Dong Jie
Beijing
Tel: (86 10) 6333-8257
Fax: (86 10) 6401-7365

COLOMBIA
Infoenlace Ltda.
Carrera 6 No. 51-21
Apartado Aereo 34270
Santafé de Bogotá, D.C.
Tel: (57 1) 285-2798
Fax: (57 1) 285-2798

CYPRUS
Center for Applied Research
Cyprus College
6, Diogenes Street, Engomi
P.O. Box 2006
Nicosia
Tel: (357 2) 44-1730
Fax: (357 2) 46-2051

CZECH REPUBLIC
National Information Center
prodejna, Konviktska 5
CS – 113 57 Prague 1
Tel: (42 2) 2422-9433
Fax: (42 2) 2422-1484
URL: http://www.nis.cz/

DENMARK
SamfundsLitteratur
Rosenoerns Allé 11
DK-1970 Frederiksberg C
Tel: (45 31) 351942
Fax: (45 31) 357822

EGYPT, ARAB REPUBLIC OF
Al Ahram Distribution Agency
Al Galaa Street
Cairo
Tel: (20 2) 578-6083
Fax: (20 2) 578-6833

The Middle East Observer
41, Sherif Street
Cairo
Tel: (20 2) 393-9732
Fax: (20 2) 393-9732

FINLAND
Akateeminen Kirjakauppa
P.O. Box 128
FIN-00101 Helsinki
Tel: (358 0) 12141
Fax: (358 0) 121-4441
URL: http://booknet.cultnet.fi/aka/

FRANCE
World Bank Publications
66, avenue d'Iéna
75116 Paris
Tel: (33 1) 40-69-30-56/57
Fax: (33 1) 40-69-30-68

GERMANY
UNO-Verlag
Poppelsdorfer Allee 55
53115 Bonn
Tel: (49 228) 212940
Fax: (49 228) 217492

GREECE
Papasotiriou S.A.
35, Stournara Str.
106 82 Athens
Tel: (30 1) 364-1826
Fax: (30 1) 364-8254

HAITI
Culture Diffusion
5, Rue Capois
C.P. 257
Port-au-Prince
Tel: (509 1) 3 9260

HONG KONG, MACAO
Asia 2000 Ltd.
Sales & Circulation Department
Seabird House, unit 1101-02
22-28 Wyndham Street, Central
Hong Kong
Tel: (852) 2530-1409
Fax: (852) 2526-1107
E-mail: sales@asia2000.com.hk
URL: http://www.asia2000.com.hk

INDIA
Allied Publishers Ltd.
751 Mount Road
Madras - 600 002
Tel: (91 44) 852-3938
Fax: (91 44) 852-0649

INDONESIA
Pt. Indira Limited
Jalan Borobudur 20
P.O. Box 181
Jakarta 10320
Tel: (62 21) 390-4290
Fax: (62 21) 421-4289

IRAN
Ketab Sara Co. Publishers
Khaled Eslamboli Ave.,
6th Street
Kusheh Delafrooz No. 8
Tehran
Tel: (98 21) 8717819; 8716104
Fax: (98 21) 8712479
E-mail: ketab-sara@neda.net.ir

Kowkab Publishers
P.O. Box 19575-511
Tehran
Tel: (98 21) 258-3723
Fax: (98 21) 258-3723

IRELAND
Government Supplies Agency
Oifig an tSoláthair
4-5 Harcourt Road
Dublin 2
Tel: (353 1) 661-3111
Fax: (353 1) 475-2670

ISRAEL
Yozmot Literature Ltd.
P.O. Box 56055
3 Yohanan Hasandlar Street
Tel Aviv 61560
Tel: (972 3) 5285-397
Fax: (972 3) 5285-397

R.O.Y. International
PO Box 13056
Tel Aviv 61130
Tel: (972 3) 5461423
Fax: (972 3) 5461442
E-mail: royil@netvision.net.il

Palestinian Authority/Middle East
Index Information Services
P.O.B. 19502 Jerusalem
Tel: (972 2) 6271219
Fax: (972 2) 6271634

ITALY
Licosa Commissionaria Sansoni SPA
Via Duca Di Calabria, 1/1
Casella Postale 552
50125 Firenze
Tel: (55) 645-415
Fax: (55) 641-257
E-mail: licosa@ftbcc.it
Url: http://www.ftbcc.it/licosa

JAMAICA
Ian Randle Publishers Ltd.
206 Old Hope Road
Kingston 6
Tel: 809-927-2085
Fax: 809-977-0243
E-mail: irpl@colis.com

JAPAN
Eastern Book Service
3-13 Hongo 3-chome, Bunkyo-ku
Tokyo 113
Tel: (81 3) 3818-0861
Fax: (81 3) 3818-0864
E-mail: svt-ebs@ppp.bekkoame.or.jp
URL: http://www.bekkoame.or.jp/~svt-ebs

KENYA
Africa Book Service (E.A.) Ltd.
Quaran House, Mfangano Street
P.O. Box 45245
Nairobi
Tel: (254 2) 223 641
Fax: (254 2) 330 272

KOREA, REPUBLIC OF
Daejon Trading Co. Ltd.
P.O. Box 34, Youida
706 Seoun Bldg
44-6 Youido-Dong, Yeongchengo-Ku
Seoul
Tel: (82 2) 785-1631/4
Fax: (82 2) 784-0315

MALAYSIA
University of Malaya Cooperative
Bookshop, Limited
P.O. Box 1127
Jalan Pantai Baru
59700 Kuala Lumpur
Tel: (60 3) 756-5000
Fax: (60 3) 755-4424

MEXICO
INFOTEC
Av. San Fernando No. 37
Col. Toriello Guerra
14050 Mexico, D.F.
Tel: (52 5) 624-2800
Fax: (52 5) 624-2822
E-mail: infotec@rtn.net.mx
URL: http://rtn.net.mx

NEPAL
Everest Media International
Services (P) Ltd.
GPO Box 5443
Kathmandu
Tel: (977 1) 472 152
Fax: (977 1) 224 431

NETHERLANDS
De Lindeboom/InOr-Publikaties
P.O. Box 202
7480 AE Haaksbergen
Tel: (31 53) 574-0004
Fax: (31 53) 572-9296
E-mail: lindeboo@worldonline.nl
URL: http://www.worldonline.nl~lindeboo

NEW ZEALAND
EBSCO NZ Ltd.
Private Mail Bag 99914
New Market
Auckland
Tel: (64 9) 524-8119
Fax: (64 9) 524-8067

NIGERIA
University Press Limited
Three Crowns Building Jericho
Private Mail Bag 5095
Ibadan
Tel: (234 22) 41-1356
Fax: (234 22) 41-2056

NORWAY
NIC Info A/S
Book Department
P.O. Box 6125 Etterstad
N-0602 Oslo 6
Tel: (47 22) 57-3300
Fax: (47 22) 68-1901

PAKISTAN
Mirza Book Agency
65, Shahrah-e-Quaid-e-Azam
Lahore 54000
Tel: (92 42) 735 3601
Fax: (92 42) 758 5283

Oxford University Press
5 Bangalore Town
Sharae Faisal
PO Box 13033
Karachi-75350
Tel: (92 21) 446307
Fax: (92 21) 4547640
E-mail: oup@oup.khi.erum.com.pk

Pak Book Corporation
Aziz Chambers 21
Queen's Road
Lahore
Tel: (92 42) 636 3222; 636 0885
Fax: (92 42) 636 2328
E-mail: pbc@brain.net.pk

PERU
Editorial Desarrollo SA
Apartado 3824
Lima 1
Tel: (51 14) 285380
Fax: (51 14) 286628

PHILIPPINES
International Booksource Center Inc.
1127-A Antipolo St.
Barangay, Venezuela
Makati City
Tel: (63 2) 896 6501; 6505; 6507
Fax: (63 2) 896 1741

POLAND
International Publishing Service
Ul. Piekna 31/37
00-677 Warzawa
Tel: (48 2) 628-6089
Fax: (48 2) 621-7255
E-mail: books%ips@ikp.atm.com.pl
URL: http://www.ipscg.waw.pl/ips/export/

PORTUGAL
Livraria Portugal
Apartado 2681
Rua Do Carmo 70-74
1200 Lisbon
Tel: (1) 347-4982
Fax: (1) 347-0264

ROMANIA
Compani De Librarii Bucuresti S.A.
Str. Lipscani no. 26, sector 3
Bucharest
Tel: (40 1) 613 9645
Fax: (40 1) 312 4000

RUSSIAN FEDERATION
Isdatelstvo <Ves Mir>
9a, Lolpachniy Pereulok
Moscow 101831
Tel: (7 095) 917 87 49
Fax: (7 095) 917 92 59

SINGAPORE, TAIWAN, MYANMAR, BRUNEI
Asahgate Publishing Asia
Pacific Pte. Ltd.
41 Kallang Pudding Road #04-03
Golden Wheel Building
Singapore 349316
Tel: (65) 741-5166
Fax: (65) 742-9356
E-mail: ashgate@asianconnect.com

SLOVENIA
Gospodarski Vestnik Publishing Group
Dunajska cesta 5
1000 Ljubljana
Tel: (386 61) 133 83 47; 132 12 30
Fax: (386 61) 133 80 30
E-mail: belicd@gvestnik.si

SOUTH AFRICA, BOTSWANA
For single titles:
Oxford University Press
Southern Africa
P.O. Box 1141
Cape Town 8000
Tel: (27 21) 45-7266
Fax: (27 21) 45-7265

For subscription orders:
International Subscription Service
P.O. Box 41095
Craighall
Johannesburg 2024
Tel: (27 11) 880-1448
Fax: (27 11) 880-6248
E-mail: iss@is.co.za

SPAIN
Mundi-Prensa Libros, S.A.
Castello 37
28001 Madrid
Tel: (34 1) 431-3399
Fax: (34 1) 575-3998
E-mail: libreria@mundiprensa.es
URL: http://www.mundiprensa.es/

Mundi-Prensa Barcelona
Consell de Cent, 391
08009 Barcelona
Tel: (34 3) 488-3492
Fax: (34 3) 487-7659

SRI LANKA, THE MALDIVES
Lake House Bookshop
100, Sir Chittampalam Gardiner Mawatha
Colombo 2
Tel: (94 1) 32105
Fax: (94 1) 432104

SWEDEN
Wennergren-Williams AB
P.O. Box 1305
S-171 25 Solna
Tel: (46 8) 705-97-50
Fax: (46 8) 27-00-71

SWITZERLAND
Librairie Payot
Service Institutionnel
Côtes-de-Montbenon 30
1002 Lausanne
Tel: (41 21) 341-3229
Fax: (41 21) 341-3235

TANZANIA
Oxford University Press
Maktaba Street
PO Box 5299
Dar es Salaam
Tel: (255 51) 29209
Fax: (255 51) 46822

THAILAND
Central Books Distribution
306 Silom Road
Bangkok 10500
Tel: (66 2) 235-5400
Fax: (66 2) 237-8321

TRINIDAD & TOBAGO, AND THE CARRIBBEAN
Systematics Studies Unit
9 Watts Street
Curepe
Trinidad, West Indies
Tel: (809) 662-5654
Fax: (809) 662-5654
E-mail: tobe@trinidad.net

UGANDA
Gustro Ltd.
PO Box 9997
Madhvani Building
Plot 16/4 Jinja Rd.
Kampala
Tel: (256 41) 254 763
Fax: (256 41) 251 468

UNITED KINGDOM
Microinfo Ltd.
P.O. Box 3
Alton, Hampshire GU34 2PG
England
Tel: (44 1420) 86848
Fax: (44 1420) 89889
E-mail: wbank@ukminfo.demon.co.uk
URL: http://www.microinfo.co.uk

VENEZUELA
Tecni-Ciencia Libros, S.A.
Centro Cuidad Comercial Tamanco
Nivel C2
Caracas
Tel: (58 2) 959 5547; 5035; 0016
Fax: (58 2) 959 5636

ZAMBIA
University Bookshop
University of Zambia
Great East Road Campus
P.O. Box 32379
Lusaka
Tel: (260 1) 252 576
Fax: (260 1) 253 952

ZIMBABWE
Longman Zimbabwe (Pte.)Ltd.
Tourle Road, Ardbennie
P.O. Box ST125
Southerton
Harare
Tel: (263 4) 6216617
Fax: (263 4) 621670

ADECO Van Diemen Editions Techniques
Ch. de Lacuez 41
CH1807 Blonay
Tel: (41 21) 943 2673
Fax: (41 21) 943 3605

010697

50°

Volga

To
Astrak

AZERB

40°

50°

0

0